D1526738

Public Choice and Constitutional Economics

POLITICAL ECONOMY AND PUBLIC POLICY, VOLUME 6

Editors: William Breit, *Department of Economics, Trinity University, San Antonio*
Kenneth G. Elzinga, *Department of Economics, University of Virginia*

POLTICAL ECONOMY AND PUBLIC POLICY

An International Series of Monographs
in Law and Economics, History of Economic Thought
and Public Finance

Edited by William Breit
Department of Economics
Trinity University
and Kenneth G. Elzinga
Department of Economics
University of Virginia

Copublished by the
Cato Institute

Public Choice and Constitutional Economics

Edited by: **JAMES D. GWARTNEY**
Florida State University
RICHARD E. WAGNER
Florida State University

 JAI PRESS INC.

Greenwich, Connecticut   *London, England*

Library of Congress Cataloging-in-Publication Data

Public choice and constitutional economics
    edited by James D. Gwartney, Richard E. Wagner.
        p.   cm.—(Political economy and public policy : v. 6)
    Five of the papers were originally developed at a symposium on
government, the economy, and the constitution sponsored by the
Policy Sciences Program of Florida State University in March 1986
and subsequently published in the Cato journal, fall 1987.
    Includes index.
    ISBN 0-89232-935-1
    1. Social choice.   2. United States—Constitutional history.
3. Liberty.   4. Individualism.   I. Gwartney, James D.   II. Wagner,
Richard E.   III. Florida State University. Policy Sciences Program.
IV. Series.
HB846.8.P83 1988   88-1915
338.973—dc19   CIP

Copyright © 1988 JAI PRESS INC.
55 Old Post Road, No. 2
Greenwich, Connecticut 06830

JAI PRESS LTD.
3 Henrietta Street
London WC2E 8LU
England

ISBN: 0-89232-935-1

Library of Congress Catalog Number: 88-1915

Manufactured in the United States of America

CONTENTS

CONTENTS

ACKNOWLEDGEMENTS

The papers of this volume represent a joint contribution. Five of the papers were originally delivered at a symposium on "Government, The Economy, and The Constitution" sponsored by the Policy Sciences Program of Florida State University in March 1986. Financial support for the symposium was supplied by the John M. Olin Foundation and the Smith Richardson Foundation. These five papers were subsequently published in the *CATO Journal*, Fall 1987. We are grateful to the Cato Institute for allowing us to reprint these papers, to James Dorn, editor of the *CATO Journal*, for his help at numerous stages of this project, and to William Niskanen, chairman of the Cato Institute, for writing the Foreword.

We are indebted to the Earhart Foundation for a grant which permitted us to prepare the rest of the book, including the writing of the first two essays. We are also appreciative for the cooperation and support supplied by the Policy Sciences Program of Florida State University and to its Director, Dr. Thomas R. Dye.

The exploration of constitutional matters from an economic perspective is something that would have seemed pure fantasy before James M. Buchanan and Gordon Tullock showed how it could be done in *The Calculus of Consent*. We shall be forever indebted to them, not only for the intellectual field they opened but also for the massive personal inspiration and support they have provided both of us.

Valerie Colvin and Harriet Crawford did an excellent job of handling the word processing. Finally, we should like to thank Barry Thornton and David Sollars for their research assistance and coordination of the many details associated with the preparation of this book.

FOREWORD:

THE EROSION OF THE
ECONOMIC CONSTITUTION
William A. Niskanen

The Constitution of the United States established the structure of the federal government, limits on the powers of the federal and state governments, the procedures for amending the Constitution, and a partial listing of the rights of individuals. The objective of the Constitution was to define the islands of government powers within the ocean of individual rights. The distinctive American contribution was to assert the supremacy of individual rights over governmental powers and, in the Declaration of Independence, "That to secure these rights, Governments are instituted among Men, deriving their just powers from the consent of the governed."

Although the United States is one of the youngest major nations, it is the oldest surviving republic. In general, the Constitution has served us very well. For two centuries, the structure of government has been remarkably stable. In general, our civil rights have been strengthened by the implicit extension of the Bill of Rights to limit the powers of state governments. There is no need, especially during our bicentennial celebration, for me to elaborate on the strengths of our Constitution, other than to reaffirm our loyalty and our thankfulness for the wisdom of the Framers.

At the same time, we should recognize that whole sections of the Constitution bearing on the economic powers of the government and the economic rights of individuals have been seriously eroded, for the most part, in our lifetime and without any formal amendment. Those who are surprised by this observation may not recognize the many provisions of the Constitution that bear on economic powers and rights. Others dismiss any concern for this condition on the basis, in the language of Justice Holmes, that "a constitution is not intended to embody a particular economic theory." Giving the benefit of the doubt to the learned Justice, one wonders whether these commentators have read the Constitution or

William A. Niskanen is Chairman of The Cato Institute

the deliberations that led to its numerous fiscal, monetary, and economic rules. The fiscal rules include the enumerated spending powers (Article I, Section 8 and the 10th Amendment) and the limitations on federal and state taxing powers (Article I, Sections 8, 9, and 10, and the 16th Amendment). Specific monetary rules are included in Article I, Sections 8 and 10. The major economic rules include the interstate commerce clause and the patents and copyrights clause (Article I, Section 8), the contracts clause (Article I, Section 10), and the rights to property (the 5th and 14th Amendments).

Any reading of the deliberations that led to the Constitution and the several amendments should lead one to recognize that these rules were specifically designed as part of the larger set of rules to secure individual rights. The Framers may not have shared a common vision about the economic system. There should be no doubt, however, that the Constitution was designed to provide a strong but limited federal role, free trade among the states, and the security of private property—however the intent of the Framers may have been changed by subsequent interpretation.

Most of these rules, unfortunately, have now been stretched beyond recognition. Only a partial listing of the changes in the effective economic constitution is sufficient to make this point.

- The few spending powers enumerated in Article I, Section 8 were expanded without limit by a 1936 ruling of the Supreme Court that "the power of Congress to authorize appropriations of public money for public purposes is not limited by by direct grants of legislative power found in the Constitution." One can state with assurance that the intitial Constitution would not have been ratified if this later interpretation had been anticipated.
- The requirement that "all duties, imports, and excises be uniform throughout the United States" has been interpreted to permit a differential "windfall profits" tax on oil and the complex web of internal tariffs that is implicit in environmental regulation.
- The power "to coin Money" has been broadened to permit a federal monopoly on paper money.
- The power "To regulate commerce . . . among the several States" has been progressively broadened to permit federal regulation of any form of commerce within individual states.
- The rule that "No state shall . . . pass any . . . law impairing the obligation of contracts" has been interpreted to permit several types of contractual impairments, including debt moratoria.
- The "public use" test for the exercise of eminent domain has been expanded to a "public purpose" test to permit the use of eminent domain for urban renewal and land redistribution among private parties.

- The "just compensation" test for the exercise of eminent domain has been restricted, until recently, to preclude compensation for regulations that substantially reduce, but do not eliminate, the value of the property to the private owners.

In these cases, the language of the Constitution is clear and specific. The effective economic constitution, however, has been changed substantially in response to political pressure, and these changes have been ratified, not by formal amendment, but by creative and compliant decisions of the Supreme Court. There is a reasonable case that some of these changes in the effective economic constitution may have been appropriate. My primary point is that these changes in the effective constitution were made by extra-constitutional procedures, by compliant courts, rather than by the Article V procedures for formal amendments that would have provided a test whether these changes were supported by a broad consensus.

The objective of the fine collection of articles in this volume is to rebuild the case for the economic constitution. The authors bring three new perspectives to bear on these issues, each reflecting important intellectual developments during the past quarter century. Public choice, by analyzing politics as exchange, uses economic theory and game theory to explain the outcomes of political processes. Constitutional economics addresses the types of rules that people would choose without knowledge or concern about the effects of specific applications of these rules to their own well-being. The rapidly developing literature on law and economics addresses the efficiency effects of a wide range of fine-grained legal rules. Each of these perspectives is well represented by its leading scholars in this volume. These articles provide both a useful introduction to each of these perspectives and some fascinating insights to specialists.

The erosion of the economic constitution and the pervasive growth of government are among the more important characteristics of our times. We do not understand these developments very well. Both individual liberty and economic efficiency are at stake. This volume provides a cornerstone on which to rebuild our economic constitution, in part by rediscovering the wisdom of those who drafted and approved our initial Constitution.

PART I

THEORY OF PUBLIC CHOICE AND
CONSTITUTIONS

1

PUBLIC CHOICE AND THE CONDUCT OF REPRESENTATIVE GOVERNMENT

James D. Gwartney and Richard E. Wagner

It remains to be enquired whether a majority having any common interest, or feeling any common passion, will find sufficient motives to restrain them from oppressing the minority. . . If two individuals are under the bias of interest or enmity against a third, the rights of the latter could never be safely referred to the majority of the three. Will two thousand individuals be less apt to oppress one thousand or two hundred thousand one hundred thousand?[1]

—James Madison (1787)

Introduction

As many of the papers in this volume illustrate, American government has undergone a dramatic transformation over the past two centuries. The original constitutional compact established a federal government with enumerated powers: the federal government could do only what it was specifically authorized to do, principally as expressed in Article I, Section 8 of the Constitution. Everything else, the Tenth Amendment made clear, was "reserved to the States respectively, or to the people". While the Constitution placed limits on the substance of governmental activity, today those limits have little force. Certainly the federal government is not limited by the Constitution's enumeration of powers. Other constitutional limitations on the federal government are often equally ignored. For instance, the Fifth Amendment prohibits the federal government from taking private property, unless it pays "just compensation" and unless the taken property is put to "public use". However, during the last 50 years the Supreme Court has gutted this protection of economic liberty. For instance, in its 1954 decision in *Berman v. Parker* the Supreme Court ruled:

The authors are Professors of Economics at Florida State University.
[1] Quote from James Madison in a letter to Thomas Jefferson, October 24, 1787. (Saul K. Padover, p.41).

3

> The legislature, not the judiciary, is the main guardian of the public needs
> to be served by social legislation . . . This principle admits of no excep-
> tion merely because the power of eminent domain is involved.[2]

Such a ruling would seem to eliminate all obstacles to legislative actions
involving the taking of private property.[3]

At least with regard to economic functions and rights, we no longer
possess a constitutionally limited government. Congressional majorities are
now largely free to legislate as they choose, with government being limited
only by the requirements of electoral competition. The framers of the
Constitution feared this situation. After conducting an extensive study on
the history of governments, James Madison warned against the gradual
erosion of individual liberty under majoritarian democracy. Madison
concluded:

> Since the general civilization of mankind, I believe there are more instances
> of the abridgment of the freedom of the people, by gradual and silent
> encroachments of those in power, than by violent and sudden usurpations:
> But, on a candid examination of history, we shall find that turbulence,
> violence and abuse of power, by the majority trampling on the rights of
> the minority have produced factions and commotions, which, in republics,
> have more frequently than any other cause, produced depotism. If we
> go over the whole history of ancient and modern republics, we shall find
> their destruction to have generally resulted from those causes.[4]

Madison sought to design the U. S. Constitution in a way that would stave
off these dangers arising from majoritarianism. Clearly he was not entirely
successful. We have moved quite far down the path Madison feared.
However, some encouraging intellectual signs of a reawakening interest
in the importance of constitutional limits on government are now observable. In this chapter, and in the next, we shall try to explain how the
scholarship in the theory of public choice that has emerged during the past
25 years supports Madison's central insight about the importance of
constitutional controls over government. In this chapter, we seek to explain
the main defects that characterize political regimes where legislative
majorities have practically unlimited ability to legislate. In the next chapter,
we explore the constitutional implications of this public choice scholar-

[2] *Berman v. Parker* (348 U.S. 26; 1954) at 32 (citations omitted).

[3] See Richard Epstein (1985 and Chapter 9 of this volume) and Bernard Siegan (1980) for
details on this point. Perhaps the most blatant evidence of the judiciary's failure to uphold
the rights of private property owners against legislative action is *Hawaii Housing Authority
v. Midkiff* (467 U.S. 229; 1984). In that case, the court permitted the State of Hawaii to use
the power of eminent domain to take land and apartments from their owners and in turn to
sell them to the previous tenants.

[4] See Padover (1953, pp. 46-47).

ship, and in so doing perhaps provide some useful perspective on many of the remaining essays in this volume.

Economic Attributes of Good Government

Many economists, as well as other scholars, have written on what they think constitutes the desirable scope of government. Despite the many specific differences that a detailed comparison of those scholars would reveal, there would also be substantial agreement that there are two primary economic functions of government: to maintain order and to provide public goods. These functions correspond to what James Buchanan (1975) conceptualizes as the protective and the productive states.The protective state refers to government's maintenance of a framework of security and order, and entails the enforcement of rules against theft, fraud, and the like. Government is assigned a monopoly on the use of violence which is to be used to protect citizens from each other and from outsiders. Thus, the protective state seeks to prevent individuals from harming one another and to maintain an infrastructure of rules within which people can interact with one another. The crucial ingredients of the latter include the enforcement of contracts and avoidance of restrictions, regulations, and differential taxes which restrain exchange.

Thomas Jefferson believed that such a protective state was the *sine qua non* of good government. In a letter to Andrew Jackson, Jefferson wrote:

> A wise and frugal government, which shall restrain men from injuring one another, which shall leave them otherwise free to regulate their own pursuits of industry and improvements, and shall not take from the mouth of labor the bread it has earned. . . This is the sum of good government.

Beyond the maintenance of order governments might also be able to enhance the wealth of their members through undertaking productive activities that cannot be organized efficiently through market transactions. This activity of the productive state is captured by Abraham Lincoln's famous dictum to the effect that the legitimate object of government is to do those things that people cannot do at all, or very well, acting in their separate and individual capacities. The theory of public goods explains why there are certain types of activities that cannot easily be provided through market transactions, principally because it is difficult, if not impossible, to restrict consumption to those who pay for the service. It is relatively easy for a painter to restrict his services to those who pay him, and so the painting of houses can be organized efficiently through market transactions. But it would be quite difficult, if not downright impossible, for someone who builds a dam to control flooding to withhold flood protection from those who do not pay. In the presence of such public goods, governments have the potential for adding to the wealth of a nation—though, as we shall explain below, that potential will not automatically be realized, but rather will be realized only to the extent that constitutional arrangements are appropriate to the task.

The Economic Competence of Government

Just because it is possible to conceptualize government normatively as fulfilling the requirements of the protective and the productive states, it does not follow that actual governments perform as those models describe. The actual conduct of government may deviate, perhaps sharply, from that characterized by the conceptual models. To say what government should do, does not itself imply that this is what governments actually will do.

For various reasons government may lack the competence required to fulfill its protective and productive functions. The problem of the state's lack of competence was expressed by George Stigler: "We can get on a bus labelled Economic Reform, but we don't know where it will take us" (1975, p. 24). The bus might not take us to its announced destination because the driver doesn't know how to get there. Alternatively, it might not take us there because the driver doesn't want to go there, regardless of the announced destination. The competence of the state may be insufficient to the fulfillment of its protective and productive tasks because it lacks the necessary *knowledge* or because it lacks the necessary *incentive*. Between these two components of the competence question, incentive has so far received the greater attention by public choice scholars. The central point of departure taken by these scholars is that the incentives contained within a particular system of government will determine whether or not government's power to tax, spend, and regulate is used as envisioned by the normative justifications.

Public choice scholars seek to explain how political processes actually work. They do not view government as some organic entity that always makes decisions in the public interest. Nor do they view it as a mechanism that automatically corrects the failings of the market process. Rather they view government as an alternative method of social organization—as an institutional process through which individuals collectively make choices and carry out activities.

In a democratic setting, individual preferences will influence the outcomes of collective decisions. Just as differences in market structures influence market outcomes, so too, differences in the structure of the political process will influence collective outcomes. Public choice scholars seek to understand the linkage between institutional arrangements—including alternative decision-making rules, political structures, and constitutional constraints—and collective choices or outcomes. To do this requires the development of a logically consistent theory linking individual behavior to collective action, analyzing the implications of the theory, and testing the implications against events in the real world.[5]

Central Elements of Public Choice Theory

Public choice analysis is to governments what economic analysis is to markets. In both cases, outcomes will reflect the choices of individuals and the incentive structure which influences those choices. In the political arena, the major players are voters, politicians, and bureaucrats. It is useful to visualize the political process as a complex set of interrelationships among members of these three groups. Like consumers in the market, voters use their electoral support, money, and other political resources to express their demand for legislation. Like business enterpreneurs, politicians are suppliers: they design and shape legislation. Finally, just as managers and employers are assigned the details of the production process in the market, bureaucrats perform this task in the public sector.

The Self-Interest Postulate

Economists have used the self-interest postulate to develop theories which enhance our understanding of how markets work. Public choice represents an extension of this postulate to politics. The self-interest postulate implies that incentives matter—that they influence personal choices in a predictable manner. If something becomes more costly, people will choose less of it. If something becomes valued more highly, people will choose more of it. The likelihood an option will be chosen by an individual is inversely related to its personal cost and is directly related to the expected personal benefits.

Since there is no evidence that entrance into a voting booth or participation in the political process causes a personality transformation, there is sound reason to believe that the motivation of participants in the market and political processes is similar. The voter who selects among political alternatives is the same person who selects among market alternatives. If Jones is influenced by expected personal benefits and costs when he makes choices in the department store, it makes sense that he will be similarly influenced by personal benefits and costs when he makes choices in the voting booth. Likewise, the men and women working in government as politicians and bureaucrats are pretty much like their counterparts in the private sector. If pursuit of such rewards as personal wealth, power, and prestige motivates people in the marketplace, there is every reason to believe that these same elements will motivate them in the political arena.

Contrary to the charges of some, the self-interest postulate does not imply

---

[5] For a thorough survey of this scholarship, see William Mitchell (1983).

that either market or political decision-makers are greedy materialists who care only about themselves. People act for a variety of reasons, some selfish and some humanitarian. The self-interest postulate implies that the choices of both the humanitarian and the egocentric change in a systematic way in response to changes in personal costs and benefits. Both types of people will be more likely to support a policy that generates benefits for others (for example: farmers, the poor, or the elderly) when the personal cost of doing so is low. Similarly, both the humanitarian and the egocentric will be more likely to discover and act upon opportunities to reduce costs the higher the personal gain from doing so.

Furthermore, the motivation for an action is not always a good indicator of its result. It is an error to suppose that actions motivated by self-interest necessarily conflict with the general interests of society. As Adam Smith noted more than two centuries ago, self-interested individuals directed by market prices tend to promote the general welfare even though they neither intend nor are aware of the extent to which they are doing so. Likewise, within government the extent to which the individual pursuit of self-interest is congruent with the general welfare depends on various features of governmental institutions. One of the primary objectives of public choice scholarship is to enhance our ability to differentiate between institutional arrangements that bring individual self-interest and the general welfare into harmony and institutional arrangements that leave them in conflict.

The Politician-Supplier

The economic theorist postulates that the pursuit of profit is the primary stimulus shaping the behavior of market suppliers. The public choice theorist postulates that pursuit of votes is the primary stimulus shaping the behavior of political suppliers. In varying degrees, such factors as pursuit of the public interest, compassion for the poor, and the achievement of fame, wealth, and power may influence the behavior of politicians. But regardless of ultimate motivation, the ability of a politician to achieve his objectives is sorely dependent upon his ability to get elected and reelected. Just as profits are the life-blood of the market entrepreneur, votes are the life-blood of the politician. Predictably, political suppliers will seek to promote an image and stake out positions on issues which will enhance their chances of electoral success.

Political competition more or less forces politicians to pay attention to how their actions influence their electoral prospects. If a politician refuses to support policies that are vote-getters, perhaps because he thinks the policies are counterproductive or morally wrong, he runs an increased risk of being replaced by a competitor who pays closer attention to the acquisition of votes. Thus, political competition presents even the most public-spirited politician with a strong incentive to make decisions in light of elctoral considerations. Just as neglect of economic profit is the route to market oblivion, neglect of potential votes is the route to political oblivion. The easiest way to win votes, both in the political arena and in the market place, is to give—or at least appear to give—constitutents what they want. A politician who ignores the views of his or her constituents is as rare as a market entrepreneur selling bikinis in the Arctic.

However, while vote-seeking politicians have a strong incentive to support policies that enhance their electoral prospects, this does not mean that they will always support the views of the majority on a specific issue. In some cases a candidate may gain more votes among an intensely active minority, willing to vote for or against candidates on the basis of this one issue, than he would gain from a dispassionate majority that is rationally uninformed on the issue. This is particularly likely to happen when, as is often the case, most voters know very little about many of the items that comprise the bundle of views the politician is offering.

Politicians must also have an eye for how their actions will influence their campaign coffers. Money is the power source of politics. While votes win elections, voters must be convinced to "want" a candidate. In senatorial, congressional, and other elections involving a large electorate, the positive attributes (for example, honesty, compassion, and effectiveness) of a candidate must be projected to the voters. Various voting groups must be informed that the candidate agrees with them on key issues. Money, staff, and expertise will be required to purchase media time and promote the candidate among the voters. But this does not mean that politicians will always be scrounging for money. Political markets are two sided. Through their ability to enact or reject legislation, politicians can influence peoples' wealth in substantial ways. As we shall explore later, those who are so affected will seek out the policitians—there will be little need for politicians to go hunting for money, although some such efforts will always be rational.

The Voter-Consumer

Just as consumers use dollar votes to demand market goods, voter-consumers use electoral support, lobbying, political contributions and organizational skills to demand political goods. There are, however, some significant differences in the settings of consumer choice and voter choice, differences that affect outcomes in the two sectors.

How does a voter decide which candidate to support? Many elements may enter into this decision. The television image, perceived honesty, communication skills and experience of alternative candidates may, in varying degrees, influence the choices of voters. However, the self-interest postulate indicates that voters, like market consumers will ask, "What can you do for me and how much will it cost?" The greater the voter's perceived net personal gain from a particular candidate's platform the more likely it is that the voter will favor that candidate. In contrast, the greater the perceived net economic cost imposed on the voter by the positions of a candidate, the less inclined the voter will be to support the candidate. Other things equal, voters will tend to support those candidates whom they believe will provide them the most political goods, services, and transfer benefits *net of personal costs.*

While voters and consumers both choose the option they regard as superior to the option they regard as inferior, there are substantial differences in range of choices available to consumers and voters. Consumers in the marketplace are in a position to make marginal adjustments and choose among virtually an infinite combination of goods from many different suppliers. Consumers can buy jeans made by Levi Strauss or Jordache; computers made by IBM or Kaypro; automobiles made by Ford or Nissan; to say nothing of the many other possible options. Consumers can pick-and-choose among competing suppliers, putting together in the process a bundle of goods that best suits their needs.

It is very different in collective choice. Voters cannot undertake the collective choice analogue of choosing one supplier for jeans, another for tomato soup, and yet another for toothpaste. They cannot choose one candidate's proposed offering on social security, a second candidate's offering on foreign policy, and yet a third candidate's offering on public assistance programs. Rather, voters must choose among the bundles of issues that the different candidates represent; there is no ability to pick-and-choose particular items from among the bundle offered by the different candidates. This *bundle purchase nature* of representative democracy substantially reduces the ability of voters to register their preferences on specific issues. It also increases the ability of government to extract taxes. It is well recognized by economists that tie-in sales or full-line forcing allows a monopolist to collect more revenue from the same output than would be possible from selling the various items individually. This revenue impact of service bundling holds for governments as well, as Wagner and Weber (1975) explain.

The Political Process and Resource Allocation

The political process can be visualized as a complex set of interrelationships among voter-consumers and politician-suppliers, who direct the actions of bureaucratic producers. Insight into the operation of the political process can be gained by comparing and contrasting it with market allocation. While persons who engage in the political process and market exchange are likely to be similarly motivated—self-interest influences behavior in both sectors—the structure of incentives and constraints on behavior differ under the two institutional arrangements. The primary insights of public choice theory reflect the analysis of how these differences influence social outcomes and the efficiency of resource use.

The Rational Ignorance Effect

Consider the incentive of individuals to acquire knowledge relevant to market and political choices. In the market, the purchaser is able to act upon additional information derived from shopping. For example, if additional shopping leads to a $2,000 savings, say on the purchase of furnishings, the market consumer could pocket the $2,000 saved—though, of course, he or she would have to bear the cost of the added shopping. In a comparable collective-choice setting, approval of the majority of voters would be required before the more economical furnishings could be purchased. Therefore, a voter could not benefit from the cost-reducing information unless he could convince a majority of voters to support the same choice. Since it will be costly to convince others to alter their choices, the net return from shopping is clearly lower when choices are made collectively.

It is similar in politics. Competing candidates are like competing stores. A consumer who investigates the offerings of competing stores to find a better deal can act directly on that knowledge. But a voter who investigates the offerings of the competing candidates can do practically nothing to act on that knowledge. He can vote on the basis of his knowledge. But citizens recognize that there is only a minuscule chance that their vote will be decisive. Since one vote is not going to decide who is elected, why should an individual study the issues and research the positions of alternative candidates? After all, the outcome will be unaffected, whether an individual voter makes an informed choice or simply chooses on the basis of current knowledge and vague impressions. Given this incentive structure, voters have little reason to invest the time and energy that would be required to cast a well informed vote. Under these circumstances, it is sensible (rational) for voters to remain uninformed on many issues—a phenomenon that has come to be called "rational ignorance" since first articulated by Anthony Downs (1957).

In failing to expend personal resources in an effort to cast an informed vote, the voter is merely exercising good judgment as to how his or her time and effort will yield the most benefits. There is a parallel between the voter's failure to acquire political knowledge and a farmer's inattention to the factors that determine the weather. Weather is probably the most important factor determining the income of an individual farmer. Still, it makes no sense for a farmer to invest time and resources attempting to understand meteorology. An improved knowledge of how weather systems work will seldom enable a farmer to avoid their adverse effects. It is the same with voters. A voter stands to gain little from the acquisition of additional information about a wide range of issues that are decided in the political arena. Since the resolution of these issues is, like the weather, out of the voter's hands, the voter has little incentive to become more informed.

Because of weak incentives to gather information, most voters simply rely on information that is supplied to them freely by candidates and the mass media. Conversations with friends and information acquired at work, from newspapers, from TV news, and from political advertising are especially important because the voter has so little incentive to spend personal time and effort gathering information. It is not surprising, then, that few voters are able to accurately identify their congressional representatives, much less identify and understand their position on issues like minimum wage legislation, tariffs, and agricultural price supports. The scanty information voters acquire merely indicates that they are responding rationally to economic incentives.

Shortsightedness In Government

The theory of property rights can be applied to enhance our understanding of how market and political processes handle the allocation of resources over time. When considering the allocation of resources across time periods, economic efficiency requires that we take account of future costs and benefits, appropriately discounted for the fact that the present value of a dollar in the future is worth less than a dollar today. When private owners possess exclusive and transferable ownership rights, they are forced to consider the present value consequences of actions that affect future costs and benefits. For example, someone who owns a farm might reduce current expenses by neglecting terrace grading that would reduce future erosion. However, the farmer cannot avoid bearing the consequences of the erosion that results. If he keeps the land, his future income will be lower. And if he sells the land, its sales price will be lower because the lower productivity of the eroded land makes that land less valuable to others.

Private investors expand their wealth by undertaking projects that generate future income of greater present value than costs, even when all or most of the costs come during the current period. For example, a tree farmer will plant and maintain trees even though those trees may not be harvested for 20, 30, or even 50 years. Of course, with the passage of time, the value of the farmer's trees will rise to reflect the increasing present value of the expected harvest-time income. Private property rights also provide resource owners with an incentive to conserve for the future. If scarcity and strong demand are expected to push up the price of a resource at an annual rate in excess of the interest rate, self-interest dictates that private owners conserve the resource for the future. When private property rights are present, prices and interest rates tie the future with the present and provide decision-makers with the information and incentive to see that resources are properly cared for and used efficiently (Gwartney and Stroup 1987, pp. 655-57)

How does the political process handle benefits and costs across time periods? What happens *prior* to the next election is of crucial importance to incumbent politicians. Since issues of public policy are usually complex, it is often difficult for voters to anticipate *future* benefits and costs accurately. Moreover, principles of rational ignorance suggest there is little payoff from doing so in any case. Instead, voters tend to rely on current conditions. To the voter, the best indicator of how well the incumbent has done may be the state of affairs close to election day. Policies that look good around election day will thus enhance the image of incumbents, even if those policies are likely to have substantial negative side effects after the election. On the other hand, policies that generate pre-election costs in order to provide long-term gains that emerge only after the next election reduce the reelection prospects of incumbents. As a result, the political process is biased toward the adoption of shortsighted policies and against the selection of sound long-range policies, when they involve observable costs prior to the next election.

Essentially, legislators have a property right to benefits (for example, improvements in the economy) that accrue *prior* to the next election, but they lack a clear property right to gains subsequent to the election. Unlike their market counterparts, politicians are unable to benefit from wise decisions that provide payoffs primarily in the future. As a result, politicians tend to exaggerate the importance of policy impacts prior to the next election and discount heavily their post-election consequences. Positive results must be observable by election day. After all, long-range policies that improve the status of the economy 6 or 12 months after the next election may well work to the benefit of a competitor one fails to defeat on election day.

Dwight Lee and Richard McKenzie (1987, p. 131) nicely summarize the myopic nature of the political process:

> Politicians . . . are in much the same position as the buffalo hunters of the 1870s. Each knew that all would be better off in the long run if everyone reduced his slaughter of the buffalo. But in the absence of private ownership, each also knew that the buffalo he did not shoot today would be shot by someone else tomorrow. Individual buffalo hunters found themselves in a situation in which there was little to gain, but much to lose, from taking a long-term perspective and exercising restraint in the extermination of the buffalo. Political decision-makers find themselves in a situation in which there is little to gain, but much to lose, by refraining from placing short)term demands on the economy that will, in the long run, exterminate much of our productive capacity.

This shortsightedness characteristic often leads to a conflict between good politics and sound economics. Policies can enhance the election prospects of politicians when the short-term results differ substantially from the effects over a longer time period. Unfortunately, this is often the case with economic issues. Examples abound. Financing government by monetary expansion is likely to stimulate employment and output in the short-run, even though inflation, uncertainty, and instability are side-effects observable in the long run. Borrowing to finance short-term programs that benefit coveted voting blocks is attractive even though the long-term result will be higher real interest rates, less capital formation, and higher future taxes. Rent controls tend to reduce rental housing prices in the short-term, even though housing shortages, black markets, and a deterioration in housing quality are the long run result. In each case, the more positive short-term effects increase the political attractiveness of policies that are generally detrimental in the long run.

Bureaucracy and Economic Waste

The day-to-day functions of government are performed by bureaus, which derive the major component of their revenues from the periodic appropriations of the legislature rather than from the direct sale of output to consumers. In effect, the legislative body supplies the bureau with a budget along with instructions for dealing with it's assigned tasks. The function of the bureau is to transform the budget into public services.

How will bureau managers and employees operate? If bureaucrats are pretty much like the rest of us—neither more nor less virtuous or self-interested, it is useful as a first approximation to view them as seeking to maximize the size of their bureau's budget (Niskanen 1971). A larger budget will enhance the opportunities and resources available at all levels. As the bureau expands, the power, prestige, salary and other benefits to bureau managers will generally increase. At the middle and lower levels of employment, a larger budget and bureau expansion will offer additional job security and possibilities for promotion. Larger budgets are also likely to generate additional funds for office space, furniture, travel, and other resources which improve the work environment of bureaucrats. Almost every bureaucrat can expect to gain something from the growth of his bureau; it is surely a rare bureaucrat who would lose as the result of budgetary expansion.

Therefore, the people who staff a bureau can be expected to develop and unite behind a strategy designed to increase the size of the bureau's budget. Interestingly, this is true even if, as is often the case, the bureaucrats have a burning desire to serve the mission of the bureau. Employees are often attracted to a bureau precisely because they want to promote the interest of the bureau's major clients. In addition, the bureau has a strong incentive to satisfy its clients since they are often an important source of political clout. Thus, it is not surprising that bureaus sometime become, in effect, a lobbying agency for interests they serve. For example, the Department of Agriculture is generally an advocate for farmers. Similarly, the Department of Defense tends to represent military suppliers and defense contractors. In budget matters the self-interest of the bureau and that of its client are parallel. Both want to enlarge the budget allocations of the bureau.

Political competition would seem to provide legislators with incentive to curb inefficient performance by public sector suppliers. Legislators who promote the efficient operation of government bureaus might seem likely to reduce their vulnerability to a challenge by potential competitors. However, there are four major reasons why it will be extremely difficult for a legislative body to control the budget of a bureau and promote opera-tional efficiency, particularly when the bureau is a monopoly supplier. First, bureaus do not have an easily identifiable "bottom line", analogous to the net income of a corporation, that might be used to judge the bureau's performance. Neither do they produce an easily quantifible output which might be used to calculate per unit costs. The absence of a well-defined index of performance provides managers in the public sector with con-siderably more leeway to gloss over inefficiency and pursue personal objectives than is available to their counterparts in the market sector.

Second, the major source of information with regard to the bureau's performance invariably comes from a biased source—the bureau itself. While the managers of the bureau know far more about the costs of alter-native outputs than anyone else, they also have a strong incentive to satisfy goals other than the minimizing of cost. A hospital administrator wants the most elaborate equipment. A university wants the finest computer. A fire chief wants the most advanced, showy fire truck. Predictably, the bureau will supply the legislative body with information indicating that it is stretched to the limit, supplying an immensely valuable service at a rock bottom cost. Dire predictions for the fate of the bureau's clients (or for society as a whole) will be projected if the bureau's budget is not increased. Of course, legislators know that bureau chiefs follow this strategy. Nonetheless, since they generally lack solid evidence capable of contradic-ting the bureau's cost estimates, legislators will find it difficult to restrain the bureau.

Third, legislative control is complicated because inefficient performance does not lead to the termination of an activity in the public sector. If a private business incurs costs in excess of the value of the service it provides, bankruptcy will eventually bring the operation to a halt. The public sector lacks a parallel process for controlling inefficiency and halting unsuccessful experiments. In fact, failure to meet objectives often generates pressure for larger appropriations in the public sector. If the crime rate is rising, the crime prevention agencies will lobby for additional funds. If the illegitimacy rate is soaring, the welfare industry will demand more funds for Aid For Dependent Children. If the Department of Defense is beset with cost overruns, you can bet that supplemental appropriations will be requested.

Fourth, bureaucrats and their clients often form a powerful coalition pressing for enlargement of the bureau. Since bureau employees and clients are highly concentrated, their interests are likely to be politically more effective than those of widely dispersed taxpayers, as we explain below. Of course, interest groups served by the bureau can be expected to be at the forefront of those advocating an expansion in the bureau's budget. In addition, the bureaucrats themselves may be a political force with which to reckon. Thus, the demand of persons *supplying* bureau services will supplement the demand of those *receiving* services from the bureau. Together these forces will tend to result in overproduction of bureau output (Niskanen 1971).

Beyond these reasons why it would be difficult for a legislative body to promote efficiency within the bureaus it oversees, it is questionable how strongly interested the legislature would be in bureau efficiency. To a substantial degree, oversight committees are comprised of those legislators who have high demands for the services of the bureaus they oversee. Agricultural committees, for instance, are likely to be staffed by legislators from rural areas; banking from urban areas with strong concentrations of financial institutions. As a result, oversight committees are more likely to favor larger budgets for the functions they oversee than the rest of the legislature.

In summary, economic analysis indicates that bureaucrats confront a perverse incentive structure that will lead to both high per unit costs and a rate of output for which the marginal value of the bureau's output is less than its cost. It is important to note that the fault lies with the organizational structure and not with the character of public sector employees. On the whole there is no reason to think that government employees are less competent, lazier, or less committed to their work than other workers. Nonetheless, given the incentive structure under which they toil, bureaucratic inefficiency is a predictable result.

Can anything be done to improve the situation? The nature of the problem does suggest a solution. Monopoly is at the core of bureaucratic inefficiency. Since bureau suppliers are generally monopolists, legislative monitors do not have alternative suppliers to provide a basis for evaluating their cost effectiveness. Both decentralization and contracting out offer an alternative to bureau production (Bish, Chapter 16 of this volume). Both would provide legislative bodies with a competitive supplier and additional information on costs which in turn could be used to improve the monitoring of remaining bureau suppliers.

The real world evidence is consistent with our analysis of public sector efficiency. The experience of Scottsdale, Arizona indicates that contracting of fire prevention services results in costs approximately 50 percent less than communities of similar size that rely on municipal production (Ahlbrandt 1973). A study by E. S. Savas of Columbia University of refuse collection in 260 cities found that cities contracting out the collection of garbage to private firms provide the service at less than two-thirds of the cost of municipal government production (Savas 1982). A more recent study by Robert Bish found that "competitive provision" of garbage collection in Canada cut costs by approximately 50 percent (Bish 1986). Just as competition works in the private sector, there is both theoretical reason and empirical evidence indicating that it also works in the public sector.

Fiscal Discrimination and Majoritarian Democracy

In the market, a consumer who wants to obtain a commodity must be willing to pay the price. The beneficiaries of market goods and services generally bear the cost of their provision. However, in the public sector, the persons bearing the cost of the activity are not always the primary or even the secondary beneficiaries.

In an earlier era, constitutional limitations effectively restrained fiscal discrimination—that is, policies which were designed to benefit various sub-groups of the population at the expense of their fellow citizens. As we discussed earlier, these constitutional limitations have eroded with the passage of time. The United States has gradually moved from a limited constitutional government with enumerated powers to a government with virtually unconstrained authority to tax, spend, and regulate—except for limitations imposed by the majoritarian political process.

Public choice theory indicates that various problems emerge from a majoritarian process that permits government to be used as an instrument to bestow fiscal favors on some while discriminating against others. This section explains the nature of these problems and indicates why they emerge naturally from an unconstrained majoritarian political process.

Fiscal Discrimination and Legislative Majorities

The simplest form of fiscal discrimination which permits one segment of society to gain at the expense of another is the use of government by a winning majority to enrich itself at the expense of a losing minority. The theory of external costs of traditional microeconomic analysis enhances our understanding of this issue. When external costs are present in a market, economic analysis indicates that excessive output can result because the parties to the transaction need not take into account the costs they impose on others. With majority rule, the same forces are present in the political arena. When a majority (either directly or through the legislative process) decides on a particular policy, the minority must accept the policy and help pay for its cost. The democratic process puts the majority in a position to send at least part of the bill to the minority. Suppose your uncle was willing to pay 49 percent of anything you purchased. You would tend to spend more on housing, clothes, food, and transportation than if you alone were paying the bill. It is the same with the budgetary choices of majorities. Since the majoritarian process does not force the majority to consider the costs it imposes on the nonconsenting minority, the majority supports wastefully large government as a by-product.

This proposition about overly-large budgets is not affected by recognition that people who win on one issue lose on others, with the income effects of winning and losing approximately offsetting one another. Someone who wins on subsidized education may lose on auto import quotas or restrictions on agricultural output. Even though the income effects of the various transfers may aggregate to zero, the substitution effects will bring about economic waste and excessive government. Furthermore, but relatedly, it is individually rational to pursue fully the opportunities available when in a winning majority, regardless of the losses that result when in the losing minority. After all, failure to exploit opportunities for gain when in the majority will merely confer benefits on others in the form a lower tax bill.

Expansion of output into the counterproductive range is also an expected result when the benefits of a project are clearly recognizable and the costs are partially concealed and difficult for voters to identify. In fact, vote-seeking politicians have an incentive to design programs and financing methods with precisely these characteristics.[6] Projects that provide highly visible benefits (for example, income transfers, low-cost housing or "cheap" irrigation) are highly attractive to politicians. In contrast, politicians will search for financing methods that conceal the cost of government and lead voters to believe that someone else is paying the bill. Viewed from this perspective, extensive use of debt-financing, indirect taxes, money creation, and unfunded retirement programs is a predictable result. As Senator Robert Dole put it, "Taxing is much like plucking a goose. It is the art of getting the greatest number of feathers with the least amount of hissing" (*Wall Street Journal*, December 16, 1983). When benefits are highly visible and the costs largely invisible, government programs will appear more attractive than is in fact the case. Adoption of inefficient programs and over-expansion of government is a side effect of the pressure on politicians to exaggerate the benefits and conceal the cost of government programs.

---

[6] Sellers in the market sector have an incentive to follow this same strategy. However, the one-to-one link between payment and receipt of goods in the market sector reduces the ability of suppliers to convince buyers that someone else is paying the bill.

Fiscal Discrimination and the Predominance of
Special Interest Legislation

A special interest issue is one that generates substantial personal benefits for a small number of constituents while imposing a small individual cost on a large number of other voters.[7] A few people benefit a great deal while almost everyone else loses a little bit. A majoritarian system of representative democracy is biased toward the adoption of special interest policies, even when those policies reduce the size of the economic pie. This can be seen by comparing the political gains a vote-seeking politician can expect by supporting the intense, concentrated interest of the few rather than the weak, diffused interest of the many. For the recipients of the concentrated benefits, the personal stake involved is substantial. Since the outcome of the issue is of such personal importance, the concentrated beneficiaries have a strong incentive to inform themselves and their allies and to let candidates (and legislators) know how strongly they feel about the issue. Many special interest voters will vote for or against politicians almost exclusively on the basis of whether they are supportive of their views. Special interests will also use financial contributions and other forms of assistance, to support politicians who are receptive to their views and oppose those who are not.

In contrast, consider the political payoff a representative could expect if he is supportive of the majority—the ordinary taxpayer if you like. Voters who have only a small personal cost imposed on them by the special interest policy will not care much about the issue. Most likely they will be rationally uninformed because the time and energy necessary to examine the issue and figure out its impact will be more costly than it is worth, particularly if the issue is fairly complex. Even if the members of the majority are informed on the issue, they will not feel very strong about it because it exerts little impact on their personal welfare. In addition, the bundle-purchase nature of the political process makes it virtually impossible for voters to register effectively their opposition on the specific issue, independent of other issues.

If you were a vote-seeking politician, what position would you take on special interest issues? Clearly, little would be gained if you supported the largely uninformed, disinterested majority. Support of their interests would not enhance your chances of getting elected. An astute politician who wants to succeed politically is strongly motivated to support narrow but intense over broad but diffuse interests. Those with intense interests are capable

---

[7] In some cases there may be well organized, intense interests on both sides of an issue. The analysis of this section applies to cases where the special interests are on only one-side of the issue.

of providing additional votes, campaign workers, and perhaps most importantly, financial contributions. In turn, the resources supplied by the special
interests can be used to buy media time and take other steps to win the
support of other voters.

Special interest policies are particularly attractive when they can be
packaged in a manner that will make it difficult for even alert voters to
recognize the cost imposed on them. The more complex the policy under
question, the more difficult it is for the average voter to figure out how
he or she is affected. There is an incentive for politicians to make special
interest issues very complex. The special interest group will most assuredly
figure out that it stands to gain from a given proposal, but the typical voter
will find it difficult to determine the seemingly complex proposal's actual
impact (Tullock 1966).

Special interest groups do not need to be large in order to be effective.
In fact, a special interest group can be handicapped by being too numerous,
and at least up to a point, it can benefit from being small in size (Becker
1981 and 1985). The smaller the interest group, the greater the leverage
it has on the majority. For example, if an interest group makes up 10 percent
of the population, it will cost the remaining 90 percent an average of $100
each to provide a subsidy of $900 to members of the interest group.
However, if the interest group is only 1 percent of the population, the same
$900 subsidy will cost other voters only about $9. Thus, the smaller the
interest group, the less it costs the rest of the population to provide the
interest group with a subsidy of any specified amount. Of course, the lower
cost will reduce the likelihood of opposition from voters in general.

The case of agriculture subsidies illustrates the importance of this leverage
effect as the size of an interest group declines. When farmers were 10
percent of the U.S. population, it would have been extremely costly to
provide them with transfers equal to one-half of their income. However,
when farmers are less than 2 percent of the population (as is now the case),
such a transfer level can be accomplished (and was in the mid 1980s)
without a substantial increase in taxes (or in the price of food products).
Viewed in this light, it is not surprising that the share of farm income derived
from subsidy programs has *risen* as the size of the farm population has
declined.

Why don't the taxpayers harmed by the transfers form a coalition and
throw out representatives who support such transfers to special interests?
There is some incentive to do this, but it is largely ineffective because the
cost of coalition formation is much lower for interest groups than for widely
dispersed taxpayers. Of course, when benefits are spread among members,
each individual member has an incentive to free ride, to let others expend
the necessary time and money to obtain the benefits. However, free riding
is easier to control among tightly knit groups like business, professional,

and labor organizations or when subsidies can be obtained which primarily benefit members who contribute. Unfortunately, taxpayers are a widely dispersed group. An individual's gain from opposing any specific special interest issue will be small. Thus, the free rider problem is more serious among taxpayers, leading to organizational costs that are generally prohibitive. Stated another way, coalitions in favor of concentrated benefits are far more efficient that those opposed to the resultant higher taxes.

What evidence is there that the power of special interest generates counterproductive policies in a democratic setting? Consider the case of the roughly 11,000 sugar farmers in the United States. The cost of producing sugar in the U.S. is three or four times higher than production costs in many other countries, particularly in the Caribbean. Nonetheless, Congress has instituted import restrictions and price supports which have pushed the U.S. price above 20 cents per pound compared to the 7 cents price on the world market. As of 1986 the average U.S. resident paid approximately $6 more for sugar each year than would otherwise have been the case, while the 11,000 sugar farmers gained $1.5 billion in gross income, approximately $130,000 per farm.[8] Of course, the average "rationally ignorant" voter is unaware that sugar farmers are among the leading contributors to politicians who exert a key impact on agricultural policy. As a nation we are poorer, because we could buy sugar cheaper than we can raise it. Nonetheless, the continuation of the program indicates that the current policy toward the sugar industry is "good politics" even if it is "bad economics".

The special interest effect helps explain the presence of other counterproductive legislation. Recent legislation paying dairy farmers to slaughter their herds and leave the industry was an effort to increase dairy prices and the incomes of dairy farmers, not to promote the general welfare. Tariffs and quotas on steel, automobiles, and textiles are designed to promote the interests of these industries, and not the citizenry in general. Regulations mandating that Alaskan oil be transported by the high cost American maritime industry reflect the industry's political clout, not its economic efficiency. Acreage restrictions and price supports on feed grains, tobacco, and peanuts generate waste and promote the adoption of inefficient production methods. Nonetheless, they survive in the political marketplace because agricultural pressure groups support such policies, while most others are largely disinterested and uninformed.

---

[8] Since domestic producers have higher production costs, their net gain is far less than the differential between the domestic and world price paid by the American consumer. In this case, as in most others, production inefficiency accompanying the transfer erodes most of the intended benefits.

Federally funded irrigation projects, subsidized grazing rights, loans at subsidized interest rates, subsidies to airports—the list goes on and on. Policy in each of these areas is rooted to the special interest effect, not sound economic doctrine. While each individually imposes only a small drag on our economy, in the aggregate they substantially diminish our standard of living.

Rent-Seeking, Political Plunder, and Economic Waste

Rent-seeking is a term used by economists to describe actions taken by individuals and groups to alter public policy in order to gain personal advantage at the expense of others.[9] The incentive to engage in rent-seeking activities is directly proportional to the ease with which the political process can be used for personal (or interest group) gain at the expense of others. When the effective law of the land makes it difficult to take the property of others or force others to pay for projects favored by you and your interest group, rent-seeking is unattractive (Epstein 1985). Under such circumstances, the benefits of rent-seeking are relatively low and few resources flow into rent-seeking activities. In contrast, when government fails to allocate the tax cost (through user fees or similar forms of financing) of its projects to the primary beneficiaries or when it becomes heavily involved in tax-transfer activities, the payoff to rent-seeking expands. Stated another way, when government becomes more heavily involved in providing benefits to some people at the expense of others, individuals and groups will invest more resources into efforts designed to shape political outcomes to their advantage.

The rent-seeking activities, which are a natural by-product of discriminatory fiscal action by the government, generate economic waste. Resources that would otherwise be used to create wealth and generate income are wasted fighting over slices of a shrinking economic pie. People will spend more time organizing and lobbying politicians and less time producing goods and services. The employment of lobbyists, expert witnesses, lawyers, accountants, and other political specialists capable of influencing public policy and/or the size of one's tax bill will expand. In contrast, engineers, architects, physical scientists, craft workers, machine operators and other workers involved in the creation of goods and services will decline as a share of the labor force (Gwartney and Stroup 1982). In response to rent-seeking by others, individuals will take defensive actions in an effort to protect their wealth. People will not stand still while they are fleeced. Of course, those defensive actions also consume valuable resources.

---

[9] The pioneering work on rent-seeking was done by Tullock (1967) and Krueger (1974). For additional information on this topic, also see Buchanan, Tollison, and Tullock (1981).

As Gordon Tullock (1967) and Terry Anderson and Peter J. Hill (1980, pp. 6-7) have pointed out, in terms of its impact on resource use, rent-seeking is similar to theft. Both rent-seeking and theft are efforts to gain income by taking from others, rather than by helping others in exchange for income. Improved prospects for personal gain via either rent-seeking or theft will expand the size of the redistributive sector and attract resources away from production. Just as an increase in the incidence of theft causes individuals to purchase more burglar alarms, safety deposit boxes, locks, dogs, and firearms, an increase in rent-seeking will lead to more defensive actions designed to resist transfers. Both rent-seeking and theft lead to negative sum activity and the social waste of resources.

In recent years, government has become more heavily involved in redistributive activities. Unsurprisingly, the growth of the redistributive sector has been accompanied by an increase in the flow of resources into lobbying—the most obvious form of rent-seeking activities. Between 1976 and 1983 the number of lobbyists registered with the federal government rose from 3,420 to 6,500, and increase of 90 percent in 7 years. As recently as 1979, New York had twice as many national trade associations as Washington. D.C. By 1983 the number of trade associations located in Washington, D.C. exceeded those located in New York by nearly 20 percent. A recent study found that 65 percent of the chief executive officers of the top 200 Fortune firms are in Washington on business at least once every two weeks, up from 15 percent a decade ago (Boaz 1983). When the political process makes transfers more likely, an increase in rent-seeking is a natural by-product.

Fiscal Non-Discrimination and The U.S. Constitution

Article I, Section 8 of the U.S. Constitution stands in contrast with the discriminatory fiscal activities and special interest politics that characterize modern majoritarian governments. That clause sets forth the general budgetary power of the federal government by proscribing:

> The Congress shall have Power to lay and collect, Taxes, Duties, Imposts and Excise, to pay the Debts and provide for the common Defence and general Welfare of the United States; but all Duties, Imposts and Excises shall be uniform throughout the United States.

As Article I, Section 8 stands, the budgetary powers of Congress are tightly constrained. Spending programs must be of *common* and *general* benefit, and may not be of special benefit only to subsets of people. Similarly, the taxes necessary to finance those spending programs must be levied in a *uniform* manner, so taxes may not be used to discriminate against some people for the benefit of others.

Public choice analysis indicates the wisdom of these constitutional provisions. If the uniformity clause were adhered to, it would prevent the taxing power of government from being used directly as an instrument of plunder, such as would happen if A, B, and C were to tell D and E that the tax burden was theirs to bear. The uniformity specification would require all five to pay taxes. In this respect it is perhaps worth noting that the top 50 percent of taxpayers currently pay about 93 percent of all federal income taxes. And if the larger number of tax exempt voters were taken into account, it would doubtless be the case that the top 50 percent of voters, arrayed by taxes paid, pay close to 100 percent of the federal income tax.

But even if all five were required to pay taxes, the majoritarian political process might allow A, B, and C (or even powerful minority interests) to appropriate general tax revenues for their own personal benefit, and thereby circumvent the protection offered by the uniformity requirement. However, expenditures for the benefit of particular subsets of the population are also prohibited by the requirement that federal spending is limited by the restriction that it be for the *common* defense and *general* welfare.

Of course, today the constitutional adjectives limiting the taxing and spending powers of Congress are ignored. As several of the authors in this book note, for all practical purposes Congress is now free to use public funds to advance the welfare of whichever *particular* groups it selects for favorable treatment.[10] Similarly, as Gale Norton points out (see Chapter 12) neither are there any effective constitutional restraints limiting the ability of Congress to impose taxes in a discriminatory manner.

But suppose this was not the case—suppose the restrictions of Article I, Section 8 were effective. With such a requirement of non-discrimination in taxing and spending, democratic political processes could turn out to be relatively efficient as well as respectful of personal liberty and private property. The development of programs which benefitted most people, if not everyone, would be accentuated. Federal programs that were efficient—those providing general benefits greater than the general taxes required for their finance—would tend to be favored by most all voters (and therefore most all legislators). Correspondingly, inefficient programs which were more costly than the accompanying benefits would tend to be rejected by most all voters. If the federal government got involved in proposals designed to benefit specific interests, it would have to finance

---

[10] For example, see Epstein (Chapters 9 and 14), Aranson (Chapter 13), Higgs (Chapter 17), and Lee and McKenzie (Chapter 18).

them with user fees rather than taxes.[11] Of course, state and local governments might undertake special interest projects, but at these levels it would
be much easier to escape any oppressive action by government. If
discriminatory fiscal activities were precluded, as intended by the constitutional provisions calling for uniformity, commonality, and generality, the
political process would yield outcomes similar to those that would emerge
from exchanges based on mutual agreement.[12]

Public Choice, Majoritarian Pathologies, and the Case for Constitutional Government

Public choice explains why various pathologies emerge from majoritarian
government. To speak of pathology requires, of course, some normative
standard to serve as a basis for comparison. Clearly, within the American
constitutional framework, that standard is something more than simply
whatever emerges from democratic processes. The standard against which
it is possible to speak of pathology within the American constitutional
framework is the Lockean standard of individual self-ownership. People's
rights of person and property are normatively prior to government. Hence,
government is not a source of rights, but is only a reflection of people's
use of their rights, as exemplified by the principles of the protective and
productive states. The task of government is, within the American constitutional order, twofold: (1) to promote the security of individual rights and
(2) to provide those services that people cannot provide for themselves
through ordinary market processes.

In other words, within the American context, mutual agreement is the
standard of comparison. Therefore, behavior that oppresses some for the
benefit of others is pathological. If two people encounter a third on the
street and demand the third person's money, that is a violation of the third
person's rights and it is the task of the protective state to prohibit such
conduct. But it is no different if the three people constitute a government,
with the two taxing the third person for their benefit. Nonetheless, as public
choice theory illustrates, the unconstrained majoritarian political process
yields outcomes of precisely this nature.

---

[11] An important feature of user fees is their ability to reveal to public sector decision-makers
evidence on how much citizens really value a project. If user fees are sufficient to cover the
cost of the government-provided good or service, this is strong evidence that the project is
worthwhile. The converse is also true. If users are unwilling to pay for the cost of a government-
provided activity, this is powerful evidence that the activity should be curtailed because it
is not valued as much as the alternative use of the resource.

[12] See W. H. Hutt (1966) for an analysis of the general equivalence of fiscal non-discrimination
and unanimity as a characteristic of the political process.

As the authors of *The Federalist* clearly indicate, the framers of the U.S. Constitution feared the pathologies of majoritarian governments. The authors of these essays both explained the pathologies of majoritarian government and argued that the Constitution they were supporting would hold them in check. Modern public choice theory indicates that checking democratic pathologies is an even more difficult task than Madison, Hamilton, and Jay envisoned. Nonetheless, the central thrust of public choice theory is congruent with that of *The Federalist*: people are essentially the same when they act publicly as when they act privately, self-interest is dominant throughout human affairs, and good government is much more a matter of having rightly constructed institutions that channel self-interest in valuable directions than it is a matter of exhorting people to deny their basic nature when acting publicly.

The intellectual folly of our Age is the view that majoritarian democracy is a sufficient condition for the preservation of a free society based on the consent of the governed. Today, Americans seem to have confidence in majoritarian democracy, but that confidence runs counter to the lessons of history. Generalizing from his study of democracy in ancient Greece, Alexander Tytler, the 18th century Scot historian concluded:

> A democracy cannot exist as a permanent form of government. It can only exist until a majority of voters discover that they can vote themselves largess out of the public treasury. From that moment on, the majority always votes for the candidate who promises them the most benefits from the public treasury, with the result being that democracy always collapses over a loose fiscal policy.[13]

The use of democratic government as an instrument of plunder is as much rooted in human nature as is theft more broadly construed. While there is surely scope for the man of the cloth in any effort to control theft or plunder, it would be foolish to rely exclusively on such efforts. Incentives must also be changed. The man of violence must restrain and punish thieves and thereby reduce the incentive to engage in theivery. It is the same with democratic government. The cultivation of civic virtues is important. But the man of the cloth cannot do the job alone. Incentives within government must also be constructed properly. This is the task of appropriate constitutional construction, as the founders of our constitutional order noted and as the growing body of public choice scholarship is showing afresh.

---

[13] As quoted in Niskanen (1978), p. 159.

References

Ahlbrandt, Roger. "Efficiency in the Provision of Fire Services." *Public Choice* 16 (1973): 1-15.

Anderson, Terry L. and Hill, Peter J. *The Birth of the Transfer Society.* Stanford: Hoover Institution Press, 1980.

Becker, Gary S. "A Theory of Competition Among Pressure Groups for Political Influence." *Quarterly Journal of Economics* 98 (August 1983): 373-400.

Becker, Gary S. "Public Policies, Pressure Groups, and Dead Weight Costs." *Journal of Public Economics* 28 (December 1985): 329-47.

Bish, Robert. "Improving Productivity in the Government Sector." In *Response to Economic Change*, pp. 203-37. Edited by David Laidler. Toronto: University of Toronto Press, 1986.

Boaz, David. "Spend Money to Make Money." *Wall Street Journal* (13 November 1983) Op-ed.

Buchanan, James M. and Gordon Tullock. *The Calculus of Consent.* Ann Arbor: University of Michigan Press, 1962.

Buchanan, James M. *The Limits of Liberty.* Chicago: University of Chicago Press, 1975.

Buchanan, James M. *The Economics of Politics.* London: The Institute of Economic Affairs, 1978.

Buchanan, James M., Robert D. Tollison, and Gordon Tullock. *Toward a Theory of the Rent-Seeking Society.* College Station: Texas A & M University Press, 1981.

Dietze, Gottfried. *The Federalist: A Classic on Federalism and Free Government.* Baltimore: John Hopkins University Press, 1980.

Downs, Anthony. *An Economic Theory of Democracy.* New York: Harper and Bros., 1957.

Epstein, Richard A. *Takings: Private Property and the Power of Eminent Domain.* Cambridge: Harvard University Press, 1985.

Gwartney, James D. and Stroup, Richard L. "Cooperation or Conniving: How Public Sector Rules Shape Decisions." *Journal of Labor Research* 3 (Summer 1982): 247-57.

Gwartney, James D. and Stroup, Richard L. *Economics: Private and Public Choice.* San Diego: Harcourt, Brace, and Jovanovich, 1987.

Hutt, William H. "Unanimity Versus Non-Discrimination (as Criteria for Constitutional Validity)." *South African Journal of Economics* 34 (June 1966): 133-47.

Krueger, Anne O. "The Political Economy of the Rent-Seeking Society." *American Economic Review* 15 (June 1974): 291-303.

Lee, Dwight R. and McKenzie, Richard B. *Regulating Government: A Preface to Constitutional Economics.* Lexington, Mass.: Lexington Books, 1987.

Mitchell, William C. "Fiscal Behavior of the Modern Democratic State: Public Choice Perspectives and Contributions." In *Political Economy: Recent Views*, pp. 69-114. Edited by L. Wade. Los Angeles: Sage, 1983.

Niskanen, William A. *Bureaucracy and Representative Government*. New York: Aldine-Atherton, 1971.

Niskanen, William A. "The Prospect for Liberal Democracy." In *Fiscal Responsibility in Constitutional Democracy*, pp. 157-74. Edited by James M. Buchanan and Richard E. Wagner. Leiden: Martinus Nijhoff, 1978.

Ostrom, Vincent. *The Political Theory of a Compound Republic*. Fairfax, VA: Center for Study of Public Choice, George Mason University, 1971.

Padover, Saul K. *The Forging of American Federalism: Selected Writings of James Madison*. New York: Harper and Row, 1953.

Savas, E. S. *Privatizing the Public Sector: How to Shrink Government*. Chatham, New Jersey: Chatham House Publishers, 1982.

Siegan, Bernard H. *Economic Liberties and the Constitution*. Chicago: University of Chicago Press, 1980.

Stigler, George J. *The Citizen and the State*. Chicago: University of Chicago Press, 1975.

Tullock, Gordon. *Toward a Mathematics of Politics*. Ann Arbor: University of Michigan Press, 1966.

Tullock, Gordon. "The Welfare Cost of Tariffs, Monopolies, and Theft." *Economic Inquiry* (June 1967): 224-32.

Wagner, Richard E. and Weber, Warren E. "Competition, Monopoly, and the Organization of Government in Metropolitan Areas." *Journal of Law and Economics* 18 (December 1975): 661-84.

2

PUBLIC CHOICE AND CONSTITUTIONAL ORDER

Richard E. Wagner and James D. Gwartney

> The great desideratum in Government is, so to modify the sovereignty
> as that it may be sufficiently neutral between different parts of the Society
> to control one part from invading the rights of another, and at the same
> time sufficiently controlled itself, from setting up an interest adverse to
> that of the entire society.
>
> —James Madison, letter to Thomas Jefferson
> —October 24, 1787

Introduction

In the same year (1776) the Founding Fathers proclaimed in the
Declaration of Independence that governments derive "their just powers
from the consent of the governed," Adam Smith described in the *Wealth
of Nations* how the inhabitants of a free society could also be more
prosperous than those who lived in a restricted, mercantilistic society.
These two documents laid the foundation for limited constitutional
government and a free market economy, the primary mechanisms of
social cooperation based on mutual agreement rather than force—on
the natural rights of individuals rather than interests of governments.
The subsequent unfolding of the American experiment with limited
government and a market-directed economy resoundingly illustrated the
merits of these arrangements—they lead to both economic prosperity
and personal liberty. But in recent decades our constitutional limits on
governmental power have been rent asunder again and again.[1] A government virtually without limits, save those inherent in the majoritarian
political process, has emerged. Reflecting the lack of restraint on the
powers of government, public sector spending has expanded from less
than 10 percent of Gross National Product (GNP) in the 1920s to

---

[1] See, for instance, Anderson and Hill (1980), Siegan (1980), Norton (1985), and Epstein
(1985).

29

more than 35 percent in the 1980s.

The massive growth of government in this century reflects to a large degree, changes in the American concept of government. Government used to be viewed as a *consensual arrangement* designed for the *mutual betterment* of all. First and foremost, it protected the lives, liberties, and possessions of all citizens from intruders—both foreign and domestic— who would take what did not belong to them. As Madison (1792) put it, "A just government impartially secures to every man whatsoever is his own." In addition, government was sometimes used to undertake projects such as construction of roads and power sources designed to capture mutual benefits that could not be achieved (or could be achieved only at a higher cost) with private action. Mutual gain was the center piece of this view of government which, until recently, was the dominant American view.

In contrast with the consensual view, today government is widely viewed as an agency through which we pursue objectives *favored by a legislative majority* (for example, a modified distribution of income, additional spending on education, or favored treatment for various interest groups). To the adherents of this view, "consent of the governed" has come to mean majority rule. Most Americans are virtually oblivious to the inherent conflict between majoritarian government and the liberty of individuals. The case of so-called entitlements—transfers of money or in-kind benefits from taxpayers to various segments of the population—vividly illustrates this conflict. If one group is granted an entitlement to food or housing, another group must be forced to labor to grow that food and supply that housing. A system of entitlements on the product side of the market must necessarily entail a system of servile labor on the factor side. Of course, entitlements and the accompanying servile labor account for much of the growth of government in this century.

While constitutional limitations protect minorities against the actions of the majority, constitutional government is difficult to maintain. In this chapter we will explore why the maintenance of a constitutional order is extremely fragile and investigate governmental structures that might make it less so.

Hobbesian Anarchy and Constitutional Order

The central economic principles of constitutional order can be seen by contrasting the conduct of economic activity under two alternative regimes.[2] One would be a system of constitutional order, under which economic activities are organized throught the legal principles expressed by the ideas of property and contract. When private property rights are clearly defined

---

[2] See, for instance, Tullock (1972, 1974) and Buchanan (1975).

and enforced, individuals are prohibited from using the property of others, including their labor, without their consent. Thus, mutual agreement is a requisite condition for social interaction. For example, someone who wants to manufacture and sell shirts must get the agreement of resource owners to supply him with the labor, materials, and other inputs necessary to produce shirts, and to sell the shirts he must get the agreement of consumers to buy them. The economic life of such a constitutional order is a complex network of trades based on consent—that is, mutual agreements between parties.

The alternative regime would be a system of Hobbesian anarchy, perhaps depicted most explicitly by the expression "anything goes." Trading would be permitted; people could cooperate with each other according to the rules of property and contract. But those rules would not be the exclusive basis for economic organization. Violence would also be permissible. A manufacturer of shirts might conscript people to work for him. Or he might try to prevent people from working in competitive outlets, such as at home. He may also try to prevent people from buying imported shirts and he may spend some time trying to take shirts that others have already produced. Whereas "trade" is the only admissible economic activity under constitutional order, "plunder" is also admissible under Hobbesian anarchy.

To say that plunder is admissible under Hobbesian anarchy does not, we should note, imply that life will truly be "nasty, brutish, and short," for as John Umbeck (1981) notes, people will always seek to avoid Hobbesian anarchy by establishing some form of order.[3] Nonetheless, this taxonomy does make it easier to visualize the purpose of constitutional regimes as well as the forces that can undermine those regimes. In the Hobbesian world of anything goes, people will, of course, expend less effort on production and trade and more effort on various forms of plunder. In fact, potential gains from plunder will generate two side effects: one is the offensive effort to take what belongs to others; the other is the defense effort to avoid being victimized by the plundering of others. But in either case the composition of human effort in a society characterized by Hobbesian anarchy will differ from that found in a society characterized by constitutional order. People will engage exclusively in production and trade in the latter case but part of their energy will be allocated to plundering under Hobbesian anarchy.

The superiority of a system of constitutional order, as well as the latent incentives that would undermine it, can be illustrated by the prisoners'

---

[3] Focusing on the development of order in California's gold mining areas between the departure of the Mexican government in 1848 and the arrival of the American government in 1850, Umbeck's work illustrates the tendency of a contractural-based government, not unlike that advocated by Spencer McCallem (1970), to emerge from anarchy.

dilemma model illustrated by Exhibit 2.1. Although the exhibit allows the portrayal of only two people, the dilemma should be understood as applying to many people, which reduces the personal element that is inherent in a two-person illustration. The model illustrates a situation in which each person can choose between two economic strategies: "trade" which entails an adherence to the common law principles of property and contract, and "plunder" which eliminates all restrictions on economic conduct, meaning that theft and other forms of violence are also admissible options. The extent to which the two options are pursued depends on their relative payoffs.

Exhibit 2.1:
ILLUSTRATIVE MODEL OF THE SOCIAL DILEMMA

	\multicolumn{4}{c}{Individual A Engages in:}			
	\multicolumn{2}{c}{Trade}	\multicolumn{2}{c}{Plunder ("anything goes")}
	A's Income	B's Income	A's Income	B's Income
Individual B Engages In:				
Trade	100	100	120	30
Plunder "anything goes"	30	120	50	50

Exhibit 2.1 illustrates a situation in which the participants are inherently equal. This is not a necessary assumption, and making it does not essentially restrict the conclusions from what would result if the participants differed in their abilities. If both parties adhere to the rules of property and contract, their income will be $100 each. On the other hand, if both parties engage in plunder as well as producing, income falls to $50 each. This reduction in income results because the participants shift some of their efforts away from production and trade into theft and protecting against being victimized by the thievery of others. The resulting diminution in the effort devoted to production and trade implies a reduction in the total income of the society. Exhibit 2.1 implicitly assumes that the reduction in income is 50 percent and that the reduction is shared equally between the two parties. The latter assumption implies that the two parties are equally capable both at trading and at plundering. The introduction of different assumptions about relative abilities would not affect the central point of Exhibit 2.1 as long as plundering adversely affects aggregate income. This

being the case, clearly both (all) participants would prefer a system of constitutional order—one that prohibited plundering—to the "anything goes" conditions of Hobbesian anarchy.

However, the preferred system of constitutional order is not a product of each individual pursuing his or her self interest, independent of all others. While all participants are better off under a system of constitutional order in which they limit their activities to trading, each individual has an incentive to engage in plunder. Thus, when each person acts independent of others, they get caught in the classical prisoners' dilemma. The outcome is the joint-plundering of Hobbesian anarchy (southeast cell). Consider the position of person A against the rest of society, everyone else, represented by B. If A assumes others will stick to the rules of trade (row one), A is better off to switch to a strategy of plunder, for his income rises from $100 to $120. The others, represented by B, are, of course, worse off. The total income in the society has fallen from $200 to $150, indicating both that A has reduced his efforts at trading and that B has perhaps done likewise, through engaging in defensive efforts to protect against being victimized by A.

Alternatively, if A assumes that the others will engage in plunder (row 2), he would be foolish to stick purely with trade, for if he were to do so his income would be only $30. But were he also to engage in plunder he could increase his income to $50. Other people are, of course, in the same situation as A. When considered from the perspective of these other people, that is person B in Exhibit 2.1, the ultimate outcome is one in which all participants come to adopt a strategy of anything goes, and so come to live under a regime of Hobbesian anarchy. Total income declines to $100 (reflecting the movement of resources from production and trade to plunder), although its distribution is unchanged, since we assume that the relative abilities of A and B are equal with regard to trading and plundering.

The Nature of Constitutional Contract

Clearly, people have an incentive to develop a constitutional order whereby they agree to abide by the rules of trade and to refrain from plunder. A constitutional contract provides a possible escape from the prisoners' dilemma in which the members of society are otherwise caught. In effect, constitutional order is a mutually advantageous treaty among what would otherwise be warring factions—a treaty which promotes the substitution of wealth-creating trade for wealth-reducing plunder. This agreement to restrict the scope of permissible economic activities—this ratification of a constitutional contract—represents, even if only metaphorically and not literally, the establishment of a government to act as an instrument for promoting production and trade through deterring the various forms of plunder. It is important to note that the central idea of constitutional government is that the creation of a constitution is not itself an act of government. Rather a constitution represents an agreement among a set of people to constitute a government. People's natural rights of person and property, as represented, for instance, by the Lockean concept of individual self-ownership, are prior to government. A constitutional contract is a reflection of people's use of their natural rights to secure improvement in their well-being. All human beings have a right, prior to the existence of government, to the protection of their life, liberty (voluntary associations based on consent), and worldly possessions acquired without the use of violence, theft, or fraud. As the Declaration of Independence states, governments are instituted "to secure these rights" and they derive "their just powers from the consent of the governed."

Since people's natural rights limit the legitimate activities of government, it follows that, as the noted constitutional scholar Charles McIlwain observed (1947, p. 21) in his historical survey of thought and practice on the notion of constitutional government: "Constitutional government is by definition limited government." The very *raison d'etre* of constitutional government is that government is subject to limits that reside in people's prior rights of person and property, and most clearly, government itself is not the arbiter of those limits.

Why is the protection of each individual's person and property acquired without the use of violence, theft or fraud so important? Such protection is the foundation of social cooperation based on mutual agreement, and in the final analysis, *mutual agreement* is the only valid test that an action is beneficial.[4] When property rights are protected—when people are restrained from invading the premises of others and taking what does not belong to them—social cooperation based on mutual agreement emerges naturally. Individuals seeking the assistance of others will offer them compensation large enough to elicit the desired cooperation. Sellers will seek out those willing to offer the highest prices for their services and products. Simultaneously, buyers will search for those offering the cheapest prices—those giving them the most value for their money. The terms of trade (the price) must be acceptable to both buyer and seller; otherwise the exchange will not take place. Thus, only mutually beneficial exchanges occur. When property rights are clearly defined, mutual consent provides powerful evidence that the action is beneficial to both the trading parties

---

[4] As James Madison (1792) argues in his essay on property, when it is broadly perceived to include one's person, opinions, and religious beliefs, as well as labor services and material possessions, indeed the protection of private property is the foundation of human freedom. For additional detail on the importance of private property to the preservation of personal liberty see the papers of Roger Pilon, Richard Epstein, and Terry Anderson and P. J. Hill in Part III of this volume.

and the economy as a whole. As Adam Smith explained more than 200 years ago, market prices will direct the participants as if by an "invisible hand" to produce, cooperate, and serve the interests of others. History indicates that this mechanism of social cooperation is also highly productive, leading to prosperity for all segments of society.

Mutual consent is the central characteristic of social cooperation through markets; it is also the central attribute of constitutional government. If a government is constitutional in reality rather than in name only, it must reflect a broad consensus among all segments of society.

Why Constitutional Government Is Difficult To Maintain

The very idea of constitutional government is that the authority of government is limited to the boundaries proscribed by the constitutional contract. But "government" is an abstract noun. Unless government is designed with built-in incentives capable of keeping it within constitutional bounds, there is no inherent reason for real governments act in the manner envisioned by the constitutional contract. Government may, for instance, become an instrument of plunder, with those who gain control of governmental authority using that authority to prey upon others, thereby leading to a reassertion of the Hobbesian dilemma.

While individuals have strong incentives to design a constitutional order prohibiting plunder, once government is established there is also a strong incentive to cheat on the constitutional contract and use government as an instrument to gain advantage over others. Thus, a constitutional order will not be easy to maintain. Exhibit 2.1 can be used to illustrate why this is the case. Suppose that A and B represent groups of individuals, each of whom agreed at the constitutional stage to abide by the rules of property and contract. Nonetheless, the basic structure of the social dilemma remains. Individuals (and groups) still have an incentive to undertake various forms of plunder, including the use of government as an instrument of plunder, if they can get away with it. Clearly, group A can gain (move to the northeast cell) if it can use government to take from B. For example, members of group A might improve their economic position by changing the rules so the members of group B will have to sell to group A at a lower price, or buy from group A at a higher price, or pay for goods that benefit group A. The potential gains will provide group A with an incentive to promote such policies. Of course, the same opportunities for using government as an instrument of plunder hold for group B. It, too, has an incentive to capture the reins of government and use this power to take from group A (a move to the southwest cell).

When one group is able to use the possession of governmental authority to prey on others, master-servant relationships arise. Those with political power rule over those without it. When the possession of the governmental authority is permanent (highly secure), as in authoritarian regimes, the outcome is represented by either the northeast or southwest cells of Exhibit 2.1 depending upon whether A or B is in control of the government. Both economic stagnation and a highly unequal income distribution are the expected outcome.

When constitutional restraints erode in a manner which permits many groups to use the powers of government to take from others, as is generally the case under unconstrained democratic regimes, the economy moves toward the joint-taking outcome illustrated by the southeast cell of Exhibit 2.1. Since everybody (or nearly everybody) is playing the "taking" game, the distributional consequences will be more egalitarian under a democratic than an authoritarian regime (compare the southeast cell of Figure 2.1 with either the northeast or southwest cells). Nevertheless, both regimes will involve an erosion of aggregate income (output) relative to the potential achievable under constitutional order because both move resources from production and trade into plunder.

Unfortunately, anarchy in the state of nature is not the only route to the Hobbesian jungle. As Chapter 1 illuminates, majoritarian legislative processes do not naturally prevent government from becoming an agent of plunder. Indeed, the prisoners' dilemma model in conjunction with the special interest effect and rent seeking theory of modern public choice analysis indicates that the substitution of plunder for trade is the "natural" (unconstrained) outcome of majoritarian legislative processes. When constitutional restraints are effectively absent, organized interests tend to exploit disorganized taxpayers and consumers. The business of government becomes the use of taxing, spending, and regulatory powers to rearrange property rights in order to achieve political gain. Politics becomes the arena in which chaotic mayhem of the Hobbesian jungle takes place. Political skills replace physical violence as the primary weapon used by individuals and groups to take from others. Nevertheless, the outcome is much the same: output suffers because resources are moved from production and trade to taking and bickering. Unless constitutional rules impose restraints, majoritarian democracy is not a move out of the Hobbesian jungle; instead it is merely a shift of the fighting to a new location.

Substantive Constraints and Procedural Design—Two Strategies For The Maintenance of Constitutional Order

The social dilemma model both (a) illuminates the mutual gains people can achieve from a constitutional order which constrains taking activities and the social waste they generate and (b) explains why such a constitutional order will be difficult to maintain. How can a people limit the scope of postconstitutional opportunism—including the use of government as an instrument of plunder? There are two major strategies to achieve this task. First, *substantive constraints* designed to limit the scope of the ordinary legislative process and protect freedom of contract and private property from all intruders, including the government itself, can be incorporated into a constitutional contract. An external authority, the Supreme Court in the United States, can be assigned the task of enforcement. The external authority becomes the arbitrator of what is constitutional and what is not. It is the function of the external authority to declare unconstitutional any legislation emanating from the ordinary legislative process which is outside of the constitutional boundary.

A second strategy, we might call it the *procedural design approach*, establishes political institutions and procedures which reduce the likelihood that governmental policies plundering some for the benefit of others will be adopted. This strategy pursues the logic of a self-enforcing constitution, under which constitutional maintenance is an *internal* process that depends on the incentives contained within the legislative process.

The two strategies are by no means mutually exclusive. The framers of the U.S. constitution utilized both. Perhaps the best example of the procedural design approach is the differing criteria for representation in the House and Senate. At the time of the Constitutional Convention, delegates from small states feared the legislative dominance of the populous states if representation were based on population. Simultaneously, the populous states feared the dominance of the small states if equal representation were granted each state. The framers crafted constitutional procedures which protected both. Each state was granted equal representation in one legislative branch (the Senate), while representation was based on population in the other (the House). Since approval of both branches was required for passage, this procedural design protected the interests of both small and large states.

Do Substantive Provisions Of The U. S. Constitution Promote Trading And Prohibit Taking?

Does the U.S. Constitution contain substantive provisions which preclude legislatively sanctioned plunder by which some people enrich themselves at the expense of others, using government as a vehicle for doing what they could not legitimately accomplish by acting as private citizens? As the recent work of Richard Epstein (1985) and Bernard Siegan (1980) indicates, one can build a strong case for an affirmative answer to this question.

The framers of the U.S. Constitution wrote a document which enumerated the various powers of the federal government. Furthermore, it was agreed, as the Tenth Amendment states, that "powers not delegated to the United States [the central government] by the Constitution, nor prohibited by it to the states, are reserved to the states respectively, or to the people." James Madison stressed this point in *Federalist* No. 45:

> The powers delegated by the proposed constitution to the federal government are few and defined. Those which are to remain with the State governments are numerous and indefinite . . . The powers reserved to the several States will extend to all the objects which, in the ordinary course of affairs, concern the lives, liberties, and properties of the people, and the internal order, improvements and prosperity of the states.

While Congress was granted the power to levy and collect taxes, these taxes were to be "uniform throughout the United States." Furthermore, revenues from the uniform taxes were only to be used for spending programs which "provide for the *common* defense and *general* welfare" (Article I, Section 8, Clause 1). The requirement of uniform taxation precludes, on a regional basis, a winning coalition from discriminating against everyone else, thereby preventing government on the taxing side of the budget from being an instrument by which some people enrich themselves by shifting tax burdens onto others. The constitutional requirement that the expenditure of tax revenues be for the *common* defense and the *general* welfare indicates that it was the intent of the framers to limit *federal* expenditures to projects which provide widespread benefits to most all citizens in all parts of the nation. This view is reinforced by the general nature of benefits emanating from functions mentioned explicitly in the constitution, including the development of a monetary system and a standard system of weights and measures; the establishment of a court system, uniform rules of naturalization, laws of bankruptcy, post offices, and post roads; and the raising up of an Army and Navy. All of this implies that it was the intent of the framers that uniform taxes be levied and that the revenues from such taxes be used only for the purpose of financing governmental activities providing generalized benefits to all (or most all) citizens throughout the nation. This arrangement would approximate the condition of fiscal non-discrimination. As our analysis of Chapter 1 illustrates, when this is the case, the political process works reasonably well.

Certainly, there is nothing in the Constitution which authorizes programs of the general nature that A and B enrich themselves at the expense of C (and possibly at the expense of D and E as well). There is nothing to indicate that the federal government is authorized to tax persons throughout the nation in order to, for example, subsidize a subway system for Washington, D.C. or a waste disposal system for Chicago, Illinois. Neither is there any authorization for the use of the uniformly levied taxes to finance programs designed to benefit wheat farmers, small businesses, large businesses, the maritime industry, sugar growers, families with dependent children or any of the literally thousand of other narrow interest groups which currently benefit from tax dollars. Such programs represent the use of public funds for *private* use. They are a violation of the public trust doctrine (see Epstein, Chapter 14 of the volume).

In addition, the U.S. Constitution also places explicit restrictions on (1) the taking of private property and (2) interferences with the freedom of contract. The Fifth Amendment states, "nor shall private property be taken for public use without just compensation." Article I, Section 10 mandates, "No State shall . . . pass any . . . law impairing the obligation of contracts." As Richard Epstein has articulated so persuasively, these sections, like the provisions with regard to the taxing and spending powers of Congress, reflect the principle that government should not be an instrument by which some people enrich themselves by infringing upon the rights of others. If two people acting privately cannot legitimately take the property of a third, neither should they be able to do so just because they form a political majority.

However, just as the social dilemma model indicates, it is one thing to incorporate substantive provisions against takings and quite another to constrain the ordinary legislative process within the constitutional boundary. Despite the internal consistency of the U.S. Constitution and the apparent clarity of key limitations on taking activities, the constitution has failed to control legislative bodies intent on the support of plunder in the guise of public policy.

Legislative actions which plunder some for the benefit of others have became such a routine element of the political process that they are often overlooked. The owners of developed property often secure ordinances from zoning boards which restrict the development of underdeveloped property (*Agins v. City of Tiburon*[5]). Not only do such zoning ordinances decrease the value of the underdeveloped property, but also, because they restrict the supply of competitive land, they increase the value of the developed property. In effect, the zoning ordinances enable the owners of the developed property effectively to rob the owners of the undeveloped property, just as surely as if the owners of developed land had forcibly prevented the owners of the undeveloped land from developing their land. As noted above, restricting the ability of people to manufacture clothing in their homes is plunder. It represents an effort by some people to restrict other people's rights of property and contract. It is just as much plunder as would be an outright raid to steal the output of people who work at home. Similarly, prohibitions on the ability of people to install lawn sprinklers, repair television sets, landscape yards, and engage in hundreds of other

[5] 447 U.S. 255 (1980).

occupations without a license constitute plunder. Such regulations deflect effort from exchange into the prevention of exchanges that would otherwise take place (Young 1987).

Under a regime of private property and freedom of contract, you could invest in a herd of diary cattle if you chose, and could make a living to the extent you could find people willing to buy your milk. It would be a violation of your rights of person and property, and of the constitutional contract, for an existing set of farmers to prevent you from engaging in the production of milk. For their efforts to do so would represent a form of plunder, just as surely as if they had confiscated part or all of what you had already produced. Nonetheless, legislative action permits the Department of Agriculture to establish marketing orders which accomplish precisely this objective—the restriction of potential entrants into the diary industry. Legislators have also been quite willing to establish restrictions limiting entry into various occupations and lines of business activity. There are now literally thousands of monopolistic enclaves embedded in our economy, making it perhaps more accurate to refer to our economic system as mercantilist or neomercantilist rather than free enterprise.[6]

As the literature on rent-seeking and the power of special interests shows, the list of predatory activities is lengthy and growing. Even through the constitutional contract in the United States elevates exchange over plunder, the legislative process is often an instrument for the latter. As a result, resources are transferred from wealth-expanding "trading activities" to wealth-reducing "taking activities" and our aggregate level of income is diminished.

Shortcomings Of Substantive Constraints

Why have the substantive provisions failed to restrain taking activities via the political process? There are three major reasons for this failure. 1. *Since judges are chosen via the political process and alternative interpretations of constitutional rules are possible, there is nothing to prevent the politicizing of the judicial process.* While we are impressed with the strength of the case that the Supreme Court has failed to restrain legislative acts that are obviously violations of the Constitution, we must admit that alternative interpretations are possible. Consider the case of transfer programs,

---

[6] One of the long-standing principles of common law is that competition is not a tort. As the owner of a bakery you can bring an action for damages against someone who drives a truck into your store, destroying 50 percent of the net worth of your bakery in the process. But you cannot bring an action against someone who opens another bakery that reduces your business, diminishing your net worth by 50 percent in the process. However, a prolix variety of recent legislation does, in effect, make competition a tort by restricting the ability of people to engage in economic activities in competition with those already established.

which use general tax revenue to make payments to farmers, the poor, and other well defined groups. These programs would appear to patently violate the public use and just compensation limitations on the taking of private property. Is it possible for someone to present an argument that has at least some plausibility that transfers of this variety are constitutional permissible? The answer is "yes." There is an economic literature that argues that charity has characteristics of a public good, and hence is subject to free rider problems.[7] Even though people may value some alleviation of poverty, they also recognize that their individual efforts will do little to deal with the problem. Therefore, like free riders in general, they will often refrain from contributing, thus leading to fewer transfers than they themselves would truly like to see. This argument about transfers being too small is of the same form as the public goods argument which provides support for action by the productive state. Moreover, an individual's claim that a transfer provides no value to him is not itself evidence for his claim, because the essence of the free rider situation is that it can be in someone's interest to claim to receive no benefit even though some benefit is in truth received.

What this means is that some judicial process by which a third party selects between competing truth claims is necessary. A proponent of a transfer program claims the program is one of common value, and not just of particular value to the recipients, while an opponent argues the reverse. It is hard to deny in this case that much depends on the predispositions of those making the judgments. A court comprised of Richard Epsteins or Bernard Siegans would in many cases rule quite differently than one comprised of Lawrence Tribes or Ronald Dworkins. The very recognition of the importance of the particular identities of the judges is itself a source of concern and suggests problems with relying upon substantive restraints and judicial enforcement.

When government is more heavily involved in taking from some and giving to others, judicial rulings increase in importance. Predictably, individuals and interest groups will make larger investments seeking to promote or block particular nominees. Controversies over nominations to the Court will take on the flavor of a winner-take-all political contest rather than the selection of a neutral referees to interpret the rules of the game. Of course, this is precisely what we have observed in recent years.

2. *It is doubtful whether the Supreme Court can resist the powers of Congress.* Further difficulties concerning constitutional enforcement of substantive restraints arise once it is allowed that the Supreme Court is largely an agent of the legislature: it rarely rules against the federal legislature, even though it does sometimes rule against the executive branch

---

[7] See, for instance, Hochman and Rogers (1969).

or state legislature. James Madison was surely generally correct in asserting in *Federalist* No. 51: "In republican government, the legislative authority necessarily predominates." Within the central features of American republicanism, Congress controls both the jurisdiction and the budget of the Supreme Court, and has the ability to eliminate all courts inferior to it. And while the President does have the ability to nominate members to the Court, those nominees must be confirmed by the Senate. And more than this, the President, and the executive branch generally, cannot act without congressional appropriations. Moreover, Congress can impeach the President, while at most the President can force the legislature to operate with a two-thirds majority through the the veto power. Without the Court having an independent source of revenue, and one that were somehow to vary directly with the degree to which it prevents constitutional erosion, it is hard to see how the Supreme Court can, other than perhaps temporarily, restrain a federal legislature that wants to overstep constitutional bounds.

3. *The legislature can often circumvent substantative restraints.* If constitutional provisions restrict one type of legislative action, the legislature often can adopt alternative approaches to achieve the same or a similar objective. Nothing illustrates this point more vividly than reflection upon possible legislative response to proposals limiting expenditures. For one thing, the definition of the government's budget is to some degree arbitrary. Many states have balanced budget requirements or limits on the amount they can borrow, and yet operate with deficits and accumulate debt beyond the constitutional limit. This is often done through off-budget transactions, as James Bennett and Thomas DiLorenzo (1983) explain. A government may wish to build a museum to honor politicians and to give them a place to donate their papers, but be constrained by a budget or debt limit. It may be able nonetheless to build the museum and yet not violate the constitutional limit, by creating an off-budget enterprise—a museum authority—that is excluded from the debt limit.

Futhermore, any pattern of resource usage that government can attain through its budget can in principle be attained through government's use of its police power. For instance, education budgets could largely be eliminated by a requirement that parents send their children to school for a stipulated number of years. But whether government provides education through such a system of commands or provides it through budgets, government's control over the use of resources in society is essentially the same. Furthermore, the distributive impact of publicly financed education could be approached through various "sponsor a child" rules that would require people without children to contribute to the education of other people's children. Predictably a budget limitation would lead to an increase in the use of regulatory powers designed to achieve resource transfers that would otherwise be accomplished through the budget. Such regulatory actions would to some degree, undermine the intent of the budget limitation. In any event, the presence of the regulatory option highlights the difficulties involved in the use of substantive constraints to control the actions of governments.

Can "Interpretation" Be Distinguished From "Amendment?"

Is there no test to distinguish between a Court decision which simply interprets the Constitution from one which represents a judicially-imposed revision or amendment to the Constitution? Must one person's reasonable interpretation be someone else's (un)constitutional amendment?

It is instructive to compare processes of constitutional enforcement with such other processes of rule enforcement as those found in organized athletics.[8] The rules of football constitute its constitution. Moreover, the authority to amend the rules belongs to the participants and not the referees. The task of the referees is to enforce the rules the participants have chosen. But how are referees, or judges, to be limited to enforcing rules and restrained from making rules? The participants may agree to a rule against unnecessary roughness. But whether or not a particular tackle constitutes unnecessary roughness requires the referees to interpret the intent of the participants.

Despite the inescapability of interpretation, it is reasonable to claim that referees do not make the rules but only enforce them. What maintains the distinction between interpretation and amendment is the *consensual process* by which referees are selected and maintain their positions. Not only are they chosen by the agreement of the participants, but also they are subject to periodic and consensual reaffirmation by the participants.

The presence of a consensual test involving a periodic reaffirmation of a referee or a judge makes it possible to determine whether the presumed neutral official is interpreting or amending the rules. A number of state judicial systems follow this procedure. When judges are reaffirmed consensually, it is reasonable to infer that rules are being interpreted rather than amended. Correspondingly, the absence of consensus among the participants implies that the rules are being amended and property rights redefined for the benefit of some of the participants at the expense of others.The actual process of constitutional interpretation and enforcement differs substantially from the type of process that is consistent with the maintenance of the constitutional contract. The Supreme Court is not in an analogous position with the officials who work a game. The members of the Court are not selected consensually by the participants. Neither are they subject to periodic reaffirmation by a consensual process. Instead,

---

[8] The argument presented here is developed more fully in Wagner (1987).

members of the Court are selected via the majoritarian political process. The judiciary has became part of this process. By and large, the processes of rule interpretation and enforcement are now indistinguishable from processes of rule selection and amendment, as the increasing controversy over federal judicial appointments attests.

Procedural Design As A Route To A Self-Enforcing Constitution

Given the difficulties involved in the maintenance of constitutional government and the shortcomings of substantive constraints, is there a better method of achieving government "with the consent of the governed?" Public choice analysis indicates that there is. The writings of James Madison and the great Swedish economist Knut Wicksell provide valuable insights on how to design a self-enforcing constitutional order—a governmental structure with built-in features capable of protecting the natural rights of all segments of society from each other and from the excesses of majoritarian democracy.

Insights of Madison

As we previously noted, Madison believed that legislative authority was the dominant center of power in republican governments. Thus, if the constitutional contract is going to be maintained, legislative procedures must be designed so that legislative coalitions will remain within constitutional bounds. In *Federalist* No. 51, Madison argued that this objective could be achieved by making sure that competing interests were represented in the legislative process. In Madison's words, "Ambition must be made to counteract ambition."

This is precisely why Madison and the other framers of the U.S. Constitution established two legislative branches with differing criteria for representation. As Madison went on to state in *Federalist* No. 51:

> The remedy for this inconvenience [the tendency for legislative authority to predominate] is to divide the legislature into different branches; and to render them, by different modes of election and different principles of action, as little connected with each other as the nature of their common functions and their common dependence on the society will admit.

The greater the dissimilarity between the two branches, the greater the support in the society at large that would be represented by concurrent majorities in the two branches. In this manner constitutional enforcement would become more of a consensual process, like the enforcement of rules in athletic contests, because the legislature would be organized more fully along consensual lines. Madison also thought the competitive process inherent in the decentralization of governmental powers would provide a self-enforcement mechanism protecting individuals from possible oppressive actions by state and local governments. Again, in *Federalist* No. 51 Madison argued:

> In the compound republic of America, the power surrendered by the people is first divided between two distinct governments [state and federal] and then the portion alloted to each subdivided among distinct and separate departments. Hence a double security arises to the rights of the people. The different governments will control each other, at the same time that each will be controlled by itself.

Madison did not envision any direct constitutional restraints limiting the tax and expenditure powers of state and local governments because he thought competition among these governments would automatically limit their ability to institute oppressive policies. For example, if New York (or any other state) sought to tax business, the rich, the poor, or any other segment of society without providing them with compensating public services, people would move from New York toward states with less oppressive (and more productive) governments. Thus, states offering people an attractive government environment—high value for their tax dollars—would grow relative to those following oppressive policies. The same would be true for local governmental units. These competitive forces would limit the ability of state and local governments to follow policies that were inconsistent with the wishes of their citizenry.

Insights of Wicksell

The work of Knut Wicksell also provides valuable insights on how to design a self-enforcing constitutional order. Although Wicksell's major work on this topic was published in 1896, it was largely unnoticed until the public choice revolution of recent decades.[9] Wicksell recognized that majoritarian democracy contained a pattern of biases which resulted in counterproductive governmental actions. If winning coalitions are allowed to place some of the costs of their preferred programs onto the others, they will adopt programs even when the projects are valued less then their cost. Wicksell provided a remedy for the waste emanating from this incentive structure: prohibit legislative majorities from foisting the cost of projects onto nonconsenting minorities.

If voters value a public sector good or service more than its cost, it will

---

[9] Wicksell's classic work on taxation (an abridged version is reprinted as Chapter 5 of this volume) was first translated into English by James Buchanan in 1958. Buchanan and Gordon Tullock credit Wicksell with the inspirations for many of the ideas they presented in *The Calculus of Consent*, a book that has became a classic in its own time. For additional detail on the relationship between Wicksell and *The Calculus* see Wagner (forthcoming).

always be possible to devise a pattern of taxes that will lead to the project's approval by all, or most all voters. Alternatively if overwhelming approval cannot be achieved, this is powerful evidence the project is counter-productive and should be rejected. As Wicksell (1958, pp. 87-88) put it:

> There are hundreds of ways of distributing the costs of a proposed state expenditure among the separate classes of people. Provided the expenditure in question holds out any prospect at all of creating utility exceeding costs, it will always be theoretically possible, and approximately so in practice, to find a distribution of costs such that all parties regard the expenditure as beneficial and may therefore approve it unanimously. Should this prove altogether impossible, I would consider such failure as an *a posteriori*, and the sole possible, proof that the state activity under consideration would not provide the community with utility corresponding to the necessary sacrifice and should hence by rejected on rational grounds.

For Wicksell as for us, "the consent of the governed" is the point of departure for the evaluation of government activities. In it pristine form, government by consent means unanimity. Wicksell recognized, however, that unanimity would be exceedingly costly to achieve, and that a small movement away from unanimity would not do serious violence to the consensual principle. To this end he suggested that a voting rule in the legislature requiring on the order of a 75 to 90 percent consent, would be reasonable and effective. In conjunction with this voting rule, Wicksell described a set of procedures for reaching budgetary decisions, procedures which included the requirement that the sponsors of any proposal for government expenditure also propose a means of paying for the project. In this way, it would be possible for people to judge whether what they were getting was worth what they were being asked to pay.

Beside suggesting that the legislative branch be bound by a rule of approximate unanimity instead of majority rule, Wicksell also proposed that it be selected under a system of proportional representation. If the legislature was selected by proportional representation and bound by a rule of approximate unanimity, the scope for a winning faction to enrich its members at the expense of everyone else would be sharply curtailed. To the extent that a system of proportional representation led to the selection of a legislature that was a representative sample of the citizenry at large, approximate unanimity among the members of the legislature would correspond to approximate unanimity among the citizenry. Hence, legislative approval would indicate that most all citizens of the society expected to gain as a result of the government action. Under these procedures, government would essentially be constrained by the same rule of property and contract that apply to other participants in the economy.

In contrast with Wicksell's consensual form of government, legislative approval under a system of majority rule and winner-take-all, single member legislative districts may be decidedly non-consensual. Suppose, for example that there are 99 legislative districts, each containing 101 voters. Furthermore, suppose that in fifty of the districts 51 of the 101 citizens own developed property, while all other voters in all districts own only underdeveloped property. Assuming each legislator reflects the majority of his constituents, a proposal to restrict development would gain majority approval (50 to 49) of the legislature even through only slightly more than 25 percent of the voters (2550 of the 9999) favored it.

Designing a Self-Enforcing Constitution

Since the analyses of both Madison and Wicksell focus on the use of the legislative process to control competing interests, they are particularly relevant in an American context. Madison's initial hope was that the House and Senate would represent different interests since they were chosen on the bases of different representation criterion. However, technological changes in transportation and communication, along with organizational changes (particularly the popular selection of senators) have eroded the differences between the two chambers. Thus, the bicameral legislative system no longer preforms the function envisioned by Madison.

Of course, it would be possible to change the basis on which the legislatures are selected, with the intent of such changes being to reduce the similarity between the two chambers. For example, one chamber might be elected by constituents with incomes below the median, while the other chamber was elected by voters with incomes above the median. Alternatively, one chamber might be chosen from voters in blue collar occupations and the other by workers in white collar occupations. Of course the point of such suggestions would be to increase the diversity between the two chambers. The greater the diversity, the more nearly true it is that legislation receiving majority support in both chambers is in fact of broad, general value rather than of narrow, factional value.

Wicksell suggests an alternative method of achieving consensual government. Choose a legislature that is broadly representative of competing interests within the society, but require consensual (supra-majority) approval for passage of legislation. This procedure would substantially reduce the ability of various interest groups to use legislative procedures to foist the cost of favored projects onto others. If broad approval was required for passage, legislators would be forced to develop compromises and design procedures that allocated costs (taxes) primarily to the beneficiaries of the action.[10] Legislative action more consistent with the principles of economic efficiency would result.

What procedures would yield a legislative body that was representative of the major interests with the society? Wicksell suggests a system of proportional representation designed to mirror the broader society.[11] Of course this would lead to a multi-party system with each party representing various interests. The representation of the parties in the legislature would be in proportion to their support in the general populace. Since approval by a supramajority (three-fourths, for example) would be required for passage, it would not be easy for an interest group to use government as a means of plunder.

If we want government to reflect the wishes of the people, we must also design procedures which will strengthen state and local governments. As more technical analysis indicates, Madison's perception that a competitive process among state and local governments causes each to act as a check on the other is essentially correct.[12] However, as the enumerated powers constraint on the federal legislature eroded, centralization of government soon denied us the benefits accompanying competition among governmental units. In recent years, state and local governments have become more like an extension of the federal government, and less like independent government units.

How could we reestablish the Madisonian concept of federalism? One possible change would be to require more inclusive majorities the higher the level of government. For example, local legislative bodies (city commissions, county commissions, regional authorities, etc.) might continue

---

[10] Critics argue that a supramajority requirement substitutes the rule of the minority for the rule of the majority. This view reflects a fundamental misunderstanding of consensual government. The purpose of consensual government is mutual agreement not exploitation. Consensual procedures are designed to restrict the ability of both simple majorities and sizable minorities from ruling one over the other. This will be the case if the consent of both a simple majority and all sizable minorities is required for legislative action. In effect, this is what the supramajority rule does. Projects must be mutually agreeable to all segments of a society if they are going to command supramajority approval. As Wicksell notes, if a project is socially productive, it will be possible to structure its financing such that it provides net benefits to all major segments of the society, majority and minority alike. On the other hand, if a project is unable to command the support of all segments of a society, and therefore a supramajority, this is strong evidence that it is socially counterproductive and should therefore be rejected.

[11] William F. Buckley, Jr. once remarked, "I should sooner live in a society governed by the first two thousand names in the Boston telephone directory than in a society governed by the two thousand faculty members of Harvard University." Within the Wicksellian framework of government as a consensual entity designed for the mutual benefit of all segments of society, statements like Buckley's make a lot of sense.

[12] See Charles Tiebout (1956), Vincent Ostrom (1971) and Robert Bish (Chapter 16 of this volume) for additional information on the importance of competition among government units.

to act with the approval of only a simple-majority, while a three-fifths majority might be required for legislative action at the state level, and a three-fourths majority at the federal level. The increasing majorities required for legislative action at higher levels of government would help remedy a deficiency of the current system—the tendency of federal and state governments to get involved with issues that are best dealt with at lower levels governments. This procedural design to strengthen state and local governments would provide for greater diversity and opportunity for experimentation with alternative approaches. The diversity would permit governments to satisfy a larger number of voters whose preferences, after all, differ with regard to the value they attach to public sector goods and services. The experimentation would promote efficiency within government since it would help both voters and public sector managers discover and emulate successful approaches. This procedural design follows from a recognition that citizens are better able to control and discipline local governments than they are a national government. Since local governments have less ability than the federal government to oppress any group of citizens, consensual approval is less important at the local than at the federal level.

A second possible change to promote federalism and consensual government would be to permit legislative action by a sizable *minority* of states— we would suggest one-third—to invalidate federal legislation.[13] This structure would protect the states from federal activities opposed by a sizable number of states. It would help assure that federal action was really based on mutual agreement. Of course, if a minority of states set aside a federal action, a national 55 mph speed limit for example, states favoring the plan could still adopt it. A majority of the states might well do so at the state level. But so long as a substantial minority is opposed, the action could not be taken at the federal level.

Consensual Government And The Redistribution Issue

Despite the attractiveness of a government based on the consent of the governed—on the mutual agreement of all major segments of a society— many well-intended citizens are reluctant to support the concept because they believe majoritarian democracy promotes egalitarianism and the interests of the poor. According to this view, majoritarian government is the great equalizer. The votes of the rich and the poor count equally. In civil societies, compassionate citizens will use the voting process to transfer income from the rich to the poor and thereby soften the sometimes harsh verdicts of both nature and markets. Of course, this may require that we

---

[13] This proposal has previously been advanced by William Niskanen (1978).

give up some economic growth in order to promote equality. So be it. As the late Arthur Okun put it, some reduction in efficiency is the price of equality.

We find this view both understandable and appealing. We ourselves accepted it for many years. However, we now believe that it is based on a false premise. Those who adhere to this view—and we believe it is a majority—*assume* that the powers of majoritarian democracy will be used to reduce economic inequality. There is neither theoretical justification nor empirical evidence to support this assumption.

Let us consider the issue from a theoretical viewpoint. At the most basic level, is should be noted that many majority coalitions are possible. While a majority coalition of the *bottom* 51 percent of income recipients is possible, so too, is a majority coalition of the top 51 percent of income recipients (or the middle 51 percent of income recipients). However, as we have previously discussed, the majoritarian process elevates the importance of special interests. Politicians will find redistribution from widely dispersed, disorganized groups (e.g. taxpayers and consumers) to easily-identifiable, concentrated interests (e.g. labor, business, farmers and the elderly) far more attractive than egalitarian transfers. Similarly, the shortsightedness effect indicates that transfers which provide easily identifiable *current* benefits while imposing future costs (e.g. slower economic growth) that are difficult to identify will be attractive to political entrepreneurs. These are the types of reshuffles one can expect from the political process. There is little reason to believe they will be egalitarian.

Of course, the skills and attributes that lead to political success differ from those necessary for success in the marketplace. If you want to become rich and powerful in a market economy, you must discover how to supply products and services that are intensely demanded relative to their cost. If you want to become rich and powerful in the tax-transfer state, you must learn how to deliver votes. There is little reason to believe that this works to the advantage of the poor. In the United States, the poor are less likely to vote than middle and upper income recipients. They are less likely than others to be well informed on political issues and candidates. They are not well organized. Neither are they a significant source of financial resources that exert a powerful influence on the political process.

Success will not come easy in either a market or political setting. That is why so few people get to the top. However, there is little reason to believe that the skills and attributes of the poor will be rewarded more handsomely in the tax-transfer state than in the competitive marketplace. In fact, the entrepreneurs and managers in a politically dominated society are likely to be pretty much the same people as those who would excel under market organization. The people with better ideas, more creative minds, and greater energy will rise to the top in most any society. They will rise to the top of a socialist bureaucracy just as they will rise to the top in the business world.

However, even if the majoritarian democratic process does pursue the transfer of income to the poor, or to any other group, it will be exceedingly difficult to do so in a manner that will significantly improve the welfare of the intended recipients. This point follows from a standard proposition of economic theory: Competitors will be attracted to activities that yield abnormally high rates of return until the abnormally high profit is eroded. Application of this proposition to politics indicates that whenever the government establishes a criteria (as it must in a world of scarce resources) that must be met in order to qualify for transfers or other political favors, competition to meet the standard will erode the opportunity for profit. Unanticipated changes in public policy will impose temporary gains and loss on various groups. However, paradoxical as it may appear, it is extremely difficult to bestow favors upon a class of recipients in a manner that will *permanently* improve their well-being (D. Friedman 1986, pp. 448-49; Gwartney and Stroup 1986).

In order to understand why it is hard for the government to help people by giving them something, consider the following simple illustration. Suppose the government decided to give away $50 bills between 9 AM and 5 PM to persons willing to wait in line at the teller windows of the U.S. Treasury. Since long lines would emerge and discourage most people seeking the transfer, the program would have a finite cost (this is essential or otherwise it could not be financed). Persons with the lowest opportunity cost would be the primary beneficiaries. Many of them would perceive that the transfer benefits were worth the wait. However, much of the beneficiary's gain would be eroded as the result of competition (to meet the criteria) for the transfer. If a person's opportunity cost of waiting several hours was $30, his net gain from the $50 transfer would be $20. The opportunity cost of the wait for some would be $49.99. In that case, virtually the entire benefit of the transfer would be eroded by the cost incurred in its acquisition.

This simple example highlights the general problem that arises when the government bestows a favor upon a group: the subsidized activity is encouraged and competition for the transfer erodes much of the net gain of the beneficiary. For example, government favors in the form of restrictions on imports, occupational licensing, and agricultural price supports will encourage more people to "invest" in an effort to meet the criteria necessary to acquire the subsidy. In some cases, the investment will be in the form of lobbying expenses, filling out forms, paying required fees, and even bribery. In others, it may involve bidding up the price of an asset (e.g., land with a wheat allotment) that is required to qualify for a special subsidy.

As people and markets adjust to the transfers, any abnormally high returns derived by recipients of government subsidies will dissipate. When one considers what one has to buy, or do, or be in order to qualify for transfers, it is clear that the net gain of the recipients is substantially less than the size of the transfers. In the case of the poor, high implicit marginal tax rates accompanying income-tested transfers severely retard the incentive of the poor to earn. Thus, the net increase in income of the poor is much less than the dollars transferred. To a large extent, the transfers merely replace income that would have been earned in their absence. The high implicit tax rates often induce the poor to drop out of the work force. When this happens the skills of the poor depreciate, further reducing their ability to support themselves and escape poverty. Government involvement in antipoverty transfers crowds out private charitable efforts by families, individuals, churches, and civic organizations. When taxes are levied to do more, predictably private individuals and groups will adjust and do less. When one considers these adjustments, it is not at all clear that the poor benefit from transfers, particularly in the long run.

If transfer programs fail to provide significant benefits to recipients beyond the windfall gains at the time the programs are instituted or unexpectedly expanded, what accounts for the continued political support for such programs? Gordon Tullock's (1975) work on the transitional gains trap provides the answer. Elimination of the programs would be costly for recipients who have adjusted to or "bought into" the programs. Thus, even though the programs do little to improve their welfare, the current beneficiaries would be harmed by elimination or an unanticipated cutback in the programs. Thus, they form a vocal lobby supportive of the programs.

Clearly, adjustment to taxes and transfers distort both the before and after tax distributions of income. Thus, it is totally illegitimate to use a comparison of the after tax-transfer income distribution with the before tax-transfer distribution as a measure of the egalitarian effects of public policy. Both of these distributions are distorted by the presence of the transfers. Thus, they do not indicate the egalitarian effects, if any, of the transfers. Similarly, data that a certain level of transfers goes to the poor does not indicate that majoritarian transfers improved that status of the poor by that amount (or any portion of that amount). Any meaningful statement linking income transfers with an improvement in the status of the poor requires a comparison of the economic position of the poor in the presence of the programs with their economic status in their absence, *taking into account the various economic adjustments and reactions emanating from the transfers.*

Of course, we cannot directly observe what the distribution of income would be at various levels of transfers. However, if the transfers significantly exert egalitarian effects, one would expect less inequality when transfers are a larger share of total income. Using this indicator, the U.S. experience provides indirect evidence that the egalitarian effects of transfers are modest, at most. Between 1950 and 1980, the size of government grew from a little more than 20 percent to more than 35 percent of GNP. Growth of transfer payments was the major source of this growth in the size of government. However, studies in this area indicate that there was little change in the distribution of income in the United States during this period. Perhaps the most detailed study of this topic was undertaken by Morgan Reynolds and Eugene Smolensky (1977). Their research covered the years 1950, 1961 and 1970. After adjusting the income data for the effects of a broad range of taxes and transfers, Reynolds and Smolensky concluded that despite the vast increase in transfers during the period, the after tax and transfer distribution of income was approximately the same at the end of the period as at the beginning.

Similarly, if transfers exert egalitarian effects, one would also expect countries with large transfer sectors to exhibit less inequality than countries with small transfer sectors. However, there is no evidence that this is, in fact the case. Studies indicate that the degree of income inequality in France exceeds that of both Japan and the United States, even though the size of government (and the transfer sector) is larger in the former than for the latter two countries. Similarly, the distribution of income in the United Kingdom is approximately the same as for the United States (and more unequal than for Japan) despite the more sizable transfer sector in the U.K. What about the case of Sweden? The income distribution in Sweden is more egalitarian than for the United States. However, the population of Sweden is much smaller and far more homogeneous than the United States. Rather than comparing with the entire United States, it makes more sense to compare Sweden with areas of the U.S. with similar populations. Interestingly, in Minnesota and Wisconsin, two states with relatively homogeneous population (and large Scandinavian communities), the distribution of income is approximately the same as for Sweden.

The statistics linking poverty rates to transfer payments also fail to provide support for the view that public sector transfer policies are advantageous to the poor. The growth of antipoverty transfers accompanying Great Society programs during the 1965-1980 period did not reduce the incidence of poverty in America. Despite the vast increase in transfer expenditures, the poverty rate of working-age Americans was higher in 1980 than 1965. Analysis of state level data also indicate that transfers are an ineffective antipoverty weapon. The states which had the highest level of transfer benefits during the 1970s experienced increases in poverty, while states with the lowest benefit levels experienced continued reductions in the incidence of poverty. The assumption that policies emanating from majoritarian democracy are egalitarian is simply false. Neither economic theory nor the empirical evidence are supportive of the assumption. Those who continue to use this assumption as a justification for their opposition to consensual democratic procedures need to reexamine their views.

Concluding Thoughts

It is common, and probably comforting, to think that the destructive consequences of contemporary, majoritarian democracy can be escaped by electing better politicians. But this is not the case. The expansion in the powers of government—particularly the federal government—and the accompanying erosion of wealth and liberty is not the result of incompetent public officials motivated by evil intentions. Rather the core of the problem emanates from the incentives that ordinary people confront within the prevailing system of majoritarian democracy.

The current system of majoritarian democracy is not the result of deliberate design; rather it reflects the evolutionary erosion during this century of substantive constraints protecting trade and limiting plunder. As a political system, majoritarian democracy is fundamentally flawed, and no less so in our day than it was when the concept was vigorously opposed by the framers of our constitutional order. It draws resources from production into political plunder. It reestablishes the bickering and chaos of the Hobbesian jungle. Since it establishes government as the maker of rules for others, rather than an adherent to the same rules as others, "political markets" naturally arise to secure favorable rules and favorable interpretations of those rules. Special interest politics dominate. Since legislative majorities are the source of law rather than being constrained by law, a system of lawless democracy arises in which the legislature "sells" favors to the highest bidders, and thereby becomes a broker of people's rights of person and property.

What is needed is not so much a change in the composition of the legislature as a change in constitutional framework to reestablish consensual government. Political outcomes depend much more on the rules of the game than on the politicians running the political plays. If consensual government is going to be reestablished, we need rules and procedures that encourage politicians, including those who are less than saints, to support policies which serve the general welfare.

While the prisoners' dilemma model illustrates nicely the potential gains from a consensual agreement to eliminate plunder, that model also illustrates that the maintenance of such a constitutional contract does not resolve itself naturally. If democracy is going to promote the common welfare, institutional procedures capable of constraining plunder—including plunder via the political process—must be designed. It is particularly important that the constitutional design place a preponderance of the legislative interests on the side of exchange rather than plunder. The more fully institutional arrangements point political power and self interest toward the enforcement of the original constitutional contract, the more likely it is that contract will be maintained. The idea of the self-enforcing constitution looks to the creation of institutional arrangements that make it unlikely that the constitution will be violated. This was central to James Madison's effort at constitutional construction, and it has been recast with contemporary modes of thought by the scholars who have created the theory of public choice.

While dissatisfaction with government abounds, current popular political opinion is largely oblivious of the relationship between majoritarian democracy and loss of liberty and prosperity. Does this mean that the western majoritarian democracies, like others throughout history, are in the process of returning to oppression and stagnation? There are powerful forces in this direction. However public choice analysis provides us valuable knowledge as to the nature of the problem. As Richard Weaver instructed, ideas do have consequences. Just as unsound ideas can lead to unsound policies, so too, can sound ideas lead to sound policies. It was a sound idea—the idea that prior to government people have rights to their person and possessions and that the primary purpose of government is to secure these rights—that led to the American system of government.

Once again the challenge before us is to get our ideas right. In the area of government, this means the discovery, or more accurately the rediscovery, of political institutions capable of bringing personal self interest into harmony with political liberty and economic propersity. As James Buchanan (1978, p. 17) argues, the challenge before us is to construct "a political order that will channel the self-serving behavior of participants towards the common good in manner that comes as close as possible to that described for us by Adam Smith with respect to the economic order." We hope the essays in this book will contribute to that objective.

References

Anderson, Terry L. and Hill, Peter J. *The Birth of the Transfer Society*. Stanford: Hoover Institution Press, 1980.

Bennett, James T. and DiLorenzo, Thomas J. *Underground Government*. Washington: Cato Institute, 1983.

Buchanan, James M. *The Limits of Liberty*. Chicago: University of Chicago Press, 1975.

Buchanan, James M. *The Economics of Politics*. London: The Institute of Economic Affairs, 1978.

Buchanan, James M. and Tullock, Gordon. *The Calculus of Consent*. Ann Arbor: University of Michigan Press, 1962.

Epstein, Richard A. *Takings: Private Property and the Power of Eminent Domain*. Cambridge: Harvard University Press, 1985.

Friedman, David D. *Price Theory*. Cincinnati: South Western Pub., 1986.

Gwartney, James D. and Stroup, Richard L. "Transfers, Equality and the Limits of Public Policy." *Cato Journal* 6 (Spring/Summer 1986): 111-37.

Hochman, Harold M. and Rodgers, James O. "Pareto Optimal Redistribution." *American Economic Review* 59 (September 1969): 542-57.

Landes, William M., and Posner, Richard A. "The Independent Judiciary in an Interest-Group Perspective." *Journal of Law and Economics* 18 (December 1985): 875-901.

Madison, James. "Property." National Gazette, I, No. 44 (March 29, 1792): 174-75. Reprinted in *Letters and Other Writings of James Madison*. Vol. 4, pp. 478-80. Philadelphia: J.B. Lippincott & Co., 1865.

McCallum, Spencer H. *The Art of Community*. Menlo Park, CA: Institute of Humane Studies, 1970.

McIlwain, Charles H. *Constitutionalism: Ancient and Modern*. Revised ed. Ithaca, NY: Cornell University Press, 1947.

Niskanen, William A. "The Prospect for Liberal Democracy." In *Fiscal Responsibility in Constitutional Democracy*, pp. 157-74. Edited by James M. Buchanan and Richard E. Wagner. Leiden: Martinus Nijhoff, 1978.

Ostrom, Vincent. *The Political Theory of a Compound Republic*. Fairfax, VA: Center for Study of Public Choice, George Mason University, 1971.

Reynolds, Morgan, and Smolensky, Eugene. *Public Expenditures, Taxes, and the Distribution of Income*. New York: Academic Press, 1977.

Siegan, Bernard H. *Economic Liberties and the Constitution*. Chicago: University of Chicago Press, 1980.

Tiebout, Charles. "A Pure Theory of Local Expenditures." *Journal of Political Economy* (October 1956): 416-24.

Tollison, Robert D. "Rent Seeking: A Survey." *Kyklos* 35 (March 1982): 575-602.

Tullock, Gordon, ed. *Explorations in the Theory of Anarchy*. Fairfax, VA: Center for Study of Public Choice, George Mason University, 1972.

Tullock, Gordon. *The Social Dilemma*. Fairfax, VA: Center for Study of Public Choice, George Mason University, 1974.

Tullock, Gordon. "The Transitional Gains Trap." *Bell Journal of Economics* 6 (Autumn 1975): 671-78.

Umbeck, John. *A Theory of Property Rights with Application to the California Gold Rush*. Ames: Iowa State University, 1981.

Wagner, Richard E. "Parchment, Guns, and the Maintenance of Constitutional Contract." In *Democracy and Public Choice: Essays in Honor of Gordon Tullock*, pp. 105-21. Edited by Charles K. Rowley. Oxford: Basil Blackwell, 1987.

Wagner, Richard E. "*The Calculus of Consent*: A Wicksellian Retrospective." *Public Choice*, forthcoming.

Wicksell, Knut. "A New Principle of Just Taxation." 1896. In *Classics in the Theory of Public Finances*, pp. 72-118. Edited by Richard A. Musgrave and Alan T. Peacock. London: Macmillan, 1958.

Young, David. *The Rule of Experts: Occupational Licensing in America*. Washington, D.C.: The Cato Institute, 1987.

3

PUBLIC CHOICE AND THE CONSTITUTION: A MADISONIAN PERSPECTIVE

James A. Dorn

I own myself the friend to a very free system of commerce, and hold it as a truth, that commercial shackles are generally unjust, oppressive, and impolitic; it is also a truth, that if industry and labor are left to take their own course, they will generally be directed to those objects which are the most productive, and this in a more certain and direct manner than the wisdom of the most enlightened Legislature could point out . . . . [A]ll are benefited by exchange, and the less this exchange is cramped by Government, the greater are the proportions of benefit to each.

James Madison[1]

I. Introduction

The problem facing James Madison and the other Framers in 1787 was to design a system of government that protected individual rights while providing for a viable democratic republic. As the chief architect of the Constitution, Madison was deeply concerned with forming a federal government that would curb factionalism. He warned against unlimited democracy and chose instead a *constitutional* democracy as the most suitable form of government for a free people.

Madison based his case for constitutional democracy on the widely held Lockean view that government is a social compact instituted to protect certain unalienable or "natural" rights. The starting point for Madison's theory of constitutional choice was self-interest, not some mythical social interest; and it was the *consent* of the parties to the social compact that justified the state. In the Madisonian vision, the powers of government are delegated and limited to those necessary to safeguard persons and property. As such, majority rule is constrained by the higher law of the Constitution,

---

James Dorn is Editor of the *Cato Journal* and Associate Professor of Economics at Towson State University.
[1] Speech in First Congress, 9 April 1789; cited in Padover (1953, pp. 269-70).

which reserves to individuals the fundamental rights of life, liberty, and property so esteemed by the Framers.

A careful examination of Madison's thought, as it relates to constitutional choice and the relationship of that choice to individual freedom and a spontaneous market order, reveals a close correspondence to modern public choice theory and constitutional economics. Madison, like James Buchanan and Gordon Tullock in their classic work *The Calculus of Consent*, explored the rational framework for constitutional democracy using an individualistic methodology and a constitutional rule-making calculus based on consent. He also recognized that unlimited majority rule would lead to chaos unless subject to constitutional limits on the coercive powers of government. Thus he favored a rule of law and a liberal social order, in the classical sense, in which the state plays a protective function as opposed to an activist social welfare state where the will of the majority or organized minorities dominates. By placing limits on democratic rule, Madison, like modern public choice economists, hoped to limit the rent-seeking process and provide a framework for collective choice that would ensure institutional stability. Individuals would then be free to pursue their own interests without trampling on the economic and noneconomic liberties vested in each individual.

This paper will explore the correspondence between the modern public choice perspective and Madison's theory of constitutional democracy— including his vision of man and the state, his conception of property and justice, and his theory of political economy. It will be seen that the public choice perspective, which incorporates a normative theory of constitutional choice based on the unanimity rule, is at base the Madisonian perspective of a liberal republican order grounded in a rational rule of law protecting the private domain.

Section II briefly reviews the major features of the public choice perspective and the importance of constitutional limits on the democratic process. Section III considers Madison's vision of man and the state in relation to the basic postulates of public choice theory. Section IV examines Madison's view of property and justice, with emphasis on the functions of a just government. The higher law background of the Constitution and the significance of the Bill of Rights, as understood by Madison, are examined in section V. Section VI discusses the role of the judiciary in protecting individual rights, with special emphasis on economic liberties. The relationship of constitutional democracy to a spontaneous market order is considered in section VII, by reviewing Madison's notion of a liberal republic along with his constitutional political economy. Section VIII contrasts the modern redistributive state with Madison's constitutional democracy and offers reasons for the transformation of a protective state into a rent-seeking polity. The concluding section reemphasizes the parallels between the public choice perspective and the Madisonian perspective of man and the state, and draws some policy implications from the preceding analysis.

II. Public Choice and Constitutionalism

The distinguishing characteristics of what Buchanan (1983) has called the "public choice perspective" are its emphasis on self-interest as the motivating force in both private and collective choice, its focus on politics-as-exchange, and its recognition that constitutional constraints are necessary to prevent majoritarian impulses from becoming destabilizing. For public choice theorists, the fundamental problem at the level of constitutional choice is analogous to that at the level of economic organization, namely, how to channel individual self-interest so as to achieve social coordination.

In *The Calculus of Consent*, Buchanan and Tullock analyze constitutional choice and the problem of nonmarket coordination. They adopt an individualistic methodology, rejecting the organic concept of the state and the "grail-like search for some 'public interest' apart from, and independent of, the separate interests of the individual participants in social choice" (1962, p. 12). For them, government is best modeled as a "set of processes" for collective choice rather than as a unitary being (p. 13). Drawing on the market-exchange paradigm and the Pareto criterion, Buchanan and Tullock embrace the Wicksellian unanimity rule or principle of universal consent as a benchmark for evaluating constitutional choice. Any change in the rules of the political game that could command unanimity implies a Pareto superior move and an improvement in the constitutional regime (see pp. 14, 319).

By considering those *changes* in the rules of the game that could command universal agreement, Buchanan and Tullock adopt a marginalist version of the classical contractarian theory of the state. Together with their acceptance of the self-interest postulate, their approach to constitutional rule-making is aptly labeled an "economic approach to a theory of politics" (1962, pp. 320, 322). In taking an economic approach, however, Buchanan and Tullock shy away from any discussion of the natural rights framework that was fundamental to Madison's vision of constitutional government; they find it more fruitful simply to accept the unanimity rule as an ethical norm and depend on this criterion to determine the relative attractiveness of alternative institutions for collective choice. Buchanan and Tullock, like their predecessor David Hume, rely on rational self-interest as the *modus operandi* for limiting majoritarianism and for creating a constitutional democracy (see pp. 14, 314-15).

Nevertheless, if the unanimity rule is reinterpreted as the right to noninterference, the Madisonian natural rights framework with its emphasis on voluntarism and individual freedom leads to a criterion for constitutional choice that is consistent with the principle of universal consent. The social compact/natural rights approach of Madison then leads to the selection of constitutional democracy as the form of government most consistent with individual freedom, an outcome consistent with the public choice perspective. Moreover, when viewed in light of the higher law background, Madison's approach to constitutional choice can be extended to include the consent of all future generations to the original compact, because the fundamental rights of life, liberty and property remain vested in individuals; the state's only legitimate function is to secure these rights.[2]

In sum, if one views the unanimity rule as a principle of voluntarism or individual freedom and grounds this rule in a natural rights framework, as Madison did, the correspondence between the public choice/constitutional perspective and the Madisonian view of constitutional choice becomes apparent. Madison accepts the self-interest postulate, rejects the organic view of the state, and, like public choice theorists, sees the rationale for limiting the majoritarian process. It is no coincidence, then, that Buchanan and Tullock have pointed to Madison as an early adherent of the public choice perspective.[3] Madison, however, extends the public choice framework by resting his case for a constitutional democracy both on moral and practical grounds—tracing back to a rational theory of rights, a social compact theory of the state, and an understanding of the interconnectedness of a liberal constitutional republic and a spontaneous market order, in which incentives to work, save, and invest are enhanced by the protection of private property and freedom of contract. It is to Madison's thought that we now turn.

---

[2] When an individual *voluntarily* enters into a social compact he loses nothing. In a just constitutional exchange no one's rights are violated; the so-called property right is merely afforded collective protection. Thus liberty is enhanced rather than sacrificed when individuals enter into a social compact; the only legitimate end of this compact being to defend pre-existing rights. These Lockean themes were generally accepted by the Framers. For an insightful discussion of the correspondence between voluntary exchange and liberty, as well as the idea that government is legitimate if and only if it uses force to defend liberty rather than to sacrifice it, see Bastiat ([1851] 1964a, pp. 456-57).

[3] Buchanan (1983, p. 14) noted:

> When persons are modelled as self-interested in politics . . . the constitutional challenge becomes one of constructing and designing framework institutions or rules that will, to the maximum extent possible, limit the exercise of such interest in exploitative ways and direct such interest to furtherance of the general interest. It is not surprising, therefore, to discover the roots of a public choice perspective . . . in the writings of the American Founders, and most notably in James Madison's contributions to *The Federalist Papers*.

See also Buchanan and Tullock (1962, pp. 24-25).

III Madison's Vision of Man and the State

Nowhere is Madison's work closer to the public choice perspective than in his discussion of man and the state. For Madison man is best viewed as rationally self-interested both in his private and public dealings. Experience, not illusion, was the basis of Madison's perspective:

> If men were angels, no government would be necessary. If angels were to govern men, neither external nor internal controls on government would be necessary. In framing a government which is to be administered by men over men, the great difficulty lies in this: you must first enable government to control the governed; and in the next place oblige it to control itself. A dependence on the people is, no doubt, the primary control on the government; but experience has taught mankind the necessity of auxiliary precautions (*Federalist* No. 51).[4]

These "auxiliary precautions," of course, were to be found in a rule of law guarding the sanctity of persons and property against majoritarian interests.

Like the Framers in general, Madison rejected the organic conception of the state and accepted Lockean political theory, which emphasized the natural rights of man and the consensual basis of legitimate government.[5] Madison undoubtedly was also influenced by David Hume, who emphasized man's rationality in the process of constitutional rule-making and the importance, therefore, of *limited* government.[6] Certainly Madison would have agreed with Hume's statement that "'twou'd be in vain, either for moralists or politicians, to tamper with us, or attempt to change the usual course of our actions, with a view to public interest" (*Treatise*, III, p. 521).[7] And Madison clearly would have agreed with Hume that it is only by observing "the three fundamental laws of nature, *that of the stability of possession, of its transference by consent,* and *of the performance of promises*...that the peace and security of human society" will be maintained (p. 526).

It was in view of his understanding of the nature of man and the state that Madison ([1829] 1865c, pp. 22-23) wrote:

> Bodies of men are not less swayed by interest than individuals, and are less controlled by the dread of reproach and the other motives felt by individuals. Hence the liability of the rights of property, and of the impartiality of laws affecting it, to be violated by legislative majorities

[4] All references to *The Federalist Papers* are to the DeKoster (1976) edition.

[5] For a discussion of the influence of John Locke's thought on the Framers, see Solberg (1958, pp. xxxvi-xxxvii).

[6] On Hume's impact on the Framers, including Madison, see Solberg (1958, pp. xi-xliii).

[7] References to the *Treatise* are to the Selby-Bigge/Nidditch (1978) edition.

having an interest, real or supposed, in the injustice. Hence agrarian laws and other levelling schemes. Hence the cancelling or evading of debts, and other violations of contracts. We must not shut our eyes to the nature of man, nor to the light of experience.

In framing a constitution, therefore, Madison warned against factionalism and the abuse of government power: "the causes of faction are . . . sown in the very nature of man" (*Federalist* No. 10); "the essence of Government is power" and that "power, lodged as it must be in human hands, will ever be liable to abuse" ([1829] 1865c, p. 51).

Madison did not believe that recourse to individual prudence, character, or religious sentiment would be sufficient to protect the rights of individuals against majoritarian impulses ([1787] 1865a, pp. 326-27). The "great danger" he saw in adopting a republican form of government was that "the majority may not sufficiently respect the rights of the minority" ([1829] 1865c, pp. 51-52). He therefore dispelled the public interest view of government— "how easily are base and selfish measures masked by pretexts of public good"[8]—and advocated limiting government to protect the private domain:

> Man is known to be a selfish as well as a social being. . . . [Reliance on] favourable attributes of the human character are all valuable, as auxiliaries; but they will not serve as a substitute for the coercive provisions belonging to Government and Law. They will always, in proportion as they prevail, be favourable to a mild administration of both; but they can never be relied on as a guaranty of the rights of the minority against a majority disposed to take unjust advantage of its power. The only effectual safeguard to the rights of the minority must be laid in such a basis and structure of the Government itself as may afford, in a certain degree, directly or indirectly, a defensive authority in behalf of a minority having right on its side ([1829] 1865c, p. 52).

Similarly, Madison argued that "it is in vain to say that enlightened statesmen will be able to adjust . . . clashing interests and render them all subservient to the public good." The real problem, as he perceived it, was one of constitutional choice and protection of individual rights, namely, "how to secure the public good and private rights against the danger of . . . faction, and at the same time to preserve the spirit and the form of popular government" (*Federalist* No. 10).

In sum, Madison's vision of man as rationally self-interested in both the private and public sector, his vision of the state as a social compact, and his recognition that to secure the pre-existing rights of individuals to life, liberty, and property in a republican government requires constitutional limits on the democratic process place him squarely in the public choice framework. This is especially true if public choice is viewed in its broader

---

[8] Madison ([1787] 1865a, p. 325).

context as the search for rules of the political game that serve to harmonize competing interests, subject to the Wicksellian unanimity rule at the level of constitutional choice. The distinguishing feature of Madison's approach to constitution-making, however, is his emphasis on the protection of economic and noneconomic liberties as the prerequisite for a just government. Like Wicksell, he viewed justice as the absence of coercion in the exchange process.[9] But the focus in Madison's work was on the underlying rights structure through which the exchange process moves—in the context of both private and collective choice. In this sense, Madison extended the public choice perspective to include a rights-based approach to constitutional choice. Like Locke, he accepted the sanctity of the property right, generally conceived, and narrowly limited state action. When individuals enter into a social compact, they do so with their private rights intact. The purpose of the compact in the Madisonian perspective is to secure liberty, not to diminish it.[10]

IV. Property and Justice in the Madisonian System

Liberty, property, and justice are inseparable in the Madisonian system. Individuals are free only insofar as their "lives, liberties, and estates"— property in the Lockean sense—are safeguarded.[11] And the just government is one that serves this vital function above all others.

Madison's Perception of Property

The best statement of Madison's conception of property is found in his *National Gazette* article of March 29, 1792.[12] In that article Madison first presented a narrow definition of property, based on William Blackstone's usage as found in his *Commentaries* (1765, p.2). According to Madison, property narrowly construed is " 'that dominion which one man claims and exercises over the external things of the world, in exclusion of every

---

[9] According to Wicksell ([1896] 1958, p. 90): "In the final analysis, unanimity and fully voluntary consent in the making of decisions provide the only certain and palpable guarantee against injustice in tax distribution." For a discussion of the parallels between Madison and Wicksell, see Buchanan (1987, p. 250).

[10] Although Madison accepted Lockean natural rights theory, he integrated it with the work of other writers to form his own distinctive approach to constitution-making—an approach that resembles the "eminent domain approach" taken by Richard Epstein (1985a) in his treatment of constitutional choice. Like Epstein, Madison would not view favorably the Rawlsian contractarian approach to constitutional rule-making, in which individuals enter the process of constitutional choice under a "veil of ignorance" and operate in an ethical vacuum. See Epstein (1985a, pp. 338-44) for a critique of John Rawl's (1971) contractarianism.

[11] For Locke's definition of property, see *Second Treatise* (para. 123).

[12] Reprinted in Hunt (1906, pp. 101-3). Page references in the text are to the Hunt reprint.

other individual.' "[13] But Madison went on to extend the concept of property along Lockean lines: "In its larger and juster meaning, it [property] embraces every thing to which a man may attach a value and have a right; and *which leaves to everyone else the like advantage*" ([1792] 1906, p. 101). The italicized phrase is significant because it points to the emphasis Madison placed on the equality of rights, an indication of Madison's acceptance of the so-called nondiscrimination principle.

Under the rubric of property, Madison would include "a man's land, or merchandize, or money," as well as the property a person has in "his opinions and the free communication of them," and especially the property a person has "in his religious opinions, and in the profession and practice dictated by them." An individual also "has property very dear to him in the safety and liberty of his person" and "an equal property in the free use of his faculties and free choice of the objects on which to employ them." In brief, "as a man is said to have a right to his property, he may be equally said to have a property in his rights" ([1792] 1906, p. 101). Property, then, is a bundle of rights with correlative obligations, the overriding one being not to interfere with the equal rights of others, in their lives, liberties, and estates; hence, the inseparability of property, justice, and freedom.[14]

Madison's perception of property, as a continuum of rights vested in individuals and pre-existing the state, was shaped by his understanding of common law and his adherence to natural rights doctrine. Yet Madison was not rigidly tied to English legal tradition. He certainly accepted the idea, stated in Blackstone's *Commentaries*, that the "absolute right, inherent in every Englishman, is that of property, which consists in the free use, enjoyment, and disposal of all his acquisitions, without any control or diminution, save only by the laws of the land" ([1765, p. 2]; in Epstein 1985a, p. 22).[15] But he rejected Blackstone's own ultimate adherence to absolutism,

[13] Cf. Blackstone's definition of property: "that sole and despotic dominion which one man claims and exercises over the external things of the world, in total exclusion of the right of any other individual in the universe" (in Epstein 1985a, p. 22).

[14] As Pilon (1983, p. 175) notes: "The free society is a society of equal *rights*: stated most broadly, the right to be left alone in one's person and property, the right to pursue one's ends provided the equal rights of others are respected in the process, all of which is more precisely defined by reference to the property foundations of those rights and the basic proscription against taking that property." Moreover, "the free society is . . . a society of equal *freedom*, at least insofar as that term connotes the freedom from interference that is described by our equal rights."

[15] Epstein (1985a, p. 22, n. 6) interprets "law of the land" to mean "only that regular procedures had to be used to deprive an individual of property, that extraordinary ad hoc procedures could not substitute for adjudication." In his opinion, "it makes little sense to read the passage as saying that property was held at the grace of the legislature." Blackstone's passage here is simply a statement of the common law tradition, not necessarily a reflection of his own views.

that is, to the supremacy of Parliament or the legislative body in vesting rights.[16] For Madison, property was a natural right—the inviolability of which was taken as axiomatic and not the object of legislative tinkering.

Examples of the natural rights tradition within which Madison wrote abound. The Massachusetts Circular Letter of 1768, which blended elements from the thought of Sir Edward Coke and Locke, stated:

> It is an essential, unalterable right, in nature, engrafted into the British constitution, as a fundamental law, and ever held sacred and irrevocable by the subjects within the realm, that what a man has honestly acquired is absolutely his own, which he may freely give, but cannot be taken from him without his consent; that the American subjects may, therefore, exclusive of any consideration of charter rights, with a decent firmness, adopted to the character of free men and subjects, assert this natural and constitutional right (in Corwin 1955, p. 79).

The Declaration and Resolves, adopted by the First Continental Congress on October 14, 1774, stated that "the inhabitants of the English colonies in North-America, by the immutable law of nature, the principles of the English constitution, and the several charters or compacts," have definite rights, the foremost of which is "that they are entitled to life, liberty and property"; and that "they have never ceded to any sovereign power whatever, a right to dispose of either without their consent."[17]

These two examples offer testimony to the importance of the natural rights doctrine in the period immediately preceding the framing of the U.S. Constitution. It is inconceivable that the "inalienable Rights" of the U.S. Declaration of Independence did not include the property right, so-called—a right enshrined in the "higher law" of the Constitution and explicitly stated in the Bill of Rights.

Justice and Government

For Madison, justice meant the protection of property, broadly conceived, and it was the primary function of a just government to afford such protection. "Government is instituted," wrote Madison ([1792] 1906, p. 102), "to protect property of every sort; as well that which lies in the various rights of individuals, as that which the term particularly expresses.

---

[16] Although Blackstone paid tribute to the natural rights tradition, says Solberg (1958, p. xlv), "his real view was that Parliament was supreme in the British system. For him the locus of sovereignty was in the lawmaking agency." So while the Framers saw Blackstone as an expert on English law, they by no means accepted his view of legislative supremacy. For a summary of Blackstone's influence on the framing of the U.S. Constitution, see Solberg (pp. xliv-xlvi). See also Corwin ([1914] 1970, p. 33).

[17] Cited in Solberg (1958, p. 11). The right to "life, liberty and property" was *unanimously* accepted by the delegates.

This being the end of government, that alone is a *just* government, which *impartially* secures to every man, whatever is his *own*."[18] In this sense, justice is seen as the prevention of injustice, namely, as the prohibition against the taking of property without the consent of the rightful owner(s).[19] There is no dichotomy in the Madisonian system of rights between property rights and human rights, as one finds, for example, in Marxian writers. According to Madison ([1829] 1865c, p. 51): "It is sufficiently obvious, that persons and property are the two great subjects on which Governments are to act; and that the rights of persons, and the rights of property, are the objects, for the protection of which Government was instituted. These rights cannot well be separated. The personal right to acquire property, which is a natural right, gives to property, when acquired, a right to protection, as a social right." Thus, he argued repeatedly that "in a just and free Government . . . the rights both of property and of persons ought to be effectually guarded" (Madison [1829] 1865c, p. 22).

When the government departs from its protective role and interferes with property rights, understood in the Madisonian sense, it becomes unjust. In the case of economic liberties—associated with one's right to private ownership and freedom of contract—Madison ([1792] 1906, pp. 102-3) states:

> That is not a just government, nor is property secure under it, where the property which a man has in his personal safety and personal liberty, is violated by arbitrary seizures of one class of citizens for the service of the rest . . . .
>
> That is not a just government, nor is property secure under it, where arbitrary restrictions, exemptions, and monopolies deny to part of its citizens that free use of their faculties, and free choice of their occupations, which not only constitute their property in the general sense of the word; but are the means of acquiring property strickly so called . . . .
>
> A just security to property is not afforded by that government under which unequal taxes oppress one species of property and reward another species; where arbitrary taxes invade the domestic sanctuaries of the rich,

---

[18] Cf. Locke: "The great and *chief end* . . . of Mens uniting into Commonwealths, and putting themselves under Government, *is the Preservation of their Property*" (*Second Treatise*, para. 124); also Thomas Paine: "the design and end of government" is "freedom and security" ([1776] 1984, p. 68).

[19] Writing in the Madisonian tradition, Bastiat ([1850] 1964b, p. 65) spells out the nature of law and justice:

> When law and force confine a man within the bounds of justice, they do not impose anything on him but a mere negation. They impose on him only the obligation to refrain from injuring others. They do not infringe on his personality or his liberty or his property. They merely safeguard the personality, the liberty, and the property of others. They stand on the defensive; they defend the equal right of all. They fulfill a mission whose harmlessness is evident, whose utility is palpable, and whose legitimacy in uncontested.

and excessive taxes grind the faces of the poor; where the keenness and competitions of want are deemed an insufficient spur to labor, and taxes are again applied by an unfeeling policy, as another spur; in violation of that sacred property, which Heaven, in decreeing man to earn his bread by the sweat of his brow, kindly reserved to him, in the small repose that could be spared from the supply of his necessities.

In his Lockean/common law view of property and justice, Madison adhered to an entitlement theory of justice, with emphasis on the rights of first possession, transference by consent, and restitution for takings. He held that:

> The principle of natural law ... vests in individuals an exclusive right to the portions of ground with which they have incorporated their labour and improvements. Whatever may be the rights of others, derived from their birth in the country; from their interest in the highways and other parcels left open for common use, as well as in the national edifices and monuments; from their share in the public defence, and from their concurrent support of the Government, it would seem unreasonable to extend the right so far as to give them, when they become the majority, a power of legislation over the landed property without the consent of the proprietors. Some shield against the invasion of their rights would not be out of place in a just and provident system of Government ([1829] 1865c, pp. 24-25).

Given his broad interpretation of the property right—to include both economic and noneconomic liberties—Madison saw the takings clause of the Fifth Amendment as applying to all sorts of property and to indirect as well as direct takings:

> If there be a government...which prides itself on maintaining the inviolability of property; which provides that none shall be taken *directly* even for public use without indemnification to the owner, and yet *directly* violates the property which individuals have in their opinions, their religion, their persons, and their faculties; nay more, which *indirectly* violates their property, in their actual possessions, in the labor that acquires their daily subsistence, and in the hallowed remnant of time which ought to relieve their fatigues and soothe their cares, the inference will have been anticipated, that such a government is not a pattern for the United States ([1792] 1906, p. 103).[20]

---

[20] On close reading, one senses Madison's anguish over the slavery issue. He never justified slavery. Slaves, he said, "should be considered . . . in the light of human beings, and not as mere property [narrowly considered]. . . .[T]he mere circumstances of complexion cannot deprive them of the character of men" ([1829] 1865c, p. 53). See also Burns (1968, pp. 76-78), who points out that Madison recommended a buy-out scheme to end slavery. The United States would sell off federal lands and use the proceeds to compensate slaveholders as their slaves were freed. The plan, however, had certain weaknesses, which Burns addresses.

The acid test for a just government, then, is that it "will equally respect the rights of property, and the property in rights," wrote Madison (p. 103).

Among Madison's contemporaries, there was widespread acceptance of the view that a just government should be limited to the protection of person and property. The "Letter of the Massachusetts House to the Agent of the Province in England," drafted by Samuel Adams in 1768 to protest the Townshend Acts, for example, declared: "It is an essential, natural right, that a man shall quietly enjoy, and have the sole disposal of his own property .... The security of right and property, is the great end of government. Surely, then, such measures as tend to render right and property precarious, tend to destroy both property and government; for these must stand and fall together" (in Solberg 1958, p.8). This same respect for individual freedom, as a private right not to be interfered with by government save to offer greater security to property, was present at the Constitutional Convention. The Framers, in general, would not have contested Locke's dictum that "*Government* . . . can never have a Power to take . . . the whole or any part of the Subjects *Property*, without their own consent" (*Second Treatise*, para. 139).

It should now be evident that Madison's approach to property, justice, and government was a principled approach, in contrast to legal positivism whereby rights are posited by virtue of the state or lawmaker. Using Bastiat's phraseology, one could say that for Madison "law is born of property, instead of property being born of law" (Bastiat [1848] 1964b, p. 99). In the Madisonian system, justice is rendered when property is protected. It is therefore a closed system of government, with specific limits placed on governmental powers. Madisonian justice is *consensual*, so that those exchanges that are forced are unjust, and where governmental takings occur, compensation must be paid. Moreover, the government must bear the burden of proof to show that the taking meets the public-use standard. Under the rights-from-law system, however, there are no discernable limits on legislative action and all property is potentially subject to taking, with the burden of proof shifted to private owners. Indeed, if it is assumed that all rights stem from government, individuals will be at the mercy of government, with their rights created and destroyed as the rulers see fit. In such a system of unlimited government, justice becomes whatever the law says it is; and with the implementation of this "end-state" view of justice, to use Robert Nozick's term, the Madisonian protective state is transformed into a redistributive regime.[21]

Although natural rights theory has been the subject of critical attack,

---

[21] On the difference between end-state justice and entitlement/procedural justice, see Nozick (1974, esp. pp. 149-82); on the implications of alternative perceptions of man and justice, see Brunner (1983).

it nevertheless provided Madison and other Framers with a foundation on which to build their case for limited government. They knew what they wanted. to constrain the power of the state and enlarge individual freedom by safeguarding economic and noneconomic liberties. Madison and the Framers therefore tacked onto their moral foundation, resting on the property right, a structure of government designed to limit the power of the majority as well as organized minorities—thus securing the equal rights of each individual to life, liberty, and estate.[22] Drawing on both "right and reason," Madison made an especially strong case for limited government. For him, as for the Framers in general, the written Constitution was encased by a higher law, a "law of justice" as Bastiat ([1848] 1964b, p. 136) would say. And it is in this light that one can view the U. S. Constitution as a "charter of freedom" and a bulwark against the interventionist "democratic" state.

V. The Constitution: A Charter of Freedom

When Madison was asked his opinion of Governor Morris, he answered that although Morris "did not propose any outline of a Constitution . . . he contended for certain articles . . . which he held essential to the stability and energy of a Government capable of protecting the rights of property against the spirit of Democracy" ([1831] 1865c, p. 168). The desire to protect property rights from the tyranny of the majority was foremost in the minds of the Framers, especially Madison. And with this basis of government being widely accepted, the most difficult task facing the delegates was to structure government so as to promote democracy while safeguarding individual rights. Their choice of a *constitutional* democracy wherein the national government's powers are delegated, enumerated, and limited—by "fundamental law," the separation of powers, and federalism— was a novel experiment in constitution-making. Yet it was an experiment that drew upon the rich heritage of common law, the English constitution, and natural rights doctrine. Indeed, to properly understand the U.S. Constitution as a charter of freedom, it is necessary to examine what Edward Corwin (1955) has called its "higher law background."

---

[22] The epistemological problems surrounding natural rights theory have been exaggerated, at least as they affect constitutional theory. Epstein (1985a) builds a compelling case for limited government using a variant of the Lockean natural rights doctrine. He emphasizes that even if there is a problem with Locke's justificatory argument, those who used Locke's theory to justify individual rights did so without questioning its validity; they merely assumed that justice required government protection of the property right (see Epstein, p. 12). Pilon (esp. 1979a, 1979b, 1981, 1983) also refines the Lockean theory and builds a rational theory of rights to justify the "right to noninterference." He argues that although the Framers lacked modern epistemological tools, they "got it right, right as a matter of ethics" (1981, p.7).

Although the American colonials initially turned to common law, the English constitution, and existing charter rights in their quest for independence and justice, they were forced by the intransigence of Parliament to rest their case for liberty on what Solberg (1958, p. lviii) describes as "the law of nature." More specifically, it was to the higher law doctrine of Coke and Locke that the revolutionary leaders turned to justify their cause. And it was with the armor supplied by Coke's "fundamental law," his system of justice based on "common right and reason," and Locke's natural rights doctrine that the Founding Fathers successfully defended individual rights to life, liberty, and property.[23]

The Law of the Constitution

The higher law of the constitution has as its sole object the prevention of injustice, that is, the *protection* of persons and property. It is what Bastiat ([1850] 1964b) meant when he wrote "law is justice" (p. 91); "law is the organization of the natural right to legitimate self-defense; it is the substitution of collective force for individual forces, to act in the sphere in which they have the right to act, to do what they have the right to do: to guarantee security of person, liberty, and property rights, to cause *justice* to reign over all" (p. 52). And it is what F. A. Hayek refers to when he uses the terms "rules of just conduct," "freedom under the law," and "constitution of liberty."[24] In particular, the higher law of the constitution must be distinguished from legislative acts propagated by the will of the majority or organized minorities to gain special favors at the expense of less favored groups, creating legal "rights" that clash with pre-existing rights of persons and property under the law of "right and reason."[25]

The priority of substantive individual rights under the higher law doctrine of the constitution—protecting persons and property against legislative intrusions—is a principle that has been recognized by constitutional scholars and was evident in the writings of Madison and others. Noted constitutional scholar A. V. Dicey, for example, argued: "Individual rights are the basis, not the result, of the law of the constitution" ([1915] 1982, p. 124). Corwin agreed, arguing in Lockean fashion that "while legislative supremacy is the normal sanction of the rights of men, it is not the final

---

[23] See Corwin (1955, secs. 3-5) for an excellent discussion of the importance of Coke and Locke in shaping the higher law background of the U.S. Constitution.

[24] See Hayek (1960; 1982, esp. chaps. 8-9).

[25] Corwin (1955, pp. 4-5) marks out the distinctive characteristics of higher law: "*There are . . . certain principles of right and justice which are entitled to prevail of their own intrinsic excellence, altogether regardless of the attitude of those who wield the physical resources of the community . . . . They are external to all Will as such and interpenetrate all Reason as such. They are external and immutable . . . .* They owe nothing to their recognition in the Constitution."

sanction" (1955, p. 69). And writing in 1765, John Adams observed: "Many of our rights are inherent and essential, agreed on as maxims, and established as preliminaries, even before a parliament existed" (in Corwin, pp. 78-79).

The idea that the law of the constitution, understood as higher law, is superior to legislative enactments—which merely reflect the interests or will of the majority instead of being rationally grounded in first principles related to the "law of nature"—traces back at least to the Stoics and, in particular, to Cicero, who held that "true law [natural law] is right reason" (in Corwin 1955, pp. 9-10).[26] In this sense, the *rule of reason* is the *rule of law*, taken as a metalegal principle.[27]

Dicey (1982, pp.120-21) attributes three meanings to the "rule of law," understood as "a fundamental principle of the [English] constitution." First, it signifies the "absolute supremacy or predominance of regular [i.e., common or private] law," as a means of limiting the discretionary power of government. Second, it connotes "equality before the law," namely, "the equal subjection of all classes to the ordinary law of the land administered by the ordinary Law Courts." And third, it means that "the law of the constitution" is "the consequence of the rights of individuals, as defined and enforced by the Courts," that is, "the constitution is the result of the ordinary law of the land."

If the higher law of the constitution is lodged in the "law of the land," that is, in private law rather than acts of Parliament or legislation, it is essential to understand the basis of this law; and for this it is sufficient to turn to Corwin ([1911] 1970, pp. 46-47) who explains that Coke equated "law of the land" with "due process of the common law." More specifically, Coke imparted both a substantive and procedural connotation to "due process," as is clear from his famous dictum: "When an act of parliament is against common right and reason . . . the common law will controul it and adjudge such act to be void" (in Corwin 1955, p. 44). As Solberg (1958, p. xxi) notes: "Neither king nor Parliament was sovereign, but rather English law, which for Coke was a constitution protecting the liberty of the subject. In this he found a guarantee similar to natural right." Similarly, Corwin (1955, p. 47) writes: " 'common right and reason' is . . . something fundamental, something permanent; it is higher law."

---

[26] According to Corwin (1955, p. 26), "The notion that the common law embodied right reason furnished from the fourteenth century its chief claim to be regarded as higher law." He goes on, however, to point out that the "right reason" underlying English common law is "*judicial* right reason," not "the right reason of all men" ascribed to by Cicero and invoked by contintental writers when discussing higher law. Thus considered, the common law of England became more and more "the act of experts." Cf. Kesler (1987, p. 12) who cites "right reason" as the basic criterion of "genuine common law."

[27] On the rule of law as a metalegal principle, see Hayek (1960, chap. 14).

In England, however, the "law of the land" and "due process" came increasingly to mean the sovereignty of Parliament and procedural due process, while Coke's higher law doctrine and substantive due process took hold in the colonies. As such, the "rule of law" of the U. S. Constitution rested on the Cokean notion of "fundamental law" and the Lockean natural rights doctrine, substantive principles that were used to deny Parliament's sovereignty as well as legislative supremacy. It is in this sense that the rule of law was carried further in America than in England.[28] Indeed, given the emphasis Madison and other Framers placed on the inviolability of property and their insistence that the primary function of a just government is to protect substantive rights of persons and property, it is inconceivable that they would have viewed the Constitution—the "supreme Law of the Land" (art. VI)—in terms of anything other than *substantive* due process. With the usurpations of Parliament and state legislatures under the Articles of Confederation fresh in their minds, the overriding aim of the Framers was to secure property as a fundamental right, not to submit it to the political process. "The great desideratum in Government," wrote Madison ([1787] 1865a, p. 327), "is such a modification of the sovereignty as will render it sufficiently neutral between the different interests and factions to controul one part of the society from invading the rights of another, and, at the same time, sufficiently controuled itself from setting up an interest adverse to that of the whole society."

The higher law of the U.S. Constitution, therefore, is not some nebulous doctrine incapable of clear exposition and interpretation by the judiciary. Rather, as Corwin ([1914] 1970, pp. 32-33) has emphasized, the principles and content of the higher law doctrine are embedded in the common law and have been explicated in legal treatises such as Blackstone's *Commentaries*—where Blackstone, even though himself a legal absolutist, recognized the rights of "personal security," "personal liberty," and "property" as fundamental rights of individuals. Indeed, Blackstone's listing of absolute rights is simply a recognition of Hume's "three fundamental laws of nature" and a reflection of the core of private or common law as generally understood; namely, the sanctity of private property, freedom of contract, and restitution for takings.[29] It is in this tradition that Dicey ([1915] 1982, p. 84) wrote: The U. S. Constitution "provides that the elementary principles of justice, freedom of trade, and the rights of individual property shall be absolutely respected throughout the length and breadth of the Union."

---

[28] See Dicey ([1915] 1982, p. 315). See Also Corwin (1955, p. 47) who points to the acceptance of Coke's higher law in America.

[29] On the basic principles of private law and their correspondence with Hume's "law of nature," as well as with Hayek's "rules of just conduct," see Hayek (1982, chap. 8, p. 40).

The Bill of Rights

The Bill of Rights, when understood as higher law, reinforces the original Constitution as a safeguard of those rights to life, liberty, and property that the Framers sought to secure against the heavy hand of government and the political agendas of organized factions. Concerned lest future legislators try to undermine the economic and noneconomic liberties embodied in the higher-law Constitution, but not explicitly mentioned in the original document, Madison led the movement in the First Congress for a bill of rights (see Burns 1968, pp. 80-81). On June 8, 1789, he introduced a number of proposed amendments, ten of which became the Bill of Rights and two of which—the Ninth and Tenth Amendments—he was "the principal author and sole commentator" (Canavan 1987, p. 26).

Madison's views on a bill of rights are forcefully expressed in a letter to Thomas Jefferson, his close friend and trusted advisor, dated October 17, 1788.[30] "My own opinion," wrote Madison, "has always been in favor of a bill of rights; provided it be so framed as not to imply powers not meant to be included in the enumeration." But Madison also stated that he "never thought the omission a material defect," and initially he was reluctant to push for a bill of rights. His reluctance was based on the beliefs that (1) "the rights in question are reserved by the manner in which the federal powers are granted"; (2) "there is great reason to fear that a positive declaration of some of the most essential rights could not be obtained in the requisite latitude"; (3) "the limited powers of the federal Government and the jealousy of the subordinate Governments, afford a security which has not existed in the case of the State Governments;" and (4) "experience proves the inefficiency of a bill of rights on those occasions when its controul is most needed."

On this last point, Madison directs Jefferson's attention to the fact that "repeated violations of these parchment barriers have been committed by overbearing majorities in every State." He then makes the following observation:

> Wherever the real power in a Government lies, there is the danger of oppression. In our Governments the real power lies in the majority of the Community, and the invasion of private rights is *chiefly* to be apprehended, not from acts of Government contrary to the sense of its constituents, but from acts in which the Government is the mere instrument of the major number of the Constituents.

It is precisely this observation—the possibility of unlimited government driven by the will of majorities—that swings Madison back toward a bill of

---

[30] Reprinted in Padover (1953, pp. 253-55). The quoted passages in this paragraph and the next two paragraphs are from the Padover reprint.

rights. In a representative democracy, argues Madison, a bill of rights will prove useful because: "The political truths declared in that solemn manner acquire by degrees the character of fundamental maxims of free Government, and as they become incorporated with the national sentiment, counteract the impulses of interest and passion."

On net balance, then, Madison favored a bill of rights and gave his full support to ensure that it would become an integral part of the Constitution. The amended Constitution would serve to strengthen the security of individual rights by specifying those rights more fully and by making it clear that no further powers were to be given to the government beyond those delegated and enumerated in the original Constitution. Madison's purpose in helping to frame the Bill of Rights was to secure pre-existing rights, not to extend democratic rule. In principle, therefore, he would likely have agreed with the Supreme Court's opinion in *West Virginia State Board of Education v. Barnette*, where the majority held:

> The very purpose of a Bill of Rights was to withdraw certain subjects from the vicissitudes of political controversy, to place them beyond the reach of majorities and officials and to establish them as legal principles to be applied by the Courts. One's right to life, liberty, and property, to free speech, a free press, freedom of worship and assembly, and other fundamental rights may not be submitted to vote; they depend on the outcome of no elections.[31]

In looking at the Bill of Rights, it is easy to discern Madison's influence. Indeed, the rights described therein are of the same fabric as those he incorporated into his broad definition of property. First Amendment rights lie side-by-side with Fifth Amendment rights to "life, liberty, and property." Moreover, at the risk of failing to enumerate rights that properly belong in the private domain as a matter of "right and reason," Madison authored the Ninth Amendment to read: "The enumeration in the Constitution, of certain rights, shall not be construed to deny or disparge others retained by the people." The emphasis here is on protecting individual *rights* against government intrusion and, as such, this amendment is consistent with Madison's view of a just government. What Madison wanted to guarantee was that those rights compatible with an individual's fundamental right to noninterference not be denied as a matter of law.[32] The Ninth

---

[31] 319 U.S. 624, 638 (1943).

[32] In a recently discovered draft of the Bill of Rights, the proposed Second Amendment reads:

> The people have certain natural rights which are retained by them when they enter into Society. Such are the rights of Conscience in matters of religion; of acquiring property, and of pursuing happiness & Safety; of Speaking, writing and publishing their Sentiments with decency and freedom; of peaceably assembling to consult their common good, and of applying to Government by petition or remonstrance

Amendment, therefore, should be viewed as entirely consistent with Madison's rights-based approach to government and is a reflection of his overarching moral and political philosophy.

While Madison framed the Ninth Amendment to afford greater protection to the property right, broadly conceived, he framed the Tenth Amendment to maintain the spirit of federalism. The emphasis here is on establishing a proper balance of power between the federal and state governments, with political sovereignty lodged in the states and ultimately in the people. This amendment reads: "The powers not delegated to the United States by the Constitution, nor prohibited by it to the States, are reserved to the States respectively, or to the people."

In sum, Madison saw the Constitution (inclusive of the Bill of Rights) as a bulwark against the state and organized interests. His aim was to protect persons and property and provide a structure of government that limited the potential for injustice, that is, for the taking of property without the consent of the rightful owner(s). Thus, he sought to limit government and provide the maximum scope for individual freedom under the higher law of the Constitution. Specific provisions to protect private property rights, freedom of contract, and First Amendment rights were only meant to sketch the higher law background; those rights not explicitly mentioned in the Constitution (as amended) were retained by the people. These private rights, however, were not unlimited; they were constrained by the requirement that they be in conformity with an individual's basic right to noninterference, which is simply the Lockean/Madisonian property right. In this sense, then, Madison's higher law Constitution is a "constitution of liberty," affording individuals equal freedom and justice under the law. Whether the U. S. Constitution (hereafter inclusive of the Bill of Rights) effectively secures private rights, however, will depend on the Supreme Court's role as guardian of the Constitution and its higher law background.

for redress of grievances. Of these rights therefore they Shall not be deprived by the Government of the United States.

And the proposed Eighth Amendment reads:

Congress Shall not have power to grant any monopoly or exclusive advantages of commerce to any person or Company; nor to restrain the liberty of the Press.

These two proposed amendments are important because they shed new light on the Framers adherence to natural rights doctrine. It is especially significant that there is a specific listing of "natural rights which are retained" by the people, and that this listing is consistent with Madison's broad definition of property as including both economic and noneconomic liberties. The proposed Eighth Amendment further strengthens the evidence in favor of the view that the Framers sought to afford equal protection to economic liberties. That is, the right to noninterference applied as much to voluntary exchange as it did to freedom of the press. For the full text of the proposed Bill of Rights, see Mitgang (1987, p. C21). According to Collier (1987), Mitgang incorrectly attributes the draft to Roger Sherman. Even though the draft was in Sherman's handwriting, authorship is still unknown. The draft was discovered in Madison's papers at the Library of Congress.

VI. The Judiciary: Guardian of the Constitution

Adam Smith, in *The Theory of Moral Sentiments* ([1759] 1976, p. 163), listed what he considered the fundamental "laws of justice," namely: "laws which guard the life and person of our neighbor"; "those which guard his property and possessions"; and "those which guard what are called his personal rights, or what is due to him from the promises of others." The jurisprudential view of Madison, and the Framers in general, reflected this Smithean view of justice and the law.[33] In their view, it was the function of the judiciary to secure the "laws of justice" against the usurpations of the political branches of government. As such, Madison argued in the First Congress for a strong federal judiciary to protect individual rights: "Independent tribunals of justice will consider themselves . . . the guardians of those rights; they will be an impenetrable bulwark against every assumption of power in the Legislative or Executive" (*Annals* 1: 439). Similarly, Dicey ([1915] 1982, p. 72) notes: In the United States, the system of judicial review "which makes the judges the guardians of the constitution, provides the only adequate safeguard which has hitherto been invented against unconstitutional legislation."[34]

The Final Arbiter

In a federalist system characterized by "supremacy of the constitution"— and "the distribution among bodies with limited and co-ordinate authority of the different powers of government"—the judiciary necessarily emerges as the final interpreter of the Constitution, observes Dicey (p. 77).[35] Indeed, within a federalist structure, the Supreme Court becomes what Dicey (p. 90) has called "the ultimate arbiter of all matters affecting the Constitution."[36] Madison, likewise, recognized the importance of the judiciary in a federalist system. He stated that although the political branches have an equal right to interpret the Constitution, "the Judicial department most familiarizes itself to the public attention as the expositor, by the *order* of its functions in relation to the other departments; and attracts most the

---

[33] The ideas of Adam Smith and other Scottish moral philosophers were imparted to Madison and other Framers who attended John Witherspoon's lectures at Princeton University. "Madison had no teacher so influential in shaping his thought as Witherspoon," writes Scott (1982, p. 15). See also Solberg (1958, p. xcix).

[34] See also Siegan (1985a, p. 279): "The federal judiciary is . . . the guardian of the Constitution. Its role is to prevent any governmental unit, branch, agency, or official from either usurping the powers of any other governmental authority or denying the people their liberties."

[35] For a general discussion of the characteristics of a federalist system and the importance of the judiciary therein, see Dicey ([1915] 1982, chap. 3).

[36] Cf. Siegan (1985a).

public confidence by the composition of the tribunal." Hence, he considered the Supreme Court, "when happily filled," to be "the surest expositor of the Constitution" ([1834] 1865c, pp. 349-50).

Under the Articles of Confederation, the state legislatures were sovereign. Madison reacted to this in the Federal Convention by supporting the idea of granting the judiciary a revisionary power to be shared with the executive. Accordingly, he held that in the absence of a Council of Revision, "the Legislature would still be an over-match." And noted: "Experience in all the States had evinced a powerful tendency in the Legislature to absorb all power into its vortex" (in Solberg 1958, p. 236). Although the revisionary power was never granted, the doctrine of judicial review provided a potentialy effective means of defending the property right against legislative intrusions.[37]

The doctrine of judicial review, as it had evolved up to the time of the Constitutional Convention, can be summarized in the following manner: "The judiciary possesses exclusive power to interpret with finality standing law, but the latter must meet the tests imposed by 'higher' law—i.e., it must be intrinsically just" (Solberg 1958, p. lxxxiv).[38] The Framers generally accepted this view, as did the ratifying conventions; the notion that the Constitution "provided for control of legislation by the courts was seldom even questioned" (Burns 1968, pp. 180-81). As for Madison, his higher-law vision of the Constitution consistently led him to support a judiciary that would protect individual rights and check the power of the lawmakers. Thus Burns (1968, p. 183) relates that Madison "never abandoned his belief in the authority of the courts to pass upon the validity of legislation, especially of the sort that affected private rights."

Judicial Protection of Economic Liberties

Economic liberties were of particular importance for Madison and the Framers. The judiciary's role was to afford equal protection for economic and noneconomic rights, so long as they were consistent with the basic Lockean property right. Madison made no distinction between the rights of persons and the rights of property; for him property was a civil right. It would make little sense to sanction freedom of the press but outlaw private presses, for example.[39] The role of the federal judiciary, then, was

---

[37] Corwin (1955, p. 89) notes that "even statutory form could hardly have saved the higher law as *a resource for individual* had it not been backed up by *judicial review.*"

[38] For a further discussion of the development of the doctrine of judicial review and its role in a constitutional democracy, see Corwin (1914) and Siegan (1987). See also Burns (1968, pp. 174-90) who places Madison's view of judicial review in historical context.

[39] On the relation between economic and political freedom, see Friedman (1962, chap.1) and Siegan (1980, esp. chaps. 10-11).

to act as a defender of individual liberties consistent with the Madisonian vision of a just government. A stable framework would then be provided for social coordination. From this perspective, Madison ([1833] 1865c, pp. 296-97) wrote: "The Federal judiciary is the only defensive armour of the Federal government, or, rather, for the Constitution and laws of the United States. Strip it of that armour, and the door is wide open for nullification, anarchy, and convulsion."

Constitutional provisions for safeguarding private property and freedom of contract include the commerce clause, the contracts clause, the clauses prohibiting ex post facto laws and bills of attainder, the takings and due process clauses of the Fifth Amendment (and later the Fourteenth), and the Ninth Amendment's sanctuary for property rights, broadly conceived. It is in light of these and other provisions, as seen from a higher law background, that Dicey ([1915] 1982, p. 91) commented: "To the judiciary in short are due the maintenance of justice, the existence of internal free trade, and the general respect for the rights of property."

In the period immediately following ratification, the Supreme Court chiefly applied natural law principles to uphold the inviolability of property (Siegan 1984, p. 41). As early as 1795, Justice Paterson in *Van Horne's Lessee v. Dorrance*[40] argued:

> The right of acquiring and possessing property and *having it protected* is one of the natural, inherent and unalienable rights of man. . . . The legislature therefore had no authority to make an act divesting one citizen of his freehold and vesting it in another, without a just compensation. It is inconsistent with the principles of reason, justice, and moral rectitude; it is incompatible with the comfort, peace and happiness of mankind; . . . and lastly, it is contrary both to the letter and spirit of the constitution.

Three years later, in *Calder v. Bull*[41], Justice Chase argued: "An Act of the legislature (for I cannot call it a *law*) contrary to the great principles of the social compact cannot be considered a rightful exercise of legislative authority. . . . [A] law that destroys, or impairs the lawful private contracts of citizens . . . or a law that takes *property* from A and gives it to B . . . is against all reason and justice."

The line of reasoning ascribed to by Justices Paterson and Chase become known as the "doctrine of vested rights" in U. S. constitutional law. Briefly, this doctrine holds that "the property right is fundamental" and "treats any law impairing *vested rights*, whatever its intention, as a bill of pains and penalties, and so, void" (Corwin [1914] 1970, pp. 33-34). It was the application of this doctrine, says Corwin (p. 35), that "gradually operated

[40] 2 U.S. (2 Dall.) 304, 310 (1795).
[41] 3 U.S. (3 Dall.) 386, 388 (1798).

to give legal reality to the notion of governmental power as *limited power."*
Thus, even though Justice Iredell disparaged Justice Chase's argument for
a principled approach to judicial review—one turning on higher law
principles in the interpretation of written law—Chase's principled approach
was the dominant one taken by the early Court.[42]

Additional protection for persons and property was afforded by the early
Court's adherence to the "doctrine of due process of law," which took on
increasing importance after ratification of the Fourteenth Amendment. By
1897, in *Allgeyer v. Louisiana*,[43] the Court could unanimously declare that
freedom of contract is an inherent part of the property right and should
be afforded equal protection under the law.[44] It was not until the 1930s,
with the decisions in *Nebbia v. New York*,[45] *West Coast Hotel Co. v. Parrish*,[46]
and *United States v. Carolene Products Co.*[47] that substantive economic due
process was abandoned by the Court in favor of a less rigorous test of the
constitutionality of legislation involving economic regulation—the so-called
rational relation (or rational basis) test. Under this lower level of scrutiny,
however, almost any statute regulating the rights of property and contract
could be held constitutional, since all that is required is that the law be
"rationally related to a conceivable public purpose."[48] Using this standard,
for example, the Court ruled in *Hawaii Housing Authority v. Midkiff*[49] that
a statute forcing party A (the landholder) to sell to party B (the leaseholder)
for the purpose of decentralizing land ownership is constitutional (see
Epstein 1984).

By abandoning substantive due process in its review of economic
legislation, the Court divorced economic rights from noneconomic rights
and paved the way for increased regulation of private property and freedom
of contract. Thus, the property right, instead of being protected as a natural
right vested in individuals and superior to legislation, became the subject
of activist legislation designed to regulate and redistribute property in the

---

[42] See Corwin ([1914] 1970, pp. 28-31). With reference to Iredell, he notes: "Iredell's tenet
that courts were not to appeal to natural rights and the social compact as furnishing a basis
for constitutional decisions was disregarded by all the leading judges and advocates of the early
period of our constitutional history" (p. 31).

[43] 165 U.S. 578 (1897).

[44] On the importance of the due process doctrine before and after the Civil War, see Corwin
(1970, chaps. 3-4) and Siegan (1980, 1985b).

[45] 291 U.S. 502 (1934).

[46] 300 U.S. 379 (1937).

[47] 304 U.S. 144 (1938).

[48] For a useful account of the demise of substantive economic due process and the ineffectiveness
of the rational basis test in protecting economic liberties, see Siegan (1980).

[49] 467 U.S. 229 (1984).

name of "social justice." Majoritarian interests therefore came to dominate private property rights, with a consequent loss of individual freedom.[50]

The change in the nature of the Court after the termination of substantive economic due process is illustrated in *Berman v. Parker*,[51] a land-use case that set the precedent for the *Hawaii* decision. In *Berman* the Court held that "when the legislature has spoken, the public interest has been declared in terms well-nigh conclusive. In such cases the legislature, not the judiciary is the main guardian of the public needs to be served by social legislation. . . . This principle admits of no exception merely because of the power of eminent domain is involved."[52] Such reasoning, however, turns the higher law of the Constitution on its head. As Epstein (1985b, pp.714-15) points out:

> [Under the] "rational basis" test . . . so long as there is some "plausible" or "conceivable" justification for the challenged legislation, it is invul-
> nerable to constitutional attack. . . . Courts [therefore] simply give up before they try, and embrace an appalling sort of ethical noncognitivism.
> Anything legislatures do is as good as anything else they might have done; we cannot decide what is right or wrong, so it is up to Congress and the states to determine the limitations of their own power—which, of course, totally subverts the original constitutional arrangement of limited government.

Siegan (1980, p. 265) concurs, noting that if the standard of constitutionality is lowered in the case of economic rights so that a statute need only be "rationally related to a public purpose," nearly all regulatory acts can be justified. In his view, therefore, "the rational relation standard essentially presupposes judicial withdrawal." By failing to offer economic rights the same protection as noneconomic rights, the modern Court has abandoned Madison's views of justice and government, and opened the door for all kinds of legislative mischief. In this respect, Siegan (1985a, p. 276) observes: "The Framers surely would never have accepted judicial review if they had thought it would be used to advance government authority and regulation."

Danger of Judicial Deference to the Political Branches

Under the pretense that the majority should rule, the judiciary has lost sight of the Constitution as a charter of freedom and a bulwark for individual rights. Without the guidance of higher law principles, the modern Court

---

[50] On the failure of the Supreme Court to protect economic liberties after 1936, see Dorn (1987, and the references therein); also Pilon (1985).

[51] 348 U.S. 26 (1954).

[52] *Id.* at 32.

has widened its proclivity to err in two directions.[53] First, in the direction of judicial overreaching as when the Court reads rights into the Constitution that clash with rights to life, liberty, and property—rights that lie at the heart of private law (or Smith's "laws of justice") and that pre-exist government and written constitutions. Second, the Court can err in the direction of judicial restraint as when it reads rights out of the Constitution that properly belong there by virtue of their conformity with "fundamental law." The constitutional text itself may be silent with regard to certain property rights, but this silence disappears when one examines the basis and structure of constitutional democracy and the higher law background of the document.[54]

It is the duty of the judiciary to uphold the Constitution as the "law of the land," but to do so requires that judges go beyond the document to its higher law background. And to perform this task satisfactorily requires a *substantive* rights-based approach to the Constitution. Without an intimate knowledge of the higher law background of the Constitution, the Court is likely to go astray—either wrongly enlarging the Constitution or wrongly shrinking it according to the preferences of judges or the interests of politically favored groups.[55] The ideal, of course, is for the Court to uphold acts that are consistent with the higher law of the Constitution but to void those acts that violate both economic and noneconomic rights, as understood by Madison and his contemporaries. The Court's role, therefore, is one of protection rather than policymaking, either directly by excessive activism or indirectly by excessive restraint.

The danger inherent in judicial deference to the political branches was well recognized by Madison. Indeed, he strongly criticized the type of judicial reasoning associated with the rational relation test and warned that without judicial protection of individual rights, constitutional democracy would be transformed into unlimited democracy with disastrous consequences for the young liberal republic. Thus, in his letter to Judge Roane, dated September 2, 1819, Madison (1865b, p. 146) argued:

---

[53] Cf. Epstein (1985b, esp. p. 717) on two types of judicial error. See also Siegan (1987) who writes in his chapter on "Economic and Property Rights," "Failure to implement existing rights is no less an error than enforcing non-existent rights. The Constitution can be transgressed either through omission or commission" (p. 81).

[54] On a more rigorous approach to justifying moral rights, see Pilon (1979b); also Epstein (1985a, 1985c). In the latter reference, Epstein writes: "Judicial restraint may call for inaction when the Constitution is silent. But that silence cannot be simply presumed, but must be demonstrated by close textual analysis"; that is, against a higher law background in which "the Constitution is a charter for limited government."

[55] Writing in the midst of the economic due process era, Corwin ([1928-29] 1955, p. 72) warned: "Without the Lockean or some similar background, judicial review must have atrophied by 1890 in the very field in which it is today most active." Cf. Macedo (1986, chap. 5) who calls for a "principled judicial activism."

> Much of the error in expounding the Constitution has its origin in the use made of the species of sovereignty implied in the nature of government. The specified powers vested in Congress, it is said, are sovereign powers; and that, as such, they carry with them an unlimited discretion as to the means of executing them. It may surely be remarked, that a limited government may be limited in its sovereignty, as well with respect to the means as to the objects of its powers; and that to give an extent to the former superseding the limits to the latter is, in effect, to convert a limited into an unlimited government.

Madison was reacting to the doctrine laid down by Chief Justice John Marshall's broad interpretation of the "necessary and proper clause" (art. I, sec. 8) in *McCulloch v. Maryland*,[56] where Marshall reasoned: "Let the end be legitimate, let it be within the scope of the Constitution, and all means which are appropriate, which are plainly adapted to the end, which are not prohibited, but consist[ent] with the letter and spirit of the constitution, are constitutional." In essence, what this came to mean was that any legislative act that is "convenient and useful" as a means of implementing an express power of the federal government will not be voided by the Court. With respect to the case at hand, J. W. Peltason (1976, p. 20) notes: "Although the power to incorporate a bank is not among the powers expressly delegated, it is a necessary and proper—that is to say, convenient and useful—means of carrying into effect such delegated powers as caring for the property of the United States, regulating currency, and promoting interstate commerce." The trouble Madison saw with Marshall's doctrine was that under it "the expediency and constitutionality of means for carrying into effect a specified power are convertible terms; and [members of] Congress are admitted to be judges of the expediency. The Court certainly cannot be so; a question, the moment it assumes the character of mere expediency or policy, being evidently beyond the reach of judicial cognizance" ([1819] 1865b, p. 144). According to Madison (p. 145), the proper route for constitutional change is through the amendment process, not the "innovations" of the Court and subsequent deference to legislative majorities. Had Marshall's broad interpretation been part of the constitutional text, Madison doubts that the Constitution would have been ratified.[57]

From a public choice perspective, Madison recognized that if the judiciary abandoned its role as guardian of the higher law Constitution, majorities and favored interest groups would undermine economic and noneconomic liberties. Without an effective constraint on government, legislation would proliferate, increasing uncertainty and upsetting social and economic

---

[56] 17 U.S. (4 Wheat.) 316, 421 (1819).

[57] For a general discussion of the context of Madison's letter, see Burns (1968, pp. 184-85).

coordination.[58] Judicial deference to the political branches, then, amounts to an attenuation of the Constitution as a *substantive* limit on government interference with an individual's liberty and property. In particular, if almost any legislative act regulating the use and disposal of property and freedom of contract can pass the test of constitutionality, based on the "rational basis" standard, expectations will change in a predicable direction. Instead of expecting a noninterventionist state, individuals will rationally expect the state to pursue their economic interests even if individual rights to property and contract are violated in the process.

When the judiciary fails in its role of securing property, in the Lockean/Madisonian sense, it becomes an instrument for redistribution, allowing rent-seekers to gain at the expense of less politically favored groups, with the result that property rights become the subject of majority vote. The failure of the judiciary to uphold the "laws of justice" can thus be viewed as a form of "government failure," namely, the failure to afford equal protection to economic and noneconomic rights.[59] It was to prevent such a failure that Madison, who Robert Rutland (1987) calls "The Founding Father," favored a strong federal judiciary. Moreover, Madison recognized that a stable government by law, protecting both economic and noneconomic liberties, would provide a sound basis for a spontaneous social and economic order in which individuals could pursue their interests without violating the equal rights of others. His constitutional democracy or liberal republic, therefore, was fully compatible with a free market order.

VII. Constitutional Democracy and Spontaneous Order

Madison pointed to the close relationship between political stability and economic stability and warned that without effective limits on legislation, constitutional democracy would deteriorate into unlimited democracy. Runaway majoritarianism was therefore a real concern for him. But he was also concerned with the rise of the Federalist Party under Alexander Hamilton, who favored an aristocratic government based on privileged positions for business interests and a strong central government capable

---

[58] Madison points to the "multiplicity of laws" in the states prior to effective constitutional constraints on legislative sovereignty and their pernicious effects on security of exchange and liberty in general ([1787] 1865a, pp. 324-25); see also Madison's "[Letter] to John Cartwright" ([1824] 1865b, pp. 355-56).

[59] The failure of the post-1936 Court to treat property rights on equal grounds with other rights has been emphasized by Siegan, (1985a, p. 289): "The most important civil rights for the framers of the original Constitution, the Bill of Rights, and the Fourteenth Amendment were those of life, liberty, and property. Contemporary Supreme Court policy largely ignores this understanding with respect to the last item of this trilogy." See also his discussion of the difference between "negative and affirmative jurisprudence" (in Siegan 1980, chap. 14).

of implementing a national industrial policy, as outlined in the "Report on Manufactures" (1791). To counter the Federalist Party, Madison (with Thomas Jefferson) formed the liberal Republican Party, also known as the Democratic-Republican Party. This new opposition party was to be a party of principle based on Madison's vision of man and the state, and his conception of justice under the higher law of the Constitution.

As a *liberal* republican, that is, one who saw the function of government as the safeguarding of liberty and property, Madison favored those institutions that limited the power of government. Like Adam Smith, Madison saw liberty of person, private property, and freedom of contract as the institutional features most consistent with Coke's "common right and reason." And like Smith and other classical liberal economists, Madison held that within a constitutional framework protecting these institutions, individual self-interest would be socially beneficial. He therefore adhered to Smith's doctrine of free trade and criticized Hamilton's inclination toward protectionism and national economic planning. In particular, he dismissed Hamilton's underlying assumption that government officials are better able to allocate resources than private entrepreneurs operating in open markets and guided by the profit motive.

Madison's emphasis was on establishing a set of constitutional rules that constrained government's economic empowerments. By limiting government to the protection of private property rights, voluntary exchange would tend to guide resources to their highest-valued uses without central direction. His view was that "property as well as personal rights is an essential object of the laws, which encourage industry by securing the enjoyment of its fruits" ([1829] 1865c, p. 22). Hamilton, however, was less trusting of markets and prices, and sought to supplement the spontaneous market order with increased government planning of industry and trade. He was, in effect, like Smith's "man of system," that is, "apt to be very wise in his own conceit, and . . . so enamoured with the supposed beauty of his own ideal plan of government, that he cannot suffer the smallest deviation for any part of it . . . . [H]e seems to imagine that he can arrange the different members of a great society with as much ease as the hand arranges the different pieces upon a chess-board" (Smith [1759] 1976, pp. 380-81).

It was Madison's stricter adherence to the Smithean principle of spontaneous organization of the market, based on voluntary exchange, that distinguished his political economy from that of Hamilton's. And it was his strict interpretation of the Constitution as a set of higher law principles, limiting the power of government, that distinguished his liberal republicanism from Hamilton's nationalism.

Madisonian Liberal Republicanism

Edward Dreyer (1987, pp. 2, 5) describes Madison as the "chief architect" and "intellectual founder" of the liberal Republican Party.[60] And Lance Banning (1974, p. 179) characterizes Madison's opposition party as one designed to "elevate the Constitution as the palladium of American liberty." While Madison was a proponent of federalism in Dicey's sense of the word (see *supra*, n. 35), and supported a national government to preserve the Union, he never favored a dominant central government that would be largely immune from popular sovereignty, or that would endanger individual property rights by granting privileged positions to special interest groups. He therefore opposed Hamilton's Federalist Party on grounds of principle.

In his essay "Charters" (*National Gazette*, January 18, 1792), Madison spelled out the meaning of liberal republicanism and provided a rationale for forming an opposition party. Essentially, liberal republicanism meant the establishment of "the efficacy of popular charters, in defending liberty against power . . . and in keeping every portion of power within its proper limits; [and] by this means discomfiting the partizans of anti-republican contrivances." By instituting a constitutional party of principle, Madison hoped to strengthen the public's love of liberty, thereby safeguarding "the *great charters* [specifically the U. S. Constitution and Bill of Rights] . . . from every attempt to add to or diminish from them." He believed that "liberty and order will never be *perfectly* safe, until a trespass on the constitutional provisions for either, shall be felt with the same keenness that resents an invasion of the dearest rights" (in Rutland et al. 1983, p. 192).

Madison pointed to the delegation and enumeration of powers as important features of a republican government (*Federalist* No. 39). Moreover, in his general approach to government, he adhered to the doctrine of vested rights and the social compact. In Madison's liberal republic, the principles of freedom, property, and justice were fully compatible with democracy, understood as an individual's freedom under the higher law of the Constitution. But in his acceptance of the Lockean natural rights doctrine, he stood at an opposite pole from Hamilton and the new Federalists.

The principles of "free republican governments" were explicated by Justice Chase in *Calder v. Bull* (1798), when he stated: "There are certain vital principles in our free republican governments which will determine and overrule an apparent and flagrant abuse of legislative power." Among these principles, he highlighted an individual's unalienable rights to protect his life, liberty, and property from governmental takings.[61] The same

---

[60] Dreyer (1987) reviews Madison's essays in the *National Gazette*, the opposition party's newspaper, and distinguishes Madison's liberal republicanism from Hamilton's nationalism.

[61] See Justice Chase's full discussion in Corwin ([1914] 1970, p. 28).

emphasis on vested rights and the social compact was voiced by Daniel Webster in 1829. Defending the principles of liberal republicanism, he argued that without "a general restraint on legislatures, in favor of private rights, there is an end to private property. Though there may be no prohibition in the constitution, the legislature is restrained from acts subverting the great principles of republican liberty and of the social compact" (in Corwin [1914] 1970, p. 31). And as Joyce Appleby (1986, p. 34) relates, those "who *claimed* republican for a party label in 1800 . . . celebrated the free individual."

Based on his vision of justice and a liberal social order, Madison scorned Hamilton's ambitious plans for artificially supporting manufacturing establishments against the free flow of industry and trade. Thus, in his essay "Republican Distribution of Citizens" (*National Gazette*, March 5, 1792), he warned against Hamilton's "experiments by power" and advocated private enterprise and freedom of contract as institutions better suited to a liberal republic, arguing that "the free choice of occupations by the people, might gradually approximate the [best] order of society" (in Dreyer 1987, p. 18).

That Madison supported a *democratic* regime is fully consistent with his liberal republican principles. He never sought an unlimited democracy based on the will of the majority as a measure of right and justice. In such a system, individual rights and justice would be turned on their heads, and the higher law Constitution subverted to legislative sovereignty. Rather, he sought a constitutionally limited democracy that would protect the equal rights of individuals, in the Lockean tradition. For Madison, as for Locke, the power of government rested on the consent of the people.[62] The liberal version of Madisonian democracy is captured in the following statement from John O'Sullivan, who in 1837 wrote:

> The best government is that which governs least. . . . [Legislation] should be confined to the administration of justice, for the protection of the natural equal rights of the citizen, and the preservation of the social order. In all other respects, the voluntary principle, the principle of freedom . . . affords the true golden rule. . . . This is the fundamental principle of the philosophy of democracy, to furnish a system of the administration of justice, and then to leave all the business and interests of society to themselves, to free competition and association—in a word, to the *voluntary principle* (in Vernier 1987, pp. 12-13).

It was in this sense, then, that Madison questioned "the fundamental principle of republican Government, that the majority who rule in such

---

[62] On the two senses of democracy and on Madison's adherence to the liberal version, that is, the version compatible with individual rights and freedom under the law, see Burns (1968, chap. 3).

Governments are the safest guardians both of public good and of private rights" ([1787] 1865a, p. 325). And it is why he proposed a liberal republicanism with constitutional safeguards, especially a strong judiciary to afford equal protection to economic and noneconomic liberties. But even a strong judiciary would be ineffective if the people themselves abandoned their love of liberty.[63]

Constitutional Political Economy

Foremost in Madison's political economy was an emphasis on the rules required for social and economic coordination and, hence, for a spontaneous market order. Taking a comparative institutions or property rights approach, Madison (at the time of the Constitutional Convention) searched alternative forms of government to discern a set of rules that would provide stable government by law and maximum individual freedom. Like Adam Smith, he recognized the overriding importance of private property, freedom of contract, and voluntary exchange in promoting a nation's wealth. He therefore opposed, as a general principle, government intervention in trade and industry. Moreover, he believed that the gains from exchange would be proportional to the freedom of trade.[64] Thus, at the core of his political economy was an understanding of the importance of institutions in shaping incentives and economic behavior, and an appreciation of the market exchange process and the notion of spontaneous order. From this perspective, Madison can well be called a pioneer in the field of constitutional political economy.[65]

The attention paid to rules of political and economic organization, and their impact on individual incentives to utilize resources efficiently and increase societal wealth, was an integral part of late 18th century political economy, with the principle of free trade dominant. Referring to the free trade doctrine of Smith and J. B. Say, Frederick List, himself having protectionist sympathies, wrote: "This doctrine . . . was embraced by the greater part of those who made politics their particular study, and after having admired a doctrine for ten and twenty years, found it difficult to divest themselves of it" (1827, pp. 5-6). He went on to remark: "The system of Adam Smith has assumed so great an authority, that those who venture to

---

[63] Jefferson's views of democracy and the principles of a liberal republic were much the same as Madison's. On these similarities, see Burns (1968, pp. 85-90). See also Vernier (1987) for a review of the literature relating to alternative interpretations of Jeffersonian liberal republicanism.

[64] Madison's acceptance of the free trade principle is reflected in the opening quote of this paper.

[65] In his modern-day appeal for a constitutional political economy, Buchanan (1983, p. 8) has referred to the "principle of spontaneous order" as the central principle of economics and has emphasized economics as "the science of exchanges."

oppose it, or even to question its infallibility, expose themselves to be called idiots" (p. 13).

Madison's views on free trade did not change much over his lifetime. Writing in 1785, he stated: "A perfect freedom [of trade] is the system which would be my choice" (in Padover 1953, p. 335). And in 1824, in letters to Henry Clay and Dr. Thomas Cooper, he wrote: "I am a friend to the *general* principle of 'free industry,' as the basis of a sound system of political economy" (to Clay); "I have always concurred in the general principle that the industrious pursuits of individuals ought to be left to individuals, as most capable of chusing and managing them. And this policy is certainly most congenial with the spirit of a free people" (to Cooper).[66]

One of the reasons Madison sought to form a federal Union bound by a national Constitution was to end the protectionist trade practices among the several states. In April 1787, in his "Notes on the Confederacy," Madison criticized the parochial spirit of the states and pointed to the discoordination caused by restrictive trade policy: "The practice of many States in restricting the commercial intercourse with other States . . . is certainly adverse to the spirit of the Union, and tends to beget retaliating regulations, not less expensive and vexatious in themselves than they are destructive of the general harmony" (1865a, p. 321). By creating a domestic free-trade zone, the Constitution contributed greatly to the economic welfare of the states and the Union.

In reviewing the economic basis of the Constitution, Siegan (1984, p. 51) notes: "The economics of our Constitution is capitalist; the economic powers of government are limited and the economic rights of individuals are protected." But it was Madison, more than anyone else, who took it upon himself to protect the economic Constitution of liberty. He was instrumental in framing the Constitution and Bill of Rights to protect the property right, and he vigorously rejected Hamilton's plea for aristocratic/monarchistic government. As a member of Congress, he strongly opposed Hamilton's "Report on Manufactures," which he viewed as a blueprint for industrial policy; he also rejected Hamilton's call for the accumulation of a large national debt, and the establishment of a national bank, which he thought would issue an excessive amount of paper currency.[67] Reacting to Hamiltonian-type policies, Madison, in his essay "Property," voiced his opposition to "arbitrary restrictions, exemptions, and monopolies" that interfered with individuals in the "free use of their faculties, and free choice of their occupations" (in Hunt 1906, p. 102). Such

---

[66] Cited in Padover (1953, pp. 272-73).

[67] See Dreyer (1987, esp. pp. 15-18, and the references therein) for a discussion of Madison's anti-Hamiltonian views.

interventions were unjust in Madison's moral universe because they violated the fundamental right to property, broadly conceived. Moreover, such interventions were destructive of social wealth because they upset the competitive market process.

Although Madison favored free trade as a general principle, he did admit to certain exceptions. His experiences as president and during wartime convinced him of the need for affording some protection to American industry. Writing in 1817, he expressed his trade policy: "Although I approve the policy of leaving to the sagacity of individuals, and to the impulse of private interest, the application of industry and capital, I am equally persuaded that in this, as in other cases, there are exceptions to the general rule, which do not impair the principle of it. Among these exceptions is the policy of encouraging domestic manufactures within certain limits, and in reference to certain articles" (in Padover 1953, p. 271). His case for limited protectionism was essentially based on the "infant industry" argument and considerations of national defense,[68] arguments that Hamilton had also utilized. Yet, it appears that even though Madison found it expedient to promote domestic industry when faced with foreign protection for manufactures and the problem of wartime interruptions, he always saw these cases as temporary exceptions to the free trade principle. Hamilton, on the other hand, seemed more willing to use the exceptions as the basis for establishing a general protectionist policy to spur his industrial policy.

Madison's general acceptance of the free trade principle is further revealed in his 1824 letter to Clay, in which he expressed his opposition to a tariff bill:

> The bill, I think, loses sight too much of the general principle which leaves to the judgment of individuals the choice of profitable employments for the[ir] labor and capital; and the arguments in favor of it, from the aptitudes of one situation for manufacturing establishments, tend to shew that these would take place without a legislative interference. The law would not say to the cotton planter, you overstock the market, and ought to plant tobacco; nor to the planter of tobacco, you would do better by substituting wheat. It presumes that profit being the object of each, as the profit of each is the wealth of the whole, each will make whatever change the state of the markets and prices may require. We see, in fact, changes of this sort frequently produced in agricultural pursuits, by individual sagacity watching over individual interest. And why not trust to the same guidance in favor of manufacturing industry, whenever it promises more profit than any of the agricultural branches, or more than mercantile pursuits, from which we see capital readily transferred to manufacturing establishments likely to yield a greater income? (in Padover 1953, pp. 272-73).

[68] See Madison's remarks in Padover (1953, pp. 270-71).

In the same letter, however, Madison stated: "On the other hand, I am not less a friend to the legal patronage of domestic manufactures, as far as they come within particular reasons for exceptions to the general rule, not derogating from its generality." What he meant was stated more clearly in his letter to Thomas Cooper, where he cautioned against those who would "convert the exceptions into the rule, and would make the Government a general supervisor of individual concerns" (in Padover, p. 273).

Madison's letter to Clay makes it clear that he recognized the importance of prices and profits as guides to resource allocation, as well as the importance of the entrepreneur. This understanding made him suspicious of the politicization of economic decisionmaking, which he thought best to leave in the hands of private individuals who had an incentive to utilize relevant information and move resources to higher-valued uses. Like Smith, Madison thought that "if industry and labor are left to take their own course, they will generally be directed to those objects which are the most productive" (in Padover, p. 269).[69] As such, Madison favored a laissez-faire approach to economic development, an approach in opposition to that of the Federalist Party.

The impossibility of centralizing the diverse information available to market participants was a problem Madison accepted as central to the difficulty of national economic planning. He argued that in the absence of government intervention, resources would be allocated "in a more certain and direct manner than the wisdom of the most enlightened Legislature could point out" (in Padover, p. 269). In this respect, he was simply following Adam Smith, who wrote: "No human wisdom or knowledge could ever be sufficient . . . [to perform] the duty of superintending the industry of private people, and of directing it towards the employments most suitable to the interest of the society" [(1776) 1937, p. 651]. Moreover, "the law ought always to trust people with the care of their own interest, as in their local situations they must generally be able to judge better of it than the legislator can do" (Smith, p. 497). By emphasizing the information, incentive, and allocation functions of market prices and profits, Madison, like Smith, was a precursor of modern public choice theory with its emphasis on the "Hayekian knowledge problem."[70]

Finally, in contrast to Hamilton and the Federalists, Madison looked unfavorably upon the accumulation of a national debt, arguing that "public debt is a public curse" (in Padover, p. 336).[71] Likewise, he was critical of

---

[69] Cf. Smith ([1776] 1937, pp. 594-95).

[70] See Hayek's classic article "The Use of Knowledge in Society" (1945); also Kirzner (1984).

[71] Cf. Jefferson, who said: "The principle of spending money to be paid by posterity, under the name of funding, is but swindling futurity on a large scale" (in Somerville and Santoni 1963, pp. 254-55).

the national bank, seeing it as an engine of inflation in the absence of a monetary rule. Anticipating monetarism, he argued that a stable value of money, in principle, could be achieved by limiting the amount of money in circulation to the needs of trade. But anticipating modern public choice theory, he doubted that the bank would follow such a rule, and thus favored covertibility as a surer means of achieving monetary stability. Writing in 1820, Madison noted:

> "It cannot be doubted that a paper currency, rigidly limited in its quantity to purposes absolutely necessary, may be made equal and even superior in value to specie. But experience does not favor a reliance on such experiments. Whenever the paper has not been convertible into specie, and its quantity has depended on the policy of the Government, a depreciation has been produced by an undue increase, or an apprehension of it" (in Padover 1953, p. 292).

And in 1831, he stated:

> The only adequate guarantee for the uniform and stable value of a paper currency is its convertibility into specie. The least fluctuating and the only universal currency. I am sensible that a value equal to that of specie may be given to paper or any other medium, by making a limited amount necessary for necessary purposes; but what is to ensure the inflexible adherence of the Legislative Ensurers to their own principles & purposes? (in Padover 1953, p. 292).

Madison also anticipated some of the arguments used by modern-day bank deregulators when he argued in 1827 that a method of making banks more responsible in conducting their activities would be to make shareholders fully liable for bank losses and provide bank directors with a cost/benefit structure that made them more accountable for their decisions. According to Madison: "Subscribers should be individually liable pro tanto and pro rata for its [the Bank's] obligations, and . . . Directors, with adequate salaries paid out of the profits of the Institution should be prohibited from holding any interest in or having any dealings whatever with, the Bank, and be bound moreover by the usual solemnity, to administer their trust with fidelity and impartiality" (in Padover 1953, p. 291).

In sum, Madison saw a close relationship between the rules of political and economic organization and the justice and efficiency of an economic system. The function of a just government is to protect persons and property so that individuals will be free to pursue their own interests in a mutually beneficial manner. Moreover, under a stable rule of law, uncertainty will be reduced compared to a discretionary regime in which legislative majorities or the ruling elite steer the economy by grants of privilege and the use of duties, bounties, and other protectionist measures.[72] For Madison, unlike Hamilton, the core principle of political economy is that rules of just conduct, affording equal protection to persons and property, create the basis for a spontaneous market order.

Madison formed his liberal Republican Party as a guard against those who would defer to an activist legislature or to a ruling elite determined to supplant individual choice with central authority. He sought to protect the higher law Constitution from Federalist Party functionaries like Hamilton, who wanted to widen the powers of the federal government and disparage the true spirit of democracy as a reflection of individual liberty. From a broader perspective, Madison formed his liberal Republican Party to safeguard individuals against the redistributive state and the rent-seeking he foresaw under unlimited democracy as well as under an elitist British-style regime.[73]

VIII. The Redistributive State vs. the Constitution

Constitutional interpretation was of key importance to Madison and a central part of the debate between himself and the Federalists. His approach to the Constitution was to focus on "the process of its formation, the peculiarity of its structure, and the limitation and distribution of its powers" ([1831] 1865c, p. 171). This approach led him to view the Constitution as a charter for limiting the power of government and protecting the private domain. Most assuredly, he did not view the Constitution as a charter for unlimited democracy and the establishment of a redistributive state. "That is not a just government," wrote Madison, "nor is property secure under it, where the property which a man has in his personal safety and personal liberty, is violated by arbitrary seizures of one class of citizens for the service of the rest" ([1792] in Hunt 1906, p. 102).

For Madison, as for the Framers in general, justice was obtained in the process of protection and destroyed in the process of forced transfers—either direct or indirect—in the name of "distributive justice." The principle function of government was to safeguard private property, not to take it for private use. Thus, in interpreting the "general welfare clause" (art. 1, sec. 8), Madison stated:

---

[72] For Madison's argument that constitutional democracy reduces uncertainty, see *Federalist* No. 51 (esp. p. 68 in DeKoster's edition). Cf. Hayek (1982, chap. 8, p. 38) who has argued: "The rules of just conduct . . . serve to prevent conflict and to facilitate co-operation by eliminating some sources of uncertainity."

[73] In his essay "Spirit of Governments" (1792), Madison pointed to what he considered the major defect of British-style government, namely, the conferring of privileges by government discretion. And this is precisely the characteristic Madison disliked about Hamilton's economic policies. See Dreyer (1987, pp. 14-15).

With respect to the words "general welfare," I have always regarded them as qualified by the detail of powers connected with them. To take them in a literal and unlimited sense would be a metamorphosis of the Constitution into a character which there is a host of proofs was not contemplated by its creators. If the words obtained so readily a place in the "Articles of Confederation," and received so little notice in their admission into the present Constitution, and retained for so long a time a silent place in both, the fairest explanation is, that the words, in the alternative of meaning nothing or meaning everything, had the former meaning taken for granted [(1831) 1865c, pp. 171-72].

This strict interpretation of the function of government under the higher law Constitution put Madison at odds with the Federalists' broad interpretation of the general welfare clause. Hamilton, for example, had argued in his "Report on Manufactures" that the scope of the general welfare clause should be "left to the discretion of the National Legislature," which would then decide what "appropriation of money is requisite and proper" (in Thompson 1917, p. 507).[74] Thus, at the beginning of the republic there was already a clash between the redistributive state and the Constitution.

In the battle of ideas and constitutional interpretation, the judiciary initially sided with the higher law Constitution, as did popular sentiment. Property rights and economics liberties, by and large, received effective judicial protection up until 1936.[75] During that period, the state remained largely a protective agency and its redistributive role remained minor, in line with a strict interpretation of the enumerated powers of the federal government—which furnish "*no* explicit authority for federal welfare programs" (Niskanen 1985, p. 2).[76] The termination of substantive economic due process after 1936, the Court's ruling in *United States v. Butler*[77] that effectively removed constitutional constraints on the scope of federal spending by adopting a so-called public-purpose test, the change in popular sentiment toward redistribution as a by-product of the Great Depression, and the rise of modern "democratic liberalism" all helped spur the rise of the redistributive state or what Terry Anderson and P. J. Hill (1980) have called the "transfer society."[78]

---

[74] On Madison's disagreement with Hamilton over the interpretation of the general welfard clause, see Burns (1968, p. 99).

[75] Siegan (1980, pp. 265-66) observes that since 1936 the Supreme Court has not struck down any economic legislation on grounds of substantive due process.

[76] See also Epstein (1985a, p. 307): "Nothing in Article I appears to confer upon the federal government the power to make transfer payments."

[77] 297 U.S. 1 (1936). For a discussion of this case and its implications for the welfare state, see Niskanen (1985, p. 6).

[78] For a general discussion of the transfer society and the conditions surrounding its rise since the 1930s, see Dorn (1986).

Of the above factors, however, the major impetus to the growth of the modern redistributive state, with its rent-seeking apparatus, was the failure of the judiciary to effectively guard the higher law Constitution in the area of economic liberties.[79] By deferring to the political branches, the judiciary gradually established the expectation that "social justice," rather than commutative justice, is the proper end of the state. But as Hayek has long argued, once the state embarks on the path of "social justice," it opens the door to all sorts of redistributive schemes and, in the process, attenuates property rights, dulls incentives, and distorts the spontaneous market process—with the end result being a loss of freedom and wealth.[80]

In Madison's writings, one finds a distinction between rights and interests, with the former receiving priority over the latter. The government's primary function is to safeguard property, and the majoritarian political process (democratic rule) is legitimate only insofar as it does not violate individual rights. Writing in the spirit of Madison, Roger Pilon (1985, pp. 831-32) elaborated on the higher law Constitution and the priority of private rights over majoritarian interests:

> Our Constitution...sets out precisely those rights that reflect the background, higher law, albeit in a general way only. That higher law is one of structure, of framework—of rights that both permit and constrain our pursuit of values [or interests], whether as individuals or collectively. But the higher law is not "neutral," any more than any of the truths of reason, strictly speaking, are "neutral." Rather, it is the law of individual freedom, of private sovereignty, and hence of laissez-faire capitalism.... [T]here is all the difference in the world between our rights and our values [or interests], between those moral relationships we derive from principles of reason and those attitudes we hold, pro and con, toward the various things of this world.

Elsewhere Pilon (1981, p. 9) ties in the concept of rights to that of property and further distinguishes rights from interests or values: "We get clear about what our *rights* are by getting clear about what our *property* is. Rights, then, are not the same as values; nor are they the same as interests .... There are many things that we value, and many things in which we

---

[79] Tumlir (1985, p. 14) notes: "If we are to explain the rise of rent seeking to a dominant form of democratic politics, we must focus on the change in constitutional interpretation." On this point, see also Anderson and Hill (1986) who argue that moral constraints, such as general acceptance of the natural rights doctrine, play an important role in checking the transfer society. When these constraints are eroded, the explicit provisions of the Constitution limiting the taking of property will be more costly to monitor and enforce.

[80] See, for example, Hayek (1982, chaps 8-9).

we have an interest, but these are not ours by right unless we hold title in them free and clear."[81]

In the strictest sense of the liberal (i.e., protective or just) state, individuals cannot be said to have any legitimate legal obligation to help others; because to imply that they have such an obligation implies that potential recipients have a right to take what is not theirs, which is inconsistent with the norm of justice, that is, the safeguarding of property. As such, "welfare rights," which entail positive obligations, cannot be justified under the higher law Constitution as substantive rights, since they attenuate private property rights and are inconsistent with the fundamental right to noninterference.[82]

The *just* state in the Madisonian sense sets only minimal requirements for morality—by requiring the protection of property, broadly conceived—while leaving individuals the maximum amount of freedom to pursue their own interests or values.[83] Under the "laws of justice," individuals have no legal obligation to help others; but they are free to do so and indeed "ought" to do so as moral persons.[84] What the rise of the modern welfare state has done is to impose its will on individuals, via the majoritarian political process, under the guise of "morality." The democratic process has become the test of justice, as opposed to the substantive law of the Constitution. But coercive actions, even if sanctioned by majority vote, are not moral actions unless in defense of persons and property; and compelled "charity" is false charity. As Smith argued in *The Theory of Moral Sentiments* ([1759] 1976, p. 155): "Beneficence is always free, it cannot be extorted by force."

A return to Madison's "just government" requires turning from the redistributive state to the higher law Constitution; thus setting strict limits

---

[81] See also Pilon (1981, p. 13): "The theory of rights is to be distinguished from the theory of value. If our rights can be grounded in principles of reason, then at least part of ethics can be secured from the skeptic. We then have both surety—in rights—and relativity—in values: the right to pursue whatever values we wish, provided only that we respect the equal rights of others in the process"; also Pilon (1982, p. 39).

[82] On the idea that a rational or substantive theory of rights yields only negative obligations and therefore a consistent set of rights, see Pilon (1979a, pp. 1184-88): "Our general rights . . . are often called our natural rights; they are logically prior and are justified as direct implications of the PGC [Principle of Generic Consistency]. These rights are all variations of the basic right entailed by the PGC, the right to noninterference; hence the correlative obligations are all negative" (p. 1188). On the nonjustifiability of "welfare rights" as substantive moral rights, see Pilon (1979a, pp. 1177-78; 1979b, pp. 1340-41; 1982, pp. 35-36).

[83] In this respect, Pilon (1982, p. 39) remarks: "Laws and governments were instituted to protect our rights, to provide a minimum but basic framework within which each of us might pursue his *own* conception of the good . . . . [L]egitimate law is not an instrument for imposing our conception of the good on others."

[84] This appears to be Adam Smith's general position. See Smith ([1759] 1976, pp. 155-60). See also Pilon (1979b, p. 1342) who states: "The theory of rights sets the strict boundaries of ethics, within which individuals may pursue whatever 'higher' morality they wish."

on takings while allowing individuals to pursue their own conception of the "good society." This change, from taking to protecting property, would once again make the Constitution a charter ensuring freedom and limited government, as envisioned by Madison. Such a change would be consistent with both right and reason: it would secure the rights of individuals and at the same time set the basis for a spontaneous market order and its wealth-creating properties.

IX. Conclusion

From a careful study of Madison's work and its higher law background, there emerge certain obvious facts, which are often overlooked in today's political environment and by the modern Court. Four facts stand out: (1) the fact that the Constitution rests on common law and Lockean natural rights doctrine; (2) the fact that the ostensible purpose of the Constitution was to limit the government and to protect individual rights, with special emphasis on the property right; (3) the fact that the Framers saw the judiciary as the final arbiter in safeguarding the rights of persons and property against the political branches and majoritarian impulses; and (4) the fact the Constitution was never meant to be either a "living constitution" or a "black hole," with rights read into the document or read out of it at the will of the judiciary. Rather it was viewed as a means of establishing a government by law within which individual rights and freedom were to be given priority over the interests of favored political groups. The amendment process was to be the escape hatch for changing the Constitution, not the judiciary or the legislature alone; and for this the Framers provided for a super-majority, in the spirit of Wicksell.

These facts, which underlie Madison's public choice/constitutional perspective, suggest that the deference of the post-1936 Court to legislative activism in the field of economic rights is really a form of government failure, namely, the failure of the judiciary to afford equal protection to economic and noneconomic liberties. In assuming that majority rule will produce rationally consistent results in the "public interest," the Court has been too willing to submit economic rights to the test of the ballot box, and it has been shortsighted in failing to recognize that self-interest is the hallmark of public as well as private choice.[85] To correct this failure requires putting the Court back in touch with Madison's higher law Constitution and bringing modern public choice theory to the Court's attention. Progress

---

[85] Riker and Weingast (1986, p. 26) argue on the basis of modern public choice theory that "judicial abdication by appeal to elections and legislatures for protection of property rights is exactly no protection at all. Furthermore, the Court's notion that majority outcomes result from a balancing of all relevant interests has no basis in theory or fact."

is slowly being made on both these fronts and the Court's recent decisions in *First English Evangelical Church v. Los Angeles* and *Nollan v. California Coastal Commission* offer some hope that property rights may once again become the focus of judicial review.[86]

Restoring Madison's principled approach to constitutional interpretation would place economic rights on an equal footing with other rights, and act as a bulwark against the redistributive state. In taking such a route, the Court would not be converted into a policymaking branch of government, conventional wisdom notwithstanding. Rather, it would simply return to its legitimate function of protecting persons and property. In fulfilling this function, it would reestablish the expectation that in cases of economic regulation and legislative overreaching, the Court would not stand idly by while Congress eroded the "economic constitution," to use Niskanen's term.[87]

While it is important to establish what Justice Scalia (1985, p. 709) has called "a constitutional ethos of economic liberty" in the general public, such an ethos must first be evidenced by the Court itself, as the guardian of the higher law Constitution.[88] If the Court errs by excessive restraint in reviewing economic legislation, it necessarily encourages legislative activism. An ethos of redistributive justice will then come to prevail among the public, fueling the modern welfare state. This has certainly been the experience of the past 50 years. To ignore this experience and wishfully entrust economic liberties to the political branches is to ignore Madison's public choice/constitutional perspective, further eroding the property foundations of a free society.

---

[86] For an analysis of these two cases and "the possibility of a judicial revolution in the takings area," see Epstein (1987).

[87] See Niskanen's foreword, "The Erosion of the Economic Constitution," in this volume.

[88] James Otis, a patriot of the American Revolution and instrumental in affirming the right of the courts to void acts of Parliament that deprived individuals of their fundamental rights, was described by John Adams as one who held it as "a maxim . . . that a lawyer ought never to be without a volume of natural or public law, or moral philosophy, on his table or in his pocket" (in Corwin 1955, pp. 77-78). In similar vein, Peter Aranson (1985, p. 721) has argued: "Courts must find doctrinal, not economic, bases for containing the growing mischief of the political branches." See also Pilon (1985, pp. 832-33).

References

Anderson, Terry L., and Hill, Peter J. *The Birth of a Transfer Society*. Stanford, Calif.: Hoover Institution Press, 1980.

Anderson, Terry L., and Hill, Peter J. "Constraining the Transfer Society: Constitutional and Moral Dimensions." *Cato Journal* 6 (Spring/Summer 1986): 317-39.

Annals of the Congress of the United States. Washington, D.C.: Gales and Seaton, 1834.

Appleby, Joyce. "Republicanism in Old and New Contexts." *William and Mary Quarterly* 43 (January 1986): 20-34.

Aranson, Peter H. "Judicial Control of the Political Branches: Public Purpose and Public Law." *Cato Journal* 4 (Winter 1985): 719-82.

Banning, Lance. "Republican Ideology and the Triumph of the Constitution, 1789 to 1793." *William and Mary Quarterly* 31 (April 1974): 167-88.

Bastiat, Frederic. "Property and Law." 15 May 1848. In Bastiat (1964b, pp.. 96-115).

Bastiat, Frederic. "Justice and Fraternity." 15 June 1848. In Bastiat (1964b, pp. 116-39).

Bastiat, Frederic. "The Law." June 1850. In Bastiat (1964b, pp. 51-96).

Bastiat, Frederic. *Economic Harmonies*. 1851. Translated by W. Hayden Boyers. Edited by George B. de Huszar. Irvington-on-Hudson, N.Y.: Foundation for Economic Education, 1964a.

Bastiat, Frederic. *Selected Essays on Political Economy*. Translated by Seymour Cain. Edited by George B. de Huszar. Irvington-on-Hudson, N.Y.: Foundation for Economic Education, 1964b.

Blackstone, Sir Willian. *Commentaries on the Laws of England*. Vol. 1. Oxford: Clarendon Press, 1765.

Brunner, Karl. "The Perception of Man and Justice and the Conception of Political Institutions." In *Reflections on a Troubled World Economy: Essays in Honour of Herbert Giersch*, pp. 327-55. Edited by Fritz Machlup, Gerhard Fels, and Hubertus Muller-Groeling. London: Macmillan, for the Trade Policy Research Centre, 1983.

Buchanan, James M. "The Public Choice Perspective." *Economia delle scelte pubbliche* 1 (January 1983): 7-15.

Buchanan, James M. "The Constitution of Economic Policy." *American Economic Review* 77 (June 1987): 243-50.

Buchanan, James M., and Tullock, Gordon. *The Calculus of consent: Logical Foundations of Constitutional Democracy*. Ann Arbor, Mich.: University of Michigan Press, 1962.

Burns, Edward McNall. *James Madison: Philosopher of the Constitution*. New York: Octagon Books, 1968.

Canavan, Francis. "Judicial Power and the Ninth Amendment." *The Intercollegiate Review* 22 (Spring 1987): 25-29.

Collier, Christopher. "Draft Bill of Rights was Most Likely Not by Roger Sherman." Letter to the Editor. *New York Times*, 5 September 1987.

Corwin, Edward S. "Due Process of Law Before the Civil War." 1911. In Corwin (1970, pp. 46-66).

Corwin, Edward S. "The Basic Doctrine of American Constitutional Law." 1914. In Corwin (1970, pp. 25-45).

Corwin, Edward S. *The Doctrine of Judicial Review*. Princeton, N.J.: Princeton University Press, 1914.

Corwin, Edward S. *The "Higher Law" Background of American Constitutional Law*. 1928-29. Ithaca, N.Y.: Great Seal Books, Cornell University Press, 1955.

Corwin, Edward S. *American Constitutional History: Essays by Edward S. Corwin*. Edited by Alpheus T. Mason and Gerald Garvey. Gloucester, Mass.: Peter Smith, 1970.

Dicey, A.V. *Introduction to the Study of the Law of the Constitution*. 1885/1915. Indianapolis, Ind.: Liberty Classics, 1982.

Dorn, James A. "The Transfer Society." Introduction. *Cato Journal* 6 (Spring/Summer 1986): 1-17.

Dorn, James A. "Judicial Protection of Economic Liberties." In *Economic Liberties and the Judiciary*, pp. 1-28. Edited by James A. Dorn and Henry G. Manne. Fairfax, Va.: George Mason University Press, 1987.

Dreyer, Edward C. "Making Parties Respectable: James Madison's National Gazette Essays." Political Science Papers, Faculty of Political Science, University of Tulsa, 1987.

Epstein, Richard A. "Asleep at the Constitutional Switch." *Wall Street Journal*, 9 August 1984, p. 28.

Epstein, Richard A. *Takings: Private Property and the Power of Eminent Domain*. Cambridge, Mass.: Harvard University Press, 1985a.

Epstein, Richard A. "Judicial Review: Reckoning on Two Kinds of Error." *Cato Journal* 4 (Winter 1985b): 711-18.

Epstein, Richard A. "Needed: Activist Judges for Economic Rights." *Wall Street Journal*, 14 November 1985c, p. 32.

Epstein, Richard A. "Private Property Makes a Comeback." *Wall Street Journal*, 23 July 1987, p. 30.

The Federalist Papers: A Contemporary Selection. Abridged and edited by Lester DeKoster. Grand Rapids, Mich.: William B. Eerdmans, 1976.

Friedman, Milton. *Capitalism and Freedom*. Chicago: University of Chicago Press, 1962.

Hayek, Friedrich A. "The Use of Knowledge in Society." *American Economic Review* 35 (September 1945): 519-30.

Hayek, Friedrich A. *The Constitution of Liberty*. Chicago: University of Chicago Press, 1960.

Hayek, Friedrich, A. *Law, Legislation and Liberty*. Reprint (3 vols. in 1). London: Routledge and Kegan Paul, 1982. (Vol. 1, *Rules and Order*, chaps. 1-6; Vol. 2, *The Mirage of Social Justice*, chaps. 7-11; Vol. 3, *The Political Order of a Free People*, chaps. 12-18).

Hume, David. *A Treatise of Human Nature*. Edited, with an Analytical Index, by L. A. Selby-Bigge. 2d ed. With text revised and notes by P. H. Nidditch. Oxford: Oxford University Press, 1978. (Originally published in 1739 and 1740.)

Hunt, Gaillard, ed. *The Writings of James Madison*. Vol. 6: 1790-1802. New York: G. P. Putnam's Sons, The Knickerbocker Press, 1906.

Kesler, Charles R. "The Higher Law and 'Original Intent.' " *The Intercollegiate Review* 22 (Spring 1987): 9-13.

Kirzner, Israel M. "Economic Planning and the Knowledge Problem." *Cato Journal* 4 (Fall 1984): 407-18.

List, Frederick. *Outlines of American Political Economy*. Philadelphia: Samuel Parker, 1827.

Locke, John. *The Second Treatise of Government: An Essay Concerning the True Original, Extent, and End of Civil Government*. In *Two Treatises of Government*. Rev. ed. With introduction and notes by Peter Laslett. New York: New American Library, 1965.

Macedo, Stephen. *The New Right v. the Constitution*. Washington, D.C.: Cato Institute, 1986.

Madison, James. "Notes on the Confederacy." April 1787. In Madison (1865a, pp. 320-28).

Madison, James. "Charters." *National Gazette*, 18 January 1792. In Rutland et al. (1983, pp. 191-92).

Madison, James. "Property." *National Gazette*, 29 March 1792. In Hunt (1906, pp. 101-3).

Madison, James. "[Letter] to Judge Roane." 2 September 1819. In Madison (1865b, pp. 143-47).

Madison, James. "[Letter] to John Cartwright." 1824. In Madison (1865b, pp. 355-56).

Madison, James. "Notes on Suffrage." 1829. In Madison (1865c, pp. 21-27). (These notes were composed at various times after Madison's departure from government.)

Madison, James. "Speech in the Virginia State Convention of 1829-'30, on the Question of the Ratio of Representation in the Two Branches of the Legislature." 2 December 1829. In Madison (1865c, pp. 51-55).

Madison, James. "[Letter] to Jared Sparks." 8 April 1831. In Madison (1865c, pp. 168-70).

Madison, James. "[Letter] to James Robertson." 20 April 1831. In Madison (1865c, pp. 171-72).

Madison, James. "[Letter] to J. C. Cabell." 1 April 1833. In Madison (1865c, pp. 296-97).

Madison, James. "[Letter] to Mr. _____ _____." 1834. In Madison (1865c, pp. 349-50).

Madison, James. *Letters and Other Writings of James Madison*. Vol. 1: 1769-1793. Published by Order of Congress. Philadelphia: J. B. Lippincott and Co., 1865a.

Madison, James. *Letters and Other Writings of James Madison*. Vol. 3: 1816-1828. Published by Order of Congress. Philadelphia: J. B. Lippincott and Co., 1865b.

Madison, James. *Letters and Other Writings of James Madison*. Vol. 4: 1829-1836. Published by Order of Congress. Philadelphia: J.B. Lippincott and Co., 1865c.

Mitgang, Herbert. "Handwritten Draft of a Bill of Rights Found." *New York Times*, 29 July 1987, pp. A1, C21.

Niskanen, William A. "A 'Constitutional' Perspective on Social Welfare Policy." Paper presented at the Ford Foundation Conference on Social Welfare Policy and the American Future, Racine, Wis., 3-5 November 1985.

Nozick, Robert. *Anarchy, State and Utopia*. New York: Basic Books, 1974.

Padover, Saul K., ed. *The Complete Madison: His Basic Writings*. New York: Harper and Bros., 1953.

Paine, Thomas. *Common Sense*. 1776. Edited by Isaac Kramnick. New York: Penguin Books, 1984.

Peltason, J. W. *Corwin and Peltason's Understanding the Constitution*. 7th ed. Hinsdale, Ill.: Dryden Press, 1976.

Pilon, Roger. "Ordering Rights Consistently: Or What We Do and Do Not Have Rights To." *Georgia Law Review* 13 (Summer 1979a): 1171-96.

Pilon, Roger. "On Moral and Legal Justification." *Southwestern University Law Review* 11 (1979b): 1327-44.

Pilon, Roger. "On the Foundations of Justice." *The Intercollegiate Review* 17 (Fall/Winter 1981): 3-14.

Pilon, Roger. "Capitalism and Rights: An Essay toward Fine Tuning the Moral Foundations of the Free Society." *Journal of Business Ethics* 1 (February 1982): 29-42.

Pilon, Roger. "Property Rights, Takings, and a Free Society." *Harvard Journal of Law and Public Policy* 6 (Summer 1983): 165-95.

Pilon, Roger. "Legislative Activism, Judicial Activism, and the Decline of Private Sovereignty." *Cato Journal* 4 (Winter 1985): 813-33.

Rawls, John. *A Theory of Justice*. Cambridge: Harvard University Press, 1971.

Riker, William H., and Weingast, Barry R. "Constitutional Regulation of Legislative Choice: The Political Consequences of Judicial Deference to Legislatures." Working Papers in Economics E-86-75, Hoover Institution, Stanford University, December 1986.

Rutland, Robert A. *James Madison: The Founding Father*. New York: Macmillan, 1987.

Rutland, Robert A. et al. *The Papers of James Madison*. Vol. 14: 6 April 1791-16 March 1793. Charlottesville: University Press of Virginia, 1983.

Scalia, Antonin. "Economic Affairs as Human Affairs." *Cato Journal* 4 (Winter 1985): 703-9.

Scott, Jack, ed. *An Annotated Edition of Lectures on Moral Philosophy by John Witherspoon*. Newark: University of Delaware Press, 1982.

Siegan, Bernard H. *Economic Liberties and the Constitution*. Chicago: University of Chicago Press, 1980.

Siegan, Bernard H. "The Economic Constitution in Historical Perspective." In *Constitutional Economics: Containing the Economic Powers of Government*, pp. 39-53. Edited by Richard B. McKenzie. Lexington, Mass.: Lexington Books, D. C. Heath and Co., 1984.

Siegan, Bernard H. "The Supreme Court: The Final Arbiter." In *Beyond the Status Quo: Policy Proposals for America*, pp. 273-90. Edited by David Boaz and Edward H. Crane. Washington, D.C.: Cato Institute, 1985a.

Siegan, Bernard H. "Economic Liberties and the Constitution: Protection at the State Level." *Cato Journal* 4 (Winter 1985b): 689-702.

Siegan, Bernard H. *The Supreme Court's Constitution: An Inquiry into Judicial Review and Its Impact on Society*. New Brunswick, N.J.: Transaction Books, 1987.

Smith, Adam. *The Theory of Moral Sentinments*. 1759. Indianapolis, Ind.: Liberty Classics, 1976.

Smith, Adam. *The Wealth of Nations*. 1776. Edited by Edwin Cannan. New York: The Modern Library, Random House, 1937.

Solberg, Winton U., ed. *The Federal Convention and the Formation of the Union of the United States*. New York: American Hertiage Series, Bobbs-Merrill; Liberal Arts Press, 1958.

Somerville, John, and Santoni, Ronald E., eds. *Social and Political Philosophy*. Garden City, N.Y.: Anchor Books, Doubleday and Co., 1963.

Thompson, Charles M. *History of the United States*. New York: Benj. H. Sanborn and Co., 1917.

Tumlir, Jan. *Protectionism: Trade Policy in Democratic Societies*. Washington, D.C.: American Enterprise Institute, 1985.

Vernier, Richard. "Interpreting the American Republic: Civic Humanism vs. Liberalism." *Humane Studies Review* 4 (Summer 1987).

Wicksell, Knut. "A New Principle of Just Taxation." 1896. In *Classics in the Theory of Public Finance*, pp. 72-118. Edited by Richard A. Musgrave and Alan T. Peacock. New York: St. Martin's Press, 1958.

4

THE CONSTITUTION
OF ECONOMIC POLICY
James M. Buchanan

I. Introduction

> The science of public finance should always keep...political conditions
> clearly in mind. Instead of expecting guidance from a doctrine of taxa-
> tion that is based on the political philosophy of by-gone ages, it should
> instead endeavor to unlock the mysteries of the spirit of progress and
> development.[1] (Wicksell, p 87)

On this of all occasions I should be remiss if I failed to acknowledge the
influence of that great Swede, Knut Wicksell, on my own work, an influence
without which I should not be making this presentation. Many of my
contributions, and especially those in political economy and fiscal theory,
might be described as varied reiterations, elaborations, and extensions of
Wicksellian themes; this paper is no exception.

One of the most exciting intellectual moments of my career was my 1948
discovery of Wicksell's unknown and untranslated dissertation, *Finanztheoretische Untersuchungen* (1896), buried in the dusty stacks of Chicago's
old Harper Library. Only the immediate post-dissertation leisure of an
academic novice allowed for the browsing that produced my own dramatic
example of learning by serendipity. Wicksell's new principle of justice in
taxation gave me a tremendous surge of self-confidence. Wicksell, who was
an established figure in the history of economic ideas, challenged the
orthodoxy of public finance theory along lines that were congenial with

This is the lecture James Buchanan delivered in Stockholm, Sweden, December 8, 1986, when
he received the Nobel Prize in Economic Science. The article is copyright © The Nobel
Foundation and published here with the permission of The Nobel Foundation. James Buchanan
is the Director, Center for Study of Public Choice and University Professor, George Mason
University. The author wishes to thank Robert Tollison, Viktor Vanberg, and Richard Wagner
for helpful comments.

[1] This and subsequent citations are from Knut Wicksell, "A New Principle of Just Taxation,"
included in R.A. Musgrave and A.T. Peacock (1958, pp. 72-118). The more inclusive work
from which this translated essay is taken is Wicksell, *Finanztheoretische Untersuchungen* (1896).

my own developing stream of critical consciousness. From that moment in Chicago, I took on the determination to make Wicksell's contribution known to a wider audience, and I commenced immediately a translation effort that took some time, and considerable help from Elizabeth Henderson, before final publication.

Stripped to its essentials, Wicksell's message was clear, elementary, and self-evident. Economists should cease proffering policy advice as if they were employed by a benevolent despot, and they should look to the structure within which political decisions are made. Armed with Wicksell, I, too, could dare to challenge the still-dominant orthodoxy in public finance and welfare economics. In a preliminary paper (1949), I called upon my fellow economists to postulate some model of the state, of politics, before proceeding to analyze the effects of alternative policy measures. I urged economists to look at the "constitution of economic policy", to examine the rules, the constraints within which political agents act. Like Wicksell, my purpose was ultimately normative rather than antiseptically scientific. I sought to make economic sense out of the relationship between the individual and the state before proceeding to advance policy nostrums.

Wicksell deserves the designation as the most important precursor of modern public choice theory because we find, in his 1896 dissertation, all three of the constitutive elements that provide the foundations of this theory: methodological individualism, *homo economicus*, and politics-as-exchange. I shall discuss these elements of the analytical structure in the sections that follow. In Section V, I integrate these elements in a theory of economic policy. This theory is consistent with, builds upon, and systematically extends the traditionally accepted principles of Western liberal societies. The implied approach to institutional-constitutional reform continues, however, to be stubbornly resisted almost a century after Wicksell's seminal efforts. The individual's relation to the state, is, of course, the central subject matter of political philosophy. Any effort by economists to shed light on this relationship must be placed within this more comprehensive realm of discourse; a summary effort is contained in Section VI.

II. Methodological Individualism

> If utility is zero for each individual member of the community, the total utility for the community cannot be other than zero. (Wicksell, p.77)

The economist rarely examines the presuppositions of the models with which he works. The economist simply commences with individuals as evaluating, choosing, and acting units. Regardless of the possible complexity of the processes or institutional structures from which outcomes emerge, the economist focuses on individual choices. In application to market or private-sector interactions, this procedure is seldom challenged. Individuals, as buyers and sellers of ordinary (legally tradable) goods and services are presumed able to choose in accordance with their own preferences, whatever these may be, and the economist does not feel himself obliged to inquire deeply into the content of these preferences (the arguments in individual's utility functions). Individuals themselves are the sources of evaluation, and the economist's task is to offer an explanation-understanding of the process through which these unexamined preferences are ultimately translated into a complex outcome pattern.

The eighteenth-century discovery that, in an institutional framework that facilitates voluntary exchanges among individuals, this process generates results that might be evaluated positively, produced "economics", as an independent academic discipline or science. The relationship between the positively valued results of market processes and the institutional characteristics of these processes themselves emerged as a source of ambiguity when "the market" came to be interpreted functionally, as if something called "the economy" existed for the purpose of value maximization. Efficiency in the allocation of resources came to be defined independently of the processes through which individual choices are exercised.

Given this subtle shift toward a teleological interpretation of the economic process, it is not surprising that politics, or governmental process, was similarly interpreted. Furthermore, a teleological interpretation of politics had been, for centuries, the dominating thrust of political theory and political philosophy. The interpretations of "the economy" and "the polity" seemed, therefore, to be mutually compatible in the absence of inquiry into the fundamental difference in the point of evaluation. There was a failure to recognize that individuals who choose and act in the market generate outcomes that, under the specified constraints, can be judged to be value maximizing for participating individuals, *without* the necessity of introducing an external evaluative criterion. The nature of the process itself insures that individual values are maximized. This "value-maximization" perspective cannot be extended from the market to politics since the latter does not directly embody the incentive-compatible structure of the former. There is no political counterpart to Adam Smith's invisible hand. It is not, therefore, surprising that the attempt by Wicksell and other continental European scholars to extend economic theory to the operation of the public sector remained undeveloped for so many years.

An economic theory that remains essentially individualistic need not have become trapped in such a methodological straight jacket. If the maximization exercise is restricted to explanation-understanding of the individual who makes choices, and without extension to the economy as an aggregation, there is no difficulty at all in analyzing individual choice behavior under differing institutional settings, and in predicting how these varying settings will influence the outcomes of the interaction processes.

The individual who chooses between apples and oranges remains the same person who chooses between the levers marked "Candidate A" and "Candidate B" in the polling booth. Clearly, the differing institutional structures may, themselves, affect choice behavior. Much of modern public choice theory explains these relationships. But my point here is the more basic one to the effect that the choice behavior of the individual is equally subject to the application of analysis in all choice environments. Comparative analysis should allow for predictions of possible differences in the characteristics of the results that emerge from market and political structures of interaction. These predications, as well as the analysis from which they are generated, are totally devoid of normative content.

III. Homo Economicus

> . . .[N]either the executive nor the legislative body, and even less the deciding majority in the latter, are in reality. . .what the ruling theory tells us they should be. They are not pure organs of the community with no thought other than to promote the common weal

> . . . .[M]embers of the representative body are, in the overwhelming majority of cases, precisely as interested in the general welfare as are their constituents, neither more nor less. (Wicksell, pp. 86, 87)

This analysis can yield a limited set of potentially falsifiable hypotheses without prior specification of the arguments in individual utility functions. If, however, predictions are sought concerning the effects of shifts in constraints on choice behavior, some identification and signing of these arguments must be made. With this step, more extensive falsifiable propositions may be advanced. For example, if both apples and oranges are positively valued "goods", then, if the price of apples falls relative to the of oranges, more apples will be purchased relative to oranges; if income is a positively valued "good", and then, if the marginal rate of tax on income source A increases relative to that on income source B, more effort at earning income will be shifted to source B; if charitable giving is a positively valued "good", then, if charitable gifts are made tax deductible, more giving will be predicted to occur; if pecuniary rents are positively valued, then, if a political agent's discretionary power to distribute rents increases, individuals hoping to secure these rents will invest more resources in attempts to influence the agent's decisions. Note that the identification and signing of the arguments in the utility functions takes us a considerable way toward operationalization without prior specification of the relative weights of the separate arguments. There is no need to assign net wealth or net income a dominating motivational influence on behavior in order to produce a fully operational economic theory of choice behavior, in market or political interaction.

In any extension of the model of individual rational behavior to politics, this difference between the identification and signing of arguments on the one hand and the weighing of these arguments on the other deserves further attention. Many critics of the "economic theory of politics" base their criticisms on the presumption that such theory necessarily embodies the hypothesis of net wealth maximization, an hypothesis that they observe to be falsified in many situations. Overly zealous users of this theory may have sometimes offered grounds for such misinterpretation on the part of critics The minimal critical assumption for the explanatory power of the economic theory of politics is only that identifiable economic self-interest (for example, net wealth, income, social position) is a positively valued "good" to the individual who chooses. This assumption does not place economic interest in a dominating position and it surely does not imply imputing evil or malicious motive to political actors; in this respect the theory remains on all fours with the motivational structure of the standard economic theory of market behavior. The differences in the predicted results stemming from market and political interaction stem from differences in the structures of these two institutional settings rather than from any switch in the motives of persons as they move between institutional roles.

IV. Politics As Exchange

> It would seem to be a blatant injustice if someone should be forced to contribute toward the costs of some activity which does not further his interests or may even be diametrically opposed to them. (Wicksell, p. 89)

Individuals choose, and as they do so, identifiable economic interest is one of the "goods" that they value positively, whether behavior takes place in markets or in politics. But markets are institutions of *exchange*; persons enter markets to exchange one thing for another. They do not enter markets to further some supra-exchange or supra-individualistic result. Markets are not motivationally functional; there is no conscious sense on the part of individual choosers that some preferred aggregate outcome, some overall "allocation" or "distribution", will emerge from the process.

The extension of this exchange conceptualization to politics counters the classical prejudice that persons participate in politics through some common search for the good, the true, and the beautiful, with these ideals being defined independently of the values of the participants as these might or might not be expressed by behavior. Politics, in this vision of political philosophy, is instrumental to the furtherance of these larger goals.

Wicksell, who is followed in this respect by modern public choice theorists, would have none of this. The relevant difference between markets and politics does not lie in the kinds of values/interests that persons pursue, but in the conditions under which they pursue their various interests.

Politics is a structure of complex exchange among individuals, a structure within which persons seek to secure collectively their own privately defined objectives that cannot be efficiently secured through simple market exchanges. In the absence of individual interest, there is no interest. In the market, individuals exchange apples for oranges; in politics, individuals exchange agreed-on shares in contributions toward the costs of that which is commonly desired, from the services of the local fire station to that of the judge.

This ultimately voluntary basis for political agreement also counters the emphasis on politics as power that characterizes much modern analysis. The observed presence of coercive elements in the activity of the state seems difficult to reconcile with the model of voluntary exchange among individuals. We may, however, ask: Coercion to what purpose? Why must individuals subject themselves to the coercion inherent in collective action? The answer is evident. Individuals acquiesce in the coercion of the state, of politics, only if the ultimate constitutional "exchange" furthers their interests. Without some model of exchange, no coercion of the individual by the state is consistent with the individualistic value norm upon which a liberal social order is grounded.

V. The Constitution of Economic Policy

> . . . [W]hether the benefits of the proposed activity to the individual citizens would be greater than its cost to them, no one can judge this better than the individuals themselves. (Wicksell, p. 79)

The exchange conceptualization of politics is important in the derivation of a normative theory of economic policy. Improvement in the workings of politics is measured in terms of the satisfaction of that which is desired by individuals, whatever this may be, rather than in terms of moving closer to some externally defined, supra-individualistic ideal. That which is desired by individuals may, of course, be common for many persons, and indeed, the difference between market exchange and political exchange lies in the sharing of objectives in the latter. The idealized agreement on the objectives of politics does not, however, allow for any supersession of individual evaluation. Agreement itself emerges, again conceptually, from the revealed choice behavior of individuals. Commonly shared agreement must be carefully distinguished from any externally defined definition or description of that "good" upon which persons "should agree".

The restrictive implications for a normative theory of economic policy are severe. There is no criterion through which policy may be directly evaluated. An indirect evaluation may be based on some measure of the degree to which the political process facilitates the translation of expressed individual preferences into observed political outcomes. The focus of evaluative attention becomes the process itself, as contrasted with end-state or outcome patterns. "Improvement" must, therefore, be sought in reforms in process, in institutional change that will allow the operation of politics to mirror more accurately that set of results that are preferred by those who participate. One way of stating the difference between the Wicksellian approach and that which is still orthodoxy in normative economics is to say that the *constitution* of policy rather than policy itself becomes the relevant object for reform. A simple game analogy illustrates the difference here. The Wicksellian approach concentrates on reform in the rules, which may be in the potential interest of *all* players, as opposed to improvement in strategies of play for particular players within defined or existing rules.

In the standard theory of choice in markets, there is little or no concern with the constitution of the choice environment. We simply presume that the individual is able to implement his preferences; if he wants to purchase an orange, we presume that he can do so. There is no institutional barrier between the revealed expression of preference and direct satisfaction. Breakdown or failure in the market emerges, not in the translation of individual preferences into outcomes, but in the possible presentation of some choosers with alternatives that do not correspond to those faced by others in the exchange nexus. "Efficiency" in market interaction is insured if the participants are faced with the same choice options.

In political exchange, there is no decentralized process that allows "efficiency" to be evaluated, deontologically, akin to the evaluation of a market. Individuals cannot, by the nature of the goods that are collectively "purchased" in politics, adjust their own behavior to common terms of trade. The political analogue to decentralized trading among individuals must be that feature common over all exchanges, which is *agreement* among the individuals who participate. The unanimity rule for collective choice is the political analogue to freedom of exchange of partitionable goods in markets.

It is possible, therefore, to evaluate politics independently of results only by ascertaining the degree of correspondence between the rules of reaching decisions and the unique rule that would guarantee "efficiency", that of unanimity or agreement among all participants. If, then, "efficiency" is acknowledged to be the desired criterion, again as interpreted here, normative improvement in process is measured by movement toward the unanimity requirement. It is perhaps useful to note, at this point, that Wicksell's own characterization of his proposals in terms of "justice" rather than "efficiency" suggests the precise correspondence of these two norms in the context of voluntary exchange.

Politics as observed remains, of course, far from the idealized collective-cooperative exchange that the unanimity rule would implement. The political equivalent to transactions cost makes the pursuit of idealized "efficiency" seem even more out of the bounds of reason than the analogous pursuit in markets. But barriers to realization of the ideal do not imply rejection of the bench-mark definition of the ideal itself. Instead, such barriers are themselves incorporated into a generalized "calculus of consent".

Wicksell himself did not go beyond advocacy of reform in legislative decision structures. He proposed a required linking of spending and financing decisions, and he proposed that a quasi-unanimity rule be introduced for noncommitted outlays. Wicksell did not consciously extend his analysis to constitutional choice, to the choice of the rules within which ordinary politics is to be allowed to operate. His suggested reforms were, of course, constitutional, since they where aimed to improve the process of decision making. But his evaluative criterion was restricted to the matching of individual preferences with political outcomes in particularized decisions, rather than over any sequence.

It is perhaps worth noting that Wicksell himself did not look upon his suggested procedural reforms as restrictive. By introducing greater flexibility into the tax-share structure, Wicksell predicted the potential approval of spending programs that would continue to be rejected under rigid taxing arrangements. Critics have, however, interpreted the Wicksellian unanimity constraint to be restrictive, and especially as compared to the extended activity observed in ordinary politics. This restrictive interpretation was perhaps partially responsible for the continued failure of political economists to recognize his seminal extension of the efficiency norm to the political sector. Such restrictiveness is very substantially reduced, and, in the limit, may be altogether eliminated, when the unanimity criterion is shifted one stage upward, to the level of potential agreement on constitutional rules within which ordinary politics is to be allowed to operate. In this framework, an individual may rationally prefer a rule that will, on particular occasions, operate to produce results that are opposed to his own interests. The individual will do so if he predicts that, on balance over the whole sequence of "plays", his own interests will be more effectively served than by the more restrictive application of the Wicksellian requirement in-period. The in-period Wicksellian criterion remains valid as a measure of the particularized efficiency of the single decision examined. But the in-period violation of the criterion does not imply the inefficiency of the rule so long as the latter is itself selected by a constitutional rule of unanimity.[2]

As noted, the shift of the Wicksellian criterion to the constitutional stage of choice among rules also serves to facilitate agreement, and, in the limiting

---

[2] In my own retrospective interpretation, the shift of the Wicksellian construction to the constitutional stage of choice was the most important contribution in *The Calculus of Consent* (1962), written jointly with Gordon Tullock.

case may remove altogether potential conflicts among separate individual and group interests. To the extent that the individual reckons that a constitutional rule will remain applicable over a long sequence of periods, with many in-period choices to be made, he is necessarily placed behind a partial "veil of uncertainty" concerning the effects of any rule on his own predicted interests. Choice among rules will, therefore, tend to be based on generalizable criteria of fairness, making agreement more likely to occur than when separable interests are more easily identifiable.

The political economist who operates from within the Wicksellian research program, as modified, and who seeks to offer normative advice must, of necessity, concentrate on the process or structure within which political decisions are observed to be made. Existing constitutions, or structures of rules, are the subject of critical scrutiny. The conjectural question becomes: Could these rules have emerged from agreement by participants in an authentic constitutional convention? Even here, the normative advice that is possible must be severely circumscribed. There is no external set of norms that provides a basis for criticism. But the political economist may, cautiously, suggest changes in procedures, in rules, that may come to command general assent. Any suggested change must be offered only in the provisional sense, and, importantly, it must be accompanied by a responsible recognition of political reality. Those rules and rules changes worthy of consideration are those that are predicted to be workable within the politics inhabited by ordinary men and women, and not those that are appropriate only for idealized, omniscient, and benevolent beings. Policy options must remain within the realm of the feasible, and the interests of political agents must be recognized as constraints on the possible.

VI. Constitutionalism and Contractarianism

The ultimate goal . . . is equality before the law, greatest possible liberty, and the economic well-being and peaceful cooperation of all people. (Wicksell, p. 88)

As the basic Wicksellian construction is shifted to the choice among rules or constitutions and as a veil of uncertainty is utilized to facilitate the potential bridging of the difference between identifiable and general interest, the research program in political economy merges into that of contractarian political philosophy, both in its classical and modern variations. In particular, my own approach has affinities with the familiar construction of John Rawls (1971), who utilizes the veil of ignorance along with the fairness criterion to derive principles of justice that emerge from a conceptual agreement at a stage prior to the selection of a political constitution.

Because of his failure to shift his own analytical construction to the level of constitutional choice, Wicksell was confined to evaluation of the political process in generating current allocative decisions. He was unable, as he quite explicitly acknowledged, to evaluate political action involving either prior commitments of the state, for example, the financing of interest on public debt, or fiscally implemented transfers of incomes and wealth among persons and groups. Distributional questions remain outside the Wicksellian evaluative exercise, and because they do so, we locate another source of the long-continued and curious neglect of the fundamental analytical contribution. With the shift to the constitutional stage of politics, however, this constraint is at least partially removed. Behind a sufficiently thick veil of uncertainty and/or ignorance, contractual agreement on rules that allow features of a constitutionally approved transfer structure cannot, of course, be derived independently because of the restriction of evaluative judgement to the process of constitutional agreement. In this respect, the application is fully analogous to Wicksell's unwillingness to lay down specific norms for tax sharing independently of the process of agreement. *Any* distribution of tax shares generating revenues sufficient to finance the relevant spending shares generating revenues sufficient to finance the relevant spending project passes Wicksell's test, provided only that it meets with general agreement. Analogously, *any* set of arrangements for implementing fiscal transfers, in-period, meets the constitutional stage Wicksellian test, provided only that it commands general agreement.

This basic indeterminacy is disturbing to political economists or philosophers who seek to be able to offer substantive advice, over and beyond the procedural limits suggested. The constructivist urge to assume a role as social engineer, to suggest policy reforms that "should" or "should not" be made, independently of any revelation of individuals' preferences through the political process, has simply proved too strong for many to resist. The scientific integrity dictated by consistent reliance on individualistic values has not been a mark of modern political economy.

The difficulty of maintaining such integrity is accentuated by the failure to distinguish explanatory and justificatory argument, a failure that has described the position of almost all critics of social contract theories of political order. We do not, of course, observe the process of reaching agreement on constitutional rules, and the origins of the rules that are in existence at any particular time and in any particular polity cannot satisfactorily be explained by the contractarian model. The purpose of the contractarian exercise is not explanatory in this sense. It is, by contrast, justificatory in that it offers a basis for normative evaluation. Could the observed rules that constrain the activity of ordinary politics have emerged from agreement in constitutional contract? To the extent that this question can be affirmatively answered, we have established a legitimating linkage between the individual and the state. To the extent that the question prompts a negative response, we have a basis for normative criticism of the existing order, and a criterion for advancing proposals for constitutional reform.[3]

It is at this point, and this point only, that the political economist who seeks to remain within the normative constraints imposed by the individualistic canon may enter the ongoing dialogue on constitutional policy. The deficit-financing regimes in modern Western democratic polities offer the most dramatic example. It is almost impossible to construct a contractual calculus in which representatives of separate generations would agree to allow majorities in a single generation to finance currently enjoyed public consumption through the issue of public debt that insures the imposition of utility losses on later generations of taxpayers. The same conclusion applies to the implicit debt obligations that are reflected in many of the intergenerational transfer programs characteristic of the modern welfare state.

The whole contractarian exercise remains empty if the critical dependence of politically generated results upon the rules that constrain political action is denied. If end states are invariant over shifts in constitutional structure, there is no role for constitutional political economy. On the other hand, if institutions do indeed matter, the role is well defined. Positively, this role involves analysis of the working properties of alternative sets of constraining rules. In a game-theoretic analogy, this analysis is the search for solutions of games, as the latter are defined by sets of rules. Normatively, the task for the constitutional political economist is to assist individuals, as citizens who ultimately control their own social order, in their continuing search for those rules of the political game that will best serve their purposes, whatever these might be.

In 1987, the United States celebrates the bicentennial anniversary of the constitutional convention that provided the basic rules for the American political order. This convention was one of the very few historical examples in which political rules were deliberately chosen. The vision of politics that informed the thinking of James Madison was not dissimilar, in its essentials, from that which informed Knut Wicksell's less comprehensive, but more focused, analysis of taxation and spending. Both rejected any organic conception of the state as superior in wisdom to the individuals who are its members. Both sought to bring all available scientific analysis to bear in helping to resolve the continuing question of social order: How can we live together in peace, prosperity, and harmony, while retaining our liberties as autonomous individuals who can, and must, create our own values?

---

[3] A generalized argument for adopting the constitutionalist-contractarian perspective, in both positive and normative analysis, is developed in *The Reason of Rules* (1985), written jointly with Geoffrey Brennan.

References

Brennan, Geoffrey and Buchanan, James M. *The Reason of Rules.* Cambridge: Cambridge University Press, 1985.

Buchanan, James M. "The Pure Theory of Public Finance: A Suggested Approach," *Journal of Political Economy* 57 (December 1949): 496-505.

Buchanan, James M., and Tullock, Gordon. *The Calculus of Consent.* Ann Arbor: University of Michigan Press, 1962.

Musgrave, R. A., and Peacock, A. T. *Classics in the Theory of Public Finance.* London: Macmillan, 1958.

Rawls, John A. *A Theory of Justice.* Cambridge: Harvard University Press, 1971.

Wicksell, Knut. *Finanztheoretische Untersuchungen.* Jena: Gustav Fisher, 1896.

PART II

SELF-INTEREST, PUBLIC INTEREST AND
CONSTITUTIONAL CHOICE

5

A NEW PRINCIPLE
OF JUST TAXATION
Knut Wicksell

I have intentionally given this essay a somewhat challenging title and, from the outset, I have taken up a rather heterodox position in opposition to the traditional doctrines. However, this essay contains not so much a new principle of just taxation as a method to ensure that such measure of justice as can be attained is in fact achieved in practice.

The principle as such is, in reality, nothing more than the benefit principle, the well-known principle of equality between Value and Counter-value. I attempt, however, to extend the range and applicability of this principle on both sides. On the one hand, I apply the modern concept of marginal utility and subjective value to public services and to the individuals' contributions for these services. In my opinion, the most important objections to the principle of Value and Countervalue are thereby removed. On the other hand, and to my knowledge no-one has done this before, I relate the tax principle itself to the form of modern tax administration, specifically the parliamentary approval of taxes. I attempt to describe the conditions in which the Value and Countervalue principle could be used more or less automatically by parliamentary tax bodies in all those situations where the principle is generally applicable.

If this principle were to be accepted, one could in my opinion transform into public activities proper many activities which today are left to private initiative or to public enterprise operating on the fee or pricing principle. This transformation could be effected without opposition and the results would be advantageous to everyone.

I am ready to admit that some will be inclined to classify much of my discussion as armchair speculation. I accept the charge happily, since it

---

This is an *abridged version* of the translation by James M. Buchanan which initially appeared in English in *Classics in the Theory of Public Finance* (London: Macmillan, 1958), edited by Richard A. Musgrave and Alan T. Peacock. The article was originally published in 1896. The editors express their appreciation to Macmillan Publishing for their permission to reprint.

was my purpose above all to construct a complete, comprehensive and internally consistent system. For this reason, I never worried about pursuing my theory to its final conclusion. How much of this—or whether any at all—may be of practical use in the near future, men of affairs may decide.

The Principle of (Approximate) Unanimity and Voluntary Consent In Taxation

The movement which has nearly everywhere shaped the political history of this century has been steady progress toward parliamentary and democratic forms of public life. One of the prime movers is modern general education in the widest sense of the term, since this enables even the lowest classes of the people to participate more and more in political life; another is the tremendous development of the press, whereby everyone has gained unprecedented access to knowledge of public affairs. In addition, there is the spectacular growth of industrial, commercial and scientific relations both within every country and among all countries of the world. These relations are as apt to promote lasting world peace as peace itself is a condition of their very existence. The old hierarchical structure of society, the origin and purpose of which were war and conquest, is becoming more and more obsolete and unnecessary.

The ultimate goal of this progressive movement is equality before the law, greatest possible liberty, and the economic well-being and peaceful cooperation of all people. It is not the purpose of the movement and indeed it would be contradictory to its guiding spirits, to have wholly or partly shaken off the yoke of reactionary and obscurantist oligarchies only to replace it by the scarcely less oppressive tyranny of accidental parliamentary majorities.

It is true that modern parliaments can hardly be reproached with any such tyrannical leanings. The petty regulations, the irksome interference in every aspect of private life have largely disappeared, or else they just linger on as the moribund residues of earlier epochs. Freedom of movement, of occupation, religion, research and of the press will, it may be hoped, remain permanent features of the civilized world.

Ordinary legislation is full of cases with only two mutually exclusive alternatives, no third alternative being practicable or even possible. If it is in the nature of things that a certain social action must either be permitted or forbidden and opinions differ as to which it shall be, then there are clearly only two alternatives: either the minority must yield to the majority or the reverse. The former may normally be regarded as the lesser evil, especially since it is very often only a matter of difference of opinion rather than of a genuine conflict of interests. It is highly probable, therefore, that a new idea, once it has passed the preliminary stage of being recognized by only a few far-sighted men and has become accepted by the majority of the current generation, will eventually permeate the entire population. Indeed this has happened in countless situations. Decision by means of a simple majority must, it seems, be the rule in this area. We do find that even in the more progressive countries decisions on particularly important questions are sometimes subject to special rules such as the requirement of a qualified majority, the veto power of the two chambers of the legislature, the veto of the executive authority etc.; however, these are clearly not designed to safeguard the interests of the minority (which in itself would be absurd in this case) but to meet the general desire for stability in political life.

In the area of tax legislation and tax approval, however, the above-mentioned dilemma hardly ever presents itself. It is singular, although well in accord with the present state of theory, that, to my knowledge, no scholar either in constitutional law or in the theory of public finance has devoted as much as one word to this important distinction.

If any public expenditure is to be approved, whether it be a newly proposed or an already existing one, it must generally be assumed that this expenditure as such, neglecting for the moment the means of covering the costs, is intended for an activity useful to the whole of society and so recognized by all classes without exception. If this were not so, if a greater or lesser part of the community were indifferent or even opposed to the proposed public activity, then I, for one, fail to see how the latter can be considered as satisfying a collective need in the proper sense of the word. If such an activity is to be undertaken at all, it should for the time being be left to private initiative. It would seem to be a blatant injustice if someone should be forced to contribute toward the costs of some activity which does not further his interests or may even be diametrically opposed to them.

We must assume, then, that the planned state activity as such must be recognized as being of general usefulness. The next step is to weigh the expected utility against the necessary sacrifice. This is a matter on which the views of the different classes of citizens will be conditioned by their varying wealth and income and the consequent varying urgency of their private needs, as well as by their varying subjective evaluation of the particular collective need. For both reasons the proposed distribution of costs is obviously decisive for the citizen's judgement on the relative value of the utility and the cost of the public activity.

Now if a given pre-determined tax distribution is considered as having sole and universal validity and is therefore to be retained in this as in all cases, it may well happen that the proposal fails to secure even the simple majority of votes which under existing rules is normally required for decisions, whereas a majority might easily have been found with some different tax distribution. And it is virtually certain that such decisions will prejudice or neglect the interests of certain groups.

This leads us to a vital point which, to my knowledge, has never received the attention it deserves from tax theorists. It is not necessary either from the theoretical or from the practical point of view that tax distribution should be so rigid and pre-determined, nor indeed that it should be independent of the approval of the expenditure itself. There are hundreds of ways of distributing the costs of a proposed state expenditure among the separate classes of the people. There is the whole range from the simple head tax or the (at least) comparable levies on flour, salt, spirits etc., to the progressive income, property or inheritance tax and the indirect tax on luxury goods. Provided the expenditure in question holds out any prospect at all of creating utility exceeding costs, it will always be theoretically possible, and approximately so in practice, to find a distribution of costs such that all parties regard the expenditure as beneficial and may therefore approve it unanimously. Should this prove altogether impossible, I would consider such failure as an *a posteriori*, and the sole possible, proof that the state activity under consideration would not provide the community with utility corresponding to the necessary sacrifice and should hence be rejected on rational grounds.

Whether justice demands any more than this may be left in abeyance for the time being. When it comes to benefits which are so hard to express numerically, each person can ultimately speak only for himself. It is a matter of comparatively little importance if perchance some individual secures a somewhat greater gain than another so long as everyone gains and no-one can feel exploited from this very elementary point of view. But if justice requires no more, it certainly requires no less. In the final analysis, unanimity and fully voluntary consent in the making of decisions provide the only certain and palpable guarantee against injustice in tax distribution. The whole discussion on tax justice remains suspended in mid-air so long as these conditions are not satisfied at least approximately.

There can be no doubt that, from the point of view of general solidarity or charity, parties and social classes should on occasion share an expense from which they expect no great or direct benefit, or should contribute beyond the measure of their own advantage. Give and take is a firm foundation of lasting friendship and even if one cannot count on the tak- ing, there are few men who are completely indifferent to the welfare of their fellows.

It is quite different matter, however, to be forced so to contribute. Coercion is always an evil in itself and its exercise, in my opinion, can be justified only in cases of clear necessity. It can hardly be said to be clear necessity if someone who has already made an advantageous exchange would of course prefer an even better bargain; and interests which can secure no hearing at all are nearly always free to turn to private initiative and voluntary association.

Indeed, this latter course has been adopted on a large scale even in spheres which are normally regarded as properly belonging to the compe tence of the State. Side by side with national army, many countries have voluntary rifle clubs and similar institutions which sometimes constitute no mean military force; or quite considerable means of warfare are sometimes raised privately and placed at the disposal of the State. Alongside the state organization for churches and schools, we find religious groups which, for their own means, support their clergy and churches and we find private schools and institutions of higher learning. Even the judicial activities of the State are accompanied by private boards of syndics, arbitration tribunals, investigating commissions and such like.

In short, as soon as a general problem enjoys a sufficiently wide interest, the means and the methods of its solution will not be lacking—least of all in our time.

If the distribution of taxes always rested on the principle of voluntary consent, it seems to me highly probable that many such activities which today can be undertaken only by private groups, would come to be incorporated into the operation of the State. The bitter opposition which now confronts the introduction of many very useful state institutions would largely disappear as soon as each individual could be certain that he would never be burdened with a larger share of their cost than he personally or his interest groups had accepted through their representative in the legislature.[1]

The practical realization of the principle of voluntary consent and unanimity, as I should like to call it, requires first of all that no public expenditures ever be voted upon without simultaneous determination of the means of covering their cost. It is irrelevant whether the means are to come from the proceeds of new taxes or from anticipated increases in the revenue from existing taxes. This procedure used to be the rule in constitutional states, but in modern budgetary systems it has fallen more and more into disuse. This is primarily due to the fact that increasing population and income levels have caused the yields of indirect taxes, such as customs and excises, to increase so rapidly that the necessary means were normally already available when a new expenditure came to be approved. At any rate this was often the case in Sweden. The decision

---

[1] It is implicitly assumed here that the legislative assembly is truly representative of all interest groups within the people. We shall presently discuss the conditions for this goal to be fully attained. Existing legislative bodies are mostly far removed from this ideal. But this does not invalidate our conclusions. On the contrary, the veto right of the minority clearly is the more necessary the less the so-called representative body reflects the true interest groupings of the population.

concerning the acceptance or rejection of an expenditure was regularly tied to the decision concerning the raising of funds only for expenditures which were in the first instance to be financed from loans rather than from taxes. This sort of joint decision is of little value, however, unless the manner of servicing the debt is voted upon at the same time.

In many cases parliaments have perforce accepted the logical connection between the approval of expenditures on the one side and the way in which the costs are to be financed on the other. When important financial innovations are proposed, it has become customary to draw up a general plan of financing for the immediate future (a plan for the successive introduction of new taxes). Or else expenditures of doubtful popularity are made more palatable by more or less solemn promises on the part of both the government and the legislature that the costs are to be met by taxes falling more particularly on the shoulders of certain tax groups, for example the well-to-do classes, etc.

Unfortunately such plans and promises are not constitutionally binding. The plan of financing need not necessarily be carried out later and the promises may be respected only until public opinion has shifted to other subjects, whereupon the old methods may be reintroduced without being noticed.[2]

Things would be entirely different if the decision concerning the allocation of the costs in question were to be made a necessary condition for the approval of any public expenditure. It could hardly be maintained that insurmountable practical difficulties stand in the way of implementing such a rule or another clearly embodying the relevant principle.

Suppose now that this principle were combined with the requirement of approximate unanimity of decisions—absolute unanimity may have to be ruled out for practical reasons. When the government or a faction of the legislature proposes a new public activity or the extension of an existing one, the motion would constitutionally have to be accompanied by one or several alternative proposals for the distribution of the costs. The other factions of the legislature might then propose amendments concerning both the magnitude of the expenditure itself and the manner in which the costs are to be covered.

Some of the proposals may be capable of being combined, others remain mutually exclusive. All of them are put to the vote on something like the following pattern:

---

[2] The reader can perhaps find examples of this practice in any country with which he is familiar; in Sweden there is no lack of them.

Tax Plan

Main bill A	{	a . . . . Vote
		b . . . . Vote
		c + d³ . . . . Vote
		e . . . . Vote
		f. . . . . Vote
Amendment A′	{	a . . . . Vote
		e . . . . Vote
		g . . . . Vote
Amendment A″	{	b . . . . Vote
		h . . . . Vote
		i + k³ . . . . Vote

If any of the alternatives presented for balloting secures the required qualified majority, say three-fourths, five-sixths or even nine-tenths of the votes cast, then this combination becomes law (for example, the main bill A with tax plan e, or amendment A″ with taxes i and k). If several alternatives secure the required qualified majority, some way must be found to choose amongst them (the simplest being to go by the relative number of votes). If none of the alternatives secures the required majority the whole proposal would be considered defeated for the time being.[4]

As we have noted on more than one occasion, the above reasoning rests on the assumption that the legislature is completely free to accept or reject the public expenditure item under consideration. When the expenditure is a necessary result of a previously existing obligation and cannot, therefore be refused, an entirely different procedure is in order. One cannot speak of taxation according to benefit when the expenditure is not made for the sake of the utility it is expected to yield to the country but rather to meet a recognized obligation. The expenditure must always be approved and if this has to be done by vote at all a simple majority is the obvious procedure. While it is highly desirable that the majority be inspired by motive of justice and equity in the distribution of this particular burden, it difficult to make any generally valid observations of detail on this distribution.

It is hard to say out of hand what public expenditures belong in this category. In the first place interest and amortization payments on the

---

[3] Obviously several tax proposals can be presented together, for example an increase in the tax on spirits and in that on beer and wine, or an increase in income tax along with an increase in inheritance tax.

[4] The technical procedure could probably be modified in many ways. In any case a much more flexible manner of voting would be required than in in general use today. A "division" in the British house is said to need no less than six hundred members. With the aid of modern electrical devices which, if I am not mistaken, the practical Americans have already put into use, perhaps two or three seconds would be enough for this procedure.

public debt come to mind. In so far as the state considers it as its main task to uphold contractual agreements and to protect legal rights, the property of the holders of government bonds and treasury bills must be as sacred as any other lawful claim. The question whether or not and to what extent the state or other self-governing bodies should meet their obligations can seriously arise only in situations when direct interference with existing property rights seems indispensable.[5]

There is usually an element of legal or moral obligation in most other state (or other public) expenditures as well. This sort of obligation appears to me, however, to be generally much less imperative and much more transitory than is often claimed. If, for example, an existing state activity becomes obsolete and had best be suspended, the redundant officials may undoubtedly claim appropriate compensation, but nothing more. The idealistic "obligations" of a state to its "mission", to the future, etc., can be left out of account. If such tasks fail to rally the whole nation, their chances of fulfillment are always poor. And those classes of the people who have such state activities most at heart, should back their faith with deeds in the field of taxation as well, lest doubts be cast on the disinterestedness of their aspirations.

I think, therefore, that except for a small number of public expenditures (which should be precisely listed in the constitution) the principle of approximate unanimity of tax approval can be applied generally—and must be so applied if tax justice is to be found anywhere else than on paper, in the books on finance theory.

The problem is comparatively simple when new expenditures are to be approved and to be financed by new taxes.

The mechanics become more difficult when a reduction of expenditures and revenues is involved, because in modern budgets the individual expenditure and revenue items do not correspond to each other. Hence it is not pre-established what revenue (tax) shall be abrogated with the cessation of a certain expenditure, and *vice versa*. The following appears

---

[5] Interest and principal of the debt are to be considered as items on the liability side of the state's balance sheet and it seems that the most appropriate way of providing for them would be to earmark the interests the state may receive from its assets. If this were insufficient, there would be a clear case for taxation based on ability-to-pay or on equality or proportionality of sacrifice. The benefit principle might be applied only in so far as the state activity for which the debt was originally contracted may have been of demonstrable special benefit to certain classes, districts, etc.

All the more unequivocally should the benefit principle be upheld in decisions concerning the alternatives of financing a planned state expenditure by loans or immediate taxes. A loan has to be serviced in the future and special safeguards for the protection of the non-propertied classes are all the more necessary as the propertied classes almost invariably derive economic gains from any debts the State incurs. This point will be discussed later.

to me as the simplest solution. The first step would be a provisional classification of budgetary revenue and expenditure, each single expenditure or category of expenditures being assigned to a definite revenue category. The relevant decisions would obviously have to be by simple majority. Once this is done, a specified faction of the legislature (say one-tenth, one-sixth or one-fourth of the total members) may be entitled henceforth to demand removal or reduction of any tax group (including taxes proper, surcharges or personal services rendered to the State) and thereby also the abolition or reduction of the state activity to which the tax revenues had been assigned. Due notice would obviously have to be given and the required period of notice laid down in the constitution. It would then be up to the other members of the legislature to choose whether they wish to satisfy the recalcitrant party by some different distribution of the tax in question or whether they prefer to agree to the proposed abolition or reduction of the state activity.

What has been said above applies also to simple tax reform, that is, to the substitution of one kind of tax for another. If such a reform is backed by a majority of the size indicated above, then the proposal will naturally be adopted without further ado. But tax reform should not be allowed to be carried by simple majority, because the interests of the minority might be severely prejudiced. If there is a group, whether it be a minority or the majority itself, which feels especially burdened by any tax, this group may try to achieve a better tax distribution by giving notice of refusal with respect to this tax and the corresponding preclassified state service (not just any state service in the group's arbitrary choice—this would clearly be absurd). In so doing, the group of course risks the danger that the service will really be abolished and the satisfaction of the collective need has to be transferred to private initiative.

Special provisions would have to be made for taxes which are bracketed with expenditures of unchangeable amount, for example, interest on the public debt. Since the expenditure cannot be stricken, a minority's refusal to pay the tax is *a fortiori* unthinkable. Nor should the initally specified or subsequently agreed manner of covering such interest payments be altered against the will of the minority. Any tax changes proposed in this connection would have to be subject to a qualified majority decision.

However strange the arrangements here proposed may appear, I do not hesitate to assert that they constitute the only way in which the two-fold problem of justice in tax distribution and the correct magnitude of the amount of taxes can be solved in a definitive manner. The suggested arrangements provide no ideal solution for the problem of tax distribution— but neither do they stand in the way of such a solution. Within the limits of the minority's tax refusal right there would, in general, be ample room for variants of tax distribution and any one of these could be chosen for reasons of equity, simplicity etc., provided it secured approximately unanimous approval by the taxpayers or their representatives. In the last resort, such approval—and it alone—constitutes a palpable and plain but reliable guarantee that the desired goal will really be achieved. As much cannot be said of all the various tax doctrines.

In terms of practical political considerations it may be pointed out that the arrangements here proposed are equally suitable for protecting the interests of the politically defenseless classes at the upper and the lower end of the scale. As things are at the moment, there is hardly a country in the world where, notwithstanding universal and equal suffrage, the lower ranks of the population can secure parliamentary representation in proportion to their numbers—not to speak of countries like Sweden, where the working classes occasionally find an eloquent champion in Parliament but do not, and under the constitution cannot, have any direct representatives of their interests. In these circumstances, the arrangements which we have suggested would mostly serve to protect the mass of the poorer classes against excessive tax burdens and therefore in fact to defend the majority against the minority.

But the tables can be turned. If once the lower classes are definitely in possession of the power to legislate and tax, there will certainly be a danger that they may behave no more unselfishly than those classes which have so far been in power. In other words, there will be a danger that the poorer classes in power may impose the bulk of all taxes upon the rich and may at the same time be so reckless and extravagant in approving public expenditures to which they themselves contribute but little that the nation's mobile capital may soon be squandered fruitlessly. This may well break the lever of progress. This danger should not be dismissed lightly nor belittled, especially not by those who feel, as I do, that the advance of democracy is so rightful an end and so much a part of progress itself that they do their best to further this advance in spite of all misgivings. There can be no doubt that the best and indeed the only certain guarantee against such abuses of power lies in the principle of unanimity and voluntary consent in the approval of taxes.

This is precisely the reason why those who yield but with bad grace and evil forebodings to the ever more insistent claims for democracy, should make every effort now to establish this principle in existing tax legislation. It is scarcely to be expected that the new ruling classes will freely impose such self-restraint upon themselves if they do not already find it embodied in the constitution. Nor should it be taken for granted that there will be much time for reflection. The day is close when the balance of political power will be overturned. Let the eye rove East or West, North or South, everywhere the center of gravity of political power is inexorably moving downwards. It is a matter of not being overtaken by events which can neither be prevented nor long delayed.

If the ideas presented here should come to be accepted, they would give a strong impulse to a reform which outstanding thinkers have advocated for half a century, but which so far has hardly progressed beyond the discussion stage. I have in mind the so-called system of proportional representation. Those who are familiar with John Stuart Mill's writings and especially with *Representative Government*, need not be reminded how much importance this sagacious mind attached to an apparently so insignificant change in election procedures and how healthy he thought it would be for various spheres of public life. However, so long as all matters in the competence of Parliament are decided by simple parliamentary majority, a few members more or less are a matter of scant importance for any party which is too small and powerless to hope that it will ever be in a position to command majority decisions. Mill's chief object was to ensure a parliamentary hearing for every opinion which could rally some thousand of adherents in the population. The point is well taken. But today political discussion is so largely conducted outside the halls of Parliament, that the advantage would be a somewhat relative one.

Things would be entirely different if, in tax legislation, the minorities possessed the right to veto any public expenditure the utility of which they did not expect to correspond to the outlay required of them. This is the only way of giving full effect to the rightful claim that everyone should be represented in Parliament only by persons for whom he has voted because he shares their views, and not by persons whose opinion on important questions may be diametrically opposed to his own and against who he has cast his vote on election day.

There can be no legitimate doubt any more that this last question can be solved in a satisfactory manner. Suffice it to point out that the system which is today so widely advocated is quite in accord with the principle of approximate unanimity in tax approval. Both approaches are rooted in the common ground of respect of personal liberty and its greatest possible ascendancy.

The most important consequence of the adoption of the system here proposed would be that taxes would cease to seem a burden. Instead they would come to be regarded as what they really should be, namely as means to procure to the community as a whole and to each of its classes particular benefits which could not be obtained in other ways. Each member of society would be happy in the knowledge that the goods which taxation withdraws from his private use are destined solely for purposes which he recognizes to be useful and in which he has a genuine interest, be it for purely selfish or for altruistic motives. Surely this would do more than anything else to awaken and maintain the spirit of good citizenship.

There would no longer be occasion for the many devious devices by which the true magnitude and significance of the tax load have in the past been concealed from the people. The fiscal principle would have to yield to the economic principle; the direct method of raising state revenues should become the rule and the indirect method the exception.

Practical Implementation

Let us now return once again to the principle of unanimity and voluntary consent in the approval of public expenditures and taxes and say a few words concerning the practical implementation of this principle.

It is a necessary condition that expenditures and the means of financing them be voted upon simultaneously. It is clear that such arrangements could be made independently and certainly without any change in the constitution. The various parties need only make use of the right, which they possess under most constitutions, to make the approval of each budgetary demand, or at least of each new one, contingent upon a specific, initially defined manner of financing the expenditure.[6]

If this procedure should become general practice, a very important practical step would have been taken in the direction of the system proposed in this essay. The requirement of the veto right of the minorities would follow sooner or later as a logical and necessary consequence. When, as today, the expenditures and the revenues are approved separately, it may in fact appear as if in both cases, but especially in the latter, decisions can only be reached by simple majority. But it would be different if expenditures and revenues were always confronted with each other, because there would then normally be a choice between many alternative possibilities. It stands to reason that a combination which satisfies everyone—and such a combination has been shown to be theoretically possible whenever a public service possesses general usefulness—must be imbued with more justice than any other which might appeal more to an accidentally greater half of those interested, but which would be at the expense of the others. Once this is conceded, the right of minority veto is already recognized in principle.

Objections can, of course, be raised against the formal inclusion of a right of this nature in the constitution. One could speak of possible abuses, obstructionism etc., by which a disloyal minority might try to press its own particular purposes. I am not denying the possibility of such results. All

---

[6] It is self-evident that this is not to suggest the introduction of special kinds of taxes for each single expenditure, let alone separate financial administration for each budgetary item. The assignment of specific revenues to specific expenditure categories could remain an accounting device; nor need it be done with more meticulous precision than is customary in the itemization of the budget generally.

It would have been superfluous to mention this if Leroy-Beaulieu, in his *Traite' de la Science des Finances* (fifth edition, Vol. I, p. 130 and elsewhere), had not exaggerated the alleged practical difficulties of a "systeme de la specialite' des taxes", the theoretical virtues of which he recognizes at least in the field of local finances. When he notes that such a system "evidently" could never be applied to the expenditures of the State, he appears to have forgotten that this was in fact done on a large scale in some of the older constitutional states.

power can be abused. But the danger would seem the more the various parties were free to take care directly of their legitimate interests. Obstructionism is a weapon of despair, the petty and mostly sterile vengeance of minorities whose rights are trampled underfoot. The abuse of power on the part of a minority, unless it be all-powerful, is in any case exposed to the threat of reprisals in one form or another, while the power of the majority is quite uncontrolled and the minority has no legal possibility of throwing off the yoke.

The constitutions of many European countries almost seem designed to offer every possible encouragement to the approval and every possible hindrance to the rejection of tax proposals.[7] However far the system here proposed may be from such constitutional provisions, I venture to suggest that it is nothing more than a logical development of the specialization of the expenditure budget. Although such specialization was introduced in many countries only after violent constitutional struggles, its usefulness would not now be queried by any serious politician. It serves as a control by the legislature over the executive. In precisely the same way the bracketing of specific revenues and expenditures, combined with the legally acknowledged right of veto, would serve as a control by each single group of the legislature over all other groups.

I am profoundly convinced that, at least in the country with which I am most familiar, such control is urgently needed, primarily to protect the interests of the lower classes. However, my proposals have not been advanced from this point of view alone. Their purpose is—and I may perhaps take credit for it—to do justice to both sides: to the side to which I belong by birth and upbringing and to the side of those with whom, in my mature years, I have come to feel more and more in sympathy.

The propertied classes undeniably include a significant share of a nation's intelligence and economic initiative, and in many a case their preferred position is due at least in part to their own efforts. These classes should not be forced by the ill-considered claims of a precipitant democracy to assume the whole burden of the community's tax load. But neither should

---

[7] Under the Swedish constitution the lower house does not even have the right to refuse to approve a new tax. If the two chambers vote with different results, the votes of both chambers (230 in the lower, 150 in the upper) are pooled and simple majority decides. Experience has shown the upper chamber to be much more open-handed and to be apt to vote as one man in such matters, so that the lower house (which incidentally is not elected by universal suffrage but one subject to very high property qualifications) actually needs a large majority— in the extreme case 5 to 1—merely to reject a new budgetary proposal!

A striking contrast is offered in the legislation of the state of New York. The governor has a provisional veto against every item of the budget. A two-thirds majority of each house is necessary to override this veto and to uphold the proposed expenditure. (See Leroy-Beaulieu, *Science des Finances*, Fifth ed. Vol II, p. 179.)

the members of the poorer classes, who after all do also possess some judgement and who are not beasts of burden but human beings, be called upon to pay for expenditures of whose utility and necessity they cannot be convinced, perhaps for very valid reasons.

It will assuredly be one of the most important tasks of the future to attenuate and eventually to eliminate the conflict between the social classes. So long as it exists, however—and it will unfortunately continue to exist for a long, a very long time—there is nothing to be gained from discussing social problems as if there were no such conflict. One must take the material as it is and see what can be made of it.

It is not the business of the science of public finance and of tax legislation to do away with the egotism of the social classes, but to assign it its proper place as a safeguard of legitimate particular interests. This force, to which so much ill will has been imputed, may then yet produce some good.

6

JUSTIFICATION OF THE COMPOUND REPUBLIC: THE *CALCULUS* IN RETROSPECT
James M. Buchanan

Elsewhere I have stated that the public choice perspective combines two distinct elements: the extension of the economist's model of utility-maximizing behavior to political choice and the conceptualization of "politics as exchange" (Buchanan 1983). *The Calculus of Consent* (1962) was the first book that integrated these two elements into a coherent, logical structure. It will be useful here to compare and contrast the argument developed in the *Calculus* to those that were present in the nascent public choice analysis of the time as well as in the then-conventional wisdom in political science.

The Model of Utility Maximization

Kenneth Arrow published his seminal *Social Choice and Individual Values* in 1951; Duncan Black's *Theory of Committees and Elections* appeared in 1958, following earlier papers published in the late 1940s and early 1950s; and Anthony Downs published *An Economic Theory of Democracy* in 1957. These three writers were all economists, as was Joseph Schumpeter whose *Capitalism, Socialism, and Democracy* (1942) contained precursory, if widely neglected, parallels to the inquiries that followed. In each case, analysis was grounded on the economist's model of utility maximization. Indeed, in the Arrow, Black, and later social choice constructions, the individual is viewed as ranking his preferences over alternative social states. Downs's work differs from the social choice strand of inquiry in that he modeled the behavior of political parties analogously to that of profit-seeking firms in a competitive market environment; but ultimately, the construction is also based on the utility-maximizing behavior of office-seeking politicians and interest-seeking voting constituents.

Cato Journal, Vol. 7, No. 2 (Fall 1987). Copyright Cato Institute. All rights reserved.

The author is Director of the Center for Study of Public Choice and University Professor at George Mason University. He is the recipient of the 1986 Nobel Prize in Economics.

The missing element in these constructions is any justificatory argument for democratic process that embodies individualistic norms for evaluation. Arrow and Black seemed to place stability and consistency in "social choice" above any consideration of the desirability of correspondence between individual values and collective outcomes. Downs seemed to be interested in the predictions of the results of majoritarian political processes independently of overriding the desires of persons in minority preference positions. Arrow dramatically proved that consistent sets of individual orderings need not generate consistent social or collective results under any rule; but he totally neglected any normative reference to the possible coercion of minority preferences or interests in any non-unanimous rule structure.[1]

The Justificatory Basis for Collective Action

These works left us with a dangling question: Why should an individual enter into a collective? The authors of these works presumed, without inquiry, that the individual was locked into membership in a political community and that the range and scope of the collective's activities were beyond the control of the individual and, by inference, beyond the boundaries of analysis amenable to any individualistic calculus. The *Calculus* differed from the precursory works in one fundamental respect, namely, it embodied *justificatory* argument. The *Calculus* sought to outline, at least in very general terms, the conditions that must be present for the individual to find it advantageous to enter into a political entity with constitutionally delineated ranges of activity or to acquiesce in membership in a historically existent polity.

The intellectual-analytical vacuum was much more apparent in relation to the early extensions of economic methodology to the political process than it seemed in then-conventional political science inquiry. Precisely because Black, Arrow, and Downs explicitly incorporated individual utility maximization in their analyses, possible differences among persons in preference orderings over political alternatives emerged as a central issue. In a model with identical preferences, the problems addressed by Arrow, Black, and Downs do not directly arise. Once preferences over political choice options are presumed to differ, however, it is but a natural extension to consider the choice among political regimes.

Normative political science in the 1950s offered a dramatically different ideational environment. Influenced in part by Hegelian-inspired idealism, the interest of the individual was treated as being embodied in the state and in politics as process. Even for many of those who could scarcely be

---

[1] Arrow's emphasis on stability and consistency in *collective* results to the neglect of individual interests was the primary target of my own criticism (Buchanan 1954).

classified as falling within the Hegelian tradition, politics was still conceived as a search for truth and goodness, a search from which a uniquely deter minate "best" result (for everyone) emerges. One important strand of positive political analysis, based largely on the work of Arthur Bentley ([1908] 1935), focused on conflicts among differing interests but in turn tended to neglect the cooperative elements that are necessary to justify playing the game at all.

If we remain within the presuppositions of methodological individualism, the state or the polity must ultimately be justified in terms of its potential for satisfying individuals' desires, whatever these might be. The state is necessarily an artifact, an instrument that has evolved or is designed for the purpose of meeting individual needs that cannot be readily satisfied under alternative arrangements. In this sense, the great game of politics must be a positive-sum game. If this fact is recognized while also acknowledging the potential for conflict among differing individual interests, the basic exchange model of the economist is immediately suggested. In this elementary model, traders enter the interaction process with distributionally conflicting interests but in a setting that offers mutuality of gain from cooperation.

Wicksell's Unanimity Criterion

This second element in the inclusive public choice perspective, that of "politics as exchange," is necessary to make any justificatory argument. In adding this element to the utility-maximizing models for individual choice behavior in politics, Gordon Tullock and I were directly influenced by the great work of Knut Wicksell (1896), the primary precursor of my own efforts in public choice and in political economy generally. Along with a few of his European colleagues, Wicksell sought to extend the range of economic analysis of resource use to the public or governmental sector. He sought a criterion for efficiency in the state or collective use of resources that was comparable to the criterion that had been formally specified for the use of resources in the market sector of the economy. In determining the value of the collective use of a resource, Wicksell adhered to the basic individualistic postulate of market exchange: individuals, who both enjoy the benefits of state-financed services and pay the costs in sacrificed privately supplied goods, are the only legitimate judge of their own well-being. From this individualistic presupposition, there emerged the Wicksellian unanimity criterion—if any proposed public or governmental outlay is valued more highly than the alternative market or private product of the resources, there must exist a tax-sharing scheme that all citizens will agree upon. If there is no tax-sharing scheme that will secure unanimous approval, the proposed outlay fails the test. Note that this basic Wicksellian proposition incorporates the epistemological humility of revealed preference as well as the Pareto criterion for evaluation, both of which emerged as independently developed ideas later.

In proposing a departure from the established majority voting rule in legislative assemblies, Wicksell was suggesting a change in the effective political constitution, the set of constraints within which political choices are made. He shifted the ground for discourse. Rather than discuss the relative efficiency of policy options under an unchanging rules structure, with little or no regard given either to what efficiency means or for any prospect for the desired option being chosen, Wicksell sought to open up the structure of decision rules as a variable that might be chosen instrumentally for the purpose of ensuring that collective action meet a meaningfully defined efficiency norm. Wicksell, of course, recognized that the strict requirement for unanimity would offer incentives for strategic behavior to all participants and that some relaxation of this requirement might be necessary for practicable operation. By reducing the requirement to, say, five-sixths of the voting members of the assembly, the incentives for strategic behavior are dramatically reduced and there is insurance against most, if not all, inefficient outlay.

Wicksell, however, did not move beyond the development of criteria for evaluating policy alternatives one at a time. He shifted attention to a change in the decision rules, from simple majority voting toward unanimity, to ensure against collective approval of projects that do not yield benefits equal to or in excess of costs, on any ordinary project.[2] Wicksell did not extend his analysis to the operation of specific decision rules over a whole sequence of time periods or separate categories of outlay, which might have allowed for less restrictive criteria for single projects.

Extension of the Wicksellian Criterion to Constitutional Choice

In the *Calculus*, Tullock and I made this extension. We were directly influenced by discussions with our colleague Rutledge Vining at the University of Virginia, who hammered home the argument that political choices are among alternative rules, institutions, and arrangements which generate patterns of results that are at least partly stochastic. We should then evaluate the working of any rule not in terms of its results in a particularized choice situation, but in terms of its results over a whole sequence of separate "plays," separated both intercategorically and intertemporally. Vining's insistence on the relevance of the analogy with the selection of the rules for ordinary games was part of the intellectual

---

[2] Wicksell exempted categories of outlay that were considered to be irrevocable commitments, for example, interest on public debt.

environment in Charlottesville, and the shift of the Wicksellian criterion from single projects to rules seemed a "natural" one for us to take.

In the confined Wicksellian choice setting, an individual, behaving non-strategically, will vote to approve a proposed collective outlay if he anticipates that the benefits he secures will exceed the tax costs. He will oppose all proposals that fail this test. If, however, the individual is placed in a genuine *constitutional* choice setting, where the alternatives are differing decision rules under which a whole sequence of particular proposals will be considered, he will evaluate the predicted working properties of rules over the whole anticipated sequence. If, on balance, the operation of a defined rule is expected to yield net benefits over the sequence, the individual may vote to approve the rule, even if he predicts that he must personally be subjected to loss or damage in some particular "plays" of the political game.

By shifting the applicability of the unanimity or consensus criterion from the level of particular proposals to the level of rules—to constitutional rather than post-constitutional or in-period choices—we were able to allow for the possibility that preferred and agreed-on decision rules might embody sizable departures from the unanimity limit, including simple majority voting in some cases and even less than majority voting in others. The constitutional calculus suggests that both the costs of reaching decisions under different rules and the importance of the decisions are relevant. And because both of these elements vary, the preferred rule will not be uniform over all ranges of potential political action.

The construction seemed to offer justificatory argument for something akin to the complex political structure that James Madison had in mind, much of which finds itself embedded in the constitutional framework approved by the Founding Fathers. There is a justification for the compound republic, for constitutional democracy, that can be grounded in individual utility maximization; but the general argument does not allow the elevation of majority rule to dominating status. This rule, whether in the entire electorate or in the legislative assembly, takes its place alongside other rules, some of which may be more and others less inclusive.

At the constitutional stage of choice among rules, our argument conceptually requires unanimous agreement among all parties. In this sense, we were simply advancing the Wicksell-Pareto criterion one stage upward in the choice-making hierarchy. As we suggested, however, agreement on rules is much more likely to emerge than agreement on policy alternatives within rules, because of the difficulties in identifying precisely the individual's economic interests in the first setting. The rule to be chosen is expected to remain in existence over a whole sequence of time periods and possibly over a wide set of separate in-period choices. How can the individual at the stage of trying to select among rules identify his own narrowly defined self-interest? How can he predict which rule will maximize his own net wealth? He is necessarily forced to choose from behind a dark "veil of uncertainty." In such a situation, utility maximization dictates that generalized criteria, such as fairness, equity, or justice, enter the calculus rather than the more specific arguments, such as net income or wealth.

This construction enabled us analytically to bridge, at least in part, the gap between narrowly defined individual self-interest and an individually generated definition of what could be called the general interest. In this construction, our efforts were quite close to those of John Rawls, which culminated in his seminal book, A *Theory of Justice* (1971). Early papers published in the late 1950s had adumbrated the essential parts of the Rawlsian construction; and while our own construction was independently developed, we were familiar with Rawls's parallel efforts.[3]

Our analysis differed from that of Rawls, however, in the important respect that we made no attempt to generate specific predictions as to what might emerge from the prospective agreement among the contractors who choose rules from behind the veil of uncertainty. Our construction suggested that no single decision rule was likely to be chosen for general applicability over the whole range of political action. We used the construction to eliminate some sets of outcomes rather than to specify those sets that would be selected. By contrast, Rawls was led (we think, misled) to attempt to use the veil-of-ignorance construction to make specific predictions. He suggested that his two principles of justice would uniquely emerge from the pre-constitutional stage of contractual agreement.

The Social Contract Tradition

When constitutional-stage politics is conceptualized as exchange among utility-maximizing individuals, we are obliged to classify ourselves as working within the social contract tradition in political philosophy. Precursors of the *Calculus* are found in the works of the classical social contract theorists rather than in the works of the idealists or the realists. What has been and remains surprising to me has been the reluctance or inability of social scientists, philosophers, and especially economists to understand and appreciate the relationships between the institutions of voluntary exchange, the choice among constitutional rules, and the operations of ordinary politics within such rules. James Madison clearly had such an understanding, which we tried to articulate in modern analytical language a quarter-century ago. There has been some shift toward recovery of the Madisonian wisdom in both public and scholarly attitudes over two and one-half decades. Perhaps

---

[3] We were not familiar at all with the construction of John Harsanyi, which had appeared in the mid-1950s, but with quite a different normative purpose.

the *Calculus* contributed marginally to this change. But both "politics as pure conflict" and "politics as the quest for truth and light" continue as dominant models shaping both public and "scientific" views on collective action.

References

Arrow, Kenneth J. *Social Choice and Individual Values*. New York: Wiley, 1951.

Bentley, Arthur. *The Process of Government*. 1908, Reprint. Bloomington: Principia Press, 1935.

Black, Duncan. *Theory of Committees and Elections*. Cambridge: Cambridge University Press, 1958.

Buchanan, James M. "Social Choice, Democracy, and Free Markets." *Journal of Political Economy* 62 (April 1954):114-23.

Buchanan, James. M. "The Public Choice Perspective." *Economia delle scelte publiche* 1 (January 1983): 7-15.

Buchanan, James M., and Tullock, Gordon. *The Calculus of Consent*. Ann Arbor: University of Michigan Press, 1962.

Downs, Anthony. *An Economic Theory of Democracy*. New York: Harper, 1957.

Harsanyi, John. "Cardinal Welfare, Individualistic Ethics, and Interpersonal Comparisons of Utility." *Journal of Political Economy* 63 (August 1955): 309-21.

Rawls, John. *A Theory of Justice*, Cambridge: Harvard University Press, 1971.

Schumpeter, Joseph. *Capitalism, Socialism, and Democracy*. New York: Harper and Row, 1942.

Wicksell, Knut. *Finanztheoretische Untersuchungen*. Jena: Fischer, 1896.

7

THE *CALCULUS:*
POSTSCRIPT AFTER 25 YEARS
Gordon Tullock

The Neglect of Constitutional Theory and Reform

Before I arrived at the University of Virginia to begin my postdoctoral fellowship, I had had only the slightest of personal contacts with Jim Buchanan. My formal background was not in economics and, indeed, I did not favor welfare economics. Buchanan rather quickly converted me, but I have always been unhappy with the Paretian apparatus. Although I have attempted to invent improvements or replacements for that apparatus, I cannot say that I have been entirely successful.

Because of my background, Buchanan and I had a different approach to our joint work. Specifically, my goal was to understand the government and, if possible, improve its functioning. For me, using economic tools was a way of reaching this larger goal rather than an end in itself. My interest in political exchange was only instrumental. All of this provided a genuine but not large difference in approach. The mild amount of tension between our approaches together with the similarity of our basic perspective contributed to the success of the analysis.

Unlike Buchanan, however, I have been disappointed by the subsequent history of *The Calculus of Consent.* Although it has sold well, been used in classes, and has affected the thinking of many people, there has been almost no further research along the same lines. This is not to say that research in public choice theory has not flourished, but Duncan Black's "median preference theorem" and Anthony Downs's work on information in politics have led to much more research and elaboration than the constitutional perspective of the *Calculus.* Also, my later discovery of rent-seeking (Tullock 1967) prompted more articles that directly attempted to

---

Cato Journal, Vol. 7 No. 2 (Fall 1987). Copyright Cato Institute. All rights reserved.

The author is Karl Eller Professor of Economics and Political Science at the University of Arizona.

apply and expand on the logic of the constitutional perspective than did the *Calculus* itself. The same could be said of Buchanan's "An Economic Theory of Clubs" (1965).

I am not claiming that no one has done any research based on the *Calculus* nor that the "simple constitutional perspective" has not had great influence.[1] But the more elaborate constitutional theory of the book has stimulated almost no research. There has been substantially no work on constitutions per se.

For example, in a recent series of papers Kenneth Shepsle and Barry Weingast (see esp. 1984) attempted to explain the functioning of the House of Representatives in terms of semiconstitutional procedural rules that the House has adopted. These rules, however, are not part of the Constitution, and the authors never really take a reformist perspective. Indeed, they seem to think that these rules are acceptable, even though they do not formally endorse them and do not suggest any improvements. Further, Shepsle and Weingast do not compare the semiconstitutional rules with the rules used by other governmental bodies such as the British legislature. From the time of the first reform act to about 1890, the British legislature used an institutional structure that was completely different from the one the authors describe (incorrectly I think) for the House of Representatives, but as far as I know, neither the authors nor modern public choice scholars have looked into the difference and attempted a comparative evaluation. The real importance of such an evaluation could be as a first step toward developing improved constitutional rules.

In undertaking comparative constitutional studies, a comparison of the Swiss and U.S. constitutions would be a useful starting point. The Swiss constitution is the strongest modern competitor with the U.S. Constitution in terms of promoting stable government by law and a prosperous economy. Although Switzerland has a concentration of public choice scholars, they have done very little work on the differences between the two constitutions. Such studies, with efforts to evaluate performance, would be particularly useful because the 1848 Swiss constitution, which was modeled on the American constitution, has many similarities and certain radical differences. Some Swiss researchers have looked into the impact of using public referenda in Switzerland, but this research is still in its infancy and has yielded no conclusive policy proposals either for Switzerland or the United States.

To consider a less significant gap, the German constitution provides for

---

[1] The "simple constitutional perspective," which Buchanan and I introduced in the *Calculus*, consists of explaining the behavior of government by looking at its basic institutions rather than its specific activities.

a compromise between the single-member constituency and proportional representation in the lower legislative house. So far as I know, no public choice scholar has analyzed its working. This is particularly impressive because the system appears to give considerably more political weight to people whose preference is a minor party (provided it has at least 5 percent of the electorate) than to those who favor one of the two major parties.[2]

The absence of any reformist drive in the constitutional area is especially noteworthy because the *Calculus* was a reformist book. Perhaps its strongest single implicit recommendation for reform was the switch from simple majority to a reinforced majority in the legislature. In the early days, conventional political scientists regularly denounced us for this proposal. There was even some research that purported to demonstrate that a simple majority was optimal. Today, people are still critical, but they just do not talk about the issue any more.

As the author of the chapter in the book on bicameral legislatures (Chap. 16), I find it notable that it too has had no discernible effect on researchers. In essence, I argued for bicameral legislatures on efficiency grounds and urged that the two houses be elected by radically different methods. Not only has this idea vanished into the memory hole, but the actual trend has been in the opposite direction. The Supreme Court, for example, decided some years after the Constitution had been ratified that although it was all right for the federal government to have a senate that was not elected according to population, it was undemocratic for anyone else to do it. In so doing, they sharply reduced the efficiency of the state legislatures without anybody, except myself, realizing that they had done so.[3] The decision was criticized because it was a pretty cloth-headed thing to do from a constitutional standpoint, but no one mentioned that it would lower efficiency.

As a particularly extreme example, most European Public Choice Society members live in societies that have proportional representation. I prefer this system, but I would really like to see a two-chamber legislature, with one chamber elected by single-member constituencies and the other by proportional representation.[4] I expected to see a good deal of work comparing the two systems, but it does not yet exist.

But that is not all I had hoped for. There was also opportunity for a good

---

[2] This is my own deduction and assumes that voters behave strategically. Since I do not read German, the possibility of error is sizable.

[3] The Swedes recently abolished one of their two houses. This was succeeded by rapid governmental growth, which should have astonished no one who had read the *Calculus*.

[4] Japan actually has something that is a distant relative of this preferred system. I would like to have some Japanese member of the Public Choice Society look into it and decide if it may be one of the reasons they have been so successful.

deal of reformist activity in the sense that public choice scholars would propose new and improved ideas for government at the constitutional level and make some efforts to popularize them. The prospect of a few scholars getting a constitutional amendment adopted was unlikely, but we should have begun even if we anticipated no real effects for many years. Keynes's remarks about the role of ideas may be exaggerated, but they are not fundamentally wrong. New ideas invented in the quiet studies of scholars sometimes do change the world.

While I appear to be criticizing the development of constitutional theory since the publication of the *Calculus*, the criticism applies to my own work as well as to others'. I have devoted a good deal of attention to attempting to improve our knowledge of constitutions and somewhat less to propagandizing what we know, but I have been unsuccessful on both fronts.

It may be, then, that the basic reason we have not progressed along the lines I have outlined is that it is very difficult. Certainly I have found it to be hard. But even if the basic reason for the neglect of constitutional theory and reform is very simple, I am not prevented from being disappointed. Given my age, I am decidedly disappointed at the failure of medicine to do very much on "life extension." But I do not blame the doctors for the failure. What I am saying here is that I am disappointed with the lack of development of the ideas in the *Calculus*, but I do not blame anybody for it. I certainly do not feel that I should have devoted more effort to developing our knowledge of public choice and pressing constitutional reforms. As a matter of fact, I have done more research than my publications in this area indicate—a case of a lot of work and little result.

I am inclined to view the *Calculus* as a sport. In all fields of science, an occasional discovery is ahead of its time due to essentially accidental factors. There is apt to be little progress in that field until the rest of science has caught up with it. Steam engines, first built in Alexandria 2,000 years ago, are an example. I hope that the theory of constitutions will be caught up in a general advance with less delay.

The Problem of Self-Enforcing Constitutions

Having noted my disappointment with the absence of progress in the constitutional theory and in the reformist application of what we know, I would also say that I am unhappy with the particular reforms that are normally pressed. As originally drawn up in Philadelphia, the Constitution has built into it a short Bill of Rights. Madison was personally opposed to adding the first 10 amendments, which he was forced to sponsor for political reasons. He preferred a government so structured that it was unlikely to trample on liberty rather than devising specific restrictions on that government.

I think Madison's position is the correct one. The view that the government can be bound by specific provisions is naive. Something must enforce those provisions, and whatever it is that enforces them is itself unbound. We have a particularly strong example of this in the history of the Supreme Court since about 1950. The comparative freedom and efficiency with which Americans were governed in the first century and a half of the Constitution depended on the structural characteristics of the Constitution, not on the Bill of Rights.

This raises the basic problem of what I call the "self-enforcing constitution." Granted that we have invented a good constitution, how do we make sure that it will work the way we have written it. The history of the United States shows many deviations from the Founders' vision. The most conspicuous one today is the Supreme Court's arrogation to itself of vastly more power than the Framers intended. How could the constitutional designers have prevented this from happening?

It used to be said that enforcing the Constitution was simple; we could leave it to the Supreme Court. The Framers relied on the amendment process as a way of changing the Constitution in the event that it became out-of-step with the times. In a way, the amendment process was the cause of the Civil War. In *Dred Scott*, Justice Taney had correctly interpreted the Constitution as it was originally written. The problem for the Southern states was the high probability that a Republican abolitionist president would prevent slavery's spread to the West. The Republicans would then admit enough Western states without slavery to permit an amendment abolishing slavery.[5]

The current situation is different. A great many people, including many law professors and at least one Supreme Court justice, argue that it is the duty of the Supreme Court to impose on the people the Constitution as they think it should be, not the Constitution as it was written. In this view, changes in the Constitution are to take place not through the amendment process, but through a change in the views of nine old men. There is, of course, a theory of government advocating that we should be ruled by "the best" instead of by the voter. I do not wish to argue here the merits of that point of view, only that clearly is not what the Founding Fathers had in mind.

If we design a new constitution, is there some way to guarantee that it will function according to design? For example, during the period of time in which the states were ratifying a constitutional amendment providing that everyone over the age of 18 could vote, the Supreme Court suddenly

---

[5] It is frequently argued that the actual cause of the Civil War was not slavery, but the economic difference between the manufacturing North and the agricultural South. The problem with this argument is that the Republican Party essentially started in the agricultural West.

decided that the Constitution already provided for it. This problem of the self-enforcing constitution has so far evaded solution. The Founding Fathers set up a constitution that remained more or less unchanged for a long time. Indeed, it was not until this century that significant changes were made in the original design.

Changes in the Effective Constitution

There does not appear to be any obvious explanation for this long period of stability, but I believe it was the result of a very strong internal conflict having been built into the Constitution. During the 19th century, for example, the Senate usually rejected treaties negotiated by the executive. This was not a government that could impose its will strongly on any objecting group. Thus, it was generally unable to expand its power, and the states remained the dominant governments in the United States. Due to internal free trade, the states were unable to carry out much in the way of rent-seeking, although they certainly tried.

In my opinion, the basic change occurred because of a quasi-constitutional revision in the terms of employment of the federal bureaucracy. The gradual extension of the Civil Service Act throughout the government from the 1890s to the time of World War I politically chang-ed the balance-of-power within government. This is one of the many cases in which the reform movement at the turn of the century went badly astray. In this case, there was a mix of well-intentioned, well-educated people who did not actually understand either the government or a special interest. In this case, the special interest was composed of existing government employees. The Civil Service System provided examinations for new employees (mainly on irrelevant subjects); but each time the exams were changed or the system was extended, the existing employees were grand-fathered in. The change from a situation where employees were completely subject to their political superiors to one where they could not be easily fired was a great step forward for civil servants.[6]

The results differed from those that the well-intentioned progressives probably intended. Civil servants ceased being dependent on their political superiors, who in turn were dependent on the voters. Further, politicians be-came partially dependent on the civil servants. They could no longer fire civil servants, but as voters the civil servants might fire the politicians. As a consequence, the politicians became partisans of their nominal employees, and civil servants became an extremely powerful special interest group.

---

[6] The reformers who attempted to improve the medical profession by once again grandfathering all existing doctors in and providing examinations for new entrants also greatly benefited existing members of the profession.

In the early days, this new power had almost no effect on civil servants' job performance, but it did have a great effect on their political activities. The spoilsmen would have been political appointees of whatever political administration happened to be in office at the time. They would probably continue to support that party after they were grandfathered into the civil service, but they were no longer dominated by the politicians because careers were safe. At first, they found it desirable to contribute to political parties and otherwise work for them in order to protect their prospects for promotion. Indeed, it seems likely that the legal restrictions on employees engaging in political activity were largely pushed by the civil servants themselves because it prohibited this unpleasant duty.

Over time the number of civil servants increased. One explanation for this was the political power held by the civil servants, whose "unions" devoted themselves to lobbying rather than to threatening strikes.[7] This may be what has led to the somewhat odd structure of pay of what is now the government's largest single organization. In general, the lower ranking civil servants are overpaid and the people at the top are underpaid. Indeed, Congress has periodically put upper limits on salaries with the result that promotion in the upper ranks does not increase wages. The reason for this restriction is clearly that there are a lot of votes in the lower ranks and very few in the upper ranks.

Thus, I believe that the Civil Service Act was perhaps the largest single change in our "effective constitution" before the efflorescence of the Supreme Court in the 1950s. In a way, the two events are coterminus, because the Supreme Court does not seem to have many differences with the Civil Service. In both cases, there has been a sharp aggrandisement of the power of the federal government and a sharp reduction in the power of the states. One way of approaching a study of this matter would be to examine cross-nationally the growth of government and the expansion of the Civil Service.

The Desirability of Comparative Constitutional Study

This brings me back to the desirability of comparing other constitutions. The Founding Fathers did make some comparisons, although the information they had available was quite limited. They knew only about the Athenian Republic, the Roman Republic, their own state governments, and the English government from which they had just revolted.[8] Even though

---

[7] The postal workers do both.

[8] Many of them seemed to learn of the English government through Montesquieu, and it has sometime been said that the American Constitution is a misunderstanding of Montesquieu's misunderstanding of the British constitution.

they had this knowledge, it seems likely that the basic structure that we now regard as efficient was accidental. The basic decentralization of the Constitution, that is, the reservation of most governmental activities to the states, came from the very simple straightforward fact that the states already existed and it was necessary to persuade them to voluntarily join the new federal government. The states were unlikely to voluntarily dissolve themselves in order to form a centralized state, although it is quite probable that Hamilton would have been happy with that result.

The diversely selected bicameral legislature was another compromise between the large states that wanted a population-based representation and the small states that wanted each state to be equally represented. It may have been important that a number of the state legislatures already had two chambers.[9] There were not only two houses, but they were also elected by different methods (which, if you accept the argument in the *Calculus*, was an efficiency characteristic). Dividing the government into executive, legislative, and judicial branches was an imitation of English government structure by way of Montesquieu.

The method of electing the President, making that office in many ways a third house of the legislature, is a particularly clear case of accidental constitutional provision. The system never worked in the way it was originally intended to, and the Constitution was amended to change the process after the 1800 presidential election. It seems likely that those who fashioned this provision of the Constitution intended that the most popular politician in the United States would be President and the second most popular to be Vice-President. If so, their draftsmanship was extremely defective.[10] It is interesting to speculate on what would have happened if the probable intent of this provision had been implemented. It is possible that the two-party system would never have developed, and certainly political partisanship would have been to some extent moderated by the existence of a Vice-President who had actually run against the President.

Although the Swiss adopted key parts of our Constitution, they specifically ruled out judicial review and provided a board rather than one person as the executive. The widespread use of direct voting and the general use of proportional representation made the Swiss constitution quite different from ours, but its basic structure remains very similar.

The main theme of this piece has been the lack of progress along the line of the *Calculus* since it was written. The twenty-fifth anniversary of the

---

[9] In a number of cases the upper chamber was part of the executive branch. For example, in Virginia under the old colonial charter, it functioned rather like England's House of Lords.

[10] Providing the same arrangements for numbers of electors but having each one cast a single vote would easily achieve the objective.

book and the two hundredth anniversary of the Federal Convention in Philadelphia is a good time to reflect on the past and resolve to do better in the future.

References

Buchanan, James M. "An Economic Theory of Clubs." *Economica* 32 (February 1965):1-14.

Shepsle, Kenneth A.. and Weingast, Barry R. "When Do Rules of Procedure Matter?" *Journal of Politics* 46 (1984):206-21.

Tullock, Gordon. "The Welfare Costs of Tariffs, Monopolies, and Theft." *Western Economic Journal* 5 (June 1967):224-32.

PART III

LAW, PROPERTY RIGHTS AND CONSTITUTIONAL ORDER

(This material is for the correction an omitted line at beginning of second paragraph, p. 151. You may want to tape the corrected page into your book.)

8

PROPERTY RIGHTS, TAKINGS, AND A FREE SOCIETY

Roger Pilon

Introduction

Over the course of our history, but especially over the twentieth century, government regulations have increasingly limited the uses that property owners might make of their holdings. Whether in the form of zoning restrictions, or rent controls, or environmental measures, whether directed to residential, commercial, industrial, or undeveloped property, these regulations have gradually reduced the rights of property owners while giving rights to others, especially "the public," that would have been unthinkable at the time of American's founding (Siegan 1980). Thus a shift in the underlying structure of property rights has resulted: over the years this increasing regulatory burden has rearranging and redistributing those rights; and in the process, as with all such redistribution, the economic consequences have set in, sometimes making the rich richer and the poor poorer, sometimes the other way around, but nearly always making us all poorer in time.[1]

If we are to critically assess these changes, however, it is not enough simply to point to the costs the regulations have brought about--with the implication that the regulations therefore be rolled back. For that would presume that the right and wrong in the matter were clear, when in fact the many regulations that have arisen, except in certain cases of disingenuous legislation, have come about precisely in the name of justice. Those who have called for rent controls, for example, or for building codes,

8

PROPERTY RIGHTS, TAKINGS, AND A FREE SOCIETY
Roger Pilon

Introduction

Over the course of our history, but especially over the twentieth century, government regulations have increasingly limited the uses that property owners might make of their holdings. Whether in the form of zoning restrictions, or rent controls, or environmental measures, whether directed to residential, commercial, industrial, or undeveloped property, these regulations have gradually reduced the rights of property owners while giving rights to others, especially "the public," that would have been unthinkable at the time of American's founding (Siegan 1980). Thus a shift in the underlying structure of property rights has resulted: over the years this increasing regulatory burden has rearranged and redistributed those rights; and in the process, as with all such redistribution, the economic consequences have set in sometimes making the rich richer and the poor poorer, sometimes the other way around, but nearly always making us all poorer in time.[1]

simply to point to the costs the regulations have brought about — with the implication that the regulations therefore be rolled back. For that would presume that the right and wrong in the matter were clear, when in fact the many regulations that have arisen, except in certain cases of disingenuous legislation, have come about precisely in the name of justice. Those who have called for rent controls, for example, or for building codes,

This article is reprinted, with minor revisions, from *Resolving the Housing Crisis: Government Policy, Decontrol, and the Public Interest*, 369-401 (M. Bruce Johnson Ed. 1982), and from the *Harvard Journal of Law and Public Policy*, vol. 6, Summer 1983, 165-95. The editors wish to thank the Pacific Institute for Public Policy Research for their permission to reprint. Mr. Pilon holds a B.A. (cum laude) from Columbia University and an M.A. and Ph.D. in philosophy from the University of Chicago. He is currently the Director of the Asylum Policy and Review Unit of the Department of Justice.

[1] For a discussion of these economic consequences, *see* the essays in M. Bruce Johnson (1982) and Kelly Ross (1983).

or for legislation prohibiting discrimination, or for the regulation of lot sizes, or for the preservation of open spaces or coastal views have done so in the name of various private and public *rights*. To go to the root of these changes, therefore, we have to raise not simply the economic and legal issues but those moral issues that in the end have led us to where we are. More precisely, we shall have to determine whether the various rights that the regulations have brought into being can be justified as a matter of basic moral theory. Or is it rather that the legal arrangements that preceded this growth of regulations reflected the rights that alone can be justified in a free society? In recognizing or creating these new rights, that is, did government simply give legal force to the underlying moral order? Or did it instead extinguish that order, putting new and spurious rights in the place of legitimate rights?

These are large questions, of course, going well beyond matters of economic efficiency on one hand or legal legitimacy on the other, for they inquire about the basic moral order — about what moral rights and obligations we have with respect to each other and with respect to the state. In the background, then, is the fundamental idea that ethics comes first, that the legal order ought not to stand apart from the moral order but ought instead to recognize and reflect, if not the whole of ethics, at least that part described by our moral rights and obligations. This idea stood at the heart of the world the Founding Fathers set forth in the eighteenth century.[2] It is an idea that continues to compel today.

With this basic view in mind — that law and legal institutions are morally legitimate only to the extent that they reflect our moral rights and obligations — I will try to sort out some of the issues that lie beneath these changing property rights. First, I will sketch and then examine the two principal theories about the connection between property rights and a free society that have vied for legal attention over the past century — the traditional theory, which argues that private property and individual freedom are inextricably connected, and the modern theory, which argues that a decrease in private and an increase in public property is the mark of a free society.[3] In the course of this analysis I will argue that the modern view is

---

[2] *See especially* the American Declaration of Independence. *See also* Carl Becker (1922); Edward Corwin (1955); and Bernard Bailyn (1967). I have discussed the distinction between the theory of rights and the theory of good (or value) and some reasons the former is especially suited to serve as the model for law in Pilon (1979a, pp. 1341-44). *See also* H. Hart (1955, p. 186).

[3] My temporal reference here is meant to denote, very roughly, the period since the rise of modern collectivist theories of property, represented most thoroughly and most forcefully by the Marxist doctrine. Of course, this doctrine has not usually been at the center of the American debate in any explicit way—not the American legal debate, at least before the rise of the Critical Legal Studies movement. Nevertheless, Marxism has systematically articulated many of the tendencies and, more important, many of the underlying justifications for the modern view, however limited the implementations of that view may still be in the American context.

fundamentally mistaken, that it ends in practice, as the theory requires, by using people whereas the traditional view is fundamentally correct, serving to sort out in a principled way the many issues that constitute the current debate about property. Second, I will apply the traditional theory to the taking issue, to the questions "When do regulations of property amount to a taking of that property such that under the taking clause of the Fifth Amendment we are required to compensate the individuals thus regulated?" and "When do regulations amount simply to an exercise of the police power, requiring no compensation to those regulated?" (see Siegan 1977). This issue has vexed lawyers and economists for over ninety years now.[4] Nevertheless, when adequately explicated, the classical theory of rights can shed important light on this question, sorting out the principles in the matter and thus further elucidating the place and scope of property rights in a free society.

It may be well to note, however, that in all of this I will be stepping back from the more concrete problems that are ordinarily the concern of the lawyer or the economist. In fact, I will be stepping into some fairly abstract and even arid regions, into the province of the philosopher, the better to get a picture of the larger issues before us. These issues are indeed large; in truth, the title of this article is the title of a substantial treatise. Accordingly, this will not be a detailed or exhaustive statement of just what our property rights are; rather, it will be a general statement only. Nor will this be a detailed statement of the complex theory that stands behind those rights; for that I will simply refer the reader to more complete discussions and hope that the treatment here, if sometimes elliptical, will not be inscrutable.

Two Theories of Property: Private and Public

It is a commonplace in the study of ideas that theories about the world will tend, more or less, to reflect the way the world in fact is: when more, they will yield insights that give order to the world; when less, they will break down in error, confusion, and disorder. This applies not only to

---

[4] *See* Joseph Sax (1971):

"Few legal problems have proved as resistant to analytical efforts as that posed by the Constitution's requirement that private property not be taken for public use without payment of just compensation. Despite the intensive efforts of commentators and judges, our ability to distinguish satisfactorily between "takings" in the constitutional sense, for which compensation is compelled, and exercises of the police power, for which compensation is not compelled, has advanced only slightly since the Supreme Court began to struggle with the problem some eighty years ago."

Ibid. (citing Justice Harlan's opinion in *Mugler v. Kansas*, 123 U.S. 623 (1887), which is generally taken as the beginning of the modern compensation law). *See also, The Supreme Court, 1979 Term* (1980, p. 205): "Judicial interpretation of the 'takings' clause of the fifth amendment is notoriously confused."

explanatory theories of science, helping us to understand what Thomas Kuhn (1970) has called the structure of scientific revolutions, but to normative theories of ethics, politics, and law as well. Thus, in the eighteenth century the two ideas of private property and a free society were thought to be so intimately connected as to be all but equivalent. Property rights, it was believed, both enable and describe our freedom, just as the free society is the society defined by the property rights that define in turn the relationships between the individuals who constitute the society (Dietze 1963, pp. 19-34 and Fellman 1942, p. 400). Drawn not only from the thought of the Enlightenment but from the long and revered tradition of English common law, these insights epitomized a theory of ethics and law that the Founding Fathers institutionalized and set in motion some two centuries ago, a theory that has provided a remarkable degree of order and stability, affording the conditions for the pursuit of happiness with which we are all familiar.[5] By virtue of this order and stability, then, an *a posteriori* justification has been conferred upon the theory of the Founding Fathers, a theory that otherwise was justified *a priori*. Taken together, in short, these justifications argue that the Founders got it right.[6]

In the intervening years, however, much has happened in the realm of ideas — the realm that has ever been the ultimate force in the shaping of history (Weaver 1948). As the democratic influence has grown, as legislature, statute, and popular will have come increasingly to succeed court, precedent, and reason, the earlier insights have gradually been lost. Rights of private property in particular have fallen out of favor; yet calls for a freer society have grown more intense. Thus, a new theory has emerged, one posing an antinomy between private property and a free society and pitting property rights against so-called "people rights" — for example, the rights of landlords to select their tenants on whatever grounds they choose against the rights of tenants to "open housing," or the rights of landowners to build on their property against the rights of the public to enjoy views running over that property.[7] And let us be clear that this

---

[5] To say that the American legal order is grounded in a respect for property rights is not to say that those rights were consistently respected in practice. Indeed, almost from the outset the so-called "inherent power" concept of sovereignty began to whittle away the foundations. Nevertheless, until the spread of restrictive zoning following the decision in *Village of Euclid v. Ambler Realty Co.*, 272 U.S. 365 (1926), and the rise of environmental law more recently, these inroads on the traditional rights of property were relatively modest. On the earlier periods, *see* generally Morton Horwitz (1977) and William Stoebuck (1972).

[6] In the discussion that follows, I concentrate upon the *a priori* justification of property rights, leaving it to economists and others to demonstrate that a society that recognizes such rights "works" (that is, is more efficient than one that does not recognize property rights).

[7] This distinction between property rights and so-called "people rights" is spurious, of course. All rights are "people rights" in the sense that they are rights *of* people; and they are also property rights in the sense that they are rights *to* property. Proponents of "people rights,"

new theory is not simply a refinement of the old; it is not a theory, that is, that evolved by some natural course from the thought of the Enlightenment, however gradually it may have insinuated itself into our law. Rather, it is a radical departure, for its concern at bottom is not with individual freedom but with so-called "collective freedom." Accordingly, it views private property not as a condition of freedom but as an outright impediment to freedom. Whether in its thoroughgoing form, in which *all* private property is at issue, or in its more modest proportions relating primarily to *uses* of property, it remains in principle the same: a theory that argues that private property is something not to be secured but to be abolished—or better, to be collectivized, thus ensuring freedom for all, the freedom of all to use that property. What is private is to be made public; uses that otherwise are individually determined are to be collectively determined — and hence to be politicized.[8]

In the broadest terms, these are the two theories about the connection between property rights and a free society that have sought the attention of the law for the better part of a century—(1) the theory of private property and individual freedom and (2) the theory of public property and collective freedom. What I want to do now is look at these two theories a bit more closely and argue, again, that the traditional theory of classical liberalism, if not always well articulated, is fundamentally correct whereas the new theory, which draws an opposition between private property and a free society, is fundamentally mistaken. This new theory, that is, does not reflect the basic moral order. Thus, it should come as no surprise that when our law and legal institutions attempt to reflect this theory, the result is error, confusion, and disorder.

The Theory of Private Property

The traditional theory holds, again, that rights of private property, far from

after all, are advocating that (certain) people be given rights to have, or at least to use, property— property that otherwise belongs to others. When A is given the right to use B's property (in specified ways), he can be said to own that use. Certainly B can no longer be said to own it, for he can no longer exclude A or prevent A from exercising the right of use that A now has. right of use that A now has.

[8] The literature here is vast. For two recent philosophical statements of differing intensity, *see* Norman Bowie (1971) and Kai Nielsen (1977); the latter calls for violent revolution to overthrow capitalism. For applications in the land use area, *see* William Reilly (1973); and Fred Bosselman, David Callies and John Banta (1973).

In the property rights context, ordinarily understood, the redistribution of rights for which the modern theory calls is not so much from private person to private person as from private person to the public, or at leat to specified classes of the public, as with renters in the case of rent controls, community residents in the case of zoning restrictions, or tourists and other interested parties in the case of coastal views. These do, then, become "public rights."

being antithetical to a free society, are at its very core; they both enable us to be free and define our freedom and hence the free society itself. That property enables us to be free was a point well understood by no less than Karl Marx and his followers; they argued that unlike the wealthy man, the man with little or no property could hardly be said to be free.[9] That, after all, is why most of us try to acquire property: so that we will have the freedom it affords. In thus stating the matter, however, Marxists glossed over a fundamental distinction, namely, that the poor man is *at liberty* to do what he wants even though he may be *unable* to do it. Nevertheless, they pointed to a basic ambiguity in the notion of "freedom," which they went on to richly exploit. That ambiguity, which upon reflection is hardly surprising, is that an individual can be said to be at once free and unfree: free from the interference of others, or *politically* free, as we would say, yet unfree in the sense just mentioned, unable to do what he wants to do. In emphasizing the latter, the "positive" sense of freedom, as it has come to be called, Marxists have tended to equate "freedom" with "power" and hence to ignore the political or "negative" sense of "freedom" that classical liberals had always sought to secure (*see*, Berlin 1969; *cf.* MacCallum 1967). Nevertheless, our ordinary language does admit of this "positive" usage; thus the liberal cannot really argue that the Marixist is misusing the language. Nor should he rest his case on so slim a reed, especially when there are stronger ones nearby and when this distinction, taken by itself, seems to argue for redistributing property when doing so would enlarge freedom for all.[10]

As a theoretical matter, however, the more crucial function of property is to *define* our freedom — and, by implication, the free society itself. For when held as a matter of moral *right*, our property serves to delineate our moral relationships with each other and with the state (Pilon 1979d, chaps. 1 and 2). It does this in the quite literal sense in which one person's rights and another's obligations begin at the same line. But it does so much more broadly as well, a point that is best appreciated when we notice that *all* rights, at bottom, are matters of property. John Locke (1963, p. 395), who more than anyone else, perhaps, can be said to have authored the American Revolution, put the matter plainly: "Lives, Liberties, and Estates, which I call by the general Name, *Property*." To Locke, as well as to many others of the Enlightenment, everything in the world, including people and their actions, could be viewed as property and hence as objects of rights claims.

Now there are subtle and far-reaching implications in this property approach to ethics, which not even the classical liberals fully appreciated.

---

[9] Like most points in Marx, this one is not made unambiguously. *See, e.g.,* Karl Marx (1977, p.79).

[10] These points are more fully developed in Pilon (1979d, chap. 1).

For the moment, however, I will focus upon the matter of consistency, which later will bear importantly upon the taking issue. In a theory of ethics or law, consistency is imperative — especially when the theory purports to be grounded ultimately in reason, as English common law did for centuries.[11] For if a theory is inconsistent — if it yields conflicting rights, for example, and hence is contradictory — then to that extent it cannot be grounded in reason and so is not well justified. When we reduce rights to property, however, thereby tying the theory to the real world, we objectify it and hence improve immeasurably our chances of being consistent.[12] We do this because *there are no contradictions in the world:* There is only what is. Contradictions exist, when they do, only in our minds — as manifest in our theories, say, or in our values. And, indeed, it was precisely the genius of the common law jurists and the men of the Enlightenment that they saw, if only inchoately, that rights at bottom are *not* matters of subjective value or interest but matters of objective *property*. In drawing the connection between rights and property, they gave us a theory of ethics and law that was, for the most part, both objective and consistent.[13]

But was that theory correct? It is one thing to develop a theory of rights that is both objectively grounded and consistent, quite another to show that that theory is *justified*. On this score, regrettably, the men of the Enlightenment, and the Founding Fathers in particular, were at their weakest — not surprisingly, for the epistemological tools at their command were altogether primitive.[14] Thus their arguments from versions of natural law, although they persuaded many, did not stand the test of time. Today, for example, we can no longer get away with saying that our rights are justified because God-given — whereas other rights, presumably, are unjustified because not God-given — for there are well-known objections to that line of argument.[15] But neither can we view our rights as justified because

---

[11] *See* Corwin (1955, p. 26):
   "Indeed, the notion that the common law embodied right reason furnished from the fourteenth century its chief claim to be regarded as higher law."

[12] In thus objectifying and grounding rights in property, we still have to specify the "property" of the world — how it arises as private property, what in particular it encompasses, how it devolves, and much else. *See infra* notes 18-20 and the accompanying text.

[13] These points are more fully developed in Pilon (1979d, chap. 2) and Pilon (1979c).

[14] It was not until David Hume, for example, who died in the year America was born, that we came to appreciate the "is-ought" problem, the point that normative conclusions cannot be derived from factual premises. *See* Hume, (188, pp. 469-70); *cf.*,Locke (1963, p. 311); and Gewirth (1974).

[15] The king, after all, invoked the divine right thesis in support of conclusions quite opposite those of his opponents. The argument from theological considerations was not the only form of the natural law argument, of course. But those other versions have likewise fared ill against the criticism of modern epistemology. *See* Pilon (1979a, 1333-34) and Veatch (1978).

assigned by the sovereign, as is often done, at least by implication, in the modern legal and economic literature; for legal positivism is no more an ultimate justification than theological positivism.[16] This is not to say, of course, that the rights of theology or of legal positivism are not in fact *justifiable*; it is to say only that these lines of argument will not do the job of justifying them (Pilon 1979a; L. Becker 1973; and Gewirth 1978, pp. 1-47). What is called for instead is an account whereby our rights are derived not as a matter of will — divine or political — but as a matter of reason, an account such as Locke (1963, pp. 310-11) only adumbrated and Kant (1950) developed a bit more fully. That work is proceeding today in philosophical circles, and not without results (for example, Gewirth 1978, Donagan 1977, and Nozick 1974).

In general, the idea is to show that certain rights must be accepted as justified such that to deny that individuals have them is to contradict oneself. This strategy was always implicit in various formulations of the Golden Rule, but it was never developed with anything like the requisite detail (Singer 1961). Some of the work going on today, however, is aimed at setting forth that detail and, in particular, at showing that rights are grounded in the normative claims inherent in the basic subject matter of ethics — human action.[17] This normative theory of action is then connected with or expli-cated over an entitlement theory of distributive justice that characterizes the world in terms of holdings or property and goes on to explain how those holdings arise or come to be attached to particular people or institutions, either legitimately or illegitimately.[18] To be legitimately held or owned, property must have been acquired without violating the rights of others. In the case of their own persons and labor, for example, individuals acquire title by a certain "natural necessity," as it were, along the lines of the theory of action just mentioned. With respect to the more ordinary kinds of holdings, something might have been acquired from the state of nature, in which it was unheld; more likely, it might have been acquired from some-one else who held it legitimately, either in exchange for something else or as a gift; or it might have been acquired from someone else or his agent in rectification for some past wrong by that other.[19] Thus, in general,

---

[16] This line of argument usually seeks its support in a background theory of political legitimacy. But here, too, there are well-known objections. See, e.g. Wolff (1970) and Riker (1980).

[17] *See especially* Gewirth (1978).

[18] The entitlement theory of property stems from Nozick (1974, p. 149-82).

[19] For an account of justice in rectification in the area of torts, *see* Richard Epstein (1973a, 1973b, 1974, and 1975). In the area of criminal law, *see* Pilon (1978).

It is often easier to state the outlines of this theory than to apply it in particular historical contexts, where the legitimacy of the titles that are transferred from time to time may be uncer-tain or dubious. Whereas the theory presumes that we start with a clean moral slate, history provides us with such a slate only more or less.

do holdings and rights to the exclusive possession and use of those holdings arise legitimately. By contrast, things are held illegitimately when they are taken by force or fraud from those who hold them legitimately — that is, when they are taken without the voluntary consent of those who rightly hold them. When what is ours has been taken without our consent, our basic right to be free from interference in our persons and property has been violated. At bottom, then, rights violations are *takings*, which means that to be clear about them we must be clear, first, about what is held and then taken and, second, about the causal process by which those holdings are taken. These are very large subjects, but both bear crucially upon the current taking issue, as we will shortly see.[20]

With this, the sketch of the traditional theory is completed. As can be seen, it is a theory of justice as *process*, not a theory of justice as result or end-state (Nozick 1974, p. 153-60). Whatever property distribution has justly arisen is justly held, even though the distribution may be unequal or may reflect the many fortuitous factors that entered into its development. On the traditional view, then, the free society is a society of equal *rights*: stated most broadly, the right to be left alone in one's person and property, the right to pursue one's ends provided the equal rights of others are respected in the process, all of which is more precisely defined by reference to the property foundations of those rights and the basic proscription against taking that property. And the free society is also a society of equal *freedom*, at least insofar as that term connotes the freedom from interference that is described by our equal rights. But the free society is *not* a society of equal freedom insofar as that term connotes the liberty or power that comes from property ownership. For in the free society there will be powerful and weak, rich and poor, haves and have-nots, reflecting everything from industry and ingenuity to our luck in the lottery of life.

The Theory of Public Property

This final point — that the free society is not a society of equal freedom, defined as power — is precisely the rub that gives rise to the new theory of property and a free society. On this view, recall, private property is seen not as the foundation of our individual rights but as an impediment to our freedom — more precisely, though not always stated this way, as an impediment to our "collective freedom." For the property rights of some stand

---

[20] For discussions of property held, and the causal processes by which property is taken, *see* Pilon (1979c and 1979d, chap. 3). For a substantial application of this background theory, *see* Pilon (1979b, pp. 1269-1365). I have tried in these works to integrate a number of partial accounts of the theory of rights, especially those by Gewirth, Nozick, and Epstein, making corrections where necessary and constructing new arguments where spaces remained in the overall theory.

in the way of others' doing what they wish with that property—whether renting it at will, or at a controlled price, or determining the numbers or kinds of structures that can be built upon it, or enjoying the view it affords, or whatever. Exponents of this position, in fact, find it quite comfortable working in the collective idiom, as when they ask, for example, what "we" should do about planning the future of "our" region, thereby disparaging, by implication at least, the property rights that might stand in the way of such central planning. In order to increase freedom or power for all, this theory calls for taking freedom or power from some. Thus the aim of the theory is to redistribute freedom, defined as power, by redistributing property. In its modest form, the theory calls for transferring only certain uses of property — from those who own the property to those who do not. In its more far-reaching forms or applications, the theory calls for transferring property itself. And in its egalitarian form, the theory advocates measures to bring about equal freedom, understood as equal power and hence as equal property, which might then be individually or, more likely, publicly held. It is important to recognize, however, that in principle there is no end to this process of redistribution, for not only does the world not stand still, especially in the face of fortuitous events, but power is every bit as much a function of the property we possess in ourselves and our talents as it is a function of the property we possess in the world.[21] Accordingly, to bring about a state of equal power, we have to take not only others' property, narrowly understood, but their persons and talents as well. We have to *use* others, in short, and all in the name of justice.

Now it should be noticed that as a distributional matter the new theory is perfectly consistent: The new rights it "discovers" supplant the traditional rights it extinguishes. Thus, it cannot be charged with yielding conflicting rights and hence with ending in contradiction — not at this level of analysis, at least. Where it goes wrong instead is both at the practical level and at the level of basic moral theory. I have just mentioned one of the practical difficulties, namely, that the redistribution the theory requires is an endless task, requiring an endless series of redistributors whose mission, in principle, will be to reach into every facet of our lives that would make for unequal power and hence for unequal freedom. Information costs alone suggest the practical impossibility of ever constructing such a Leviathan (Hayek 1945 and 1973, pp. 11-15), which is not to say that much damage will not be done in the attempt. Yet when redistribution proceeds not from person to person but from person to public, as is common in the case of land-use restrictions, here too the practical problems are immense — not simply the problems of ensuring and encouraging economic

---

[21] For an eighteenth-century statement of this point, *see* Hume (1948, p. 194).

efficiency, defined as a measure of so-called "social wealth," but the problems of use or rights of use. Individually held property is used at the will of the owner, by right of the owner. The analogy to collectively held property breaks down, however, as soon as we realize that our collective rights over the property are informed by a collective will that simply does not exist (Hospers 1971, pp. 81-94 and Anderson 1967, pp. 105-07). Whether the Public Broadcasting System should air opera or baseball and whether Yosemite National Park should admit recreational vehicles or backpackers only are not idle questions. And when we turn to the democratic device to try to settle how "we" should use "our" property, we face the notorious fact that that device rarely yields a majoritarian preference, an embarrassment of no small proportions for proponents of the new theory (Riker 1980 and Wolff 1970, pp. 58-67). Moreover, even if a majoritarian preference were produced, the democratic device suffers from the further embarrassment of being unable to recognize the rights of the minority over what is, after all, "their" property.

This leads us to a few of the more obvious moral difficulties of the new theory, which promises liberty or power for all but ends, as it must, by giving power to some, which it can do only by taking power from others. This point holds with respect to decision-making over collectivized property, as just noted; and it holds *a fortiori* with respect to the initial collectivization and redistribution of property. For in those initial steps, the individual whose property is taken is simply *used*. This is patent in the far-reaching versions of the new theory, which argue for the literal use of individuals and their efforts: sending students to the cane fields, for example, or doctors or lawyers to do *pro bono* work. But the same objection applies to the more modest versions, which call for using only the individual's property, ordinarily understood. For that property represents past efforts, which are used by that expropriation every bit as much as present efforts are used by the conscription of labor. In the name of "collective freedom," then, we end up with anything but a free society. And in all of this, let us be clear, the justificatory argument is positively primitive. At best we are told that "need" or "want" entails "is entitled to," concerning which one need simply note that the logical gap is yawning — certainly in contrast with the gap in the traditional theory between "freely acquires" and "is entitled to." In short, the new theory has located no real support at all in moral theory; on the contrary, it has been shown to be utterly immoral (*see, e.g.,* Nozick 1974, pp. 167-74).

The Taking Issue

Notwithstanding its many difficulties, both practical and moral, the modern theory of public property, especially as it involves public rights over nominally private property, has found its way into vast areas of our law. Not surprisingly, the practical and moral difficulties that plague the theory in the abstract do not disappear when the theory is put into practice in the world. In this part of my discussion, then, I will try to show how the traditional theory of ethics and law sorts out a few of the problems that are the concern of the new law, giving principled solutions to the conflicts raised by that law, all of which will lead ultimately to the taking issue.

Procedure and Substance

The place to begin is with a few of the complex but critical procedural matters and, in particular, with a brief look at how procedure and substance go together on the traditional view. As a substantive matter, recall, the classical theory of rights argues that generally related individuals have a right to pursue their ends, individually or collectively, provided only that in doing so they respect the equal rights of others — that is, that they not take what belongs to others, whether lives, liberties, or property. This means that as between strangers, we can use our property however we wish and the burden falls upon others to show that particular uses violate their rights by taking what is theirs. As a procedural matter, that is, there is no general obligation to obtain the permission of others before we act or even an obligation to seek that permission — e.g., to demonstrate the "feasibility" of our acts. For were there such obligations, this would amount to there being a preemptive right of those to whom the demonstration had to be made to *prevent* us from acting, a logically prior right to interfere with the performance of those acts by refusing permission, with or without cause, when in fact it is acts of *interference* that must be justified, not action per se. And acts of interference are justified only *with* cause — e.g., to prevent other acts of interference. (Acts of "interference" are also justified when the interference does not amount to a taking of wholly owned property, as in the view and competition examples I will develop shortly.) ·

This result, however, presupposes a world of perfect information, which of course is not the world in which we live. It is not always clear, for example, whether given acts interfere in such a way as to constitute a rights violation or, if they do, whether they do so with cause and hence do not amount to a rights violation. Accordingly, within certain limits we allow individuals to interfere with others as a *procedural* matter: We recognize procedural rights, that is, rights that allow particular individuals — along with the rest of us — to determine whether other individuals are, in fact, interfering with them as a *substantive* matter and, if so, whether those others have a substantive cause for thus interfering. In other words, ordinarily, general substantive rights are simply *exercised*; when they are *asserted* — if they are — it is usually *defensively* ("What right have you . . . ?"), by way of calling for the warrant for an actual or anticipated and, presumably, unjustified interference of another (Hart 1955, pp. 187-88). Only thus does the *dispute* between the parties get off the ground, a dispute that the procedural rules help to sort out. It is important to notice, however, that even though the acts complained of may indeed turn out to be unjustified acts of interference, the *initial* burden of proof rests with the party who asserts the procedural right to interfere with those acts, not with the party whose acts may be interfering as a matter of substance.[22] And that burden, on the classical theory, is one of showing that the acts complained of do, in fact, interfere as a matter of substance by taking something wholly owned by the complainant. Once that burden is discharged, however, once the complainant (or plaintiff) makes out a *prima facie* case by showing that the acts of the other do in fact interfere in the requisite way, he thereby demonstrates his substantive cause of action — he justifies *his* interference —and the burden shifts to the other party to show why *his* interference may be justified.[23]

In general, then, this is the way in which procedure and substance go together in the traditional view. Now I raise these issues because they are not always clearly articulated as they apply to the matters before us. In particular, procedural criticisms are sometimes advanced when substantive criticisms are really in order. In the case of restrictive zoning, for example, it is not so much that the burden of proof has shifted in this century from legislatures or municipalities to the individuals restricted, as some have suggested.[24] For with *any* legislation thought to be illegitimate, the initial burden to make out a *prima facie* case will rest with individual upon whom the legislation falls. As a procedural matter, it does not fall to the

---

[22] "Burden of proof" is used here in a less than strict juridical sense. In the ordinary juridical context, the plaintiff is asking the court to intercede on his behalf; thus the burden of proof is discharged to the court. In the text, however, I do not mean to move to the juridical context just yet; rather, I simply want to indicate at what point or how the initial *justificatory* burden arises, even if we were in, say, a state-of-nature context, where presumably that burden would be owing to the party whose interference, actual or anticipated, is being called into account. Here again, not only at the substantive but at the procedural level as well, our law ought ideally to reflect the moral order. We are very far, however, from having a well-worked-out theory of state-of-nature procedural justice.

[23] For a discussion of several of these issues, *see* Epstein (1973a).

[24] *See, e.g.,* Johnson (1977, p. 70):
"In effect, the reasonableness of the legislature's actions falls under the due process clause; anything the legislature does is reasonable unless someone can show the contrary. The burden of proof has shifted from the legislature to the individual."
See also Siegan, *Ibid* at 17:
The courts will presume that the ordiance adopted by the locality is a reasonable exercise of police power, and the burden is on the challenger to prove otherwise.
"In all kinds of litigation it is plain that where the burden of proof lies may be decisive of the outcome." (quoting *Speiser v. Randall*, 357 U.S. 513, 525 (1958)).
See also Siegan, *Ibid* at 56 n. 84.

legislature to justify its enactments before enacting them, any more than individuals have to justify their actions before performing them; rather, those enactments are justified, if at all, in the adversarial context, which arises only when someone challenges them.[25] Where the problem *has* arisen in this century, however, is at the *substantive* level. The burden of those who have sought to overturn restrictive zoning, for example, has been made onerous and often impossible to discharge not because courts presume exercises of the police power to be reasonable but because "reasonable," as a *substantive* matter, has been so broadly and variously interpreted.[26]

Perhaps these points could be sharpened as follows. It might be thought that courts should presume nothing when cases are brought before them. In truth, however, there is always a background presumption, namely, that the defendant — the legislature in this case — is "innocent," that it acted legitimately, that it acted within the law. (Assume for the present that the background law is clear.) It is the plaintiff's burden, then, to overcome that presumption, to show that in fact the legislature did not act within the law, just as he would have to do against any private defendant.[27] But this is a *substantive* matter, accomplished, if it is, in light of the facts and the law in the case. The plaintiff makes out his *prima facie* case, that is, not simply against some formal presumption of reasonableness or innocence but in light of the facts and against the background law that informs that presumption. If it happens, however, that the court has imbued its presumption with certain substantive colorations of its own making — as the opinions often bring out[28] — then the plaintiff's argument must appeal not simply to the facts and the law of the case but to the court's substantive constructions as well. In that event, the plaintiff may indeed have an onerous burden to overcome — depending upon the exact presumptions the court has made. That burden, however, will be a function of *substantive*, not procedural, considerations. In introducing substantive presumptions of its own, the court will have introduced new law, which it is now the burden of the plaintiff to overcome, if he can.

Ultimately, then, it is to the substantive issues that we will have to look

---

[25] This discussion assumes the straightforward case in which an individual plaintiff brings suit to invalidate a legislative enactment. In the more complex case, in which the municipality brings suit to enforce a legislative enactment against an individual defendant, the municipality is the plaintiff and must make out the *prima facie* case, which it does simply by showing failure to comply with the statute. To show that the statute is invalid, the defendant must then offer an affirmative defense, showing that the statute amounts to an unjustified interference, as indicated earlier.

[26] *See, e.g.,* notes 31-33, *infra.*

[27] *See* note 25, *supra.*

[28] *See* note 31-33, *infra.*

if we are to clarify the many uncertainties that have surrounded our property law in this century.[29] Now in the preceding remarks on the procedural issues, I have simply assumed that the background substantive law on these matters was clear. In fact, it seldom is. This is especially true in the case of the police power doctrine, which of course is nowhere to be found in our Constitution.[30] And indeed it is through this doctrine in particular, especially in the case of zoning or other forms of land use regulation, that the new law has most often been introduced. In presuming legislative enactments to be reasonable exercises of the police power, that is, rather than defer, by way of explicating this presumption, to the background law alone — and in particular to the classical theory of rights as this stands behind the Fifth, Ninth, and Fourteenth Amendments, which of course *are* in the Constitution — the courts have increasingly understood "reasonable" in a broad policy sense, which has enabled them to rewrite our law as a function of the pursuit of policy. Sometimes they have done this rather more by default, by way simply of a broad definition of the police power, which has enabled the legislature to do the more particular rewriting of the law.[31] On other occasions, however, the courts have themselves developed the particulars of policy by asking not the principled question—"What are the *rights* in this case?" — but the evaluative question — "What is a 'reasonable' balancing of interests, or a 'reasonable' trade-off of costs

[29] Once again, it is not in this century alone that these uncertainties have arisen. *See* note 5, *supra.*

[30] Indeed, the police power doctrine owes its construction to a series of nineteenth-century cases that introduced it in the course of working out a theory about the attributes of sovereignty, especially as this involved the power of eminent domain. *See, e.g.,* E. Freund (1904) and Corwin (1911).

[31] *See, e.g., Mid-way Cabinet Fixture Mfg. v. County of San Joaquin,* 257 Cal. App. 2d 181, 186, 65 Cal. Rptr. 37 (Sup. Ct. 1967):

> Theoretically, not superimposed upon but co-existing alongside the power of eminent domain is the police power, unwritten except in case law. It has been variously defined — never to the concordant satisfaction of all courts or legal scholars — and frequently it has been inconsistently applied by different courts; ... sometimes, to our disbelief, by the same court, the police power is described more readily than it can be defined. It has been said to be no more "than the powers of government inherent in every sovereignty ... the power to govern men and things within the limits of its dominion.

For an opinion that fairly invites the rewriting of law by the legislature, there is the dictum of Justice Douglas in *Berman v. Parker,* 348 U.S. 26, 33, 35, 36 (1954):

> We do not sit to determine whether a particular housing project is or is not desirable. The concept of public welfare is broad and inclusive .... It is within the power of the legislature to determine that the community should be beautiful as well as healthy, spacious as well as clean, well-balanced as well as carefully patrolled ....
> Once the question of the public purpose has been decided, the amount and character of land to be taken for the project and the need for a particular tract to complete the integrated plan rests in the discretion of the legislative branch.

and benefits?" — which they have decided by reference to their own utility schedules.[32] In the first instance, the courts seem to have construed police power questions as, in essence, questions of policy and hence as not for them to decide, thinking perhaps that the legislative enactment already reflects a utilitiarian caculus arrived at through political consensus.[33] In the second instance, they have construed police-power questions identically but have had no reservations about deciding the policy issues themselves. On one hand, the courts have abdicated their function of deciding cases on the law; on the other, they have done what they have no business doing. Thus does policy triumph over justice, whether pursued by the legislature or by the courts; for in either case the policy considerations through which the modern theory of property has worked its way into our law have led to the extinction of many of our traditional rights.

The Declaration of Independence and State-of-Nature Theory

In order to clarify the substantive issues before us, then, we are going to have to clarify the nature and scope of the police power, at least at a general level. More precisely, we will have to discover how the police power arises and functions within the context of the classical theory of rights. Within that context, clearly, police-power questions are *not* questions of policy, at least not fundamentally. In the end, that is, the issues these questions raise are not issues to be decided simply by asking what "we" should do in pursuit of certain "social goals" — as though society were a single actor seeking to maximize its welfare according to some cost-benefit analysis. Rather, the police power, if it is to be legitimate, must itself flow from and be justified by the theory of rights; and it must be exercised within the constraints set by that theory. For if governments are indeed instituted

---

[32] *See, e.g., Lionshead Lake v. Township of Wayne,* 10 N.J. 165, 173, 89 A.2d 693, 697 (1952): Has a municipality the right to impose minimum floor area requirements in the exercise of its zoning power? Much of the proof adduced by the defendant Township was devoted to showing that the mental and emotional health of its inhabitants depended upon the proper size of their homes. We may take notice without formal proof that there are minimums in housing below which one may not go without risk of impairing the health of those who dwell therein . . . . But quite apart from these considerations of public health which cannot be overlooked, minimum floor-area standards are justified on the ground that they promote the general welfare of the community . . . .
For egregious cases of the pursuit of policy through the courts, see the so-called "exclusionary zoning" cases: for example, *Southern Burlington County NAACP v. Township of Mt. Laurel,* 67 N.J. 151, 336 A.2d 713 (1975); *Berenson v. Town of New Castle,* 38 N.Y. 2d 102, 341 N.E. 2nd 236, 378 N.Y. S. 2d 672 (1975).

[33] *See, e.g., Miller v. Board of Public Works* 195 Cal. 477, 491, 234 P. 381, 385-86 (1925).

among men to secure their rights, then even that policy of securing rights, and the power that attends it, must conform to the constraints set by those rights.

But an inquiry into the police power is, of course, an inquiry into the foundations of sovereignty — hence, into the fundamental roots of political authority. In the American context, this brings us face to face with state-of-nature theory and, in particular, with the objections from anarchism.[34] So profound are those objections that no one to date has succeeded in meeting them at a basic level.[35] In the absence of primordial unanimous consent, that is, which of course has ever been a fiction, or short of a satisfactory invisible-hand theory of political legitimacy,[36] we are left with mere consequentialist arguments[37] and, indeed, with the conclusion that was held by many in the eighteenth century, namely, that far from being a fundamentally legitimate institution, the state *cannot* be justified in any ultimate sense, that it is a forced association, an expedient only, constituted because of the profound *practical* problems of individual self-rule in a state of nature — and constituted in violation of the rights of those who would choose not to enter into the association.[38] Running through the state at its very core, then, is a fundamental air of illegitimacy, creating a strong presumption against doing things through government. Because of its inherently coercive nature, the state is ill suited to be an institution through which to pursue good — contrary to the view so prominent in the twentieth century. Rather, it is an imperfect institution constructed to prevent evil, to

---

[34] *See supra* note 2 and the accompanying text. It should be mentioned that state-of-nature theory does not presuppose that anything like a state of nature ever existed in historical fact — although early America, setting aside the problem of the Indians, closely resembled this theoretical starting point. Rather, the state of nature is a theoretical posit, intended simply to help us get a clearer picture of the moral world generally and of the political world in particular.

[35] *See especially* Wolff (1970).

[36] This was Nozick's (1974, Part I) strategy in his heroic attempt to overcome the anarchist's objections. I have criticized that argument in Pilon (1979d, chap. 4).

[37] Consequentialist arguments, such as utilitarianism, appeal ultimately to subjective values rather than to principles of reason; thus they have located no real epistemological support.

[38] Notice that a common objection to this line of argument will not work, namely, that the individual who would choose not to enter into the political association is always at liberty to leave. (This is the "love it or leave it" objection, which leads to the argument for political obligation from "tacit consent" — "You stayed; therefore you consented to be ruled" — which can be found at least as early as Plato's *Crito*.) For the issues of political authority cannot be argued by analogy to the authority of a private association, which one may or may not join. Rather, the issue is whether one may rightly be put to the choice: "Join our association and live by its rules (for example, yield up your rights of self-enforcement) or leave where you are, for where you are is to come under our rule." By what right does the group put the individual to a choice between two of his entitlements — his right not to associate and his right to stay where he is?

which powers are to be given with the greatest of caution and mindful always that those powers are exercised with less than unanimous consent and, indeed, contrary to the wishes of many. For however elegant our social-contract theories of hypothetical consent may be, in the end they are second-best arguments, attempting to make palatable, or even attractive, what at bottom cannot be justified.[39]

Nevertheless, we do live with the state, and we do construct second-best theories aimed at justifying various of its powers. We construct theories referring to the good consequences that ensue from the state's having those powers, for example, which in truth are third-best theories and hence are hardly adequate at all, owing to the well-known problem of the incommensurability of interpersonal comparisons of utility.[40] And again, we construct justificatory theories referring to hypothetical consent, to the rights that we *would* choose to yield up to the state to be exercised by it — if we were "rational" or "prudent" individuals. A fundamental point in the more thoughtful versions of the argument from hypothetical consent, then, is simply this, that we cannot yield up to the state rights that we do not first *have* to yield up. Thus, in order for a particular power of the state even to be a *candidate* for legitimacy, it is necessary that that power have been held first as a right by individuals in the state of nature such that they had the rights to yield up at all, quite apart from whether they ever did. In this fundamental and limiting way, then, does moral theory serve as the background for political and legal theory.[41]

Eminent Domain

Nowhere are these several points more sharply illustrated, perhaps, than in the case of eminent domain, the "despotic power" as it was often called in the eighteenth and nineteenth centuries. For in exercising this power against an unwilling individual, the state simply *takes* private property for public use. The association is forced and blatant, and no amount of compensation to the victim will alter that fact when he is unwilling to part with his justly held property. As a matter of fundamental moral theory, then, there is no justifying this power. It cannot be justified in particular applications for the reasons just cited. And it cannot be justified in general for the reasons mentioned earlier: First, no primordial unanimous consent to

---

[39] The most elegant attempt of this kind to come forth recently is from John Rawls (1971).

[40] *See also* note 37, *supra*.

[41] *See* Nozick (1974, p.6): "Moral philosophy sets the background for, and boundaries of, political philosophy. What persons may and may not do to one another limits what they may do through the apparatus of the state, or do to establish such an apparatus."

be ruled under this power can be located — much less a consent that binds heirs; and second, because there is no *private* right of eminent domain, there could hardly be a *public* right either, for, again, individuals cannot give to the state rights they do not first have to give.[42] What justification the power of eminent domain enjoys, then, must be taken from considerations of necessity, which are compelling only in exceptional cases and never from considerations of right. In those cases, moral theory requires, as a matter of simple justice, that whatever in-roads the state must make on private rights must be accompanied by just compensation, compensation that in truth should reflect not only the physical but the moral facts of the matter as well. Given these moral facts about the power of eminent domain, then, there exists a strong presumption *against* its use and, once the burden has shifted to the state, a heavy burden of proof before it is used.

The Police Power

When we turn to the police power, however, the issues are slightly different. Here too, of course, there is no unanimous consent to which to point to justify the exercise of this power by the state. Nevertheless, police power *can* be justified as a *private* right; in the state of nature, that is, individuals *do* have rights of self-enforcement; hence, in theory, at least, these rights might have been yielded up to the state to be exercised *by* the state on behalf of its members. (Thus do governments derive their just powers from the consent of the governed.) Now again, no such unanimous consent can be located as a matter of historical fact; at best, if we are in a republican democracy, we can point to imperfect consent given through surrogates. Nevertheless, in the case of the police power, unlike that of eminent domain, there *is* a legitimate power to yield up, quite apart from whether it was ever in fact yielded. Accordingly, save for the problem that we did not all ask the *state* to exercise the police power for us, the power is otherwise legitimate.

This much, of course, addresses the theoretical *foundations* of the police power. But it also provides an insight into its legitimate *scope* and hence into the taking issue itself. For if the police power has its origins in the enforcement rights of the individual, then that power, if it is to be exercised legitimately, can be no more broad than those original rights. Setting aside the consent problem, that is, the state can do no more *by right* than any individual could rightly do in a state of nature. For again, where would the state get such rights if not from the individuals who constitute it? Indeed, precisely here, in its legitimate foundations, are the legitimate boundaries of the police power.

---

[42] Notice that primordial unanimous consent *would* entitle the state to take private property for public purposes (with or without compensation), at least if we set aside the problem of heirs. That power of the state would be legitimate, but it would *not* be the power of eminent domain, for the prior consent would make the whole arrangement contractual.

Takings, Legitimacy, and Compensation

In general, then, and arguing by analogy from the case of eminent domain, the basic taking question — "When is the state required to compensate those it regulates?"[43] — can be answered as follows. First, when the activity prohibited is a rights violating activity, no compensation is required, for the activity is illegitimate to begin with. Second, when the activity is legitimate, the state has no right to prohibit it. But, third, when the state does prohibit such an activity anyway, in order to achieve some "public good," then it is required to compensate those from whom the rightful activity was taken, every bit as much as in eminent domain. And in all of this, the same presumptions and burdens of proof should obtain as apply in eminent domain.

Thus, in the end, the question whether prohibitory regulations are "takings" is really quite irrelevant; for *all* prohibitions are takings — of activities otherwise possible and hence otherwise "held" by those who hold the material conditions that make them possible.[44] The landowner who is prohibited from building on his land, for example, has had that use taken from him. But likewise, the gun owner has certain uses taken from him by the criminal code that prohibits those criminal uses. In the first case, compensation is owing, for the state has no right to take justly held property, including justly held or legitimate activities. In the second case, however, no compensation is owing, for the criminal use of the gun is illegitimate to begin with and hence can rightly be prohibited or taken by an exercise of the police power.

When we apply these findings to various of the regulations that constitute our current property law, we discover that many of those restrictions are illegitimate as a matter of right and hence should be abolished.[45] Failing that, those restricted should at least be compensated for the uses prohibited to them and hence taken from them. For if some "public good" is indeed achieved by those restrictions — if a scenic view, for example, is a public good — then let the public pay for that good rather than take it from some

---

[43] *See* note 44, *infra.*

[44] I am arguing, therefore, that the usual "taking question" ("When does a regulation go so far as to amount to a taking and hence require compensation?") is fundamentally misstated. For if *all* prohibitions are takings, then the real question is how to distinguish a legitimate from an illegitimate taking—which is *not* a matter of degree, of the "extent" of the regulation, but a matter of kind. And *this*, in turn, will answer the question about when compensation is owing.

[45] I speak here of "restrictions," although many regulations set requirements or affirmative duties. In that case, of course, the burden may be even more onerous, for the individual is then required to contribute to the "public good" not simply with his omissions but with his substance as well, when the omission to do so might otherwise be perfectly legitimate. I have discussed the issue of negative and positive duties at some length in Pilon (1979d, chap. 1).

individual member of the public.[46] Similarly, except when issues of endangerment arise,[47] regulations of lot sizes, set-back requirements, or restrictions on types of construction are all illegitimate. For the prohibited uses, were they permitted, would take nothing that belongs to others and hence would violate no rights. We have no rights to preserve particular neighborhood styles, for example, not unless we create those rights through private covenants. Likewise with rent controls or antidiscrimination measures: private individuals have a perfect right to offer their properties for sale or rent to whomever they choose at whatever prices they wish. For neither discrimination, on whatever grounds, nor offers, of whatever kind, can be shown to take what belongs free and clear to others; opportunities that depend upon the holdings of others, though perhaps measurable as a matter of *costs*, are not themselves freely held and hence are not objects of *rights*.[48] Again, not even regulations that preserve private views can be justified if those regulations prohibit activities otherwise legitimate. For a view does not "belong" to someone unless he owns all the conditions of the view; views that run over the property of others, even lovely ones, are not "owned" but are merely "enjoyed" at the pleasure of those others, who have a perfect right to block them by exercising any of their own freely held uses. In general, whether it is a view, a certain neighborhood style, or whatever, these and other such goods have to be wholly owned in order to be secured as a matter of right. Asking the government to step in to fully secure these goods is nothing less than acquiring them by taking what rightly belongs to others. If the individual has no right to do this on his own, then he has no right to do it through the government.

Sources of Confusion

If the broad lines of the taking issue are this straightforward, why has so much confusion surrounded it? There are at least two reasons, I believe. First, the language of the Fifth Amendment, around which the discussion revolves, is less than complete, like so much else in the Constitution. In particular, it seems to require either a narrow interpretation, in which property taken is limited to physical property proper, or the broad interpretation of Locke and others, in which property includes not only physical

---

[46] This is, of course, the welfare state idea in reverse. Rather than being transferred from the many to the few, wealth is flowing from the few to the many. The public, in short, is *using* those individuals from whom it takes to enrich itself, as brought out in the earlier discussion.

[47] The normative issues of endangerment, like those of nuesance, are extremely complex. For the broad outlines of the endangerment issue, *see* Pilon (1979b, pp. 1333-35).

[48] For a fuller discussion of the discrimination issues, *see* Pilon (1979b, pp. 1327-31); on opportunities, *see* Pilon (1979b, pp. 1277-84).

property but liberties or uses of property as well. On the narrow interpretation, property could be rendered all but useless by regulation and yet no compensation would be owing, the absurd result advocated by some today (Reilly 1973; Bosselman, Callies, and Banta 1973). But on the broad interpretation, at least if we limit ourselves to the Fifth Amendment, the state would have to compensate murderers, muggers, and others for any restrictions it imposed upon "their" activities, which is equally absurd. Yet those are the polar positions we get when we focus exclusively upon the text of the takings clause. This dilemma will be resolved, let me suggest, neither by "balancing" values or costs in particular cases, whatever that may ultimately mean,[49] nor by any other form of economic analysis, but only by going behind the Constitution to the moral theory that informs it.

A second reason for the confusion surrounding these general matters, I believe, is that the criteria for required compensation are often uncertain in *specific* cases, and that in turn vitiates our *general* view of the matter. Nowhere is this more clear, I submit, than in the economic treatments of the subject, especially as they relate to so-called externalities. Methodologically reluctant to turn to normative criteria, and rarely distinguishing deontological from evaluative criteria, or rights from values, the economist turns instead to considerations of efficiency, as in the well-known Coasean account (*see,* Coase 1960), which is translated as *social wealth maximization* on the Posnerian view.[50] Now as a matter of pure economics, of course, the class of externalities need not be limited to the standard nuisances (*see, e.g.,* Moore 1969, p. 536; and Johnson 1977, pp. 74-83). Why not restrict First Amendment activities, for example, if they offend and hence are costly to others? And, indeed, if all is reduced to costs and benefits alone — and hence, let us be clear, to subjective value — the answer appears to be: Indeed, why *not* restrict First Amendment activities when they offend?

The traditional theory of rights explains "why not," I submit, and does the further job as well of fleshing out the issues in even the troublesome nuisance cases. More fully, the generative, causal, consistency, and property theories that constitute the theory of rights all serve to sort the issues out in a morally principled way, which a theory of value — including a theory of economic value — has as yet been unable to do. None of these constitutive theories can be developed here, of course, but I do want to give a glimpse, at least, of the kind of thing I have in mind. The basic idea is this: The generative theory of action yields rights claims and shows in the process that ethics is fundamentally causal, concerned with which

---

[49] Once again we are up against the incommensurability of interpersonal comparisons of utility.

[50] *See especially* Posner (1979). I have criticized these views in Pilon (1979a, p. 1335-38).

actions do what to whom and, in particular, with which actions take what
from whom, all of which is fleshed out as a descriptive account of property
rights and all of which, if it is to conform to canons of reason, must yield
a consistent set of rights. Thus, in general, do each of the constitutive
theories go together. Again, it is takings of wholly owned property that constitute rights violations. Thus, the theory must yield an account both of
wholly owned property and of wholly owned property rights, which it does
at a generic level, from which more specifically described rights are derived
deductively.

   These generic rights are rights to be left alone, or passive rights of quiet
enjoyment; rights of action, or active rights, provided again that others are
left alone; and rights of association or contract. These overarching rights
and their specifications exhaustively describe the worlds of general and
special relationships; thus, they inform the traditional law of torts as well
as the laws of contracts and associations, under the first of which our First
Amendment liberties, for example, can be shown to be rights and hence
to be immune from being forcibly taken. And the theory can handle what
are often thought to be problematic cases as well, such as view or competition cases; in this last connection, for example, even though entering
into competition with someone may impose costs on him, it is not a taking
of his trade because his trade is not really *his* but is enjoyed by him simply
because third parties contribute with *their* trade, which they have a perfect
right to give to others. Thus, there is a perfect right to enter into competition — costs or harms to others notwithstanding.

   In the overwhelming number of cases, then, the theory of rights yields
answers to the question — "Why not treat *all* activities as candidates for
prohibitory regulation and hence for taking?" — which is the question that
arises when we focus upon costs and benefits or externalities alone. We
cannot because many of those activities are performed by *right* — that is,
they take nothing that is wholly owned by others. Thus, by right they cannot be forcibly taken, even with compensation.

The Emergence of Public Law

   But while the theory of rights handles the overwhelming number of cases,
it comes to its principled end in the difficult areas of nuisance, endangerment, remedies, and enforcement generally. Nevertheless, even in these
domains the theory yields *broad* principles, which I will sketch now in the
nuisance area in order to try to get a little clearer about the two questions:
"When is a nuisance a right violation?" and, hence, "When can it be prohibited without compensation?" And let us have in mind such typical
nuisances as noise, smoke, odors, vibrations, and so on. Now, in general,
recall, the plaintiff has a burden to show that the defendant's activity takes
a use of the plaintiff that does not itself take in turn. This means, then,

that passive uses enjoy a privileged place in the theory of rights, both for causal reasons and for reasons of consistency. The causal reasons are straightforward enough: Passive or quiet uses, the most quiet of which is mere ownership, crowd out neither other passive uses nor active uses.[51] Because passive uses do not crowd out, adjacent property owners can exercise their passive rights at the same time and in the same respect, as a result of which the canons of consistency are satisfied.

Now it may be objected that passive uses do indeed crowd out active uses by preventing them through successful pleas for injunctive relief. We come then to Coase's (1960, p. 2) reciprocal causation thesis. "The traditional approach," he argues,

> has tended to obscure the nature of the choice that has to be made. In the typical nuisance case, the question is commonly thought of as one in which A inflicts harm on B and what has to be decided is; how should we restrain A? But this is wrong. We are dealing with a problem of a reciprocal nature. To avoid the harm to B would inflict harm on A. The real question that has to be decided is: should A be allowed to harm B or should B be allowed to harm A? The problem is to avoid the more serious harm.

In other words, if B is to enjoy his passive "activity," let us say in order not to beg the question, A cannot enjoy his *active* activity, which is thus prevented or crowded out by B's passive activity.

I would suggest, along with several other non-economists who have looked at this passage (e.g., Epstein 1973b, pp. 164-66), that Coase has simply got it wrong here, that his reduction of matters to harms and costs has understandably obfuscated the issues, and that a more fine-grained approach should help to clarify them. Now prior to any determination of rights in this case, A's active activity does *in fact* crowd out B's passive activity; it is not B who is harming A, that is, for as a matter of empirical fact, A can go right on enjoying his active activity whereas B, if A does, can no longer enjoy the passive activity that A's active activity has crowded out. To this point, then, the causation — the *taking* — has gone in only one direction. Now in *reaction* to this taking, B gets an injunction, and *then* the causation goes in the other direction. But this is simply to cancel or reverse the initial taking. Thus, it is *not* the passive activity but the *injunction* that does the taking of the active activity. The injunction *does* constitute a taking, then. But as the theory of rights shows, the injunction is

---

[51] My use of "passive" and "active" here is not meant to be precise. By definition, a passive use does not crowd out the uses that others make of their property—that is, as a matter of *fact*, others can use their property however they wish and the passive use will not interfere. Active uses, however, except when conducted in sufficient isolation, may crowd out passive uses or even other active uses, depending upon any number of factual conditions, including the sensitivity of the individuals involved. But in general, "passive" and "active" are meant to denote the two halves of a continuum, not two distinct classes.

legitimate because it takes or prevents an activity that *itself* takes an activity that does not *in turn* take anything. With this, we have the causal analysis that both conforms to the facts and, when joined with the generative argument, yields a consistent set of rights.

Those rights, however, are passive rights, which brings us at last to the practical question, namely: "Can we live with these results?" The purely principled world, that is, is one in which the exercise of passive rights can be only as active as will not crowd out others in their enjoyment of their passive rights. To be sure, the theory of rights permits the exercise of active rights, but only if that exercise does not interfere with others. This result can be achieved either by conducting the activity in sufficient isolation or insulation from others[52] or by purchasing the consent of those otherwise interfered with, which the theory of course allows. But absent those conditions, the principled world is likely to be a very quiet place — and a very peaceful place too.

Nevertheless, for whatever reasons, these results have been found difficult to live with.[53] Thus, as a practical matter, the common law made certain inroads on the principled picture in the domain of nuisance. Most generally, it devised an "ordinary man" standard of nuisance, which precluded the supersensitive plaintiff from getting relief and hence from shutting his neighborhood down (Gregory, Kalven, and Epstein 1977, pp. 528-32). Similarly, it devised locality rules, which sought to make nuisance lines context specific (Gregory, Kalven, and Epstein, pp. 532-36). As a general matter, then, it moved in the direction of *public* lines that defined when an activity was sufficiently active to take the peace and quiet of others such that its abatement would not have to be purchased but could be obtained by right. These were uneasy solutions, however, because they *did* constitute inroads upon rights of quiet enjoyment. Nevertheless, they remained second-best *principled* solutions in that they *did* not have to appeal to the relative values or costs in particular cases, much less to aggregate concepts like "social value" or "social wealth," but instead, at their best, could be understood simply as definitions of lines describing the point beyond which no man

---

[52] For a judicial statement of this point, relating not to private but to public uses (the principles are the same in either case), *see Thornberg v. Port of Portland*, 235 Or. 178, 194, 376 P. 2d 100, 107 (1962):

> In effect, the inquiry should have been whether the government had undertaken a course of conduct on its own land which, in simple fairness to its neighbors, required it to obtain more land so that the substantial burdens of the activity would fall upon public land, rather than upon that of involuntary contributors who happen to lie in the path of progress.

See also Kretzmer (1978).

[53] For one explanation for why the law made inroads on the principled position, *see* Horwitz (1977, pp. 74-78).

need bear the taking costs of another man's activities, whatever the broader costs to that other of his forbearance (see, Pilon 1979b, pp. 1335-39).

But these common-law results were always haphazard and never constituted reliable predictors for future activity except in cases of gross invasion by nuisance. With the emergence of a public environmental law, however, many of these uncertainties and unpredictabilities are being addressed, sometimes slowly and uncertainly, sometimes with a very heavy hand. Nevertheless, there *is* a legitimate place for at least some environmental law; in addition to addressing large-number problems, as in automobile pollution, its legitimate function is one of drawing the public lines that give us notice as to the point at which the exercise of one man's property *uses* starts to take another man's property *rights*.[54]

Conclusion

There is a great deal more to be said on the many issues covered in this article than I have been able to say here. In particular, the details of causation and of how this combines with a descriptive account of passive and active uses need to be worked out much more fully. Nevertheless, I believe I have sketched at least the outline of a normative resolution of the taking issue, one that in the end can be justified — and can be lived with as well.

In sum, I have tried to show here that property rights are at the very heart of a free society, serving to define the normative relationships among its members and to enable those individuals to pursue their various ends free from the interference of others. I argued also that many of the regulations of property we currently suffer — such as restrictive zoning, or rent controls, or various prohibitions in order to secure "public goods" — are illegitimate as a matter not simply of efficiency but of right. Finally, I have tried to indicate how the traditional theory of rights, which is the theory of property rights, serves to shed light on the difficult taking issue, ordering it in a principled way such that the rights that are the foundation of the free society are protected.

[54] For a fuller discussion of several of these issues, *see* Epstein (1979) and Kmiec (1981).

References

Anderson, Martin. "Cost-Benefit Analysis for Government Decisions: Discussion". *American Economic Review* Proceedings 57 (1967): 101-08.

Bailyn, Bernard. *The Ideological Origins of the American Revolution.* Cambridge: Harvard University Press, 1967.

Becker, Lawrence. *On Justifying Moral Judgments.* New York: Humanities Press, 1973.

Becker, Carl. *The Declaration of Independence.* New York: Peter Smith, 1922.

Berlin, Isaiah. "Two Concepts of Liberty". In *Four Essays on Liberty.* London: Oxford University Press (1969): 118-72.

Bosselman, Fred, Callies, David, and Banta, John. *The Taking Issue.* Washington: U.S. Government Printing Office, 1973.

Bowie, Norman. *Towards a New Theory of Distributive Justice.* Amherst: University of Massachusetts Press, 1971.

Coase, R. H. "The Problem of Social Cost." *Journal of Law and Economics* 3 (October 1960): 1-44.

Corwin, Edward S. "The Doctrine of Due Process of Law before the Civil War," *Harvard Law Review* 24 (1911): 366-85.

Corwin, Edward S. *The "Higher Law" Background of American Constitutional Law.* Ithaca, N.Y.: Great Seal Books, 1955.

Dietze, Gottfried. *In Defense of Property.* New York: Henry Regnery Co., 1963.

Donagan, Alan. *The Theory of Morality.* Chicago: University of Chicago Press, 1977.

Epstein, Richard A. "Pleadings and Presumptions." *University of Chicago Law Review* 40 (1973a): 556-82.

Epstein, Richard A. "A Theory of Strict Liability." *Journal of Legal Studies* 2 (1973b): 151-204.

Epstein, Richard A. "Defenses and Subsequent Pleas in a System of Strict Liability." *Journal of Legal Studies* 3 (1974): 165-215.

Epstein, Richard A. "Intentional Harms." *Journal of Legal Studies* 4 (1975): 391-441.

Epstein, Richard A. "Nuisance Law: Corrective Justice and Its Utilitarian Constraints." *Journal of Legal Studies* 8 (1979): 49-102.

Fellman, David. "Property in Colonial Political Theory." *Temple University Law Quarterly* 16 (1942): 388-406.

Freund, Ernst. *The Police Power: Public Policy and Constitutional Rights.* Chicago: Callaghan and Co., 1904.

Gewirth, Alan. "The 'Is-Ought' Problem Resolved." *American Philosophical Association Proceedings and Addresses* 47 (1974): 34-61.

Gewirth, Alan. *Reason and Morality.* Chicago: University of Chicago Press, 1978.

Gregory, Charles, Kalven, G. Harry, and Epstein, Richard. *Cases and Materials on Torts.* 3rd ed. Boston: Little, Brown and Co., 1977.

Hart, H. L. A. "Are There Any Natural Rights?" *Philosophical Review* 64 (1955): 175-86.

Hayek, F. A. "The Use of Knowledge in Society." *American Economic Review* 35 (September, 1945): 519-30.

Hayak, F.A. *Law, Legislation, and Liberty.* Vol. I London: Routledge and Kegan Paul, 1973.

Horwitz, Morton. *The Transformation of American Law, 1780-1860* Cambridge: Harvard University Press, 1977.

Hospers, John. *Libertarianism.* Los Angeles: Nash Publishing, 1971.

Hume, David. *Treatise of Human Nature.* Reprint ed. Oxford: Clarendon Press, 1888.

Hume, David. *Enquiry Concerning the Principles of Morals,* edited by H. Aiken. La Salle, Ill.: Open Court Publishing, 1953.

Johnson, M. Bruce. "Planning Without Prices: A Discussion of Land Use Regulation Without Compensation." In *Planning Without Prices,* edited by Bernard Siegan. Lexington, MA: Lexington Books, 1977.

Johnson, M. Bruce, ed. *Resolving the Housing Crisis: Government Policy, Decontrol, and the Public Interest.* Cambridge, MA: Ballinger, 1982.

Kant, Immanuel. *Groundwork of the Metaphysic of Morals,* translated by H. J. Paton. New York: Barnes and Noble, 1950.

Kmiec, Douglas W. "Deregulating Land Use: An Alternative Free Enterprise Development System: *University of Pennsylvania Law Review* 130 (1981): 28-130.

Kretzmer, David. "Judicial Conservatism v. Economic Liberalism: Anatomy of a Nuisance Case." *Israel Law Review* 13 (1978): 298-325.

Kuhn, Thomas. *The Structure of Scientific Revolutions,* 2nd ed. Chicago: University of Chicago Press, 1970.

Locke, John. "The Second Treatise of Government." In Locke's *Two Treatises of Government,* revised ed. Edited by Peter Laslett. Cambridge: Cambridge University Press, 1963.

MacCallum, Gerald C. "Negative and Postive Freedom." *Philosophical Review* 76 (1967): 312-34.

Marx, Karl. "Economic and Philosophical Manuscripts." In *Karl Marx: Selected Writings.* Edited by David McLellan. London: Oxford University Press, 1977.

Moore, Thomas G. "An Economic Analysis of the Concept of Freedom." *Journal of Political Economy* 77 (1969): 532-44.

Nielsen, Kai. "On Justifiying Revolution." *Philosophy and Phenomenological Research* (1977): 516-532.

Nozick, Robert. *Anarchy, State, and Utopia.* New York: Basic Books, 1974.

Pilon, Roger. "Criminal Remedies: Restitution, Punishment, or Both?" *Ethics* 88 (1978): 348-57.

Pilon, Roger. "On Moral and Legal Justification." *Southwestern University Law Review* 11 (1979a): 1327-44.

Pilon, Roger. "Corporations and Rights: On Treating Corporate People Justly." *Georgia Law Review* 13 (1979b): 1245-1370.

Pilon, Roger. "Ordering Rights Consistently: Or What We Do and Do Not Have Rights To." *Georgia Law Review* 13 (1979c): 1171-96.

Pilon, Roger. "A Theory of Rights: Toward Limited Government." Ph.D. dissertation, University of Chicago, 1979d.

Posner, Richard. "Utilitarianism, Economics, and Legal Theory."*Journal of Legal Studies* 8 (1979): 103-40.

Rawls, John. *A Theory of Justice.* New York: Oxford University Press, 1971.

Reilly, William K., ed. *The Use of Land: A Citizen's Policy Guide to Urban Growth.* New York: Crowell, 1973.

Riker, William. "Implications From the Disequilibrium of Majority Rule for the Study of Institutions." *American Political Science Review* 74 (1980): 432-46.

Ross, Kelly. "Losing Ground in Oregon." *Reason* (April 1983): 40-44.

Sax, Joseph L. "Takings, Private Property and Public Rights." *Yale Law Journal* 81 (December 1971): 149-86.

Siegan, Bernard. *Economic Liberties and the Constitution.* Chicago: University of Chicago Press, 1980.

Siegan, Bernard, ed. *Planning Without Prices.* Lexington, MA: Lexington Books, 1977.

Singer, Marcus G. *Generalization in Ethics.* New York: Knopf, 1961.

Stoebuck, William B. "A General Theory of Eminent Domain." *Washington Law Review* 47 (August 1972): 553-608.

Supreme Court, 1979 Term. "Takings Without Just Compensation." *Harvard Law Review* 94 (November 1980): 205-14.

Veatch, Henry B. "Natural Law: Dead or Alive?" *Literature of Liberty* 1(4) (1978): 7-31.

Weaver, Richard. *Ideas Have Consequences.* Chicago: University of Chicago Press, 1948.

Wolff, Robert P. *In Defense of Anarchism.* New York: Harper and Row, 1970.

9

TAXATION, REGULATION, AND CONFISCATION
Richard A. Epstein

I. General Theory

The recent studies on regulation have underscored an emerging truth in
the study of law and economics. The traditional modes of classification and
analysis no longer suffice to organize the study of legal institutions and legal
rules. In a former day it was quite fashionable to place public and private
law into rigid, separate compartments, each governed by its own set of rules.
Within the area of private law, it was possible to draw sharp and clear lines
between contract, tort, property and restitution. Within public law, it was
fashionable to study the various techniques of social control in isolation
from one another. Taxation could be placed in one box, regulation of wages
and prices in another, and licensure of all forms of activities in still a third.
These traditional typologies do identify the relevant techniques, but they
must not be allowed to conceal the larger structure of government action.
The key point is a simple one: all of the various means of social control,
public and private, can be applied, either alone or in combination, to any
designated set of activities. Each remedy is, or may be, a close substitute
for each of the others, such that the strength and effectiveness of the one
must be evaluated in its relationship to all the others. In one sense this
observation serves as a charter of emancipation for the policy analyst, as
it makes explicit the rich array of tools available to encourage or discourage,
mandate or prohibit, various forms of social activity, all without apparent
limitation. A set of original endowments may be turned at will to maximize
some defined set of outputs in a world in which policy is king.

© *Copyright* 1982, Richard A. Epstein.

Richard Epstein is the James Parker Hall Professor of Law at the University of Chicago. This
article presents a condensed version of the major arguments Professor Epstein articulated in
his widely acclaimed *Takings: Private Property and the Power of Eminent Domain*. Cambridge:
Harvard University Press, 1985. The article initially appeared in the *Osgoode Hall Law Journal*
20 (1982): 433-43.

Into this picture of uncontested hegemony, I should like to inject a note of doubt. It must be asked by what warrant, by what title, does the public policy analyst proceed on the implicit assumption that all entitlements lie within the public domain? At the very least the question deserves some sort of an answer because of the way in which the study of law and economics —even that of a conservative stripe—cuts against the ideals of limited government, individual liberty and private property, which, especially in the American context, have deep and powerful roots of their own. At the root of this conception is the persistent fear of abuse of power— that persons, clothed in official garments, will convert a limited delegated authority into an absolute source of power over others.[1] This fear is so pervasive that it colors our view of social institutions. Government is viewed not as an inherent kind of good, but as a necessary evil required to ward off the greater evils of aggression and despoliation by self-interested individuals. The task of constitutional theory, then, is to organize political institutions in ways to prevent the state from becoming an organized menace greater than the individual misdeeds that it is designed to control.

To achieve this ideal of limited government, the powers of government can be parcelled out in different layers, as in a federal system. Within each layer of government, the principle of the separation of powers can place the premium on caution instead of on speed. Complicated voting rules and procedures can limit further the ability of a transient majority to impose its will upon the population as a whole. The effective constraints upon the power of government, however, need not be only structural and procedural. There is still the substantive question: what ends should government serve? Here it does seem clear, to one not nourished upon the British tradition of parliamentary supremacy,[2] that some explicit individual safeguards against government and the will of the majority should be entrenched in a bill of rights. At the same time it seems equally clear that the individual rights so entrenched should not be so vast and extensive as to paralyze all government action.

How then do taxation and regulation fit into this skeptical view of government powers? Here we can start with the received wisdom that each is a close substitute for the other, and note that the differences between them all go to matters of detail and technique, rather than to basic principle. Now push that equivalence one step further. Regulation and taxation both may be used as instruments of confiscation, because both are the equivalent of the (partial) taking of private property. To understnad this, it is necessary only to accept two propositions. The first is that the loss of any right in

---

[1] See, for example, Madison, *The Federalist* No. 10 (p. 54).

[2] See generally, Dicey (1965; pp. 39-86).

property is like a loss of property itself. To deny that proposition is to say that the state can take sticks in the bundle of rights one by one without compensation, when compensation would be required if the taking of the entire bundle were compressed into a single step.[3] Here the central point remains obvious. It is insufficient to control the obvious abuses of outright confiscation if its close substitutes are left unregulated and uncontrolled. There is no sense to a system which allows the government, under the guise of regulation, to take interests in real estate—for example covenants or easements—worth ninety percent of the land itself without paying a dime, when the government is required to pay full value for the land, if taken outright. In effect, the distinction between complete and partial losses sets up a sharp discontinuity in the costs to government of the different modes of acquiring interests in real property. Under the banner of regulation it can acquire, without cost to itself, a limited interest in property worth ninety percent of the fee. In the alternative it can acquire the full fee for its market value. As it sees matters, therefore, the full cost of the property is embedded in the acquisition of its last tenth. It is no wonder then that the government will not purchase the fee when it can take the limited interest.

The second proposition is that the taking from many individuals at the same time does not insulate the state from the charge of a taking any more than it does a private individual. Thus murder is a wrong and so too is genocide. The thief is not purged because he has taken from all the members of a group instead of only one, and the unfortunate private defendant who runs down a busload of children cannot escape his liability because he has damaged many persons instead of one. The progression from the single to the many on the question of what constitutes a taking of property—in whole or in part—is itself a matter of simple summation. There is no subtle interaction of the parts which allow takings from many to be viewed as something else solely because they are directed to a large number of individuals at any given point in time. Efforts have been made to avoid that conclusion, and thereby to restrict the reach of the eminent domain clause in American constitutional litigation. It has been said for example that the power of eminent domain is one thing, and the power of taxation is quite another,[4] and so too the police power has been said to be one thing, the eminent domain power quite another.[5] These rigid schemes of classification are designed to blunt the compensation requirement of the eminent domain

---

[3] A taking by government in the exercise of its power of eminent domain must be accompanied by just compensation: U.S. Const., amend. V. See infra note 9 and accompanying text.

[4] See, for example, Brushaber v. Union Pacific R.R. Co., 240 U.S.1, 60 L.Ed. 493, 36 S.Ct. 236 (1915).

[5] Megler v. Kansas, 123 U.S. 623, 31 L.Ed. 205, 8 S.Ct. 273 (1887).

principle and historically, with taxation and regulation, they have largely succeeded to that end. On intellectual grounds, however, the strategy simply will not work. An eminent domain provision in any scheme of constitutional government is not a grant of additional power to government. Instead it places a limitation upon the powers of government that are already in place, including both general powers of taxation and regulation. In both cases, that limitation upon government will be idle if by persuasive redefinition the state can defeat the obligation to compensate that it otherwise should incur. Taxes and regulation are forms of taking, to be examined under principles applicable to all other takings.

To say this much, however, is not to insist upon a strict equivalence between taxation, regulation and confiscation.[6] Indeed, to equate taxation and regulation with theft is to condemn all government at the outset, as there is none that could function without resort to these powers. How can we avoid this extreme result, steer a middle course, and identify those forms of taxation and regulation that should survive, and those that should be condemned?

To approach this question it is best to consider the simplest form of the taking of property, say the taking of land for use as a post office, and ask what differentiates it from the illicit confiscation of that same land. That some difference exists seems clear enough; we all understand that killing and murder, although related are very different affairs. While killing may be justified, for example, in self-defense, calling a particular killing murder means that the possibility of justification in the particular case has been excluded. So too with the analogous relationship between the taking of property and the theft of property; the first admits the possibility of justification that the second precludes. With this much said, the relationship between taking and confiscation can be captured by the following proposition: the taking of private property is *prima facie* confiscation.[7] So too its close substitutes, the partial takings by way of regulation and taxation. But to treat the taking as only a *prima facie* wrong is to omit the possibility of justification.

With government it seems proper to recognize two separate justifications, one of which it shares with the private individual who wishes to acquit himself of the charge of theft, and one of which is unique to its special status as the monopolist of force within the jurisdiction. The first of these

---

[6] The term confiscation is not used in the sense that is appropriate when, for example, government officials confiscate stolen property or smuggled goods. Those cases are best understood as instances in which the taking, although called confiscation, is justified by the police power given the prior wrong of the individual against whom the power is directed. That form of justification is, however, far removed from the concerns here.

[7] On the use of presumptions, see Epstein (1973).

generally goes in public law discussions under the name of the police power and can be defined quite simply as the power of the state to prevent the commission of wrongs—for example the taking of property, the use of force or fraud—by one individual against another.[8] The principles that govern taxes and regulations directed towards this end are difficult enough in their own right, and I will not dwell upon them here, except to note that there is no principled way that the exception, so useful in nuisance control matters, can account for the comprehensive revenue measures and the major forms of social regulation—price controls and the like—in issue here. The crux of the matter therefore lies in the second justification: that of making compensation, explicit or implicit, for a taking for a public purpose brought about against the will of the owner.

In most cases the easiest way to tender compensation is with money, but there is no strict requirement for its use, even if it is invariably used, with say, the taking of an isolated parcel of land. More importantly for these purposes, this cash remedy will not work in every case. Taxes and regulation are partial takings, either from all individuals or a very large group of them. There is at this point a circular and self-defecting quality about any insistence upon explicit compensation. The money raised in taxes must now be returned to the very individuals from whom it was collected. A regulation would require the imposition of additional taxes to compensate the regulated parties for their losses, which in turn makes the taxes levied themselves uncompensated takings. Therefore, with coordinated takings from a large number of individuals, explicit compensation can no longer be the norm, but the rare exception. What must be reckoned as the compensation for the property taken are the benefits received from the government operations, be it in the provision of roads, of police protection, or in the administration of justice, or whatever.

In a well-ordered state there is some reason to believe that the benefits derived from taxation and regulation will exceed the correlative costs. But it is one thing to make the assertion and quite another to demonstrate its truth. The nub of the difficulty is that any shift from explicit to implicit compensation makes it quite difficult to calculate the size of the benefits received, even if (itself a somewhat doubtful assumption) the costs in question can themselves be calculated precisely. The question is whether these difficulties make it necessary to retreat to one of two extremes, both of which seem quite untenable. Either *no* taxation or regulation is allowed, or *all* taxation and regulation is allowed. Either government ends, or the constraints imposed upon it lie in the political process, where the unfairness found in regulation or taxation is to be beaten back or endured. Follow

---

[8] The classic discussion of this topic is contained in Freund (1904).

the line and the policy analyst has his domain at last, at least that portion of it—comprehensive control—that he covets most.

In general, this second alternative has been embraced, even in the United States with its strong constitutional tradition and its explicit eminent domain provision. "[N]or shall private property be taken for public use, without just compensation."[9] While it is possible to find grudging concessions by American judges that certain forms of regulation and taxation can go "too far,"[10] the more basic truth is that the supposed limits are never reached no matter what the form of government exaction.[11]

The only way to blunt this massive rejection of limited government on economic matters is to find some intermediate position that:

(a) allows limited supervision of the powers to tax and regulate,

(b) escapes the burdens of direct measurement, and

(c) blunts the greatest abuses of government.

Here the central insight is contained in a principle of American eminent domain law,[12] whereby the *disproportionate impact* of a tax or regulation functions as an indirect measure of the adequacy of compensation. Although used in some contexts, this test to date has not been applied seriously to taxation and regulation, largely because of the occupational hazard of lawyers which prevents them from taking a comprehensive approach to the various forms of social control.

---

[9] *U.S. Constitution.* amend. V. Note that the same argument can to some extent be made in the American context from the language of the taxing power, in U.S. Constitution, art. I, s.8, cl.1:

    The Congress shall have Power to lay and collect Taxes, Duties, Imposts and Excises, to pay the Debts and provide for the common Defense and general Welfare of the United States; but all Duties, Imposts, and Excises shall be uniform throughout the United States.

    The references to "common," "general," and "uniform" all hint at the disproportionate impact test which itself has been incorporated into the eminent domain clause.

[10] *Pennsylvania Coal Co. v. Mahon,* 260 U.S. 393 p.415, 43 S.Ct. 158 p.160 (1922).

[11] See, for example, *A. Magnano Co. v. Hamilton,* 292 U.S. 40, 78 L.Ed. 1109, 54 S.Ct. 599 (1934); *Alaska Fish Salting & By-Products Co. v. Smith,* 255 U.S. 44, 65 L.Ed. 489, 41 S.Ct. 219 (1921).

[12] See, for example, *Armstrong v. United States* 364 U.S. 40 p. 49, 80 S.Ct. 1563 P. 1569 (1960): "The Fifth Amendment's guarante that private property shall not be taken for a public use without just compensation was designed to bar Government from forcing some people alone to bear public burdens which, in all fairness and justice, should be borne by the public as a whole." See also, *Louisville Bank v. Radford,* 295 U.S. 555 p. 602, 55 S.Ct. 854 p. 869 (1935), for a similar expression of the basic sentiment. In one sense, the *Radford* case is the more relevant one here, for in it the Supreme Court struck down on eminent domain grounds legislation that destroyed the existing liens of a very broad class of creditors against a very broad class of debtors. The special legislation involved in that case was akin to a tax because it possessed a degree of generality that was not found in *Armstrong, supra,* where what was in issue was a subcontractor lien on several uncompleted boats.

The extension of the disproportionate impact principle to taxation and regulation would not be sufficient in and of itself to strike down all unfortunate forms of regulation and taxation. But the rule, even if underinclusive, does provide strong incentives to control the behavior of the state. Within rough practical limits, the prohibition against disproportionate impact is designed to insure that no one will be able to obtain benefits that exceed costs without extending these same benefits to all other individuals who are also subject to the regulation. The rule therefore helps prevent the creation of a situation in which the proponents of a tax or regulation enjoy benefits in excess of costs while others are made to bear costs in excess of benefits. To be sure, the rule does nothing to prevent a situation in which a general tax or regulation leaves everyone in the system—be they proponents or opponents of the new regime—worse off than they were under the old: if everyone were left worse off, then the impact, while undesirable, would not be disproportionate. Nonetheless, it is doubtful that the unfortunate state of affairs created by such a law would be stable over time, in as much as it leaves all persons net losers. If all (or nearly all) persons are left worse off under the regulation or tax, then no one would have any incentive to work for its adoption or preservation. The principle therefore exerts powerful incentives to ensure adoption of only those measures that advance collective welfare, however defined. On the other hand, it prevents the paralysis that follows from adherence to a unanimity requirement for social change, as the state power to force exchanges means that the "hold-out" person may be bought out, not for his asking price, but for some price which leaves him at least as well off as he was under the previous legal regime.

To state the general thesis in this fashion is, however, not to answer all the objections that can be raised against it. The initial set of difficulties comes at two levels. The first concerns the potential reach of the disproportionate impact test. The second concerns its consequences: when it applies, will the test impose any real restriction upon the power of government to take from some and to give to others?

First, deciding whether a given tax or regulation is disproportionate will not normally be a simple affair. It is, for example, very difficult to determine in the abstract whether a head tax or a proportionate income tax is required, or whether a progressive income tax—whose possibilities for abuse are manifest—is permitted.[13] Indeed the possible scope of the principle goes further, to reach all the protean forms of taxation that have been used by government from time immemorial to raise the revenues of the state. Special taxes upon certain commodities—for example, liquor—have long been a

[13] See, for example, Blum and Kalven (1952).

staple in the government arsenal. Distinctions between various forms of property—for instance, differential tax rates for commercial and residential real property—have become a standard feature of municipal taxation. Special rules for certain industries, such as insurance, or certain forms of voluntary associations, partnerships, corporations, or trusts, have always been adopted.

Yet while the attack on current practices may be extensive, this alone does not furnish any reason in principle to shrink from the general consequences of this position. At most, invalidation mandates a general simplification and unification of taxation and regulation. It does not, however, limit the level of government expenditures or taxation, or even require anything like a balanced budget. To be sure, it goes against long-standing practices in a great number of instances, but this itself only means that it is an instrument that limits the long-standing abuses of government power. Unlike most efforts at aggressive constitutional action, for example, busing, the eminent domain principle operates only as a constraint against legislative or administrative action, and not as its spur.

It may be said as well that the constraints, even if imposed, will be of no real consequence. But a single constraint upon the operation of government power, if the right one, can bite hard. To deny its force in the context is somewhat like saying that the principle of "one man, one vote" should be rejected because it still leaves government officials a certain amount of freedom to gerrymander voting districts. But although some degree of freedom is left, the area in which it operates is sharply circumscribed. In the analysis that follows, three recent special taxes are considered: those against mining companies for the benefit of black lung disease victims, the windfall profits tax, and the Montana coal severance tax. The sums of money involved in each case are so substantial, and their incidence so skewed, that it is quite unlikely that any government could pass neutral legislation governing income that had anything like the distributional consequences of these taxes. There would be no way in which to target the tax against the same persons, and the revenues so derived from indirect measures would be difficult to calculate and would in any event fall into the general pool where they could not be earmarked for any specific purpose or group. And if various government officials tried to strike up a deal to reintroduce the prohibited scheme "by the back door," ample documentary and testimonial evidence would help pierce the new artifice; all abuses would not be eliminated, but many could be curtailed. The old ways of doing business could not last in the new constitutional order. In an ideal constitutional system more explicit constraints upon powers to tax and regulate might be appropriate, however difficult to formulate. But as a general matter, even the limited protection provided by the eminent domain clause is preferable to no protection at all.

Administrative matters to one side, a further challenge might be made: why is it that disproportionate impacts are regarded as improper in taxation and regulation when they are tolerated in the original acquisition, as by first possession,[14] and in subsequent voluntary transfers of rights? Here the answer lies in the very different function of the two types of rules. The original rules of acquisition operate in an environment in which no person has vested rights in external things. Likewise a voluntary transfer of admitted rights is not a violation of the rights of others; for A to sell his house to B is not to commit a tort against a stranger, C. Under these circumstances there is simply no occasion to address the question of whether certain private acts have disproportionate impacts, for the issue of compensation to others, to which the disproportionate impact test applies, simply does not arise. Only after a wide-spread taking of private property—a wrong by the state—has been established does that question become relevant as an indirect measure of the levels of compensation that are required by the eminent domain principle.

But to all this it could be said that it is improper to look at the matter from such a narrow and incremental view, as the chief normative objection to the eminent domain principle itself is that the current distribution of entitlements has been obtained by improper and illicit means. What is needed, the argument continues, is not the protection of the rights now asserted, but a return of property to the persons with superior title to it. That such may be a legitimate attack on certain holdings of wealth cannot in principle be denied. The original entitlements of the various Indian tribes is one case in which the argument might well have powerful bite. Yet what is interesting about most schemes of taxation and regulation is that they are not justified by challenges to the legitimacy of the current holdings of the parties so taxed or regulated. No one in support of price controls, minimum wage laws, or various forms of special taxation is prepared to assert, let alone establish, that the original parties improperly acquired such holdings. Indeed if their acquisition has been tainted, these property possessors, not being owners, would not have been simply regulated or taxed. Instead their property would have been taken away by main force without regard to the residual interest left to the aggrieved party. In short, prior wrongful acts of any given party will justify state responses commensurate with the wrongs in question. But this will not justify any massive system of taxation or regulation that does not allege, let alone establish, such wrongful conduct.

The last objection to the disproportionate impact test is in reality an objection to the larger requirement of compensation when the government

[14] See, for my view on this subject, Epstein (1979).

takes private property. Quite simply, the point is the wealth redistribution is a proper function of the state, one that is precluded by a systematic adherence to the eminent domain principle. In one large class of cases the point can, I think, be easily turned aside. It is very difficult to think of an intelligible moral principle which tolerates wealth transfers from some well-to-do individuals to other persons of the same class, or, as is often the case through taxation and regulation, from the poor to the rich. In preventing, therefore, the voters in a local municipality from imposing extensive land use restrictions upon the isolated owners of undeveloped lands, the eminent domain principle works at its best by blocking (*de facto*, through the insistence upon payment of compensation) a set of measures that causes a capricious transfer of wealth from some individuals to others, and dissipates overall wealth by inducing expenditures of resources either to secure or to resist the passage of the regulation in question.

This first reply is, however, not decisive across the board because it does not address the efforts to redistribute wealth from rich to poor as part of a comprehensive welfare scheme. In truth, the case for such redistribution by compulsory means is far from clear, as it must be explained why poor individuals are entitled to obtain through the intervention of the state those benefits which they could not individually claim directly from the rich themselves: need alone never generates an entitlement, because it never shows which person should pay, or why. The institution of welfare may be defended on the ground that its universal acceptance points to an over-whelming social consensus in its favor, a consensus that serves as a close enough substitute to the ideal of individualized and unanimous consent demanded by a rigourour theory of individual rights. Yet this rationale itself suggests that redistribution is principled only if it satisfies at least one stringent condition. It will simply not do for the poor—by votes—to place unlimited exactions upon the rich. If it is the consent of the donors that matters in principle, then the preferences of the donees, even if registered in votes, can hardly be decisive, whether on the amounts of the coerced transfers or the conditions on which they should be made Nor are matters made better if some rich join in the demands of the poor, especially if they contrive the passage of special taxes or regulations that fall exclusively on others in the population opposed to the general redistributive scheme. The principled limitation upon the power of the state has, however, been met and exceeded by a whole host of recent special taxes and regulations, whose disproportionate impacts are evident from the face of the legislation itself. In this paper I shall discuss four such systems of special legislation: black lung disease compensation programs, the windfall profits tax on crude oil, special state severance taxes upon coal and the Canadian regulation of foreign investment. The first two programs in large measure deal with redistributions from rich to poor, while the second two do not. Yet even if allowances are made in the first two cases for redistributive goals, all four schemes should be condemned in any system that respects both private property and the need for limited government.

II. Applications

A. Black Lung Compensation Program

The black lung disease compensation program was enacted by the United States during the early 1970s in order to establish a special fund for the compensation of those coal mine workers disabled by black lung disease.[15] The funds for the programme originally came in part from general revenues and in part from special charges imposed upon mines in order to make disability payments to former employees in the individual mines. To the firms so burdened, the payments in question were like a special tax on established mines. The competitive differential between old and new mines became so great, however, that Congress thereafter modified the program to require all mining companies to contribute to the fund on the same basis, including newly established mines that had never employed any workers benefiting from the plan. In imposing the particular tax, it was conceded that there was no unsatisfied legal obligation running from the mines (old or new) to the covered workers, as all claims in tort or under workers' compensation law were properly barred, if ever valid. While there was some causal nexus (at least in the case of the old mines) between the injury to the workers and the mines, the nexus was wholly insufficient (and recognized as such) to support any form of legal responsibility whatsoever.

In dealing with the black lung disease compensation program, the United States Supreme Court in *Usery v. Turner Elkorn Mining Co.*[16] sustained the tax on grounds that fulfilled the dreams of the policy analyst intent upon securing his widest domain. In effect, it recognized that the tax was unfair; that being retroactive it could have no incentive effects, desirable or otherwise; and that the current exposures to dangerous substances were extensively controlled by other regulatory systems. It stopped short of calling the tax a taking from one class of individuals followed by a gift to another, although that is what it was.

Let it be agreed that some redistribution by the state is permitted; it still does not follow that there should be no constraints upon the appropriate

---

[15] Title IV of the *Federal Coal Mine Health and Safety Act of 1969*, Pub. L. No. 91-173, 83 Stat. 792 (1969), as am. by the *Black Lung Benefits Act*, 30 U.S.C, 901 *et seq.* (1979 & Cum. Sup. May 1982).

[16] 428 U.S. 1, 49 L.Ed. 2d 752, 96 S.Ct. 2882 (1976).

patterns of redistribution. As noted above, the ability to generate special benefits without any constitutional limitations—one half the policy analyst's dream—should only spur demand for effective limitations upon the collection of the wealth to be redistributed. No narrow segment of the rich should be singled out for special burdens, even if some narrow segment of the poor is selected for special benefits. There will be some greater effort for legislative responsibility if the funds in question must be drawn out of general revenues than if they can be taken from one narrow group of the population, whose members receive none of the monies so collected. It is better by far that as many as possible of those in favor of the redistribution be made to pay their pro rata share, for one is apt to be somewhat less generous when the coercion of another comes at the price of payment by one's self. Therefore, to permit complete freedom as to both the objects of taxation and the beneficiaries of the tax is to allow a comprehensive scheme of confiscation which should not escape either constitutional condemnation (in the American system) or moral condemnation (everywhere). The grander the scheme of redistribution, the greater the need for its social control.

B. Windfall Profits Tax

The principles used to analyze the black lung disease compensation program can be carried over in straightforward fashion to the analysis of the American windfall profits tax upon crude oil.[17] The tax itself, when reduced to its essentials, is imposed upon the difference between the fair market value of the crude oil, and the price for which it could be sold under the previous scheme of direct controls. As regulated prices for all forms of oil were originally set quite low in the name of consumer protection, the diffential between the market value and the regulated price became quite substantial after the major rise in world energy prices during the 1970s. As the tax ranges from sixty to seventy-five percent, it is evident that billions in revenue are at stake.

Standing alone, the windfall profits tax places a disproportionate burden upon one class of property—to wit, crude oil. The forbidden redistributive aspects of the tax are even more evident when two additional points are noted. First, large portions of the tax are designed to go into general trust funds, with an eye toward the improvement of transportation, the condition of the aged, and the like. There is thus no possibility of arguing that the tax is imposed in order to offset some special benefit to the oil industry. Second, the supporters of the tax note with great pride that the owners

---

[17] Pub. L. No. 96-223, 94 Stat. 229 (1980).

of crude oil cannot pass the tax forward to consumers.[18]

Under existing American case law there is no effective way to challenge the tax. But taking the case on its merits, the disproportionate burdens condemn the tax. To this charge it might be answered, the legislative intention notwithstanding, that the tax is passed forward and thus falls generally upon the public at large, that benefits and burdens do match after all. Here it would be pointless for any court to attempt to assess the precise ways in which this particular tax works itself into the fabric of the economy. The real question therefore is what attitude it should take if it is serious, as it should be, about making sure that taxation is not a disguised form of confiscation—even on the generous view that allows some redistribution to the poor not financed by special taxes. In my view, the risk of error should fall squarely upon the government because it has adopted the means which make it so difficult to trace out the consequences of the taxes that it wishes to impose.[19] How can the government object if it is required to impose the very general revenue tax—here a broadly based income tax—which it claims, in effect, to have imitated?

There is no question that the ordinary conception of ownership includes the rights to possess, use and dispose of the thing in question.[20] Should the state demand that some oil not be sold at all, it will have taken from the original owner an incident of ownersip which is valued at the difference between the value of the oil in exchange and its highest value in use to that particular owner. Where the government allows the oil to be sold, but at a regulated price below fair market value, the principle does not change,

[18] "The committee believes that this tax will reduce profits of oil producers and royalty owners, rather than be passed on to consumers as higher prices." S. Rep. No. 96-394, 96th Cong. 2d. Sess. 2, reprinted in (1980) U.S. Code Cong. and Ad. News (p.414).

The reasoning behind this position is that, as the tax is only upon profits, the seller will maximize his return by selling at the same price at which he would without the imposition of the "windfall tax." The argument is weak insofar as it does not take into account the important, if obvious, point that the tax in question will reduce the amount of oil which will be produced from the wells it covers, which will in turn raise the market price because of the reduction in the overall supply. Yet this effect, whose magnitude I cannot begin to estimate, is not important for our discussion. What is important is that there is strong evidence of motive which shows what is apparent on the face; that there is no effort to match in even the vaguest way the benefits and burdens of this tax.

[19] There is a parallel argument in the tort literature from the law of negligence. Thus, where a defendant is negligent, and his negligence has destroyed some evidence that is necessary to establish the linkage between his negligence and the plaintiff's harm, the court will shift the burden of proof to the defendant on the question that his own wrong has made more difficult to answer. The leading American case on the issue is Haft v. Lone Palm Hotel, 3 Cal. 3d 756, 478 P. 2d 465, 91 Cal. Rptr. 745 (1970). The analogous case for Canadian Law is MaGhee v. National Coal Bd., (1972) 3 All E.R. 1008 (H.L.).

[20] See, for example, Honore (1961).

even if that which has been taken[21] from producers is given to consumers, or, for that matter, wholly dissipated. The incident of disposition is not wholly removed, but compensation for that part of the incident which is taken must be made nonetheless. To this it might be suggested that it is odd in the extreme to speak of the taking by the government "of a part of a part," especially when the government as such does not keep the part so taken. But there is confiscation if the government says to a landowner that it will take a half of a half of his land, just as when it says it will take a quarter thereof. And it would make no difference if it gave the land to some group of worthy individuals instead of keeping it for itself, or ruined it for cultivation. Why then should there be any difference when we speak of the right implicit in ownership to sell the oil in question? Here the market price is the only proper benchmark against which regulation or taxation should be measured because it is the only price which respects the unfettered right to dispose (to those who wish to purchase) that counts as part of the original bundle of ownership rights. The regulation is the wrong benchmark against which to measure the entitlements of the individual owner against the state. To be sure, the invalidation of the tax would lead to a contraction of all government programs and services, including those with redistributive ends. But this counts as a strength and not a weakness of the position, as it only denies certain groups in society the luxury of directing government force against those unable to defend themselves in the political process.

C. State Severance Taxes

The third of the special taxes is the state severance tax of up to thirty percent "of the contract sales price" imposed by the state of Montana upon coal removed from the ground.[22] The tax was sustained by the United States Supreme Court in *Commonwealth Edison Co. v. Montana*.[23] The tax in question was levied upon all coal so removed, whether from federal or from state lands, and whether intended after sale for local use or for use in other states. The tax worked out to be about a seven-fold increase over the previous severance taxes—taxes based on tonnage and not on value—imposed by the state. The increased levels were explicitly justified by the Montana state legislature on the ground that the state held within its borders a portion of the low sulfur coal large enough so that demand for its coal

---

[21] That is, the amount obtained by applying the windfall tax rate to the amount by which fair market value exceeds the regulated price.

[22] Mont. Code Ann. pp. 15-35-101 et seq. (1981).

[23] 453 U.S. 609, 101 S.Ct. 2946 (1981).

would not dry up once the tax was imposed.[24] In a manner reminiscent of the windfall profits tax, at least one-half of the monies collected were placed into a special trust fund, [25] the principal of which could be spent only with the approval of three-fourths of the members of each house. [26] The revenues generated by the tax were sufficient to permit Montana to reduce, as it in fact did, both its personal income and property taxes.

In the Supreme Court case, the challenge relevant here was that the tax offended the so-called negative implications of the commerce clause[27] because it constituted a barrier to free trade between the states.[28] In determining what these negative implications of the commerce clause are, the Court has made it very clear that the extreme position—no tax at all on goods in interstate commerce—cannot be sustained. Instead, operating under the credo that "[e]ven interstate business must pay its way,"[29] the Court fashioned rules which in some rough sense at least guarantee that goods in interstate commerce are not subject to any special burden from which local competitive goods are exempt.[30] The economic rationale behind this general position is clear enough, for the rule prevents the substitution from superior to inferior goods that would take place as a matter of course if taxes were imposed solely upon out-of-state goods. The general formulation of the rule was expounded in *Complete Auto Transit, Inc. v. Brady*,[31] where it was held that a state tax does not offend the commerce clause if it "is applied to an activity with a substantial nexus with the taxing State, is fairly apportioned, does not discriminate against interstate commerce, and is fairly related to the services provided by the State."[32]

In this formulation, the first two elements are essentially irrelevant to our inquiry because they are always satisfied: everything turns on the last two. The fourth prong of the test restates in fairly clear form the general benefit test of taxation, which requires some commensurate benefit to the

---

[24] *Supra* note 22, pp. 15-35-101 (e)

[25] *Id.*, Section 15-35-108 (1).

[26] *Id.*, Section 17-6-203 (5).

[27] "The Congress shall have Power . . . To regulate Commerce . . . among the several States . . ." *U.S. Constitution.* art I, s. 8, cl. 3.

[28] The United States Supreme Court has been prepared to look at discriminatory regulations under the negative commerce clause. *Robbins v. Taxing District of Shelby County*, 120 U.S. 489, 30 L.Ed. 694, 7 S.Ct. 592 (1887).

[29] *Western Live Stock v. Bureau of Revenue*, 303 U.S. 25] at 254, 58 S.Ct. 546 at 548 (1933).

[30] See, for example, *Colonial Pipeline Co. v. Traigle*, 421 U.S. 100, 44 L.Ed.2d 1, 95 S.Ct. 1538 (1974); *Evansville-Vanderburgh Airport Auth. Dist. v. Delta Airlines*, 404 U.S. 707, 31 L.Ed. 2d 620, 92 S.Ct. 1349 (1972).

[31] 430 U.S. 274, 51 L.Ed. 2d 326, 97 S.Ct. 1076 (1977).

[32] *Id.* at 279 (U.S.), 1079 (S.Ct.).

taxed. The third element, moreover, can be read in harmony with the fourth, if the element of "discrimination" in treatment is regarded as a rephrasing of the disproportionate impact test—our indirect measure of benefits provided for an admitted taking.

With this much said, the severance tax in question can be viewed from two vantage points. The first goes to federalism. It may be quite impermissible to have a court pass upon the tax under a negative commerce clause analysis. It is undisputed that Congress has full and plenary power to regulate the shipment of coal in interstate commerce, and, to achieve that end, to regulate the coal which remains in intrastate commerce as well. If there is some nationwide outrage against the tax, the matter can be resolved in Congress, sparing the courts the heavy burden of intervention.[33] The basic position can then be reinforced by a second observation that once a court gets into the business of striking down particular taxes it will never be able to extricate itself from the perils of standardless litigation.[34] The reply to the first point is that the stakes are so high that coalitions among special interest groups will block sensible legislative action, so that judicial intervention to create the free trade zone is welcome as a matter of principle, here as in the many other cases where the negative powers have been invoked. The reply to the second is that underinclusive tests that permit the invalidation of some taxes should not be spurned if they admit of workable application solely because they cannot reach every abuse which state legislatures can contrive. A detailed analysis of the economic impacts of the taxes involved here is not necessary to condemn them on this ground. The obvious motive of the legislature in singling out a single commodity for differential taxation without so much as a colorable justification calls for at least some intervention.

This federalism question need not further detain us, as the tax may be challenged from the second vantage point of individual rights: have any individuals, either the original owners of the coal or the purchasers thereof, been subjected to an uncompensated taking of their coal? On this matter, the general power of the Congress over commerce is of no importance. Instead, two questions of individual rights arise. The first asks whether individuals who are outside the taxing jurisdiction are required to pay special taxes for which they receive no comparable benefits. The second asks with equal force whether individuals within the taxing jurisdiction, who have some rights of participation in the local political process, are nonetheless victimized by its outcome.

As regards both producers and buyers, the ultimate issue of this eminent

---

[33] See Williams (1982).

[34] For a forceful statement of this view, see Hellerstein (1982, p. 55).

domain analysis is: was the tax fairly related to the services provided by the state? Looking at the matter in the abstract, it is clear that something must be amiss. If the original severance tax was proper, then it is doubtful that its replacement—seven times its size, and wholly different in its mode of collection—could well match the constant set of benefits provided by the state. It could, of course, be argued that the original tax furnished some sort of subsidy for the producers and consumers of coal in that the original rates were set too low. But as there is no indication of what services, apart from general policy protection, were provided by the state, this possibility should be accepted only upon very strong evidence—evidence not to be found in the record of the case.

The Court in *Commonwealth Edison* did not, however, make the slightest pretence of identifying or valuing the services rendered by the state. Instead, the opinion at its critical point[35] abandons the benefit test by quoting an extensive passage from *Carmichael v. Southern Coal & Coke Co.*,[36] the gist of which is that "[t]he only benefit to which the taxpayer is constitutionally entitled is that derived from his enjoyment of the privileges of living in an organized society, established and safeguarded by the devotion of taxes to public purposes." But this simply will not do. By adopting some version of the benefit test, it must be understood that a given tax—or regulation— can in principle flunk the test so announced. Yet here there is no question but that every person will receive some scrap of benefit from every tax, however imposed, no matter how outlandish its rates, no matter how bizarre its purposes. Any inquiry into the operation and effect of a tax is barred in effect as long as society continues to function. The level of the benefit received for property taken should be treated as a question of fact, on which it is wholly improper to erect a conclusive presumption of adequacy. Yet after the value of benefits received is made relevant, then this tax must fail. Unless there is some special benefit of the severance tax to the owners or purchasers of the coal beyond the provision of the usual police protection and the like, already paid for by other taxes, then the tax must be struck down.

To satisfy the benefit test, it might be urged that the increase in the value of the mined coal increases the value of the state services rendered to the aggrieved parties. So much can be conceded, but it will not save this severance tax under the sensible tests announced for passing on its validity. If it turns out that coal properties are far more valuable because of the increased demands for energy than they were before, there are at least two ways that the state can capture its fair portion of that increase in value

---

[35] *Supra* note 23 at 628 (U.S.), 2960 (S. Ct.).
[36] 301 U.S. 495 at 522, 57 S.Ct. 868 at 878-79 (1937).

without resorting to the special severance tax. It can tax the increased amount of the gain on sale as part of the general income tax; as the gain creases so will the tax dollars collected. Or it can in more powerful fashion capture the gain as part of the general sales tax—roughly comparable for all commodities—or as part of a real estate tax based upon overall valuation, which is not, it must be added, restricted to those minerals which are severed from the ground, but which reaches all those which are in place. With these principled alternatives available, there is no reason to sanction the imposition of a tax, be it on producers or consumers, which is wholly abusive.

Commonwealth Edison, then, is an easy case given any rough estimate as to the match between the benefits and burdens of the tax. Nor are matters better if disproportionate impact is the only ground upon which the tax could be struck down. Here again it is necessary to distinguish the position of the producers from that of the out-of-state consumers. With regard to the former, it seems clear that the portion of the tax which producers cannot pass forward is a disproportionate and therefore prohibited burden. In essence, the argument is that the national market in coal is highly competitive so that, where existing contracts themselves do not call for an automatic pass through of the tax increase, the producers will have to absorb most, if not all, of the tax, in order not to lose sales to producers elsewhere.[37]

The argument for consumers is a bit more complex. Here on first appearance it might seem that there was no illicit discrimination because the tax was, as the Supreme Court noted, the same on local consumers as on out-of-state ones. But this wholly ignores two points. First, where the taxes are passed through under prior contracts, there is the strong likelihood of disproportionate burden unless it can be also shown that coal sold in domestic markets is subject to the same type of contractual provision. The second point applies to all these contractual arrangements. Of critical importance here is the parallel reductions in income and property taxes for local residents only. These reductions were made possible not by a reduction in internal state spending, but by the increase in the revenues derived from the severance tax upon coal. To be sure, the severance tax was imposed upon coal used for internal consumption as well. But the key point is that the two taxes were part of an integrated plan. So viewed it is clear that the decrease in the local income and property taxes functioned as a rough equivalent of a rebate to the severance tax. Here there will be no perfect correlation in the reduction of property and income taxes and the increase in severance taxes, but the match is close enough, especially since it is only local citizens who have a chance, not to say a near certainty,

---

[37] See Hellerstein (1982, p. 30) and Williams (1982, p. 291).

of participating in the windfall. If the tax reforms are taken as a package, as they were no doubt viewed in the legislature, the severance tax must be condemned not because it is discriminatory in itself, but because it was part of a comprehensive plan whose impact was disproportionate. On this view, therefore, the question of how much of the tax is passed forward and how much is not is quite immaterial. No matter which view of the transaction is taken, some group of individuals—it matters not whether they are local producers or out-of-state consumers—is subject to illicit burdens.

What then are the permissible powers of taxation? Here I do not suggest that some excise tax could not be imposed upon coal. As a first approximation, it is clear that the state is in fine shape if the tax it imposes is no greater than the sales tax which it imposes upon other commodities. As a further refinement, additional taxes could well be justified by showing that there are certain greater burdens imposed upon the state by the removal of coal from the ground—although none are even suggested in *Commonwealth Edison*. What is prevented is a justification for tax that quite simply asserts—as did Montana—that the state may tax its coal because it wants the revenue very much. To make the argument is to insist not upon sovereign control held over all property by the state but the private ownership of this coal by the state. It is therefore to confiscate by assertion alone. The moral for Canada should be obvious. The division of proceeds over the sale of Canadian oil should not be regarded solely as a political power struggle between the provincial and federal governments. Where the oil in question is in private hands (as is the case with roughly twenty percent of the Albertan oil) neither the provincial nor the federal government should be allowed to subject it to special discriminatory taxes. Where the ownership is vested in the province of Alberta,[38] the federal government should not engage in partial acts of confiscation by subjecting that oil to special federal charges. Unless it can find some way to undermine the original distribution of rights, its claim to the oil rests upon greater might, not superior right.

D.Canada and the United States: Price Controls and Foreign Investment

The general principles used to distinguish the permissible from impermissible forms of taxation and regulation have thus far been illustrated exclusively with materials drawn from the American experience. The principles themselves, however, are subject to no particular territorial limitation. Even though the constitutional framework of Canada is quite different from that of the United States, the normative portions of the

---

[38] Alberta has retained ownership and extraction rights in petroleum and natural gas in most public land devised to private owners. See the *Public Lands Act*, R.S.A. 1980, c. 297, s. 34.

arguments survive even if the textual portions of the argument do not. Indeed, the normative element of the discussion is, if anything, somewhat more important in a system without entrenched individual rights: when everything is left within the political domain, legislative self-restraint has a greater importance than it does in a constitutional democracy.

With this said, it seems clear that in Canada, as in the United States, the ideal of self-restraint has not been able to survive the massive shock to the political and economic systems resulting from the energy crisis. At one level, the arguments are on grounds of economic policy that are not tied to the system of individual rights referred to above. As a matter of policy, the best thing that any government can do in response to sudden and unanticipated shifts in the prices of vital goods brought on, say, by a cartel, is nothing—nothing at all. Inaction by the government will make it clear that private responses to the external changes are required, and these in turn can be made with greater accuracy in light of the reduced political uncertainty. On the demand side, major individual efforts can find substitute ways of doing business that blunt the effect of the price rise. On the supply side, alternative forms of energy, previously uneconomical, become viable financial propositions under the price umbrella created by the cartel. Some might think that this prescription is too dramatic, for an alternative, imposing tariffs on the importation of foreign oil, might capture domestically some of the cartel rents. But the tariff levels must be precisely set, and there is always the risk that domestic producers, with expenditures of real resources, will be able to keep them in place even after the cartel ceases to function. The temptation to fine tune the response to external shifts in market conditions should therefore be resisted; cartels should be left to fall of their own weight. Institutions like OPEC will become mired in frustration when they are unable to control markets as they had done in earlier years. This process of degeneration has taken place in the last year or two.[39] It could have begun even sooner if the American government had just kept its hand out of the energy business.

The point of this essay in not to elaborate, however, what I think to be the appropriate choices that I as a policy analyst should choose to make. It is, instead, to identify the appropriate normative boundaries to the set of permissible choices. When, therefore, I criticize both American and Canadian forms of price control over crude oil, I do not do it solely on the ground that I think them inefficient. I do so also on the ground that the system of controls depends for its very survival on the government confiscating large sources of private wealth without compensation. The great

---

[39] Since the Conference at which this article was presented, there have been major cuts in both prices and outputs in the spring of 1982, further confirming the general position taken here.

battles over state, provincial or federal regulation—of which *Commonwealth Edison* is but one—are only debates over *which* level of government should be allowed to confiscate the most from private hands. If a government— Canadian, American, state, provincial, federal—wants to get into the business of regulating the price of oil and gas alone, it can do so by simply buying at market prices as much oil and gas as it chooses to, paying for supplies purchased out of the general revenue funds. If thereafter it chooses to sell the oil and gas at below-market prices on some type of rationed basis, it has not offended the normative principles against confiscation even if it has engaged in a policy which is a variety of economic reason wholly self-destructive. Placing this burden of purchase upon the government would make clear the real costs of its programmes at a very early stage, such that the likelihood that the policy would continue becomes remote in the extreme. Yet even this prediction should not be confused with the normative judgment. If it is thought that some symbolic, political or national concern justifies this general loss of both liberty and wealth, then the state can pursue this to the bitter end, so long as it does not resort to selective pressures against one group of individuals.

There is of course another alternative to price controls over crude oil. The government could simply confiscate outright some portion of the oil in place and then dispose of it as it see fit. Here there is an issue of equity in theft, for the outright confiscation could be of the total ownership interests of some, or it could be spread *pro rata* over the ownership interests of all. The difference in incidence simply determines who is entitled to protest the takings involved, for even a widespread confiscation of oil, without reciprocal benefits to the owners, can in no way convert confiscation into a legitimate form of government action. Notwithstanding the strong moral case against this form of action, there is something to be said on its behalf, not in comparison to the proper system of purchase, but in comparison to the confiscation occurring under the applicable price regulations. Quite simply, straight confiscation interferes far less with the operation of markets than does the alternative system of price regulation. The government takes it oil interests and exploits them to maximize the wealth of the whole, confining its distributional decisions to matters with little or no effect upon the productive side of the enterprise. The government simply becomes an owner or partner in certain oil interests. The only reason that this is not done is because the overt nature of the confiscation makes it impossible to conceal its illicit natures behind a fog of words. Governments always prefer the hidden taxes that should be condemned for institutional reasons. The indirect forms of confiscation are therefore preferred even though they are less efficient because they make plausible a government denial of the truth which has great symbolic value for most of us, who do not want to face the hard moral questions raised by its conduct. The system thus runs by an internal, if destructive, logic that no intellectual clarification can displace.

A parallel analysis is appropriate for another recent form of Canadian regulation, which unlike price controls over crude oil, is not found in the United States. I refer to the elaborate system of review which is established under the *Foreign Investment Review Act (FIRA)*.[40] In essence, the statutory plan is designed to tolerate further foreign investment into Canada in whatever form only if an administrative board determines that the proposed investment will provide, all things considered, some "significant benefit to Canada . . ."[41] The tests which are used to determine this particular result cannot be purely economic. If they were, there would have to be a well-nigh conclusive presumption against a system which in turn will reduce the levels of employment and economic activity within the country. To be sure, a scheme with this far reaching impact must confer a net benefit upon a few individuals, but these will be quasi-monopolists who, protected from foreign competition, will be able to market inferior goods and services at higher prices. No one can question the power to any nation to take strong steps whenever there is a substantial threat to its own national welfare and safety. But it is quite premature to assume that foreign investment in productive activities ever presents that sort of immediate threat. In almost every conceivable case, all important interests of national security can be effectively protected by a more tailored set of restrictions.

The question still remains, however, whether there can be any principled challenge to the *FIRA* on moral grounds. As regards future investment of foreign capital, these seem to be minor. The disadvantage wrought by the status is advertised in advance, so that foreigners can steer clear of even approved investments if they think that the supplemental investments, necessary to the success of their overall plans, will be blocked by Canadian administrative actions. Canadians will share in whatever political or symbolic benefits are generated by the actions in more or less equal proportions. Without the direct measure of gains and losses, the non-discriminatory effects of the statute save it from a powerful moral attack.

There is, however, one class of claimants who have a more powerful case against application of the statute on normative grounds: the individual foreign firms which have already made investments prior to the passage of the statute. The issue was raised as a matter of statutory construction in *Dow Jones & Co. v. Attorney-General of Canada*,[42] where the Court had to decide whether the statute applied to the transfer of a Canadian

---

[40] S.C. 1973-74, C.46 as am. by S.C. 1976-77, C. 52, S. 128.

[41] *Id.*, s. 2(1).

[42] (1980), 113 D.L.R. (3d) 395, 11 B.L.R. 18 (F.C.T.D.).

subsidiary for one non-Canadian company to another. Dow Jones, an American corporation, in a complicated set of transactions designed to obtain favorable tax treatment under American law, acquired Irwin U.S., an American corporation, and its wholly-owned Canadian subsidiary, Irwin Dorsey. It was agreed on all sides that the statute in question did not reach Dow Jones' acquisition of Irwin U.S., as such, but only the acquisition of its Canadian subsidiary, Irwin Dorsey. The Court held that the transaction was nonetheless caught by the notice and reporting provisions of the statute. The Court was obviously concerned about charges of retroactive application of the statute, which it thought unfounded:

> There can be no doubt that the Act is not retroactive in that it does not affect acquisitions of control of Canadian business enterprises which had been fully accomplished by non-eligible persons before the Act came into force unless and until that business is resold to another non-eligible person.[43]

It then answered the possible charge of discrimination under the statute as follows:

> No distinction is made in the Act between an acquisition by such [non-eligible] persons of a Canadian-owned business and an acquisition from one who is a non-eligible person but who obtained such control before the Act was in force or from non-eligible person who obtained the required consent after the Act came into force.[44]

As a matter of principle, however, these observations, although true, do not meet the challenge. With respect to investments already made, the rules of the game have been changed in mid-play in ways that necessarily decrease the value of foreign holding of Canadian property. Whereas once there was a robust market for the shares of the foreign corporations, today that market is effectively limited to Canadian purchasers. It is true that Canadians are subject to the same restriction when they seek to sell to foreigners, but the Canadian companies, in addition to symbolic benefits, continue to enjoy two rights that the statute systematically denies to foreign corporations: A Canadian company can always make fresh infusions of capital, and it can acquire the Canadian subsidiary of a foreign corporation without approval. It therefore has both special rights and special duties; the foreign corporation only has special duties. The entire position can, moreover, become more distressing if there is any concerted pressure on the part of Canadian or provincial government officials to induce the foreign shareholders of the Canadian companies to sell their shares at distress prices, as by other forms of tax or regulation.

---

[43] Id., p. 400.

[44] Id.

Looking therefore at the *FIRA* as a whole, its review procedures function as a powerful instrument to force the shift of existing investment from foreign to Canadian hands at below-market prices. While the general depressing effects of this legislation on the Canadian economy may be only cause for lamentation, its application to existing foreign investment is but another form of confiscation.

III. Conclusion

The purpose of this paper has been to draw attention to the question of which forms of government control should be regarded as within the domain of permissible policy choices, and which should be regarded as disguised confiscations. In dealing with this theme, it is quite clear that while all forms of regulation and taxation are subtle forms of the taking of private property, they are not necessarily confiscatory in and of themselves. Instead they are subject to two forms of justification: the police power and implicit in-kind compensation. There is within the American framework some faint recognition that the problem can be analyzed in the particular fashion, which is however followed by the implicit conclusion that with taxes and economic regulations the broad terrain of the *prima facie* case is fully occupied by its two principled exceptions. The point of this article is to show that in the context of recent retroactive and special legislation there are instances in which the *prima facie* case is not blunted by these two exceptions, even when broadly construed. The propositions in question are illustrated by consciously taking easy cases in which state conduct should in principle be attacked as illegitimate (in the Canadian context) or as illegitimate and unconstitutional (in the American context). As an historical matter, government legislation of this form has been with us for a long time. The greater stakes of modern regulation give the issue a new urgency, but do not require any change in either the analysis or outcome. Unchecked confiscation, total or partial, is always inconsistent with the ideal of limited government.

References

Blum, Walter J., and Kalven, Harry Jr. "The Uneasy Case for Progressive Taxation." *University of Chicago Law Review* 19 (Spring 1952): 417-520.

Dicey, Albert V. *Introduction to the Study of the Law of the Constitution*, 10th ed. reprint 1959. London: MacMillan and Co., 1965.

Epstein, Richard A. "Pleadings and Presumptions." *University of Chicago Law Review* 40 (1973): 556-82.

Epstein, Richard A. "Possession as the Root of Title." *Georgia Law Review* 13 (1979): 1221-43.

Freund, Ernst. *The Police Power: Public Policy and Constitutional Rights*. Chicago: Callaghan and Co., 1904.

Hellerstein, Walter. "Constitutional Limitations on State Tax Exportation." *American Bar Foundation Research Journal* 1 (Winter 1982): 1-77.

Honore, A.M. "Ownership." In *Oxford Essays in Jurisprudence*, pp. 107-47. Edited by Anthony Guest. Glasgow: Oxford University Press, 1961.

Madison, James. *The Federalist* (No. 10). New York: Holt and Co., 1898.

Williams, Stephen F. "Severance Taxes and Federalism: The Role of the Supreme Court in Preserving a National Common Market for Energy Supplies." *University of Colorado Law Review* 53 (Winter 1982): 281-314.

10

CONSTITUTIONAL CONSTRAINTS, ENTREPRENEURSHIP, AND THE EVOLUTION OF PROPERTY RIGHTS
Terry L. Anderson and Peter J. Hill

I. Introduction

There are a variety of reasons for constitutional constraints on government action, many of which are discussed in this volume. Such constraints can be useful in protecting individual liberties, restricting government to its proper sphere, and providing stability in the political order. In order to achieve such ends advocates of constitutional government usually argue for a written document that is interpreted rather narrowly, that is, one in which the provisions as originally written are enforced by judicial review. Such documents are also seen as relatively permanent in that procedures for change require a lengthy ratification process or something more than simple majority approval.

However, such constraints come at a cost. The modern world is one of rapid change. As witnessed in the United States, the ratification of the Constitution brought the necessary institutional stability to generate a "release of energy" in the nineteenth century. With this release came rapid changes in relative prices, new technologies, new third-party effects, and exploitation of old resources for new uses as well as the use of new resources. With these transformations came demographic change and new social structures which dramatically altered the functioning of the economy. Ideological shifts also rendered ineffective previous moral constraints, making social control difficult. Thus the need for flexible institutions to respond to an ever-changing economy is evident. However, to the extent that a constitution is effective in limiting the options of government, the ability of the state to respond to change will be less.

The desire to maintain options and to have a government that is able

The authors are Professors of Economics at Montana State University and Wheaton College, respectfully. They are also Senior Associates with the Political Economy Research Center of Bozeman, Montana.

to respond to new situations has led several jurists and scholars to argue for a much more flexible interpretation of the U. S. Constitution. For instance, Associate Supreme Court Justice William J. Brennan contends:

> [t]hose who would restrict claims of right to the values of 1789 specifically articulated in the Constitution turn a blind eye to social progress and eschew adaptation of overarching principles to changes of social circumstance.
>
> For the genius of the Constitution rests not in any static meaning it might have had in a world that is dead and gone, but in the adaptability of its great principles to cope with current problems and current needs [Brennan, 1985, p.36].

Justice Brennan makes clear in his remarks that traditional formulations of rights may well be inadequate in a changing world and therefore the Supreme Court should be actively involved in reinterpreting the Constitution in view of such changes.

These individuals are correct in their desire to have a set of institutions with built-in flexibility. However, one can also make cogent arguments for constitutional constraints to provide protection of basic freedoms and to enhance predictability. We shall argue that these two sets of conflicting ends can be best resolved in a constitution that clearly defines and enforces property rights; one that makes changes in those property rights extremely difficult at the legislative and judicial levels. Appropriate flexibility comes from entrepreneurs who envision new uses and combinations for well established property rights and who, through market processes and innovative contracts, act on their perceptions of previously unexploited opportunities.

The paper proceeds by discussing the nature of property rights and entrepreneurship in a dynamic society. Section III puts the important elements of the U. S. Constitution in the context of this property rights paradigm and section IV examines two cases where entrepreneurial contracting responded to changing economic conditions. In each of the cases, however, legislative and judicial responses in the late nineteenth and early twentieth centuries have been substituted for entrepreneurial responses. We argue that this substitution has reduced appropriate flexibility in the system, and at the same time has introduced an undesirable amount of instability in the rights accompanying ownership of property.

II. Property Rights and Entrepreneurship

Property rights are rules that determine access to and use of resources, including one's own mind and body. In order for these rules to effectively coordinate human action, property rights must be definable, defendable, and divestible. Of course all of these elements of property rights are a matter of degree because there can be different amounts of effort devoted to definition and defense, and the right of divestiture can be complete, non-existent, or some intermediate position between the two extremes. The amount of effort which must be expended on each element of property rights will vary depending on such things as physical characteristics, social norms, technology, and the legal system. In this setting, one purpose of a constitution is to lower the cost of defining, defending, and divesting property. By laying out the framework within which property rights are enforced and traded, the constitution brings the stability to a socio-economic system necessary for people to plan and take actions that produce wealth. Consider the role of a constitution in each of the three areas.

Effective definition of property rights requires two things. First, the holder of property rights must be free from physical invasion or the threat thereof. This means that individuals can take actions as long as those actions do not physically encroach on the rights of others. In the case of land or other real property, the notion of freedom from physical invasion is obvious. The holder of property rights in land has the right to be free from trespass by others. Similarly the owner of human capital has the right to be free from physical invasion of that property. What is important about the physical invasion criterion is that it limits the areas where people can claim harm from others. For example, defining property rights in terms of physical invasion eliminates the possibility of individual A claiming harm from the knowledge of individual B's actions simply because B's actions do not fit A's preferences. Rights defined in this way do not represent legal claims to income or status. By constitutionally limiting property rights to freedom from physical invasion, the possibility of using governmental coercive powers to limit the freedom of others is greatly curtailed.

The second criterion for effective definition is that property rights must be legitimate. If the rules governing who has access to and use of resources are not accepted by a sufficiently large portion of the society, pressure will build to change the rules. For example, at the time of the writing of the U. S. Constitution, a significant proportion of the population considered property rights in other humans, i.e. slavery, legitimate. With time, the perceived legitimacy of these property rights changed until ultimately it took a civil war to settle the issue. One common method of initially resolving the legitimacy issue is to use a natural rights philosophy or to grant rights to property to individuals who have mixed their labor with that property which is not already held by others. To be sure, questions of legitimacy will be continually open for debate, but a constitution offers a focal point for the debate.

A well constructed constitution also reduces costs of social interaction by providing a framework for defending property rights. The justice and police systems serve to allow individuals to use the coercive powers of government to accomplish this purpose. In the absence of these two governmental functions, it is likely that the cost of defending property rights would be extremely costly because the system would degenerate into a Hobbesian jungle.

Finally a constitution is an integral part of a property rights system because it reduces the cost of exchanging property rights. An effective property rights system requires that holders of property rights be allowed to recombine their rights so long as the rule of willing consent is obeyed. When individuals perceive rights which are of greater value than the ones currently held, a basis for gains from trade exists. These gains can only be realized if rights can be exchanged through freedom to contract. With the subjective values of individuals constantly changing, a constitution which allows the freedom to exchange well defined and enforced property rights provides the opportunity for individuals who perceive the potential for gains from trade to act upon their perceptions.[1]

It should be noted that this type of flexibility in a dynamic world provides a process through which new end states will be achieved, but the end states themselves are not at all predetermined. Thus a constitution that protects property rights is one that makes no attempt at predicting the future. It is based on a very real humility with respect to the ability of a society to know much about future generations and their desires. Instead of attempting to specify solutions to presently unknown problems, it puts in place an institutional framework that allows individuals to take actions in response to changes in the economic and social environment.

By establishing a constitution which reduces the costs of defining, defending, and exchanging property rights, individual foresight and creativity are allowed to respond to changes in a dynamic economy. Individuals or entrepreneurs who perceive previously unseen opportunities for gains from trade are encouraged to exploit opportunities which are not distributed evenly among members of society. These entrepreneurial perceptions are not equivalent to information that is bought and sold in the marketplace, but are what F. A. Hayek (1945, p.522) has referred to as "the knowledge of the particular circumstances of time and place." This knowledge is not and cannot be given "to a single mind which deliberately solves the problem set by these 'date' " (p. 520). Since constitution makers are not capable of having this knowledge, it is not possible for them to make decisions dependent upon it. What the constitution can do is provide the environment for entrepreneurs to act on the knowledge of the special circumstances as they unfold with time.

---

[1] Of course transaction costs may be high enough to prevent some positive sum trades from taking place. Epstein (1985) discusses how constitutional constraints should be interpreted so as to give adequate power to the state to facilitate such trades without destroying all protection of property rights.

After the fact it may appear that entrepreneurs have been engaged in the obvious—resources were more valuable in some other use or combination and all that person did was react to that situation. However, there are a myriad of opportunities for bringing a dynamic world into greater harmony. Which opportunities the entrepreneur capitalizes upon depends on his specific perceptions, and the perceptions which are not acted upon are never known to others in society. Some actions prove superior as measured by the survival test and contribute to the process of wealth generation while others fall by the wayside. The exchange of property rights and the possibility of gaining from that exchange provides the incentive for the implications of all perceptions to be carefully considered.

In addition to perceiving new possibilities for gains from trade, the successful entrepreneur also must contract with others to establish rights to the distribution of new gains. Once the entrepreneur has acted upon his superior perception and created an above-normal rate of return, that will serve as a signal for others to copy his actions. Contracts, which are a set of institutional arrangements for determining how new gains from trade are divided, are necessary for the protection of what the entrepreneur has created. In a sense these contracts become new property rights or rules determining who has access to resources. If the entrepreneur cannot successfully protect at least some of the wealth he creates through his perceptions of economic imbalances, he will be much less likely to act upon those perceptions.

Therefore the successful entrepreneur is both a perceiver of new values and a developer of contracts or property rights to protect those values. By constructing innovative contractual forms he prevents the complete dissipation of entrepreneurial returns. It is this creation of new property rights through entrepreneurship that enables a society to have the flexibility necessary to cope with changing perceptions of what is of value. For instance, as we shall see in the U. S. context, it was freedom of contract that allowed the formation of new business organizations in the nineteenth century. Such organizations were necessary to coordinate the use of large amounts of labor and capital, and it was the contractual innovations that made such combinations of inputs possible.

Despite the importance of entrepreneurial responses to the changing circumstances of time and place, one can still question the desirability of significant constraints upon government. Why not allow entrepreneurs to take their actions in response to their perceptions, but also allow legislatures and the judiciary to alter property rights to account for changes in the economic and social environment? Would not such a combination provide the optimal amount of both stability and flexibility?

The problem with this approach is that the ability of entrepreneurs to respond effectively on the basis of their perceptions depends upon a stable property rights framework. If individuals do not have an assurance that their property rights will be protected, they are not as likely to seek gains from trade. This is particulary true of the entrepreneur who is involved in innovative contracting to create new rights. If that entrepreneur believes that such newly created rights or contracts will not be enforced, he will be less willing to risk his resources in creating such rights. Many entrepreneurial actions are taken in anticipation of long term gains. Therefore it is necessary that the property rights framework be stable in the present and in the future. If legislatures can rearrange and reassign property rights by majority rule, uncertainty is a likely result with the effect of stifling entrepreneurial activity. Although such alterations can provide needed flexibility in the public sector, they will seriously hamper private initiative that is also responding to changes in the social and economic environment.

It is also important to note that flexibility in the public sphere means something quite different than it does in the private sector. There are three characteristics of collective or governmental decision-making which generate results quite different from private decision-making. First, by virtue of the fact that government bodies can use coercive power to gain control over resources, the true opportunity cost of taking a course of action is oftentimes ignored. If an entrepreneur wants to take a resource from a certain use and make it available to another party where she thinks its value will be higher, she must outbid all other potential users. Not so when coercive power can be used. Government can move resources from higher valued to lower valued uses without the decision maker having to bear the full cost of such reallocation. Although some have argued that political decision making is adequately constrained through the voting booth, the first two chapters of this volume outline numerous reasons we would not expect governmental action to represent sound economic policy.

The second problem with governmental alterations in property rights is the presence of rent-seeking, or efforts by individuals or groups to gain control over property rights through the political process. If legislative bodies are allowed to alter property rights, people will attempt to influence the process to make sure they are the beneficiaries. In both the private and the public spheres, control over property is desired. However, in the private arena such control is achieved by bidding with resources that are received by someone. The bid is made, and, if accepted, the amount bid is received. However, in contrast, in the political arena, bids that are made for resources are not received (or if they are we call it corruption). People bid by expending resources to put themselves in "deserving" categories for government grants, they lobby, stand in line, and engage in negative-sum activities as they fight over the slicing of a shrinking (relative to what could be achieved) economic pie. It is almost impossible for government to be in the business of altering property rights without encouraging a vast amount of resource waste by people attempting to be on the receiving end of the new property rights holdings.

Finally, government is less able than the entrepreneur to respond to time and place specific information. In order to survive, entrepreneurial action must meet the "market test." It must be based upon accurate assessment of conditions and must also be designed to take advantage of sudden changes in the economic environment. Governmental action, on the other hand, requires a much more cumbersome process to bring about change in response to relative prices. If majority decision making is applied, fifty percent of the voting group must be convinced that the change is appropriate. For an optimistic entrepreneur to take action on his perception, he can either use his own resources or he can convince another owner of capital that his perception is worthwhile. In neither case does a significant portion of society have to approve of his actions. Innovative actions in the public sector, however, require a consensus which can be costly to achieve.

Furthermore, it is much more difficult to recover from mistakes in government policy. Once a program is in place there are identifiable individuals who will lose if the program is abandoned; therefore, change from the status quo becomes very costly. Although the particular circumstances of time and place may dictate an appropriate change in the allocation of resources, carrying this reallocation out through political process means that the ability to respond to future changes will be limited.

Thus, in a world of uncertainty, entrepreneurial response to change property rights represents the best tool for dealing with an unknown future. However, in order to be effective, such responses must be based upon a set of well defined and enforced property rights that are freely transferable. Legislative or judicial reformulations of rights are much less likely to reflect effectively the needs of as dynamic economy and are also likely to hinder entrepreneurial action.

III. Property Rights Protection In the U.S. Constitution

In 1787, when the delegates to the Constitutional Convention met in Philadelphia they had several problems to deal with. They were to revise the Articles of Confederation in order to better empower the federal government to carry out its necessary functions, but they also had a clear understanding of the dangers of unrestrained power in the hands of the state. They chose to draft an entirely new document rather than to revise the existing one and in the fall of that year the Constitution was submitted to the states for ratification.

The Constitution was based upon three fundamental principles. Freedom and liberty were seen as the fundamental goals of society; goodwill alone was not sufficient to achieve liberty because of man's selfish nature; and government, while necessary to reconcile the first two, was itself imperfect and in need of constraint.

As a way of protecting liberty and constraining government, the Constitution gave strong emphasis to the sanctity of property rights.[2] Several parts of the document were important in providing for such rights: the contract clause (Article I, Section 10), which provides that "no state shall . . . pass any Bill of Attainder, ex post facto law or law impairing the Obligation of Contracts"; the commerce clause (Article I, Section 8) which gives Congress the power "to regulate Commerce with foreign nations, and among the several states, and with the Indian Tribes"; and the due process amendments, first the Fifth and later the Fourteenth, which provide that no person shall "be deprived of life, liberty or property, without due process of law."

As we have described above, property rights must be transferable in order for an economic system to function well. If entrepreneurs cannot bid for assets they believe will be more valuable in another use, their actions are severely constrained. Likewise, freedom of contract is necessary for entrepreneurial innovation in contracts that protect newly created wealth. The contract clause, at least as originally interpreted, served as an important constraint on the ability of government to interfere with agreements between parties.

The commerce clause was used as a negative check on state control of interstate trade and therefore significantly limited governmental interference with economic transactions across state borders. Due process was also an important constraint on legislative meddling with property rights, although its most effective era came late in the nineteenth century and the first part of the twentieth when some of the other restrictions on government alteration of rights had been removed.

Even more important than the specific provisions that protected property rights was the fact that the entire document was based on the concept of natural rights. The Founding Fathers were well acquainted with Locke and other natural rights theorists and the sanctity of property rights was an important component of their political philosophy. Both the Declaration of Independence and the Constitution clearly represent government as an institution designed to protect already existing rights, rather than the source of such rights. Siegan argues that "during the initial period of federal constitutional history, which closed about 1830, leading judges and advocates accepted the ideas of natural rights and the social compact as bases for constitutional decisions" (Siegan 1980, p. 27). Thus the doctrine of vested, or natural rights, served as both the basis for writing the Constitution and for early interpretations. This meant property rights were held in high

---

[2] For a more complete discussion of the relationship between the Constitution and property rights; see Anderson and Hill (1980), Epstein (1985), Paul (1987), and Siegan (1980).

regard and were extremely difficult to alter through legislative action.

As Siegan suggests, the Supreme Court was also an important agent in protecting property rights. Every document needs interpretation as specific applications of general rules are considered. One of the first issues that had to be settled after the adoption of the Constitution was the issue of judicial supremacy; did the Court have the right to review and negate both state and federal legislation that violated constitutional standards? The Judiciary Act of 1789 and several early court cases answered that question in the affirmative. The Court then played an active role in examining legislation, and was an important element in preserving private property rights through its willingness to declare unconstitutional legislation that violated those rights.

However, despite the fact that the Constitution constrained the power of government to alter property rights or to interfere with their transfer, those constraints have gradually eroded. The first significant change came in 1827 when, in *Ogden v. Saunders*, the Supreme Court ruled that the contract clause protected freedom of contract only from retrospective legislation. In other words, if laws were passed which impaired the obligation of future contracts, the Constitution was not violated. Fortunately, other protections of freedom of contract still remained, and the negation of the contract clause did not immediately open the floodgates for legislative interference.

The commerce clause continued, throughout much of the nineteenth century, to serve as a significant barrier to the states in their attempts to impair contractual freedom. Although the commerce clause, in effect, duplicates the contract clause in that it protects property rights holders from legislative interference with commerce, or more precisely, economic transactions, it proved an important barrier to state action. In a series of cases the Supreme Court nullified numerous state laws that attempted to restrict property rights. For instance, in 1824 the Court ruled that New York could not grant monopoly privileges to a steamship company. In 1827 it also denied Maryland the right to impose taxes on goods imported from other states.

Although the commerce clause was an important limit to state action, it did not provide a barrier to federal interference with freedom of contract. As the national congress became more interventionist the commerce clause ceased to be as important a constraint on government alterations of property rights. In 1877 another attenuation of private rights occurred in the case of *Munn v. Illinois*. At issue was the power of the Illinois state legislature to set grain storage rates for elevators. Although price setting is a clear violation of contractual freedom, the Court ruled that such freedom could be abrogated when the property was used in a way that was "affected with a public interest." The distinction between public and private interests is an ambiguous one since all property rights that are a part of economic transactions affect the public. Therefore the opportunities for continual legislative interference with contracts were greatly expanded.

Another doctrine served for a time, however, to preserve some semblance of freedom of contract. In 1868 the Fourteenth Amendment to the Constitution was ratified, and it extended the due process protections of the Fifth Amendment to state laws. For a time due process was interpreted simply in a procedural fashion, but starting in 1897 the Supreme Court used due process to provide substantive protection to property rights and the purchase and sale of those rights. Thus again another substitute for the basic protection of the contract clause was found, but this too was short lived. In 1934, in *Nebbia v. New York*, the Court upheld general price regulations as constitutional. This case set ample precedent for legislatures to pass laws that imposed significant restrictions on economic transactions. This position of non-interference with legislative acts that altered property rights was further strengthened in 1937 and 1938 in several other Supreme Court decisions.

Two more recent cases have added to this continual attenuation of rights. In 1954 the Court effectively removed the public use limitation on government takings of property. Prior to that time, eminent domain power could not be used to transfer property from one person to another for clearly private purposes. In *Berman v. Parker*, the Court held that under the guise of urban renewal property could be taken from one party, even if it were made available to private developers, a use that previously would have been considered outside of the definition of public use. This was made even more explicit in *Hawaii Housing Authority v. Midkiff* (1984) when a statute that permitted the state to condemn land and sell it to the occupying tenants was ruled constitutional.

Thus today the Constitution provides few effective barriers to legislative alterations of property rights. The Supreme Court has declined to review economic legislation under the takings or just compensation sections of the due process amendments, acceding almost completely to the will of the legislature. Neither the contract nor the commerce clause provide significant barriers to governmental action. The police power and the power to tax have both been expanded so as to justify much more radical interference with private rights than was previously authorized. Therefore efforts to meet the need for flexibility have resulted in an ever changing framework of government, but as we shall argue in the next section, have also severely constrained the ability of entrepreneurs to respond to the need for new formulations of property rights.

IV. Entrepreneurial Response to the Property Rights Framerwork

The release of energy during the nineteenth century was the result of a set of institutions, including the U. S. Constitution, which created the proper incentive structure to channel resources to higher valued uses. Rapid economic, geographic, and demographic change were characteristics of the era. Numerous economic histories of the period have focused on the ways in which entrepreneurs responded to these changes with innovative technologies. What is often missing from these histories is a description of the multitude of innovative contractual arrangements that evolved. In the case of corporations these arrangements consisted largely of recombinations of existing rights, but in the case of the western frontier, entrepreneurs were producing new property rights in response to conditions dramatically different from those previously experienced. We turn to these two examples.

A. The Rise of the Modern Firm

Certainly one of the most significant alterations in the American economy has been in the appropriate organizational forms for producing and distributing goods and services. At the time of the writing of the Constitution it is doubtful if anyone had any idea of the dramatic transformation that would take place in the next two centuries in the size and structure of the firm. Alfred Chandler (1977) describes well the dramatic transformation:

> The multiunit enterprise administered by a set of salaried middle and top managers can then properly be termed modern. Such enterprises did not exist in the United States in 1840. By World War I this type of firm had become the dominant business institution in many sectors of the American economy. By the middle of the twentieth century, these enterprises employed hundreds and even thousands of middle and top managers who supervised the work of dozens and often hundreds of operating units employing tens and often hundreds of workers. These enterprises were owned by tens or hundreds of thousands of shareholders and carried out billions of business annually. Even a relatively small business enterprise operating in local or regional markets had its top and middle managers. Rarely in the history of the world has an institution grown to be so important and so pervasive in so short a period of time (pp. 3-4).

Despite the fact that the need to completely reform the standard production unit was not foreseen, the Constitution, with its protection of property rights, served well the needs of the economy. The alterations in firm structure were the result of numerous entepreneurial actions responding to the need for new institutional forms. Firms can best be viewed as a set of contractual relationships that supplement the market in coordinating the use of inputs and the sale of outputs (Coase 1937, Alchian and Demsetz

1972, Cheung 1983). However, new contracts do not appear automatically, but are the result of entrepreneurial innovation and contracting. The legal framework of the nineteenth century allowed such action, and individuals with the appropriate vision responded with dramatic alterations in contractual form. Thus despite the lack of specification of the exact type of response to change that would occur, the Constitutional framework served well the need for flexibility in a dynamic economy.

As Cheung (1983, p. 3) describes it, "The firm emerges [when] . . . the entrepreneur or the agent who holds a limited set of use rights by contract directs production activities without immediate reference to the price of each activity." But what changed in the economics of production to alter so dramatically the contract forms necessary to coordinate the use of inputs? The firm, viewed as a set of contractual relationships under which one individual directed the actions of other inputs had long existed. But the large scale firm of the nineteenth century that used numerous managers, relied upon stockholder ownership, and consisted of numerous units, was a new phenomenon.

Alchian and Demsetz (1972) argue that it is the difficulty of monitoring and measuring team production that leads to an organization with a residual claimant who carries out the monitoring process. This residual claimant is also the central party who is common to all contracts with inputs and can, without permission from other input owners, alter the membership of the team.

In the nineteenth century several things happened that led to new institutional structures to carry out the monitoring process. First, new sources of energy, largely steam power fueled by coal, allowed concentration of more tasks in a given workplace. Concurrent technological change required the use of more machinery and the division of work into numerous repetitive tasks. As markets grew the scale of operation could be profitably expanded. Each of these factors made team production more profitable, but that also meant new transaction costs were introduced into the process. Measuring the marginal productivity of each worker became more difficult with the introduction of more machinery and the greater division of labor. Central coordination and assignment of tasks was necessary to capture the returns to scale. As a result of these influences the nature of the firm changed dramatically, and each change required a new entrepreneurial innovation in the contracts governing the relationships between inputs. Price discovery costs meant that markets no longer sufficed to coordinate as many interactions as previously.

A major shift was in the labor market, with fixed wage payments replacing piece-rate wages. As the complexity of team production increased it became more and more difficult to design a piece-rate system that accurately reflected productivity and provided adequate incentives. At first glance it would appear that transaction costs would be lower under a system of payment on the basis of individual marginal product since such a system requires little third party monitoring. However, that is the case only if productivity can be easily measured. With the increase in team production it became more profitable to institute a monitoring system that replaced measurement of the output of each input with the direct observation of input action and the central direction of tasks.

Cotton textiles was one of the first industries in which centralized, large-scale production took place. A system of putting-out, where materials were supplied to workers who conducted their tasks in their homes dominated much of the industry in the eighteenth century. In 1814 Francis Cabot Lowell built the first integrated mill, where both spinning and weaving were carried out, in Waltham, Massachusetts. The mill was initially capitalized at $100,000 and employed three hundred workers (Chandler, p. 58). Why would workers be willing to assign the rights to control their labor to a central manager, and also consent to a pay system that was not geared to individual productivity? The returns from large-scale team production were such that the fixed wage payments exceeded piece rates by enough to compensate the workers for a decrease in their degrees of freedom. However, such alterations in the contracts governing input relationships were not an automatic response to new sets of relative prices. Entrepreneurial vision and the ability to freely contract with input owners were necessary components of the new forms of production.

Lowell was responsible for numerous other organizational innovations that also would have been impossible without a set of well defined and enforced property rights that were transferable. He constructed his own machine shops, thus further integrating the production process. In order to have access to sufficient capital, he and his associates incorporated the firm. They also changed distribution patterns for the finished product dramatically, consigning the entire output to a single agent for a fixed commission.

The separation of ownership from management was another innovation that required extensive alterations in property rights structures through voluntary contracts. As late as 1840 firms were mostly single proprietorships or partnerships, with management carried out directly by the owners. Railroads were the first enterprises to require sufficient coordination so as to be clearly beyond the capacity of a few individuals. As Chandler (1977, p. 94) puts it:

> Obtaining the full potential of the new technology called for unprecedented organizational efforts. No other business enterprise, or for that matter few other nonbusiness institutions, had ever required the coordination and control of so many different types of units carrying out so great a variety of tasks that demanded such close scheduling. None handled so many

different types of goods or required the recording of so many different financial accounts.

For a time the railroads did not own the cars, but instead simply hauled them for merchants. The actual ownership of the input provided superior coordination however, and soon all railroads put that part of the operation under their direct control. The massive scale of other coordination problems was such that numerous supervisors were required, so an organizational structure that employed salaried managers evolved. Precise accounting procedures to keep track of shipments and to provide accurate estimates of costs were also developed. Interfirm coordination was also essential so that goods could be moved from one line to the other without high transaction costs. By the 1870s contracts had developed such that a car loaded in one city could go to anywhere that railroads served, on numerous lines owned by various companies, without being unloaded and the goods placed on another car.

The contractual innovations in textiles and railroads are simply illustrative of the massive private sector responses to change in a dynamic economy. Each of the changes discussed required extensive alterations in contractual form, or, if you will, in the property rights structure. Because of such alterations, the economic landscape of the latter part of the twentieth century bears little resemblance to that of two hundred years ago. It is difficult to argue that the U. S. Constitution, as conceived by the Founding Fathers and interpreted in the first part of the nineteenth century, was too rigid and made too little allowance for change. As illustrated by historical experience, the Constitution provided for stability and predictability in that it made property rights definable, defensible, and divestible. However, these same protections also provided for a great deal of flexibility through entrepreneurial recombinations of rights.

As discussed in the previous section, the Constitutional protection of property rights has, in the last century, gradually eroded. Thus the opportunities for entrepreneurs to respond to changes in the economy through the purchase and sale of property rights and through contractual innovations has been significantly restricted. This is as much evident in the limitations on the structure and ownership of firms as anywhere.

Many social critics have expressed concern about the lack of ownership control of managers in the modern corporate structure. Numerous stockholders each with insufficient holdings to exercise real control, and the existence of a salaried managerial hierarchy has meant that managers had a considerable degree of discretion. In such an environment, it is argued, management may be able to satisfy its own desires rather than representing the wishes of the stockholders. However, a very real check on managerial malfeasance exists in the market for corporate control. If an individual or group of individuals believes the corporation's resources are being badly used, i.e. they could be made to yield a higher return, purchase and redirection of those assets is an attractive option. The recent flurry of hostile takeover activity represents entrepreneurial response to a particular institutional structure, one where many firm owners may not find it in their interests to engage in extensive monitoring of managerial activity. The entrepreneur who can mount a successful takeover has engaged in at least some monitoring, however, and will undoubtedly engage in more in the process of reformulating the company he now controls.

Despite the fact that such takeovers represent an effective entrepreneurial response to very real transaction cost problems, both the federal government and numerous state legislatures have found such a process undesirable. For instance, the Williams Act, which requires public notification of intent when an individual's stockholdings reach five per cent of any given firm, is a significant obstacle to an efficient market for corporate control. Furthermore, the U. S. Supreme Court, in an April 21, 1987 decision upheld an Indiana law that denies voting rights to a bidder who acquires 20 per cent or more of a corporation, unless the remaining stockholders expressly grant those rights. Six other states have similar laws. States have also passed legislation restricting the types of offers raiders can make for stock. All of these laws represent substantial restrictions on freedom of contract and hence an attenuation of property rights.

One should also note that if the changes discussed above were desired by stockholders, legislative action would not be necessary. Entrepreneurs could offer stock for sale in a firm under just such rules. Innovative contracts offer adequate protection to shareholder interests, since entrepreneurs will provide and shareholders will choose the contractual form that best represents their wishes. However, the massive reformulation of property rights through legislative action rather than private sector initiative has occurred. The Supreme Court has chosen not to declare such reformulations unconstitutional, a result not unexpected in view of the diminution of the protection of property rights by the Court.

Other restrictions on contractual freedom are either in place or have been suggested. Senator Kennedy introduced in the 1987 Congress legislation requiring employers to provide a minimum level of health insurance to all employees working 17.5 or more hours per week. Another substantial alteration in the contracts governing inputs has been argued for through "labor-management councils" which would allow workers to "participate in company decisions about physical capital, helping choose the direction and magnitude of new investment in research, plant and machinery" (Reich, 1983, p.248). Such mandated worker participation is seen as an enhancing productivity and reducing worker alienation. Although these proposals have been subject to vigorous debate in the public arena, almost no one has raised the issue of the constitutionality of such measures, evidence that substantial legislative alterations of property rights faces few constitutional strictures. Again it is important to note that freedom of contract and entrepreneurial response to workers' desires means such legislation is unnecessary. If workers want their total wage package to contain a different mix of benefits and dollar income than presently exists, the firm that offers a better combination will find it easier to hire workers. Likewise, the traditional organization of relationships between owners of capital, managers, and workers is not a mandated one. Rather it has resulted from numerous individuals attempting to structure contracts so that optimal combinations of risk, transferability of assets, monitoring, and income are made available to input owners. Since, under a private property rights regime, these input owners have veto rights over the use of their property (this includes the property workers hold in themselves), voluntary exchange and entrepreneurial action lead to mutually advantageous contractual arrangements.

B. The Evolution of Property Rights on the Frontier

In a dynamic economy there will be a continual need for new formulations of property rights, and, in many cases, new property rights themselves will need to be created. Again, there are two possible avenues for the creation of such rights. Government can be the agent of change, actively involving itself in the process of establishing property rights. However, a second means is also available. Entrepreneurs, responding to changing relative prices, will find it profitable to formulate new rights. A constitution, or a set of basic rules establishing the general property rights framework will be helpful in setting the stage for entrepreneurial action. However, it is the entrepreneur acting upon the particulars of time and place who actually defines the rights and, in some cases, even establishes the rules governing their defense and divestiture. The American frontier is an interesting example of such entrepreneurial action.

As Professor Demsetz (1967, p. 354) has pointed out, "property rights arise when it becomes economic for those affected by externalities to internalize benefits and costs." Since the early settlers (entrepreneurs) arrived in the West before much of the legal machinery of state and federal government could be established, they found it necessary to generate their own rules. Since the presence of government was minimal, those rules depended on voluntary agreement in the form of innovative contractual arrangements among the settlers. Wagon trains formed constitutions before leaving on the long journey across the plains. These constitutional contracts defined who had what rights, how disputes over rights would be settled, and even when coercive power by the wagon master was legitimate. Land claims clubs in the mid-West also drew up constitutions to establish property rights to land before the federal government played a formal role. Contracts among the members specified the boundaries of land claimed by the club, the system by which land rights would be defined, and the effort members had to put into the definition and enforcement process.[3] Farther to the west, cattlemen's associations and mining camps served the same role for their respective resources. Cattlemen banded together to divide up the range, to agree on methods of marking the cattle with brands, and to use the round-up to take advantage of economies of scale in the gathering of cattle. Miners held meetings in their camps to establish processes for claiming ore deposits and to settle disputes over established mining claims.

> Following a tradition of collective action on the mining frontiers of other continents, the miners formed districts, embracing from one to several of the existing "camps" or "diggings" and promulgated regulations for marking and recording claims. The miners universally adopted the priority principle, which simply recognized the superior claims of the first-arrival... The miners' codes defined the maximum size of claims, set limits on the number of claims a single individual mights work, and established regulations designating certain actions ... as equivalent to forfeiture of rights (McCurdy 1976, pp. 236-37).

In each of these cases, it was entrepreneurial foresight that produced the innovative contractual arrangements which prevented chaos on the frontier. These arrangements defined and enforced property rights to new resources and allowed the exchange of those rights so as to maximize the possibilities for gains from trade.[4]

The role of contracting was especially important in the evolution of western water rights.[5] To the frontiersmen entering the Great Plains, it was clear that access to water had to be a prime factor in considering a location. Hence, initial settlement patterns can be traced to the river and stream bottoms. If an individual found that a stream location was already taken, he simply moved to another water supply. Under these circumstances, the rights to use the water accrued to whoever owned the stream bank and had access to it by virtue of first position. Such a riparian water rights system was nearly identical to that of the East and was adopted by westerners because it fit the resource conditions as long as land with adjacent water was abundant relative to the number of settlers. The benefits of changing the existing institutions governing water were not sufficient remuneration for the time and effort required to initiate the change.

Two factors worked to change the benefits and costs of altering property rights over time. First, mining technology required that water be taken

---

[3] For a more detailed discussion, see Anderson and Hill, 1983.

[4] For a more complete discussion of these examples, see Anderson and Hill, 1975.

[5] This discussion is based largely on Anderson 1983, chapters III and IV.

from the stream and moved to nonriparian locations. Since the riparian rules gave all owners the right to an undiminished quantity and quality of water, diversions for mining and irrigation were not feasible. Second, a great deal of nonriparian agricultural land could be made more productive if irrigation water could be moved to it.

Since the California mining camps were the first to feel major population pressure, it is not surprising that miners played an important role in the evolution of the prior appropriation doctrine. The miners quickly realized that gold was found in places other then streambeds, where only a pan and shovel were needed to extract the precious mineral. When deposits were discovered several miles from water, it made economic sense to appropriate water from the streams. "It universally became one of the mining customs that the rights to divert and use a specified quantity of water could be acquired by prior appropriation" (McCurdy 1976, p. 254).

With an efficient set of water institutions in place, individuals undertook projects to deliver water where it was demanded. Well-defined exclusive rights provided the necessary tenure security to stimulate private investment. A variety of organizational structures were used to mobilize capital for building dams to store the water and aqueducts to deliver it. Irrigation and mining activities received most of the water, but population growth meant that municipal demands also had to be served. The leaders of the federal reclamation movement at the turn of the century were correct in asserting that without the application of water, lands west of the 100th meridian would not be very productive. They failed to recognize, however, how effectively private institutions and markets could serve this purpose. Thousands of miles of ditches were constructed and millions of acres blossomed as a result of entrepreneurial efforts to use water efficiently.

The original mining law was aimed at establishing private rights to water through appropriation, but disputes over rights still led to court cases, which in turn led to conflicts with the riparian doctrine of common law. From eastern water law came such concepts as usufruct, beneficial use, and reasonable use, all of which represented legal restrictions on the newly established rights. From the western mining camps and cattle ranges came absolute property, equal footing for uses, and transferable ownership of water rights. The doctrine of appropriation established ownership rights that were clearly defined, enforced, and transferable. Rights were absolute and not co-equal. As a result, markets were left to determine the value of water. However, under riparian doctrine rights were not generally transferable and the possibility of water marketing was restricted.

The tensions between eastern and western water law and the federal intervention into reclamation through the Reclamation Act of 1902 eventually substituted political determination of who had rights to water for market allocation. By the late nineteenth century, western state common law had come to recognize prior rights, but state constitutions and statutes were moving toward the establishment of public ownership of water. Appropriators received only a usufructuary right (a right to use the water), not an actual ownership right, so state legislatures felt free to declare that the corpus of water was state property. With the water publicly owned, it is not surprising that political allocations of rights came to dominate the process. Eventually political restrictions broke apart the foundation of a water allocation system based on well-defined, enforced, and transferable water rights that was hammered out by the entrepreneurs of the "lawless West."

> It is evident that the long-term trend . . . has been to mobilize financial, administrative, political, constitutional and judicial resources . . . to gain . . . control of western states . . . The appropriation doctrine has been virtually expropriated and converted into licenses or permits, and control over Western waters has been centralized in state and federal governments (Cuzan 1983, pp. 20-21).

Just as limits on appropriation doctrine hindered water markets, political reclamation replaced much private enterprise and created a bureaucratic pork barrel that continues to thrive even when other public funds are cut. In his *Report on the Lands of the Arid Region*, John Wesley Powell (1878, p. 45) expressed concern that water rights would be "gradually absorbed by a few. Monopolies of water will be secured, and the whole agriculture of the county will be tributary thereto—a condition of affairs which an American citizen having in view the interest of the largest number of people cannot contemplate with favor." This concern, coupled with the argument that markets were not efficient enough to fund reclamation projects, led bureaucratic entrepreneurs to seek political funds for their large-scale plans to reclaim the American West. The result was that hundreds of dams and thousands of miles of canals were built with federal funds and large subsidies to irrigators. With this water supplied by the Bureau of Reclamation, it is not surprising that its use also was controlled by the federal government.

Between court cases and political reclamation efforts, there was little room left for the market allocation of water. In most western states, water is the constitutionally declared property of the state, the people, or the public. As a result of this political determination of rights, Hirshleifer, DeHaven, and Milliman (1960, p. 249) concluded that:

> the current trend . . . runs strongly against the development of a system of water law based on individual choice and the market mechanism . . . [I]t is the product of the common though incorrect opinion that the public interest can be served only by political as opposed to market allocation . . .

Constitutionally and culturally based support for freedom of contract allowed entrepreneurs in the mining camps, cattle ranges, and productive farms to respond to the special circumstances of time and place to produce new property rights to scarce resources. Political limits on this freedom to contract at the turn of the century, however, replaced this evolution with politically determined allocations.

V. Conclusion

The United States Constitution established a framework of private property rights that unleashed tremendous creative energy. That energy, in conjunction with other forces of modernization, produced enormous alterations in the American economy. Such alterations required significant institutional changes, and entrepreneurs responded with numerous contractual innovations that reformulated existing property rights and established new ones. However, constitutional protection of property rights gradually deteriorated, thus substantially reducing the incentives for entrepreneurs to be creatively involved in institutional change.

The last several decades has seen a renewed call for constitutional flexibility to meet the needs of a rapidly changing economy. It is argued that legislatures must not be constrained in their ability to reformulate property rights and the judiciary should be active participants in the process of creating new rights. Such a concern is misplaced. The costs of such flexibility are vastly underestimated. Also underestimated is the ability of entrepreneurs to respond to new situations with contractual innovations that reduce common pool problems, lower transaction costs, and lessen externalities. However, such entrepreneurial responses depend upon a constitutionally mandated framework of stable property rights. It is time to return to such a framework.

References

Alchian, Armen A., and Demsetz, Harold. "Production, Information Costs, and Economic Organization." *American Economic Review* 62 (December 1972): 777-95.

Anderson, Terry L. *Water Crisis: Ending the Policy Drought.* Washington, D.C.: Cato Institute, 1983.

Anderson, Terry L. and Hill, Peter J. "The Evolution of Property Rights: A Study of the American West." *Journal of Law and Economics* 18 (April 1975): 163-79.

Anderson, Terry L. and Hill, Peter J. "Privatizing the Commons: An Improvement?" *Southern Economic Journal* 50 (October 1983): 438-50.

Brennan, William J. Speech at Georgetown University, October 12, 1985; excerpts printed in *New York Times*, October 13, 1985, p. 36.

Chandler, Alfred D. *The Visible Hand: The Managerial Revolution in American Business.* Cambridge, Mass.: Harvard University Press, 1977.

Cheung, Steven N.S. "Contractual Nature of the Firm." The *Journal of Law and Economics* 26 (April 1983): 1-21.

Coase, Ronald H. "The Nature of the Firm." *Economica* 4 (1937): 386-405.

Cuzan, Alfred G. "Appropriators vs. Expropriators: The Political Economy of Water in the West." In *Water Rights: Scarce Resource Allocation*, Bureaucracy, and the Environment. Edited by Terry L. Anderson. Cambridge: Ballinger Press, 1983.

Demsetz, Harold. "Toward a Theory of Property Rights." *American Economic Review* 57 (Papers and Proceedings) (May 1967): 347-59.

Epstein, Richard A. *Takings: Private Property and the Power of Eminent Domain.* Cambridge, Mass.: Harvard University Press, 1985.

Hayek, F.A. "The Use of Knowledge in Society." *American Economic Review* 35 (September 1945): 519-30.

Hirshleifer, Jack, DeHaven, James C., and Milliman, Jerome W. *Water Supply: Economics, Technology, Policy.* Chicago: University of Chicago Press, 1960.

Kinney, Clesson S. *Law of Irrigation and Water Rights and Arid Region Doctrine of Appropriations of Waters.* San Francisco: Bender-Moss, 1912.

McCurdy, Charles W. "Stephen J. Field and Public Land Law Development in California, 1850-1866: A Case Study of Judicial Resource Allocation in Nineteenth-Century American." *Law and Society Review* 10 (Winter 1976): 235-66.

Paul, Ellen Frankel. *Property Rights and Eminent Domain.* New Brunswick, NJ: Transaction Books, 1987.

Powell, John Wesley. *Report on the Lands of the Arid Region of the United States,* 45th Cong., 2d sess., House of Representatives Ex. Doc. 73. Washington: GPO, 1878.

Reich, Robert B. *The Next American Frontier.* New York: Times Books, 1983.

Siegan, Bernard H. *Economic Liberties and the Constitution.* Chicago: University of Chicago Press, 1980.

Webb, Walter Prescot. *The Great Plains.* New York: Grosset and Dunlap, 1931.

11

REFLECTIONS ON A NORMATIVE ECONOMIC THEORY OF THE UNIFICATION OF LAW

Peter Bernholz and Malte Faber

The subject we are addressing is a difficult one because, to our knowledge, it has not been examined by economic theory, except for the theory of federalism,[1] the theory of organizations,[2] and the theory of property rights.[3] Beyond this, the legally-trained reader should bear in mind, ". . . that the ideas of economic science and its concepts and models often have a different meaning and serve a different purpose from those of jurisprudence. We are dealing with two different fields of thought, the ideas of which are difficult to transfer from one field to the other and are difficult to combine."[4] We will derive here theses of how from an economic perspective the legal system should be organized. Subsequently we shall examine the significance and extent of the unification of law. Since our effort is normative, we will not elaborate on the developments of the legal system to be expected from the application of economic reasoning. We will, moreover, not discuss how the legal system we lay our could emerge. We begin by developing in detail, from the perspective of static economic theory, what the legal system should look like?[5] This will be done in Section I,

This article was originally published in German in *Rabels Zeitschrift fuer auslaendisches und internationales Privatrecht* 50 (1986): 35-60. Translated by Birgit W. Strauch.

The authors are Professors of Economics at the Universities of Basel and Heidelberg, respectively. We should like to thank Martin Wagner of the University of Basel, Gunther Stephan and Franz-Josef Wodopia of the University of Heidelberg, and Friedrich Bayer of the University of Osnabruck for helpful suggestions.

[1] W.E. Oates, *The Political Economy of Fiscal Federalism*, (New York: Harcourt Brace Jovanovich, 1977).

[2] O.E. Williamson, "The Modern Corporation: Origins, Evolution, Attributes," *Journal of Economic Literature* 29 (December 1981): 1537-68.

[3] A. Schueller, *Property Rights und okonomische Theorie*, (Muenchen: Vahlen, 1983).

[4] W. Schmeder, *Die Rechtsangleichung als Integrationsmittel der Europaeischen Gemeinschaft* (Koeln: Carl Heymann, 1978), p. 47.

[5] In contrast to the dynamic economic view, observations of static economics are limited to a single time period. Hence, e.g. questions about cycles and growth are not addressed.

where we also consider the implications of our ideas for the European Community. In Section II, we extend our analysis to incorporate a dynamic economic perspective. Finally, in Section III we will consider connections with the literature on jurisprudence.

I. Formation of the Legal System: A Static Economic Perspective

Protective State and Productive State

We are assuming that the economic system and the legal order of a state should be constructed so that four conditions can be realized: (1) efficiency in production and consumption (Pareto-Optimality),[6] (2) freedom, (3) justice, and (4) security.

It is appropriate at this time to point out that it would also be possible, instead of starting from these four postulates, to assume the following postulate: the fullest possible achievement of the goals of one or more of the members of society. Given the scarcity of resources, this requirement would also lead to efficiency in production and to an approach towards Pareto-Optimality. Because of problems concerning information and motivation, the efficient pursuit of the aforementioned goals would require a certain decentralization of the economic system even if it were combined with a dictatorship or an oligarchy. Moreover, decentralization requires some degree of freedom and justice. With this approach the problems of information and motivation would weigh more heavily as reasons for decentralization of decision-making than if one would start from a postulate of freedom for all.

We proceed here from a decentralized organization based on independently deciding individuals. With respect to the four postulates mentioned above, we have to show how both the freedom of the individual and the extent of decentralization should be limited. To a certain extent, both approaches lead to similar conclusions regarding the organization of the state.[7] Only the extent of decentralization or centralization, freedom and justice, should depend upon the approach taken. Subsequently, we will concern ourselves above all with the first three postulates, and will consider the last one only indirectly. First, however, we formulate our main thesis: for the protective state a unification of law is desirable in principle, whereas this is true for the productive state only to a limited degree. Before we establish this thesis, we must define some concepts like protective and productive state according to their functions.

---

[6] Pareto optimality exists when it is impossible to make one person better off without making someone else worse off.

[7] It would be interesting to explore the circumstances under which both observations could lead to the same conclusions.

a) Three Pairs of Concepts.

By "mandatory" law we refer to rules that prescribe exactly what each individual has to do. Examples of mandatory law are the draft or the compulsory form of contracts for the purchase of real estate. "Subsidiary" law, on the other hand, applies when the parties to a contract determine that they have incompletely specified their relationship. Therefore in a dispute between a lessee and a lessor, general principles of rental law are applied. Mandatory law confines the choices of the individuals and the process of competition within the market system. Examples of this are the forms of organizations that are prescribed by building and real estate law.[8] The subsidiary law, by contrast, leaves room for creative arrangements in the forms of contract among the parties and thus, among other things, promotes competion. Instead of subsidiary law one speaks also of "optional" law.

Lachmann distinguishes between "outer" and "inner" institutions.[9] "Outer" institutions are specified in the constitution of a country. They are "the necessary framework of the competitive market order."[10] Examples are the Parliament and the central bank. "Inner" institutions, on the other hand, are created and possibly abandoned within the framework of the market order. Examples are the banking system and the stock exchange. The inner institutions adapt themselves to the outer institutions, and, in contrast to the outer institutions, are subject to selection through competitive processes.[11] The development of the inner institutions can be explained historically or functionally. In the latter case we assume that they are based on individual considerations of utility and cost, and could be changed or even abandoned.[12] In this manner it is possible to explain endogenously the emergence of organizational forms.

There exist an external and an internal law related to these institutions. The first concerns the outer institutions, which include both the mandatory law and the subsidiary law. The internal law, by contrast, can be freely formed both within and among the internal organizations. An example of such a formation is the development of the limited partnership, which within the limits of the external law was created and designed by private parties.

[8] A. Schueller, *Property Rights,* p. 153.

[9] L.M. Lachmann, "Wirtschaftsordnung und wirtschaftliche Institutionen," *Ordo* 14 (1963): 66ff.

[10] Lachmann, p. 66.

[11] As we will explain below, a market-related form of coordination is in certain areas superior to an entrepreneurial-related form. In other areas the opposite holds (Schueller, p. 152). With time these circumstances could change.

[12] Harold Demsetz, "Toward a Theory of Property Rights," *American Economic Review,* Proceedings, 57 (May 1967): 347-59. A detailed description of the external and internal institutions is presented by Schueller, pp. 145-70.

b) Tasks of the Protective State.

We want first to describe the tasks of the protective state.[13] The most important task is to allow each individual as much freedom as possible, without interfering with the freedom of others. While the first part of this task refers to our second postulate, the second part relates to our third postulate. This implies, among other things, the existence of property rights and a criminal law, to determine first who can rightfully control certain objects and second to prevent the members of the community from resorting to force against each other. One of the most important tasks, therefore, is the prevention of "Hobbesian anarchy." Beyond this, a free development of the members of society is possible only if noncompliance with contracts is punished through the legal order.

From the general, fundamental demand for justice, more concretely formulated principles of law like "universality of law" and "equality before the law" can be derived. The legal order of the protective state affects exclusively the aforementioned external law, including, for instance, human rights, civil and procedural law, criminal law, and administrative law. So far as necessary and possible, the protective state must further offer rules to prevent negative external effects of the actions of individuals on third parties, as well as seek to promote certain principles of distributive justice.

The main agents of the protective state are the legislature, the courts, the police, and other supervisory authorities. Once the external law of the protective state has been created, its agents have to limit themselves to enforcing laws, discovering violations of rights, including those of contracts that were concluded between private parties, and punishing those violations. Beyond this, the external law must adjust to environmental changes. It is self-evident that this should happen only within the framework of the four postulates named above. Also, changes should be kept to a minimum, mainly because of the postulate of efficiency but also because of the postulate of security, as we will show below.

c) Tasks of the Productive State.

The main task of the productive state is to provide such goods and services that the private sector, due to the free rider problem, and magnified by the indivisibility of certain goods (like defense and networks of communications), cannot provide sufficiently or even at all. We are dealing here with the problem of the existence of public goods. With public goods, it has to be determined both how much of such a good should be produced and how much each individual should contribute. Further tasks of the produc-

---

[13] To clarify, when the meaning we give to this conception does not agree with that of jurists, we will put it in quotation marks.

tive state include the avoidance of negative external effects and the support of groups in distress, on condition that these tasks cannot be solved within the framework of the protective state.

Decisions are therefore necessary on two interrelated levels.[14] The decisions themselves must be carried out through political processes, which must often be implemented through prohibitions and orders that refer to specific people, and which are not generally valid. For instance, administrative agencies will issue certain orders to be carried out, as in building a public school or in calling up draftees within a certain age group.

In legislation concerning the tasks of the productive state, we are therefore dealing with a different kind of law than that of the protective state. Hayek even states: "The major part of the so-called laws are merely instructions of the states to their officials about the manner by which they must conduct the state machinery and the means that are available to them."[15] This could also lead to specific instructions to private parties as, for instance, in the case of foreign exchange controls and the draft. In this connection Hayek considers whether there should not be two legislative bodies: one that formulates those laws that have only the character of instructions and one that deals with genuine laws that concern the protective state. The implementation of this approach would be consistent with our ideas, because in this way a separation between the protective and the productive state could be accomplished.

It is useful to point out that from the point of view of economic policy the protective state refers to the creation of the rules of an economic order, while the productive state refers to ordinary economic policy within given rules. Within the latter we include all discretionary interventions undertaken by government agencies to influence the economic process. Our concept of the productive state is clearly related to those of the social state and the welfare state. However, we have not used these alternative concepts, because the former does not quite coincide with our concept of the productive state and the latter is more extensive—and in some cases has even a negative connotation. It seems, moreover, that the welfare state, due to political and economic circumstances, has an inherent tendency to expand, in total contrast to the tasks of the productive state. In so far as the welfare state becomes even more encompassing through usurping the redistribution of income, this task should better be attached to the protective state. One could, for example, envision that the degree of income tax progression would be regulated by the constitution.

---

[14] It must be decided on the constitutional level which tasks the productive state has to perform, and on the operational level how these tasks should concretely be carried out.

[15] F.A. Hayek, *Die Verfassung der Freiheit* (Tuebingen: Siebeck, 1971), p. 269. (English: *The Constitution of Liberty*).

2. Foundations of our Theses

a) Reasons for the Protective State.

(1) *Freedom, Security, and Efficiency.* Our attention is focussed on those countries whose economies are mainly free enterprise and market oriented, and whose political systems are democratically organized. A unification of law would have three essential tasks for the protective state. First, it would help to secure the freedom of the individual. A uniform law that ensures the free choices of individuals means that those who have sufficient income will have satisfactory leeway to decide their own affairs. Their dependence on certain other persons is in this way minimized. Private and public sectors are clearly defined. In the private sector an individual has only to obey the rules, which are the same for all, and to keep his contracts. An especially strong anchorage of human rights, of the security of law, and of private law afford the protection under which the majority is prevented from forcing its will upon minorities. From the analysis of the political process we also know that under certain conditions a minority can force its will on the majority.[16] Examples of this derive from the institution of indirect democracy, and also from situations in which the majority is insufficiently or falsely informed, and thus vote against their true interests (or because of disinterest or the costs of voting do not vote at all). For these reasons, the political process should be limited as much as possible.

Second, through the unification of law, the certainty of law and the knowledge of the law would grow. The decisions of the courts could be more easily determined in an area with uniform law. By contrast, in a decentralized state with differing rules of law one must bear considerable expense to become informed. Furthermore, the suitable information would be subject to greater uncertainty than would be the case if uniform law existed. At this point it is useful to point out that, from an economic point of view, law has the property of a public capital good.[17] On one hand, the principle of exclusion does not hold.[18] Just as is true with money, law becomes more useful the larger its jurisdiction. On the other hand it is also true that with law as with a capital good, a lump-sum investment is necessary: namely, the costly process of enactment, promulgation, and enforcement. However, once these have taken place a law, like a road, serves

---

[16] See, for instance, Peter Bernholz and F. Breyer, *Grundlagen der politischen Oekonomie* (Tuebingen: Siebeck, 1984): 254.

[17] J.M. Buchanan, *The Limits of Liberty: Between Anarchy and Leviathan* (Chicago: University of Chicago Press, 1974): 123-26.

[18] The exclusion principle states that no one can be excluded from the use of a good once it has been produced. This concerns, for instance, radio broadcasting, protection by a dam, and defense readiness. Such situations as these lead to free riding.

the public for many periods. This view of the relationships also explains why laws do not always have to be changed when they no longer suit the circumstances: changing the law could require investment and transaction costs that are higher than the value of the changes.

Third, the economic organization would be improved by a unification of law. An essential prerequisite for the functioning of a market economy is the legal regulation of property relationships according to the principle of justice, which implies a decision about who has the right to decide over goods.[19] Such a legal order makes possible, under certain conditions, the efficient production of goods as well as their Pareto-Optimal consumption. To be able to internalize external effects, there must exist unified property rights and rules for indemnities have to be created. These permit on their part the corresponding formation of extensive markets.

(2) *References to the European Community.* Before we turn to the productive state, we would like to present a few thoughts about the conditions in the European Community. We know from the analysis of the logical basis of a constitutional democracy that constitutional questions have to be solved almost unanimously.[20] An important prerequisite for this is a "certain equality" of the citizens.[21] Coing, as well, sees equality as an essential condition for an internal unification of law:

> This national unification of law is carried by the pathos of the centralized state and its presupposition of political unity and its enforcement of national sovereignty against power-sharing. This national unification of law takes the place of the pluralism of the sources of law—territorial and feudal as was characteristic of the middle ages and even of the ancient regime prior to the French revolution. It is therefore not accidentally connected with the creation of a unified bourgeois class and the leveling of feudal estates, which had characterized the old society.[22]

Based on the differences of the populations of the countries of the European Community and the absence of equality that followed, it was decided in the 1950s not to unite Europe institutionally, but to do so functionally.[23] This means that one did not undertake to restructure the system once and for all, but preferred a gradual process of unification, starting with import duties and agriculture. The process of constitutional

[19] Schueller, pp. 150-56.

[20] J.M. Buchanan and G. Tullock, *The Calculus of Consent: Logical Foundations of Constitutional Democracy*, (Ann Arbor: University of Michigan Press, 1962): 85-96.

[21] M. Faber, " Einstimmigkeitsregel und Einkommensumverteilung" *Kyklos* 26 (1973): 52-54.

[22] H. Coing *Methoden der Rechtsvereinheitlichung*, in *H. Coing* et. al. eds., "Arbeiten zur Rechtsvergleichung" (Frankfurt: Metzner, 1974): 9.

[23] Schmeder, p. 42.

unification is not yet completed, for the most important decisions at the Council of Ministers are always taken unanimously, though this is no longer required by the Treaty of Rome.[24]

This corresponds with our argument to aim at the unification of law only for limited specific areas, thus leaving room to facilitate an integration of Europe through competition among the different systems of internal rights. Our view coincides with that of Schmeders:

> On the national level, the economic constitutions of the individual member states are still so different that their integration into a common economic constitution comprising an economic and monetary union cannot be promoted solely by legislative action, but at the same time have to be expected patiently through a long process of integration and growth of the community as a consequence of the Customs Union.[25]

b) Reasons for the Productive State.

The productive state should in our view be limited to undertaking only subsidiary tasks in case private individuals or their organizations are unable to do so given a suitable legal order. This is because, first, individuals, or groups of members of society, should, because of the postulate of freedom, be able to decide their own affairs as far as possible. Exceptions to this rule can only be justified by the other postulates. This is the case when the members of society are willing in principle to accept a restriction of their freedom as, for example, to achieve a better provision of public goods, to avoid external effects, or to secure a fair distribution of income. Of necessity, this limitation between the protective state and the productive state must be embodied in the constitution. Independent of the postulate of freedom, there also follows secondly, from the postulate of efficiency, the demand for an as far-reaching limitation as possible of the productive state.

Individuals and small groups are generally best informed about their environment and their possibilities, as well as being motivated through self-interest to appropriate take action. For this reason, decentralized cooperation leads generally, in the absence of public goods and external effects, to a better provision of goods then does centralized decision-making by administrative agencies. From an economic point of view, the state must mainly deal with those public goods, indivisibilities, and negative external effects that cannot be regulated solely by private individuals. This is always the case when a solution based on voluntary exchange is impossible, which

---

[24] M. Faber and F. Breyer "Eine oekonomische Analyse konstitutioneller Aspekte der europaeischen Gemeinschaft," *Jahrbuecher Sozialwissenchaften* 31 (1980): 219.
[25] Schmeder, p. 42.

in turn is especially likely when transaction costs are so high as to prevent exchanges,[26] in which case the so-called Coase Theorem does not hold.[27]

However, information and transaction costs depend upon the structure of established law. In some cases it could be possible, for example, by the fullest possible development of property rights, tort law, or the use of charges and fees, to solve the problems of external effects and public goods within the setting of the protective state.[28] In many other cases, however, the framework of rules of the protective state will not be sufficient, and intervention by the productive state becomes necessary. These include, for example, the negative effects of a "public nuisance," where many people are affected in only a minor way, in which event an individual has no incentive to seek compensation for damages. The situation is similar if many agents are present, especially if their behavior is difficult to determine, making control difficult. Such conditions are often present with environmental problems. An example is damage to forests, where there are many concerned people and many sources of damage. Here the state must intervene. But at the same time, it is true for all environmental problems that regional differences in the self-revitalizing capacity of the environment, due to different natural and economic circumstances, require different solutions. Therefore, such solutions should be found by regional legislative bodies elected by those concerned, as far as this is compatible with the general framework of environmental law. These general laws are enacted within the setting of the protective state and contain such general principles as those of causation and foresight. Moreover, the domain of state regulation is limited by the respective domain of the external effect.

We turn now to public goods. Here again, aside from the application of general principles, there should be no central legislation. We want to give particular emphasis to one of these principles: those who benefit from a public good should be the same people who pay for it. Otherwise, if the financing of the public good is shared with people who receive no benefit, an oversupply will result. With this principle we have established a criterion that allows us to determine concretely over an extensive area, in which cases and how far common interests are present regarding a particular

---

[26] Bernholz and Breyer, p. 120.

[27] The Coase Theorem states that is absence of transaction costs individual solutions will lead (with either damage awards or compensation) to the same social optimum as ideal government regulation would produce. R.H. Coase, "The Problem of Social Cost," *Journal of Law and Economics* 3 (October 1960): 1-44. See also, E. Schanze, "Der Beitrag von Coase zu Recht und oekonomie des Unternehmens" *Zeitschrift fuer die gesammte Staatswissenschaft* 137 (1981): 95-111.

[28] J.M. Buchanan and R.L. Faith, "Entrepreneurship and the Internalization of Externalities," *Journal of Law and Economics* 24 (April 1981): 95-111.

matter. In all of these cases different legal proceedings can be undertaken within the framework of general principles. An example for this is the building of a dike. Which type of construction should be used, how large it should be, and whether it should be built and maintained by governmental or private agencies are questions that can be treated differently in each region. Individual communities and states could through competition develop the most suitable legal form. The citizen even has the possibility, by migrating and thus voting with his feet, to choose the legal form preferred by him. A variety of legal forms can therefore exist for the provision of public goods, and new ones can be created if necessary. This position agrees with that of Gleichmann, who writes: "There is no ambition in the sense of art for art's sake, to plan all law for the community. On the contrary, we are happy about all of the diversity that can remain."[29]

3.Organization of the State

a) Federalism.

The preceding remarks show already that the principles we have derived also imply certain rules for the organization of the state. Our analysis of external effects and public goods offers a possibility to establish economic principles of federalism. A central principle is that the beneficiaries of public goods, or those affected by external effects, should alone decide upon taxes, rates, fees, or intervention by the state, and also which measures should be undertaken in each particular case. From this principle follows a regional or functional organization of the organs of the state. For example, the smaller the affected area the smaller should be the jurisdiction of public measures. Zoning restrictions, therefore, are best enacted by individual communities. On the other hand, the more international a matter is, the more far-reaching should be governmental regulation. Air transportation rights should therefore be standardized centrally.[30] Neuhaus and Kropholler conclude similarly their analysis about the results of the unification of law, when they speak about a "formula of relativity":

> The more predominately international the object of standardized law is (e.g., law of the sea), the more the standardization of law will improve the law. And the weaker the internationality of the object (e.g., case law), the more convincing must be the quality of uniform law to be regarded as improved law. This follows because with an international object there exists already a value to international uniformity, while such uniformity is without practical significance for strictly national objects.[31]

[29] K. Gleichmann, "Methoden der Rechtsangleichung und Rechtsvereinheitlichung innerhalb der EWG." In *Methoden der Rechtsvereinheitlichung*, p. 37.

[30] E. Noam, "The Choice of Governmental Level of Regulation," *Kyklos* 35 (1982), p. 279.

[31] P.H. Neuhaus and J. Kropholler, "Rechtsvereinheitlichung-Rechtsverbesserung?" *Rabels Zeitschrift* 45 (1981), p. 83.

b) Division of power and government compulsion

As we explained above, it follows from our postulates that the protective state and the productive state must be clearly distinguished. Practically, this means most of all an unequivocal separation of judicial, legislative, and administrative functions. Furthermore, a possible introduction of independent legislative bodies for the concerns of the protective state and the productive state is advisable.

According to the postulates of freedom and efficiency, the tasks of the productive state should only be carried out with the government acting as an equal market partner. Therefore, the productive state should as much as possible forego the use of force. In this case, therefore, public law should not be applied. Since the free rider problem arises with the provision of public goods, which means that government must be financed through taxes, fees, and dues, the use of force cannot be completely renounced, to be sure. And the same holds in circumstances that require orders or prohibitions because of negative external effects.

II. Formation of the Legal System: A Dynamic Economic Perspective

Until now we have limited ourselves to a static economic point of view, as far as it has significance for the organization of society and law. Probably even more significant, however, is an analysis of the problem from a dynamic point of view, especially of questions concerning the formation of incentives for the search for and use of already existing information, as well as for the discovery of new information.

1. Fundamental Theses

In addition to the four postulates stated above, we require two further postulates for dynamic analysis. These are (5) political-economic systems should encourage experimentation and innovation, and not hinder them, and (6) a trial introduction of limited innovations into the political-economic system is preferable to planning totally new systems.[32]

In our view there is no economic system that can solve all problems satisfactorily; every existing system has room for improvement. It is, therefore, imperative to find regulations that are flexible and which permit changes based on the aforementioned postulates, so that innovations in institutions, organizations, and decision processes are facilitated.

For a better understanding, it may be helpful to lawyers if we compare our political-economic point of departure to that of a student of jurisprudence. To this end we once again quote Schmeder:

---

[32] Bernholz and Breyer, pp. 452-54.

> To stay alive and well and to remain so, the European legal community must strive to preserve its identity in space and time, and at the same time to support and accommodate historic changes. In the lively oscillating circuit between these two poles, the life of the community is preserved. If it desires only the static preservation of its identity, its life will become rigid. If the dynamic desires for change are overemphasized, it will dissolve. . . . The dynamic drive for development and growth is justified if, when intensively developing political and constitutional law they keep it open and flexible through the principle of integration. The principle of integration, which is the basis of the European treaty represents a principle of growth and evolution, and thereby is a denial of too rapid changes of the community.[33]

We agree with Schmeder that persisting and dynamic forces should stand together in a well balanced relationship. Beyond this, Schmeder concludes as we do:

> At the boundary of the economic regime it is most notable that, because of the dynamic diversity and continual change in its subject matter, the real economic and political situation is to a certain degree out of the reach of fixed regulations, particularly of enduring regulations of fundamental characteristics.[34]

Exactly because this is so, we need to develop principles that can guide us to find our way within a complex reality. In particular, the fundamental principles of external law represent a necessary prerequisite for allowing individuals and groups the leeway necessary for bringing about the innovations and the required changes in the internal law.

In the legal awareness of the European nations the most important principle and the highest standard is: "justice is seen as the constant intention to grant people what is due to them. This principle occupies the first position in the Corpus Juris of Justinian. It dates back to Aristotle, was developed and studied by the scholastics of the middle ages, and even today is the ideal foundation of positive law."[35] While the idea of justice is rather general, the principles of law, like the principle of equality, are much more concrete.

Theoretical analysis and empirical examination show that a system is the more fully innovative the more fully agents are in competition with each other in seeking to solve new problems, especially when those agents themselves must bear the gains and losses of their actions. This holds, for example, for the development of new production methods and new

---

[33] Schmeder, p. 41

[34] Schmeder, p. 46.

[35] Schmeder, p. 31f.

products, but it also holds for the development of new types of organizations, new markets, and new legal forms. It therefore follows from the postulate of an improving supply of goods that the legal order should be shaped so as to promote innovations, and for this reason should give the widest possible room for private property and decentralization.

Before we proceed to derive these theses, it is important for what follows to show how with the help of internal law the boundary is drawn between enterprise and market. There are four essential reasons for the existence of enterprises, as the literature on property rights[36] and organization theory[37] have shown: (a) economies of scale, (b) specialization, (c) opportunistic behavior[38] and (d) negative external effects.[39]

Because of these advantages, enterprises can compensate under certain conditions for their disadvantages, which arise through their internal, more or less hierarchical and not market-coordinated, organization. These disadvantages by which enterprise-related forms of coordination are inferior to market-related forms are due to (1) absence of an incentive structure, (2) information problems, and (3) lack of efficient controls. However, since these circumstances can change, it is important that the internal law leave enough room to accommodate the transition from enterprise to market (and vice versa). The same holds for the choice between different legal forms of enterprise, as exemplified by the development of new types of enterprises. The wider the latitude there is, the larger is the domain for innovation and the stronger is the pressure of competition.

2. Information, Motivation, and Innovation

It can hardly be disputed that in comparison to a market economy, the creation and especially the application of new information is hampered considerably in centrally administered economies. It is also well-known that economic agents have weaker incentives within these systems, because their behavior is neither rewarded by higher income or profits nor is it punished by losses. The Hungarian economist J. Kornai established that since World War II the most significant new products were overwhelmingly developed in capitalistic and not in socialistic countries. "It should be noticed that with the exception of a few initiatives no socialist country figures among

---

[36] See the summary cited in fn. 3.

[37] See the article by Williamson mentioned in fn. 2.

[38] Opportunism means in this connection the short-term pursuit of self-interest, which leads in the long run to an erosion of the efficient economic organization.

[39] Negative external effects are negative results on an economic subject B, which are promoted through actions of an economic subject A, and are not included in market transactions. An example is the pollution of water through an enterprise A, which lessens the catch of fisherman B.

those introducing the product in question for the first time . . . a similar situation [is true] regarding revolutionary new products."[40] This is similarly valid for the efficient search for and use of information already present in the system.

What are the sources of these advantages of the market economy? First should be mentioned the information function of the free market. Relative shortages of goods are signaled by prices, without economic agents having to know where and why certain goods important to them have become more or less scarce. These advantages of a market system arise only through adequately developed private-property rights, under which the participants themselves both bear the losses and enjoy the gains of their actions. They are thereby motivated to look for information and to use it most efficiently. This process is emphasized through competition, because competitors can always gain an advantage through an intensive search for and better use of information, as well as through the introduction of cost-lowering production processes and new products. Such successes of competitors would, however, decrease their own profits or income, or could even change them into losses.

Since private property allows the unrestricted buying and selling of goods, it has further advantages in the use of information. In many cases the owners of essential information will not be identical with the owners of the means of production. In such cases, it is often possible for the latter to buy the information from the former. It is possible, however, that such a transfer of knowledge is in many cases impossible, too costly, or reveals valuable information to third parties. In all these cases, there exists the possibility with private property that the owners of information could themselves obtain the necessary means of production. This possibility would generally be foreclosed with public property.

On the other hand, it should not be overlooked that the coordination through markets using the information function of prices, i.e., through selling and buying, will not represent the only, and sometimes not the best, possibility to search for information and to use it. The existence of private organizations and of firms of diverse corporate form, which internally do not have markets and have only weak internal property rights, proves the superiority of these forms of organizations relative to markets in solving specific problems. Enterprises are able to realize the advantages of mass production through an appropriate expansion of capacity, as well as through the acquisition of other firms or in merging with them to internalize negative external effects. Furthermore, the merger of different production and marketing entities in an enterprise often leads to better

---

[40] J. Kornai, *Anti-Equilibrium* (Amsterdam: North Holland, 1971), p. 288.

control, a better use of resources, and an increase in the chance of survival through risk-sharing. The producer of a commodity that requires complex service cannot be certain that an independent marketing network of individual retail businesses would not sacrifice service for short-term gains, thereby harming the long-term sales of the product. In such a setting it may be prudent to forego the cost-lowering properties of market coordination, and to purchase retail businesses to attain better control. Correspondingly, it may be efficient and profitable from an economic point of view to build a conglomerate, because the capital market exerts insufficient control over the management of the acquired companies. Also, certain problems in searching, purchasing, and using information can make a centralized organization through a firm a profitable venture. It is often necessary to combine in production very specific and non-transferable knowledge of different specialists. In this respect one thinks of the construction of homes or computers. In principle it is surely correct that an entrepreneur can bring together the relevant partial sets of the necessary knowledge through piecemeal purchases:

> ... the knowledge could be assembled on the basis of individual exchanges . . . . But the evidence suggests that *quid pro quo* knowledge transfers are dominated by employment contracts. . . . Such contracts tend to be general in nature — the contents of the exchange are not precisely specified . . . . Single proprietors who contract on a case by case basis for production and application of all the knowledge it takes to operate on any but the smallest scale would soon find themselves swamped by transaction costs. The value of certain kinds of knowledge to competitors or potential competitors is another reason for long-term employment relationships. . . . Finally, longer run relationships encourage individual participants to invest in . . . specific knowledge — knowledge which has little or no value except within the particular organization.[41]

3. Conclusions for the Legal Order

What conclusions can be drawn from this analysis of the legal order? First, free markets and property rights should be offered the widest possible scope. Only in this way is it possible for an economic system to achieve its full capacity for innovation and to set strong incentives for the creation and use of information. These factors are decisive for economic growth through new and improved products and better processes of production. Public property, limitations of the freedom of private decision-making, and government regulation should thus be limited as far as possible. A unification of law that would generalize such interventions should be rejected.

---

[41] W.H. Meckling and M.C. Jensen, "Knowledge, Control and Organizational Structure," unpublished manuscript, June 1984, p. 10f.

It is also to be observed that in reality new markets are constantly being created and becoming better organized. One thinks, for example, of money markets, option markets, futures markets, insurance markets, and markets for leasing and factoring. The significance of new markets for the overall system can be verified only through empirical trial and error. This therefore leads to a second conclusion: the economic framework set by the state through prohibitions and orders should try to influence the creation, elimination, and development of markets only in the case of grave abuses.

The preceding reflections have shown that innovations are not limited to technical discoveries and their applications. They also cover markets, forms of enterprises, new types of internal organization within the firm, and new legal institutions. Also, the boundaries between markets and more or less centrally-organized enterprises depend not only on such things as type of goods, techniques of production, and external effects, but also on the type and organization of the market, of enterprises, and of legal institutions. Therefore, it is of decisive importance that legal institutions, including corporate law, offer sufficient scope for further private developments that do not limit competition. This implies a third conclusion: the internal law of the system should reach as far as possible, and should be available as disposable and subsidiary law. Only in this way is it possible to secure the system's high capacity for innovation. Legal assimilation thus occurs through competition, so to speak, among the various privately-developed legal institutions, resulting in the selection of better suited institutions.

A particular facet of this development results in the gradual development of common business practices, and of private and possibly international courts of arbitration. This type of unification of law through private action should by all means be viewed as a sensible experimental innovation, so long as the aim of the private parties neither clearly discriminates against the weak nor decisively hinders competition.

In closing let us say a few words about the law of patents and licenses. In order not to eliminate the incentive to create and apply new knowledge through excessive and premature competition, protection is necessary through mandatory patent and licensing laws, which belong to the external law. On the other hand, this protection should not be obtained for too long a time, since it would otherwise prevent competition from eventually bringing about cost-lowering imitations. To be sure, it remains an open question of how it might be possible to find a good patent and licensing law.

4. Innovation and Competition Among Communities and States

We have seen what significance internal and subsidiary law has for the capacity to innovate within a society and its evolutionary development, as well as for the choice of better suited legal institutions given an adequate "civil law order." Such possibilities, including the private development of law, are not present for the external and necessarily coercive law. Here we leave open whether and how far a positive development of external law is to be expected through the administration of justice and through the competition between courts. The limited possibilities for innovation, which the external law shares with bureaucratic authorities and with political institutions, are precisely a reason for the recommendation that the range of external law, as well as that of political and administrative decision-making, should be limited as far as possible in favor of internal law, of markets and private organizations.

Proceeding from this point of view, one asks whether and how it could be possible to bestow, at least to some extent, an ability to innovate upon government agencies, political decision-makers, and the external law. Our answer leads here also, as did our static analysis, to the recommendation of the most extensive federalism possible, on both a spatial and a functional basis, the boundaries of which should be drawn according to the ideas presented above.

Federalism on a regional basis also requires freedom for the formation of the corresponding compulsory external law. Federalism thus excludes a unification of law either through regulations by the central government or through agreements among the member states and communities of the federation. In this way a certain competition arises among the communities and member states, not only over the efficiency of public output and the size of the fiscal burden, but also over appropriate organizations and legal institutions. Given the right to emigrate, this competition is supported through a "voting by feet," in which private organizations and firms compete to attract people. This way of looking at things leads naturally to a broad rejection of financial transfers among communities and member states, which are therefore referred to their own independent sources of taxation. It is obvious that in such a system legal assimilation can succeed only through an imitation of those institutions that prove themselves superior through competition.

Similar considerations hold for competition among the public authorities that are engaged in similar functions within the same federation. While within the productive state a particular good is today often supplied by only a single authority, according to a proposal by Niskanen it should be possible for several agencies to compete with one another in the supply of public goods. Government and parliament would each year raise or lower the budget of a bureaucratic organization, according to its acheivements.[42] It

---

[42] W.A. Niskanen, "Nichtmarktwirtschaftliche Entscheidungen—die eigentumliche okonomie der Burokratie," in *Politische okonomie des Wohlfahrtsstaates*, ed. by H.P. Widmair (Frankfurt: Fischer Athenaeum, 1974), p. 221ff.

is obvious that under such circumstances a certain pressure would arise for innovation regarding the organization of government agencies and their procedural rules.

We close with reference to a problem that is difficult to solve. It was shown and emphasized earlier that a unification of the external law of a federal state can certainly be desired. But what happens to the capacity for improvement through innovation in this necessarily irrevocable legal framework, if it were unified among all states? Further problems necessarily arise concerning the boundary between the irrevocable external law and internal law among federal states, member states, and communities, and between the productive state and private, unhindered activity. It is apparent that these boundaries should also depend on the state of technical and organizational knowledge. But how can the rules for the aforementioned boundaries be adopted in a meaningful and perhaps even efficient manner, if there is no possible process that through competition and incentives steers innovation and choice? Because of this and the previously mentioned problem, are judicial and legislative processes of adaptation sufficient to bring about a movement in a desired direction?

III. Observations on Jurisprudence

1.References to the Literature on Legal Assimilation

We do not want to present here a summary of this literature. Rather, we will survey certain references from the literature on jurisprudence, and also show how our approach can be integrated into this literature. Kegel has summarized the historical evolution of the unification of law as follows:

> 1. The modern style of the unification of law is rooted in the Enlightenment and thus in the law of nature and reason; thus one does not appreciate in principle why similar circumstances should be handled differently.
> 2. The vitality of the unification of law cannot be abated. There are breaks; for instance, a hiatus after the large codifications in the beginning of the 19th century until the middle of the century. But then the development resumed, and is especially strong today. One may see in this fact either the victorious march of a grand idea or simply a practical necessity.
> 3. Unification of law is not a question of power, but a question of conviction. Power can help, as it did with the great codifications about 1800, or as it does today in the East block. But it also works without codification, to some extent through constitutional amendment at the federal level, as in Germany and Switzerland, and to some extent without constitutional amendment on the level of the individual states, as in the United States.
> 4. The transition from the national to the international unification of law at the start of the century is a difference of degree and not of substance. To be sure, the unification becomes more difficult as one approaches its boundaries, because of:

a) national sensitivities,

b) ignorance of foreign laws,

c) differences in language,

d) differences of legal terminology and legal education, and

e) differences both in actual circumstances and in the political assessment of the same circumstances, differences that are in turn rooted either in the stage of social development or in religious or political ideas. Religious conceptions oppose the unification of law, for example, in Islamic law, in Israel, and in the strict Christian laws of matrimony of southern Europe and Latin America (except for Uruguay and Mexico). Political ideologies oppose it in countries where the substitute religion of communism dominates.[43]

This discussion shows that our subject is not only of significance for the European communities but rather is of fundamental significance. The conceptions of "coordination," "harmonization," and "assimilation" which were used in the treaty establishing the European Economic Community on March 25, 1957, have not been precisely defined in their meaning relative to each other.[44] Besides this, it is also true that the concepts of the unification of law and the assimilation of law have not been used coherently in legal scholarship.[45] Therefore, we have been following the recommendation: ". . . to select the assimilation of law as the controlling concept, and to understand the unification of law as a special and the most thorough form of the assimilation of law."[46]

Let us now turn to the position of jurists with respect to the question of how far the law should be standardized. Coing explains it this way: ". . . that it should not be treated as a uniform problem, but as a question that plays a role in particular areas of legal life, and actually plays very different roles . . . . There are rather specific interests that propel the demand for a unification of law."[47] For example, Coing names the international protection of technical inventions and the interest in harmonious decision-making. With reference to the different levels, he mentions international organizations, multi- or bilateral agreements among individual states, as for instance in the European Community, and, finally, agreements among such non-governmental organizations as the International Chamber of Commerce and Industry or the Associations of Banks.[48] Because of the

---

[43] G. Kegel, "Sinn und Grenzen der Rechtsangleichung," in *Angleichung des Rects der Wirtschaft in Europa*, (Koeln: Koelner Schriften zum Eroparecht 11, 1971), p. 39f.

[44] G. Philipps, *Erscheinungsform und Methoden der Privatrechts-Vereinheitlichung* (Mainz, 1963): 71-88.

[45] Schmeder, p. 5.

[46] Schmeder, p. 6.

[47] Coing, p. 7.

[48] Coing, *ibid.*

multitude of circumstances and the complexity of the subject, the Society of Comparative Law organized in 1973 a convention to examine the methods for the unification of law, based on three case studies: the United Nations, the Scandinavian States, and the European Community.[49] Coing drew six conclusions regarding different aspects of unification. One of them referred to the interests that stand behind the efforts of unification.[50] Schmeder also deals with this question,[51] and states: ". . .that the center of every legal norm is the lawmaker's valuation of different interests, which is the solution of a conflict of interest. The interests are those of all men in the necessities of life and of human communities to satisfy all essential wants of life."[52] This formulation is closely related to our postulate asking for an improving provision of goods.

While Coing emphasizes aspects that are based on the three case studies,[53] Schmeder remains very general.[54] This also is true for his analysis concerning the "highest value," justice, as well as for the general principles of law that he uses for the assessment of conflicts of interests.[55] Also in such other contributions to jurisprudence as those of Ficker[56] and Zweigert,[57] the argument starts from cases as well as general principles. As a rule it is assumed that interests in unification are present. Apart from certain cases, however, it has not been examined when such interests would exist. This question, however, stands at the very center of our theses. To be sure, we did not discuss the conditions under which the political prerequisities for our ideas on the unification of law could be realized.

2. Observations on the Conflict of Laws

We have not considered the conflict of laws here because, on the one hand, we do not know enough about it, and on the other hand, in light of the following statement by Neuhaus and Kropholler:

> A determination of the decisions of courts through clear and strict rules, as they are generally desired in uniform law in the interests of a uniform

---

[49] See the volume cited in fn. 22.

[50] Coing, p. 15-17.

[51] Schmeder, pp. 25-28.

[52] Schmeder, p. 25.

[53] Coing, p. 7.

[54] Schmeder, p. 27f.

[55] Schmeder, pp. 31-35. The second part of his book goes into great detail.

[56] H.C. Ficker, "Zur internationalen Gesetzebung," In V. Caemmerer et al., eds. *Vom deutschen zum europaeischen Recht* (Frankfurt: Metzuer, 1963) II, pp. 35-63.

[57] K. Zweigert. "Grundsaetze der europaeischen Rechtsangleichung, ihrer Schoepfung und Sicherung," in V. Caemmerer et al. eds., pp. 401-18.

application, is especially dangerous in international private law. The conflict of laws is not only through historical coincidence but of necessity the area of law that has the most gaps. It has, as it were, a codification-resistant character.[58]

Because of this last mentioned reason, it is our opinion that international private law definitely has to be a part of the protective state.

3. The Necessary Cooperation Between Jurists and Economists

Our thoughts on an economic theory of the unification of law could, because of the voluminous extent of the subject, only be sketched. This should form a starting point from which jurists and economists together can continue to examine the related problems.

In closing we refer once again to an assessment by Schmeder, which should be taken into consideration in applying our thoughts to the European Community:

> Europe is surely much more than her law and very much more than her economy, and European integration is surely much more than the assimilation of national legal systems and the elimination of national economic borders. The community is not a nuclear conglomeration of economic trading relationships, which are mechanically timed to follow one another, and which technically function like a machine. Only a rational, mechanical conception of state and society can commit the error to initiate processes automatically through norms of law and to decree and regulate their functions. The community is rather a concrete vital entity, a political corporation, and a social reality, which is connected through the common interests of its members.[59]

---

[58] Neuhaus and Kropholle, p. 89.

[59] Schmeder, p. 40.

PART IV

GOVERNMENT, THE ECONOMY AND
THE CONSTITUTION

12

THE LIMITLESS FEDERAL TAXING POWER

Gale Ann Norton

That a tax is too high, unwise, oppressive, burdensome, restrictive or even destructive does not provide a basis upon which the courts can void a tax invoked by Congress.[1]

I. Introduction

The constitutional principles governing taxation generally reflect the law school adage, "If Congress will pass it, it's constitutional." Courts overwhelmingly rely upon democratic institutions to remedy abuses in taxation, rather than exercising a strong hand in judicial review.[2] It has been noted that "[t]he power to impose taxes is so unlimited in force and so searching in extent, that the courts scarcely venture to declare that it is subject to any restrictions whatever, except such as rest in the discretion of the authority which exercises it." (Thomas Cooley 1927, p.986).

The goal of this article is to provide a background for the debate surrounding proposed federal constitutional amendments to balance the budget or limit taxation. An examination of the status quo may assist scholarly and public policy efforts to identify viable judicial standards for evaluating taxes. To this end, the following discussion describes the current status of constitutional doctrines in the context of taxation, including

---

This article is reprinted with minor revisions from the *Harvard Journal of Law and Public Policy*, 8 (Summer 1983). Gale Ann Norton is a practicing attorney and former Associate Solicitor for the Department of the Interior. The article was prepared while the author was a National Fellow of the Hoover Institution on War, Revolution, and Peace of Stanford University, Stanford, California. Much of the underlying research derives from the author's litigation as a Senior Attorney for Mountain States Legal Foundation in Denver, Colorado. The views expressed are entirely her own and do not necessarily reflect the views of Mountain States Legal Foundation or the Hoover Institution.

[1] *Ptasynski v. United States*, 550 F. Supp. 549, 555 (D. Wyo. 1982), rev'd on other grounds, 462 U.S. 74 (1983).

[2] "The power to tax may be exercised oppressively upon persons, but the responsibility of the legislature is not to the courts, but to the people by whom its members are elected." *McCray v. United States*, 195 U.S. 27, 57 (1904); *accord A. Magnano Co. v. Hamilton*, 292 U.S. 40 (1934).

apportionment, due process, equal protection, eminent domain, and uniformity. In addition, it discusses the procedural hurdles that hamper constitutional challenges to taxation. Given the breadth of the topic, the primary emphasis is on summarizing the relevant principles rather than on in-depth analysis.

In the early days of our nation, the judiciary's primary concern in setting tax policy was to nourish a fledgling government. The nation's experience with the Articles of Confederation demonstrated the dangers of a minuscule government denied the ability to tax (Randolph Paul 1954 and Dwight Morrow 1910). However, America has come far from the age when a few import and excise taxes supported the entire federal government.[3] The days before the 1913 adoption of the income tax amendment have virtually faded from our national memory. The fragile, fledgling government of yesteryear is now a bloated giant, feeding upon the sustenance produced by and intended for its citizens. To reduce the giant's diet would not cause starvation, but would restore its health and vigor.

In light of these changing circumstances and the mounting political pressure to amend the Constitution, it is time to reexamine whether we are justified in relying solely on elected officials to halt excessive taxation. If existing constitutional provisions fail to provide workable standards, we should consider this fact in evaluating the need for future constitutional amendments.[4]

II. The Crude Oil Windfall Profit Tax

The Crude Oil Windfall Profit Tax Act of 1980[5] provides a suitable example for analyzing several constitutional theories. Briefly reviewing the general outlines of the tax is necessary before embarking on constitutional analysis.

The Windfall Profit Tax was billed as the largest single tax ever adopted in the United States.[6] Accordingly, the recent lawsuit challenging the

---

[3] In fact, during considerable periods, no internal revenue taxes were levied, including a 43-year period from 1818 to 1861. See Codification of Internal Revenue Law, ix (1939), reproduced at 26 U.S.C.A. xix-xx (West 1982).

[4] See S.J. Res. 5, 98th Cong., 1st Sess. (1983) (Balanced Budget Amendment); and Martin Anderson (1983).

[5] Pub. L. No. 96-223, 94 Stat. 229 (codified at 26 U.S.C. Sections 4986-4998 (1982) and in scattered other sections of 26 U.S.C.).

[6] 125 Cong. Rec. S16,843 (daily ed. Nov. 16, 1979). The statute set a target amount of revenues to be collected: $227.3 billion. 26 U.S.C. Section 4990(d)(2). Actual revenues proved to be considerably less than expected because the price increases Congress expected from oil price decontrol ever materialized. Congress apparently expected oil prices in the 1980's to be almost twice the actual current price levels. See estimated congressional oil price projections, Brief of Association Appellees at 17 n.19, *United States v. Ptasynski*, 462 U.S. 74 (1983).

constitutionality of the tax, *United States v. Ptasynski*,[7] was almost certainly the largest dollar value case the Supreme Court ever heard.[8] The size of the taxpaying population, in contrast, was very small.[9]

Congress enacted the Windfall Profit Tax Act to capture "windfall" profits resulting from deregulation of oil prices.[10] The oil industry was suffering from extreme political unpopularity at the time Congress passed the Windfall Profit Tax Act. Statements about the "extortionate,"[11] "unconscionably high,"[12] and "skyrocketing"[13] profits of the oil industry sprinkled congressional debates. Profit margins for the oil industry were, however, no higher than the overall average for American industry.[14] The structure of the tax also reveals congressional assumptions about high oil industry profits. It is not actually a tax on "profits" in the same manner as an income tax, where expenses are taken into account. The "windfall profit" is based on a statutory calculation that is, for the most part, unrelated to actual profits.

For purposes of this article, most of the complex provisions of the Windfall Profit Tax Act are irrelevant.[15] It is noteworthy only that the tax created an administrative burden of immense proportions while imposing a massive tax,[16] and the Act exempts oil produced in the North Slope of Alaska

---

[7] 462 U.S. 74 (1983).

[8] See Brief of the United States at 12 n.16, *United States v. Ptasynski*, 462 U.S. 74 (1983). At issue in the case were tax revenues totalling approximately $26 billion. Ibid.

[9] The tax was specifically designed to prevent producers from passing the tax on to consumers through higher prices. H.R. Rep. No. 304, 96th Cong., 1st Sess.2 (1979). (The extent to which the tax's authors achieved this objective is unclear.) The tax originally applied to approximately two million royalty owners, mostly farmers and ranchers who owned land on which oil wells were drilled. Later amendments alleviated the impact on small royalty owners. Omnibus Reconciliation Act of 1980, Pu. L. No. 97-34, 96 Stat. 1 (codified in scattered sections of 26 U.S.C.). See Craig Reese (1982). Thereafter the tax was borne almost entirely by the nation's 20,000 or fewer domestic oil producers. Statistics on the number of shareholders and other individuals affected directly by the tax are not available.

[10] Price controls on oil were a carryover from President Nixon's wage and price controls imposed in 1971 under the Economic Stabilization Act of 1970, Pub. L. No. 92-921, 85 Stat. 743. These controls regulated all commodities, but most controls were dissolved in 1973. Only oil price controls continued until the 1980's.

[11] 126 *Cong. Rec.* S3142 (daily ed. March 27, 1980) (Sen. Church).

[12] 126 *Cong. Rec.* H1797 (daily ed. March 12, 1980) (Rep. Hughes).

[13] 126 *Cong. Rec.* (daily ed. March 13, 1980) (Rep. Shannon).

[14] For studies of profit margins during periods preceding passage of the Act, see H. R. Rep. No. 304, 96th Cong., 1st Session, 83 (1979), (Minority Views of Rep. Conable, et. al.); *Proposed Windfall Profit Tax and Energy Trust Fund: Hearings Before the Committee on Ways and Means, House of Representatives*, 96th Cong. 1st Sess. 516, 622, 695, 788 (1979) (studies by Citibank and Chase Manhattan Bank). See also A. Saterdal & Jay Glenn Marks (1980).

[15] For in-depth discussions of the tax, see D. Larry Crumbley & Craig Reese (1982); Dennis Drapkin & Phillip Verleger (1981); Douglas Robison (1980); Barry Miller & Dan Easley (1980).

[16] Tax rates range up to 70% of the statutorily defined windfall profit on some categories of oil.

from taxation.[17] It is this latter point which formed the basis of litigation challenging the Windfall Profit Tax Act.[18]

Congress exempted Alaskan oil from taxation because the exceptionally high production costs, extreme climatic conditions, and high transportation costs associated with Arctic oil production meant that a heavy tax might deter further exploration and development.[19] The resulting exemption created a major deviation from pure geographic uniformity. The Act exempted from windfall profit taxation oil produced in about three-fourths of Alaska (equal to roughly ten percent of the total United States land mass). The Alaska exemption is also large in terms of oil production and reserves; it exempts what may become the second largest oil field in the United States.[20] The exempt area of Alaska is estimated to contain over 20%,[21] and perhaps as much as 50%, of the undiscovered oil reserves in the entire United States (see National Petroleum Council 1981).

The Independent Petroleum Association of America and its thirty cooperating oil and gas associations, six Wyoming taxpayers, and the states of Texas and Louisiana challenged the constitutionality of the Windfall Profit Tax. Judge Ewing T. Kerr of the Wyoming federal district court held the tax unconstitutional.[22] His opinion found that the Alaska exemption violated the constitutional requirement of uniform taxation.[23] The district court,

---

[17] See I.R.C. Section 4994(e) (1982):

> For purposes of this chapter, the term "exempt Alaskan oil" means any crude oil (other than Sadlerochit oil) which is produced—
> (1) from a reservoir from which oil has been produced in commercial quantities through a well located north of the Artic Circle, or
> (2) from a well located on the northerly side of the divide of the Alaska-Aleutian Range and at least 75 miles from the nearest point on the Trans-Alaska Pipeline System.

[18] Allegations that this exemption violated the Uniformity Clause of the Constitution are discussed in the following section.

[19] H.R. Rep. No. 817, 96th Cong., 2d Sess. 103 (1980). See also H.R. Rep. No. 304, 96th Cong., 1st Sess. 30 (1979).

[20] See *Oil & Gas Journal*, July 12, 1982, at 81; see also United States Geological Survey Estimates of Undiscovered Recoverable Conventional Resources of Oil and Gas in the United States, Circular 884 at 17 (1982). This field, the Kuparuk River oil field, is so large that it produces more oil than most states. Only Texas, Louisiana, Oklahoma, California, Wyoming, and the non-exempt portions of Alaska produce more oil than the Kuparuk River field.

[21] United States Geological Survey Estimates of Undiscovered Recoverable Conventional Resources of Oil and Gas in the United States, Circular 860 at 74-79 (1982).

[22] *Ptasynski v. United States*, 550 F. Supp. 549 (D. Wyo. 1982).

[23] *Ibid.* at 553. "The Constitution only requires that in each state where crude oil is found, the production and removal of that crude oil be subject to the tax and taxed at the same rate. The windfall profits tax ignores this requirement. The Act, on its face, says that one state, Alaska, is not subject to the same tax, at the same rate, as all the other states. This is a clear violation of the constitutional requirement of uniformity."

however, refused to adopt Fifth Amendment arguments asserted by the plaintiffs.[24]

On direct appeal, the United States Supreme Court reversed.[25] Justice Powell, for a unanimous Court, found the tax to be constitutional. This decision will be discussed in more detail below.

III. Explicit Constitutional Limitations on Taxation

A. Uniformity

Article 1, section 8, clause 1 of the Constitution grants Congress the power to tax. It provides:

> The Congress shall have power to lay and collect taxes, duties, imposts and excises, to pay the debts and provide for the common defense and general welfare of the United States; but *all duties, imposts and excises shall be uniform throughout the United States.*

This provision gives Congress the power to enact "every form of tax appropriate to sovereignty."[26] The latter phrase of this grant of authority is known as the Uniformity Clause, one of the Constitution's two explicit limitations on the federal taxing power.[27]

Because the uniformity requirement applies specifically to only three types of taxes, it is necessary to define these taxes. In general, an "excise" tax taxes the exercise of a privilege, most often the production of a good or service. Excises include "taxes laid upon the manufacture, sale, or consumption of commodities within the country, upon licenses to pursue certain occupations, and upon corporate privileges."[28] The terms "duty" and "impost" are "commonly applied to levies made by governments on the importation or exportation of commodities."[29] These three types of taxes are to be contrasted with direct taxes and income taxes, discussed below.

The Uniformity Clause has consistently been interpreted to require "geographic" uniformity. Geographic uniformity means that an item is taxed in the same way wherever it is found; there is no geographic variation in

---

[24] *Ibid.* at 555.

[25] *United States v. Ptasynski*, 462 U.S. 74 (1983).

[26] *Charles C. Steward Machine Co. v. Davis*, 301 U.S. 548, 581 (1937); see also *Brushaber v. Union Pacific Ry.*, 240 U.S. 1, 12 (1916) (The authority "embraces every conceivable power of taxation . . .").

[27] *License Tax Cases*, 72 U.S. (5 Wall.) 462, 471 (1866); *McCray v. United States*, 195 U.S. 27, 56 (1904).

[28] *Flint v. Stone Tracy Co.*, 220 U.S. 107, 151 (1911).

[29] *Ibid.* An inheritance tax is generally viewed as a type of duty or excise. *Knowlton v. Moore*, 178 U.S. 41 (1900).

the rule of tax liability. Geographic uniformity is best understood when compared with "intrinsic" uniformity, which requires that a tax fall equally upon all areas, regardless of whether the particular object of taxation is equally distributed. As originally proposed in the Constitutional Convention, the Uniformity Clause also required that taxes be "equal" throughout the United States.[30] The word "equal" was stricken to "prevent the implication that the duties, imposts, and excises which were to be uniform throughout the United States were to be placed upon rights equally existing in the several States."[31]

Early cases interpreting the Uniformity Clause involved attempts to challenge tax schemes because intrinsic uniformity was lacking. Plaintiffs argued in *Hylton v. United States*,[32] for example, that a tax could not be imposed on carriages because there were more carriages in New York than in less populous states such as Virginia. As a result, the tax would bear more heavily upon New York than Virginia. The Supreme Court rejected this argument, finding that the Uniformity Clause required "geographic" uniformity, not intrinsic uniformity.

Intrinsic uniformity was also explored in the *Head Money Cases*: "Is the tax on tobacco void, because in many of the States no tobacco is raised or manufactured? Is the tax on distilled spirits void, because a few States pay three-fourths of the revenue arising from it?"[33] The Court again rejected an intrinsic uniformity approach, noting instead that "[t]he tax is uniform when it operates with the same force and effect in every place where the subject of it is found."[34]

Geographic uniformity means that the rules of federal tax liability are the same throughout the nation. "[T]he tax levied cannot be one sum upon an article at one place and a different sum upon the same article at another place. The duty received must be the same at all places throughout the United States. . . . If, for instance, one kind of wine or grain or produce has a certain duty laid upon it, proportioned to its quantity, in New York, it must have a like duty, proportioned to its quantity, when imported at Charleston or San Francisco. . . ."[35] In the leading case interpreting the

---

[30] *Knowlton*, 178 U.S. at 104.

[31] *Ibid.* at 109.

[32] 3 U.S. (3 Dall.) 171 (1796).

[33] 112 U.S. 580 (1884).

[34] *Ibid.* at 594; see also *Knowlton*, 178 U.S. 41 ("[W]hat the Constitution commands is the imposition of a tax by the rule of geographic uniformity, not that in order to levy such a tax objects must be selected which exist uniformly in the several states.")

[35] *Pollock v. Farmer's Loan & Trust Co.* 158 U.S. 601 (1895); see also *Florida V. Mellon*, 273 U.S. 12, 17 (1927) ([T]he law shall be uniform in the sense that by its provisions the rule of liability shall be alike in all parts of the United States.") *LaBelle Iron Works v. United States*, 256 U.S. 377, 392 (1921); *Billings v. United States*, 232 U.S. 261, 272 (1914).

uniformity clause, *Knowlton v. Moore*, the Court stated the rule as follows: "[W]hatever plan or method Congress adopts for laying the tax in question, the same plan and the same method must be made operative throughout the United States; that is to say, that wherever a subject is taxed anywhere, the same must be taxed everywhere throughout the United States, and at the same rate."[36]

The Uniformity Clause resembles two other clauses in the Constitution. It is illuminating to compare the interpretation of the Uniformity Clause with that of these other provisions.

The Uniformity Clause originated in conjunction with the Port Preference Clause.[37] The Constitution's Framers intended both provisions to prevent discrimination that would handicap industry in various states. A tax or regulation applicable to ports is constitutional when it "applies to all *ports* alike, and evidently gives no preference to one over another, but is uniform in its operation in all ports of the United States."[38] The Port Preference Clause, however, was not designed to prevent Congress from undertaking activities, such as the construction of lighthouses or the improvement of rivers and harbors, that would necessarily benefit only one port.[39] The courts avoided an impracticable interpretation of the Clause by holding that it prohibits discrimination between states, not between ports.[40]

The second clause that parallels the Uniformity Clause is the uniformity requirement in the Bankruptcy Clause. In a recent Supreme Court case, the Court employed the provision to strike down a federal bankruptcy statute.[41] The Court stated that the uniformity requirement was not a "strait jacket that forbids Congress to distinguish among classes of debtors," and that it "does not deny Congress power to take into account differences that exist between different parts of the country, and to fashion legislation to resolve geographically isolated problems."[42] However, bankruptcy laws

---

[36] *Knowlton*, 78 U.S. at 84. However, the fact that a federal statute derived it definitions in part from state law (and thus had a different impact in different states) did not create a constitutionally impermissible lack of uniformity. *Florida v. Mellon*, 273 U.S. 12 (1927).

[37] U.S. Constitution, Article I, Section 9, Clause 6 provides: "No preference shall be given any Regulation of Commerce or Revenue to the Ports of one State over those of another; nor shall Vessels bound to, or from, one State be obliged to enter, clear, or pay Duties in another."

[38] *Head Money Cases*, 112 U.S. 580, 595 (1884).

[39] *Louisiana Public Service Comm'n v. Texas New Orleans R.R. Co.*, 284 U.S. 125, 131 (1931).

[40] *Ibid.*; *Pennsylvania v. Wheeling & Belmont Bridge Co.*, 59 U.S. (18 How.) 421, 433 (1856).

[41] *Railway Labor Executives' Ass'n v. Gibbons*, 455 U.S. 457 (1982).

[42] *Ibid.* at 469. This statement originated in the Regional Railroad Reorganization Act Cases, 419 U.S. 102, 159 (1974), upholding a bankruptcy statute applicable only to bankrupt railroads in the northeastern states. In that case, the statute in fact applied to all railroads undergoing bankruptcy proceedings at that time, since all of the railroads were located in the Northeast. Thus it is permissible to establish a facially geographic classification if it does in fact include the same subject whenever it is found, as required by the *Head Money Cases*, 112 U.S. 580 (1884).

must at least apply uniformly to a defined class of debtors; to allow otherwise would be tantamount to congressional repeal of the Constitution's uniformity requirement.[43]

The Supreme Court in *United States v. Ptasynski*[44] relied extensively on analogies to the bankruptcy uniformity clause when it analyzed the tax uniformity clause. The bankruptcy requirement received a stricter interpretation than the tax uniformity requirement, although the rationale for uniformity in bankruptcy legislation is less central to American constitutional law than the rationale for uniform taxation. The Founding Fathers intended the bankruptcy provision to remedy the problem of private bankruptcy laws which allow particular debtors to avoid their debts.[45] They hoped a uniform nationwide treatment of bankruptcy would prevent this type of debt avoidance. Bankruptcy uniformity, however, was grounded essentially on practicality, not on any overriding notions of federalism or constitutional checks and balances.

In contrast, the Framers viewed the uniformity clause as an important guarantee given to the states to induce centralization. They sought to prevent not just the favorable treatment of particular individuals, but also seriously divisive regional jealousies. Thus the origin of the tax uniformity requirement probably lay more in respect for principles of state sovereignty[46] than on a desire to assure equal treatment for taxpayers throughout the country. The Founding Fathers, mindful of the rivalries between the states, attempted through the Uniformity Clause to prevent states from "ganging up" to impose discriminatory taxes against less powerful states.[47] Justice Story's rhetoric provides a succinct statement of these concerns in *Commentaries on the Constitution of the United States* ([1873] 1970). This early analysis of the Uniformity Clause stated:

---

[43] *Gibbons*, 455 U.S. at 473.

[44] 462 U.S. 74, 83 n. 13 (1983).

[45] *Gibbons*, 455 U.S. at 472.

[46] See *Downes v. Bidwell*, 182 U.S. 244, 278 (1901) (the object of the Uniformity Clause was "to protect the States which united in forming the Constitution from discriminations by Congress, which would operate unfairly or injuriously upon some states and not equally upon others."); *Knowlton*, 178 U.S. at 89 ("[T]he possible discrimination against one or more States was the only thing intended to be provided for by the rule which uniformity imposed upon the power to levy duties, imposts, and excises."); see also *United States v. Ptasynski*, 462 U.S. 74, 80-81 (1983). However, a contrary assumption underlies *Florida v. Mellon*, 273 U.S. 12 (1927) (state denied standing to question the uniformity of federal tax).

[47] See *Hylton v. United States*, 3 U.S. (3 Dall.) 171, 179 (1796) ("The truth is, that the articles taxed in one state should be taxed in another; in this way, the spirit of jealousy is appeased, and tranquility preserved; in this way, the pressure on industry will be equal in the several states . . .").

The agriculture, commerce, or manufactures of one State might be built up on the ruins of those of another; and a combination of a few States In Congress might secure a monopoly of certain branches of trade and business to themselves, to the injury, if not to the destruction of their less favored neighbors . . . New York and Pennsylvania might, by an easy combination with the Southern states, have destroyed the whole navigation of New England. A combination of a different character, between the New England and the Western states, might have borne down the agriculture of the South; and a combination of a yet different character might have struck at the vital interests of manufactures. (1970, p. 683).

How much validity should concern for regional rivalries retain, given the virtual abandonment of "states' rights" principles in American jurisprudence?[48] The concern should retain at least some vitality, since it is based on sound economic and political policy. Although Congress enjoys nearly unrestricted ability to provide "boondoggles" for local legislative districts,[49] a firm tax uniformity requirement could restrict at least one avenue of preferential or discriminatory treatment. While subsidies and other benefits may be allocated unevenly, based on the relative political power of the states, the Uniformity Clause requires that taxes must be levied in the same manner throughout the country. For instance, if a member of Congress wishes to structure an excise tax to benefit an industry within his district, he must be able to make a logical distinction between the industry in his district and the same industry in other areas. If no distinguishing characteristics exist other than the location of the business, then the tax must fall with the same force on his constituents as on the rest of the country. Thus if the Uniformity Clause were interpreted strictly, the taxing power could not easily be used to confer a competitive advantage on one segment of an industry. In the aftermath of the weak interpretation of the Uniformity Clause in *United States v. Ptasynski*,[50] special regional legislation may be passed more readily. The State of Texas predicted in the *Ptasynski* litigation, "If this Court upholds the Alaska exemption, it will be an amazingly short time before the Texas delegation in Congress begins pressing for comparable geographic exemptions for Texas production."[51]

The reasons for requiring geographic uniformity may be analyzed from an economic perspective. For virtually any industry, some areas of the country are more economically suited to profitable production than other

---

[48] See, for example, *Hodel v. Indiana*, 452 U.S. 314 (1980); *Federal Energy Regulatory Comm'n v. Mississippi*, 456 U.S. 742 (1982); *EEOC v. Wyoming*, 462 U.S. 226 (1983).

[49] Uniformity is not required under the commerce power, *Hodel v. Indiana*, 462 U.S. at 332.

[50] 462 U.S. 74 (1983).

[51] Brief for the State of Texas at 11, *Ptasynski*, 462 U.S. 74 (1983).

areas. For example, a hypothetical Maine orange industry would be hampered by high costs and high risks. Maine would not be able to produce fruit as efficiently as its southern competition. Commercial orange groves in Maine would exist only if they were granted special treatment vis-a-vis that given to the citrus industry in Florida. The Uniformity Clause was designed to protect against discriminatory tax treatment that alters the realities of economic advantage.[52] In essence, preferential treatment by government substitutes artificial, political advantages for real economic advantages. The cost of these governmental advantages is inevitably borne by consumers in the form of less efficiently produced and more costly goods.

In the Windfall Profit Tax context, Congress justified the Alaska exemption with the assertion that oil production and transportation are considerably more expensive in Alaska than in other parts of the country.[53] According to the American Petroleum Institute, the average cost of an onshore Alaskan well was over $3 million, while the next highest cost was $232,000 in Louisiana.[54] The opponents of the Windfall Profit Tax disputed the high-cost argument. For example, the Revenue Commissioner for the State of Alaska testified in congressional hearings, "[W]hile [the tax] prudently exempts Arctic production to provide an incentive for development, it fails to do so for other areas with comparably high costs and risks. In the deep-water OCS (Outer Continental Shelf) off Louisiana, a single production platform may run into hundreds of millions of dollars. One exploratory well in the Baltimore Canyon may cost over $20 million, while a well in the gulf of Alaska can easily be even more expensive."[55] Tax opponents also pointed out that the cost disparity disappeared when analyzed on a per-barrel basis, since Alaskan wells generally yielded many times more oil than new wells in long-developed areas.

The Supreme Court adopted the high-cost production rationale as a sufficient justification for non-uniformity, adopting the view that the average cost of drilling a well in Alaska may be as much as 15 times greater than elsewhere in the United States.[56] The Court concluded that Congress viewed Alaskan oil production as a "unique class of oil that . . . merit[s] favorable treatment."[57]

---

[52] See *Florida v. Mellon*, 273 U.S. at 17 ("Congress cannot . . . control the diverse conditions to be found in the various states which necessarily work unlike results from the enforcement of the same tax . . .").

[53] See H.R. Rep. No. 817, 96th Cong., 2d Sess. (1980).

[54] *Ptasynski*, 462 U.S. at 78 n. 7.

[55] Crude Oil Tax: Hearings on H.R. 3919 Before the Senate Comm. on Finance, 96th Cong., 1st Sess. (1979).

[56] *Ptasynski*, 462 U.S. at 78.

[57] Ibid. at 85.

As a direct result of the exemption, Alaska attracted several billion dollars in oil industry investment that might otherwise have gone to other portions of the country. Atlantic Richfield Company, as amicus curiae in *Ptasynski*, stated that it had invested almost $700 million in the Kuparuk River oil field, and planned an addition $4 billion in expenditures. "Atlantic Richfield has increased the scope of its Kuparuk investments and accelerated their timing in reliance on the 'Alaskan oil' exemption."[58] In contrast, production in other oil-producing states was discouraged by the tax.[59]

Critics of the Windfall Profit Tax argued that disparities in the cost of oil production were not fundamentally a governmental problem, but an economic one. In *Ptasynski*, they asserted that the Alaska exemption rendered the tax non-uniform. The oil producers argued that Congress directly violated the requirement of geographic uniformity by defining the exemption in geographic terms, rather than through distinctions based directly on climate or high production costs.[60]

The government asserted in the Windfall Profit Tax litigation that the Windfall Profit Tax neither raised fears of regional jealousies nor contradicted the spirit of the Uniformity Clause.[61] The government claimed that the Alaska exemption posed a unique situation: instead of a coalition of forty-nine states imposing a tax on the minority state of Alaska, the exemption arose from forty-nine states choosing to benefit the remaining state. Futhermore, the Alaska exemption stemmed from a national decision to exploit resources located in one section of the country.[62]

The oil industry's rejoinder was that a coalition of oil-*consuming* states imposed the tax on oil-*producing* states. That thirteen of the sixteen senators from the top oil-producing states voted against adoption of the Windfall Profit Tax supports the oil industry's position.[63] The plaintiffs in *Ptasynski* asserted that the Alaska exemption was the bargaining point upon which the Act's proponents gained the support of some opponents. Had Alaskan

---

[58] Brief Amicus Curiae of Atlantic Richfield Company at 2, *Ptasynski*, 462 U.S. 74 (1983). The oil industry was not united in its criticism of the Windfall Profit Tax. Major oil companies tended to support the tax as the best possible compromise, since it did not tax imported oil. Two of the handful of oil companies operating in the exempt area of Alaska, Atlantic Richfield and Sohio, appeared as amicus curiae in *Ptasynski*.

[59] See Interstate Oil Compact Commission (1980).

[60] *Ptasynski*, 462 U.S. at 79-80.

[61] Brief for the United States at 23-39, *United States v. Ptasynski*, 462 U.S. 74 (1983).

[62] The government also characterized the Alaska exemption as a paperwork reducing device, since the high costs of Alaskan production meant that no taxable windfall profit would exist anyway, and thus there was no point in forcing Alaskan producers to file tax forms. *Ibid.*

[63] 126 *Cong. Rec.*S3151 (daily ed. March 27, 1980). The debate prior to passage of the Act primarily followed "regional lines with legislators from oil producing states opposing the Act and those from non-producing states supporting it." Miller and Easley (1980).

producers been forced to share the same tax burden as the remainder of the country, the tax rates would have been significantly less, or the tax might not have passed at all.[64]

The lower court found that the Uniformity Clause created a type of per se rule, demanding invalidation of any geographically non-uniform tax.[65] The Supreme Court rejected this approach. In fact, it established an inverse per se rule: whenever a tax is defined in non-geographic terms, the Uniformity Clause is satisfied.[66] It is only when Congress defines a tax in explicitly geographic terms that the Court will examine the classification.

The Court did not lay out a precise rule for determining which geographic classifications are permissible and which violate the Uniformity Clause. Based on the factors evaluated in *Ptasynski*, it appears that the Court would consider: (1) Whether a classification was based on "neutral factors,"[67] (Presumably this means that Congress had a rational basis for believing that a geographically isolated problem existed or that the item accorded special treatment was so unique that it constituted a separate subject of taxation) and (2) Whether Congress acted "for reasons that would offend the purpose of the Clause,"[68] or in other words, whether the enactment constituted "actual geographic discrimination."[69] Challengers of a tax would have to prove that a congressional desire to grant an "undue preference at the expense of other . . . states" motivated Congress to enact the challenged tax.[70] This unacceptable legislative intent would be difficult to prove given the Court's definition of the burden on taxpayer plaintiffs: to disprove all possible rational, proper justifications that Congress *could have* used to justify the tax.

Beyond the difficulty of proving an overriding congressional desire to discriminate (evidenced perhaps by "down with Louisiana" speeches on the House floor), improper motives are unlikely to play a significant role

---

[64] "Without the Alaska exemption, the present Windfall Profit Tax would not have obtained congressional approval. All the seriously considered bills in one form or another exempted Alaskan oil. Not only did every serious proposal effectively exempt Alaska oil, but the adoption by the Senate of an explicit Alaskan exemption was critical both to the Senate's decision to extend the tax to newly discovered oil and to resolution of the stalemate in which the tax bill had become trapped." Brief of Taxpayer Appellees at 3, *Ptasynski*, 462 U.S. 74 (1983) (citations omitted); see also Matthew Dow (1983).

[65] *Ptasynski v. United States*, 550 F. Supp. 555 (D. Wyo. 1982).

[66] *United States v. Ptasynski*, 462 U.S. at 84-85.

[67] *Ibid.* at 85.

[68] *Ibid.*

[69] *Ibid.*

[70] Note that this departs from the historic judicial reluctance to inquire into legislative intent. See, for example, *A Magnano Co. v. Hamilton*, 292 U.S. 40, 44 (1934).

in the motivation for preferential or discriminatory tax treatment, as some economic justification would undoubtedly be presented. However, it is doubtful whether the Founding Fathers would have been satisfied with an economic justification for taxation favoring various states. Implicit in the Uniformity Clause is a protection for those industries that do enjoy natural economic advantages. The Clause expresses a preference for allowing natural advantages to prevail, without government realignment of advantages.

Following the Supreme Court's decision in *Ptasynski*, it is no longer necessary for Congress to apply the same tax rules to a single industry across the country. It appears that members of Congress are now free to assist the dominant industries in their states, not only at the expense of other industries, but also at the expense of competitors in other states. Virtually any of the economic realities that give one area an advantage over another area for the development of particular specialized businesses could be utilized as a rational justification for differential tax treatment. *Ptasynski* has effectively created fertile new ground for political entrepreneurship.

B. Apportionment

The Constitution's Apportionment Clause (article I, section 9) is the second explicit constitutional limit on the taxing power. It provides:

> No Capitation, or other direct, Tax shall be laid, unless in Proportion to the Census or Enumeration herein before directed to be taken.

A parallel prohibition against unapportioned direct taxes appears in article 1, section 2. The Clause requires that certain taxes be apportioned, i.e., levied among the states according to population, such that the more populous states must pay a heavier tax.

The Apportionment Clause applies only to "capitations" or other "direct" taxes. Therefore, in order to analyze the Clause's operation, one must define the taxes it addresses. A poll or capitation tax is a specific sum levied on a per person basis, without regard to property or income.[71] The phrase "direct tax" probably originated with Adam Smith's *Wealth of Nations*.[72] Unfortunately, the meaning of the term is far from clear. Apparently, the definition of "direct tax" was not even clear to the Founding Fathers.[73]

---

[71] Poll taxes were often, but not always, levied as a requirement for voting. See *U.S. Constitution*, amend. XXIV; *Harper v. Virginia Board of Elections* 383 U.S. 663 (prohibiting use of poll taxes as requirements for voting).

[72] See David Hutchinson (1975).

[73] "[T]he authoritative opinion of those who have examined the records is that there was no definite meaning agreed upon in the convention and that it was a vague term." (J.H. Riddle 1917). This lack of clarity is illustrated by an entry in Madison's Journal of the Constitutional

The generally accepted meaning of a direct tax is one imposed on the existence of a right, referring almost exclusively to real estate taxes and poll taxes.[74] Such a tax "falls upon the owner merely because he is owner, regardless of his use or disposition of the property."[75] A broader interpretation of "direct taxes" was adopted briefly in the late Nineteenth Century, when the Supreme Court expanded the definition to include taxes on real or personal property and taxes on the income from property. In *Pollock v. Farmer's Loan & Trust Co.*[76] the Supreme Court invalidated the 1894 federal income tax. The Court examined the tax on income from real estate and personal property. It found that a tax on income from property could not be separated from a tax on the property itself. The income tax was characterized as a form of federal property tax, which was thereby subject to the apportionment requirement. Although the income tax in *Pollock* bore some relation to the population of the states, there was no attempt to allocate the tax burden in each state exactly according to population. The Apportionment Clause thus foiled the income tax in its first modern incarnation. Passage of a constitutional amendment[77] was necessary to resurrect the federal income tax.

Courts have essentially abandoned the permissive interpretation created in *Pollock*.[78] Subsequent cases have viewed the Sixteenth Amendment as a rejection of *Pollock's* definition of "direct tax."[79] The apportionment requirement again applies only to real estate and capitation taxes. Even if the Sixteenth Amendment is not viewed as narrowing the definition of direct taxes, it at least introduces an additional consideration to analysis

Convention for August 20, 1787: "Mr. King asked what was the precise meaning of direct taxation? No one answered." Quoted in Dwight Morrow (1910, p. 379). But see *Pollock v. Farmer's Loan and Trust Co.*, 158 U.S. 601 (1895) (asserting that the meaning of the phrase was clearly understood by the Framers).

[74] *Springer v. United States*, 102 U.S. 586, 602-03 (1880). In *Hylton v. United States*, 3 U.S. (3 Dall.) 171 (1796), one of the participants in the Constitutional Convention, Justice Paterson, helped illuminate the meaning of the Clause's terms. The case limited direct taxes to poll (capitation) taxes and land taxes. Accord *The Federalist* No. 21 (A. Hamilton) (noting that direct taxes "principally relate to lands and buildings").

[75] *Fernandez v. Wiener*, 326 U.S. 340, 362 (1945). This excludes, for example, taxes prompted by the sale of property, which would be "indirect" excise taxes.

[76] 158 U.S. 601 (1895).

[77] The Constitution's Sixteenth Amendment provides: "The Congress shall have power to lay and collect taxes on incomes, from whatever source derived, without apportionment among the several States, and without regard to any census or enumeration."

[78] See *New York Trust Co. v. Eisner*, 256 U.S. 345 (1921); *Flint v. Stone Tracy Co.*, 220 U.S. 107 (1941); *Spreckles Sugar Refining Co. v. McClain*, 192 U.S. 397 (1904).

[79] See, for example, *Brushaber v. Union Pacific R.R. Co.*, 240 U.S. 1 (1916) ("there is no escape from the conclusion that the [Sixteenth] Amendment was drawn for the purpose of doing away for the future with the principle upon which the Pollock Case was decided.").

under the Apportionment Clause. For the Court to strike an unapportioned tax, plaintiffs must establish not only that a tax is direct tax, but also that it is not in the subset of direct taxes known as an income tax.[80]

The original purpose of the Apportionment Clause is not entirely clear. The Constitutional Convention's initial motivation for adopting the Clause may have been the same as that underlying the Uniformity Clause: "the protection of the states, to prevent their being called upon to contribute more than was deemed their due share of the burden."[81] However, a closer examination of the Apportionment Clause's origins calls into question assertions that the Founding Fathers attributed nothing but tax policy implications to the Clause. Some members of the Constitutional Convention conceived the apportionment of taxes as a mechanism for resolving a conflict over whether slaves should be counted to determine states' representation in Congress.[82] After the conflict was resolved, a proposal to delete this provision from the final draft of the Constitution was introduced and defeated.[83] Rather than a concern for pure tax policy, the Framers were probably guided by the broader principle that "what was just in representation was also just in taxation," (Paul 1954, p. 52).

Despite the dramatic impact of the Apportionment Clause in striking the income tax in *Pollock*, it is unlikely that the Clause will have much effect on future federal tax policy. The regressive nature of both real estate and capitation taxes make it unlikely that these direct taxes would be adopted on a national basis, at least in significant amounts. Both will probably remain the exclusive province of state and local governments.

IV. Traditional Constitutional Challenges as Applied to Taxation

Courts have historically been unwilling to apply the same constitutional standards of equal protection, due process, and just compensation when scrutinizing congressional acts under the taxing power as they have applied to other congressional actions. The courts have repeatedly acknowledged

---

[80] See *Eisner v. Macomber*, 252 U.S. 189 (1920).

[81] *Knowlton v. Moore*, 178 U.S. 41 (1900); see also *Pollock v. Farmer's Loan and Trust Co.*, 157 U.S. 429, 543-45, on rehearing, 158 U.S. 601 (1895). This protection has been characterized as "important and appropriate." *Eisner v. Macomber*, 252 U.S. 189, 206 (1920).

[82] "Governeur Morris proposed that taxes be allocated on the basis of a state's proportionate share of representation in Congress. His intention was to undercut the South's desire that slaves be counted for representative purposes for, if they were, the South's proportionate share of taxes would increase accordingly. Morris attempt to second-guess the Southern States proved off the mark, however, for they accepted the prospect of higher taxes in exchange for increased representation." (Greg Johnson 1982, pp. 719-20). See also David Hutchinson (1975).

[83] See Johnson (1982) p. 720.

a unique standard for analysis of tax questions. [84]

Some case have seemingly gone so far as to hold that the Fifth Amendment provides absolutely no limitation upon the taxing power. For example, *McCray v. United States*[85] held that the Fifth Amendment "does not withdraw or expressly limit the grant of power to tax conferred upon Congress by the Constitution."[86] This appears to be more of an inaccurate choice of wording than a true analytical standard. A similar statement occurs in *Barclay & Co. v. Edwards*,[87] where the Court stated, "The Power of Congress in levying taxes is very wide, and where a classification is made of taxpayers that is reasonable, and not merely arbitrary and capricious, the Fifth Amendment cannot apply."[88] Nevertheless, the *Barclay* Court engaged in a cursory analysis of the reasonableness of the congressional classification. A more accurate statement of the rule would be that a higher standard applies to the taxing power, and therefore taxes may be stricken as violating the Fifth Amendment only in "rare and special instances."[89] Only when shown to be highly arbitrary and capricious may a tax statute be declared unconstitutional, but it remains theoretically possible for a tax to violate this standard.[90]

The reasons for distinguishing between taxes and other legislation have never been fully explained by the courts. One apparent reason is the fear that weakening the taxing power could destroy, or at least seriously disrupt, the federal governmental structure.[91] This concern for government

---

[84] See, for example, A. *Magnano Co. v. Hamilton*, 292 U.S. 40, 44 (1934); *City of Pittsburgh v. Alco Parking Corp.*, 417 U.S. 369 (1974); *McCray v. United States*, 195 U.S. 27, 57 (1904).

[85] 195 U.S. 27 (1904).

[86] *Ibid.* at 63.

[87] 267 U.S. 442 (1924).

[88] *Ibid.* at 450.

[89] A. *Magnano Co. v. Hamilton*, 292 U.S. 40, 44 (1934) (citations omitted).

[90] "That a federal statute passed under the taxing power may be so arbitrary and capricious as to cause it to fall before the due process of law clause of the Fifth Amendment is settled." *Heiner v. Donnan*, 285 U.S. 312, 326 (1932). The Supreme Court has been more willing to find violations of due process and equal protection principles by state taxing statutes. The Court recently invalidated an Alabama tax that discriminated between in-state and out-of-state insurance companies. *Metropolitan Life Ins. Co. v. Ward*, 470 U.S. 869 (1985). No legitimate state purpose justified Alabama's discriminatory taxation, and hence the tax violated equal protection.

[91] See *Nicol v. Ames*, 173 U.S. 509, 515 (1899):

> The power to tax is the one great power upon which the whole national fabric is based. It is as necessary to the existence and prosperity of a nation as is the air he breathes to the natural man. It is not only the power to destroy, but it is also the power to keep alive.

See also *Knowlton v. Moore*, 178 U.S. 41, 60 (1899):

> [I]f a lawful tax can be defeated because the power which is manifested by its imposition may when further exercised be destructive, it would follow that every lawful tax would become unlawful, and therefore no taxation whatever could be levied.

preservation overrides concerns about the recognized destructive nature of taxation.[92] It is difficult to distinguish limitations on such an inherent intrusion into individual rights that would not halt taxation altogether,[93] and therefore courts intervene only in particularly egregious cases.

A second reason for the unique standard of review courts utilize for federal taxation is their reliance upon democratic processes within Congress to resolve tax inequities. "The only security against the abuse of [the taxing] power, is found in the structure of the government itself. In imposing a tax, the legislature acts upon its constituents. This is, in general, a sufficient security against erroneous and oppressive taxation."[94] This deference is considered appropriate because the members of a legislature presumably enjoy a familiarity with local needs and conditions that the courts do not share.[95]

However, an exaggerated differentiation between tax matters and other federal regulatory matters may not withstand detailed scrutiny. Governmental discouragement of an undesirable activity can be formulated either as regulation or as taxation of that activity. The regulatory formulation would be subject to judicial review based on standard constitutional analysis, while its tax-law twin would be essentially immune from review.[96]

A. Due Process and Equal Protection

Equal protection, taking, and due process all bear a considerable similarity and all stem from the Fifth Amendment.[97] The Due Process Clause imposes on the federal government requirements comparable to those placed on

---

[92] "[I]n most instances for which taxes are levied, as the support of the government, the prosecution of war, the National defense, any limitation is unsafe. The entire resources of the people should in some instances be at the disposal of the government." *Citizens' Savings & Loan Ass'n v. Topeka*, 87 U.S. (20 Wall.) 655, 663 (1875); see also *McCulloch v. Maryland*, 17 U.S. (4 Wheat.) 316, 428 (1819) ("It is admitted, that the power of taxing . . . is essential to the very existence of government . . .").

[93] "The right of taxation, where it exists, is necessarily unlimited in its nature. It carries with it inherently the power to embarass and destroy." *Austin v. The Adlermen*, 74 U.S. (7 Wall.) 694, 699 (1868).

[94] *McCulloch v. Maryland*, 17 U.S. (4 Wheat.) at 428; see also *Pacific Ins. Co. v. Soule*, 74 U.S. (7 Wall.) 433, 443 (1868) (quoted in *McCray v. United States*, 195 U.S. 27, 57 (1904) ("Congress may prescribe the basis, fix the rates, and require payment as it may deem proper. Within the limits of the Constitution it is supreme in its action. No power of supervision or control is lodged in either of the other departments of the government.").

[95] *Regan v. Taxation with Representation*, 461 U.S. 540, 547 (1983); see also *Madden v. Kentucky*, 309 U.S. 83, 88 (1940).

[96] This point is developed in detail in Richard Epstein (1982).

[97] The relevant portion of the Fifth Amendment to the U.S. Constitution provides, "No person shall . . . be deprived of life, liberty, or property, without the due process of law . . ."

the states by the Fourteenth Amendment, including the requirement of equal protection.[98] This section discusses various types of due process claims, including those involving equal protection in the formulation of tax classifications, rationality in the purpose and operation of tax schemes, and challenges to the sheer enormity and destructiveness of a tax.

The most common Due Process Clause claim is that discriminatory tax categories violate equal protection. Legislative tax classifications will be invalidated when "palpably arbitrary" or "invidious."[99] In evaluating tax classifications, "[t]he question always is . . . whether there is any reasonable ground for it, or whether it is only and simple arbitrary, based upon no real distinction and entirely unnatural."[100] An alternative statement of the rule is that a classification "must rest upon some ground of difference having a fair and substantial relation to the object of the legislation."[101] Courts may strike down taxing schemes that are "clear and hostile discriminations against particular persons and classes, especially such as are of an unusual character, unknown to the practice of our governments . . ."[102]

Nevertheless, "an iron rule of equal taxation" is not required.[103] Courts have traditionally given Congress considerable leeway in creating categories for tax purposes.[104] This broad discretion extends to tax exemptions and deductions which are "a matter of grace [that] Congress can, of course, disallow . . . as it chooses."[105] Inequalities that result from singling out a particular class for taxation or exemption do not infringe upon constitutional

[98] *Regan v. Taxation with Representation*, 461 U.S. at 542 n.2 (citing *Schweiker v. Wilson*, 450 U.S. 221, 226 n.6 (1981)); cf. *Bolling v. Sharpe*, 347 U.S. 496, 499 (1954). But see *LaBelle Iron Works v. United States*, 256 U.S. 377, 392 (1921) ("The Fifth Amendment has no equal protection clause; and the only rule of uniformity prescribed with respect to duties, imposts, and excises laid by Congress is the territorial uniformity required by Art. 1, Section 8.").

[99] *Lehnhausen v. Lake Shore Auto Parts Co.*, 410 U.S. 356, 360 (1973) (citing *Allied Stores v. Bowers*, 358 U.S. 522, 530 (1959).

[100] *Nicol v. Ames*, 173 U.S. 509, 521 (1899) (citations omitted).

[101] *Allied Stores v. Bowers*, 358 U.S. 522, 527 (1959) (quoting *Royster Guano Co. v. Virginia*, 253 U.S. 412, 415 (1920)); see also *Welch v. Henry*, 305 U.S. 134, 144 (1938) ("Any classification of taxation is permissible which has reasonable relation to a legitimate end of government action."); *Fox v. Standard Oil Co.*, 294 U.S. 87 (1935).

[102] *Bell's Gap R.R. Co. v. Pennsylvania*, 134 U.S. 232, 237 (1890).

[103] *Ibid.* at 237. "The difficulty of adjusting any system of taxation so as to render it precisely equal in its bearing is proverbial . . ." *LaBelle Iron Works v. United States*, 256 U.S. 377, 392 (1921).

[104] *Regan v. Taxation with Representation*, 461 U.S. at 547-48; *Fernandez v. Wiener*, 326 U.S. 340, 352 (1945); *Madden v. Kentucky*, 309 U.S. 83, 88 (1940); *Kahn v. Shevin* 416 U.S. 351 (1974) (upholding differing treatment for widows and widowers in state tax law).

[105] *Comm'r v. Sullivan* 356 U.S. 27, 28 (1958) (quoted in *Regan v. Taxation with Representation*, 461 U.S. at 549).

rights. A taxing authority may "impose different specific taxes upon different trades and professions and may vary the rate of excise upon various products. It is not required to resort to close distinctions or maintain a precise, scientific uniformity . . . "[106] Tax laws may even make distinctions between members of the same class if there is a rational basis.[107] Furthermore, administrative convenience or relatively great expense in collecting or measuring a tax may justify different treatment (such as exemptions for small companies or small incomes).[108]

To modern eyes, an extreme illustration of arbitrary, yet still constitutional, line-drawing occurred in *McCray v. United States.*[109] Congress imposed a one-quarter cent per pound tax on white oleomargarine while imposing a ten cent per pound tax on yellow oleomargarine. Yellow oleomargarine created stiff competition for real butter, while white oleomargarine presented the unappetizing appearance of lard. Plaintiffs argued that the tax was imposed only because the dairy industry had persuaded Congress to suppress its competition. Nevertheless, the Supreme Court upheld the taxing scheme. It refused to dwell upon the potential motivation of legislators, and relied only upon the broad discretion of Congress in drawing lines between various categories of taxation.

> The right of Congress to tax within its delegated power being unrestrained, except as limited by the Constitution, it was within the authority conferred on Congress to select the objects upon which an excise should be laid. It therefore follows that, in exerting its power, no want of due process of law could possibly result, because that body chose to impose an excise on artifically colored oleo margarine, and not upon natural butter artificially colored.[110]

One of the most recent cases addressing equal protection in taxation is *Regan v. Taxation with Representation.*[111] A nonprofit organization challenged the extension of tax-exempt status to veterans groups engaged in lobbying, because similar tax-exempt status was denied to other lobbying organizations. The court rejected the plaintiff's equal protection argument. The Court of Appeals had applied a "high-level of scrutiny" because the

---

[106] *Allied Stores v. Bowers*, 358 U.S. at 527. "Where the public interest is served one business may be left untaxed and another taxed, in order to promote the one, or to restrict or suppress the other." *Carmichael v. Southern Coal Co.*, 301 U.S. at 512 (citations omitted).

[107] *Carmichael v. Southern Coal Co.*, 301 U.S. at 509 ("A legislature is not bound to tax every member of a class or none. It may make distinctions of degree having a rational basis . . .").

[108] *Ibid.* at 511. 513.

[109] 195 U.S. 27 (1904).

[110] *Ibid.* at 61.

[111] 461 U.S. 540 (1983). Both First and Fifth Amendment claims were raised, but only the Fifth Amendment aspects will be examined herein.

fundamental right of speech was affected,[112] but the Supreme Court adopted a minimum rationality standard. It characterized the issue as congressional subsidization of some, but not all, speech.[113] The court found that it was not irrational for Congress to favor veterans' groups. The Court reaffirmed the general principles applicable in equal protection challenges to tax statutes:

> Traditionally classification has been a device for fitting tax programs to local needs and usages in order to achieve an equitable distribution of the tax burden. It has, because of this, been pointed out that in taxation, even more than in other fields, legislatures possess the greatest freedom in classification . . . [T]he presumption of constitutionality can be overcome only by the most explicit demonstration that a classification is a hostile and oppressive discrimination against particular persons and classes.[114]

The standards for equal protection in taxation have remained surprisingly constant for well over a century. The underlying thread is a judicial acceptance of the legislative need for flexibility in tailoring tax statues to differing situations. To require absolute equality of taxation "would render nugatory those discriminations which the best interests of society require, which are necessary for the encouragement of needed and useful industries, and the discouragement of intemperance and vice . . ."[115] The assumption is that fairness and administrative efficiency in taxation are not achieved by generally applicable rules of liability, but by standards tailored to fit particular classes of taxpayers.

In summary, the legislative branch is free to set different tax rates, create exemptions, or impose single-commodity taxes, so long as some rational justification can be found (and this justification may be provided by the courts' retrospective inquiry). A more exacting standard is required only where a suspect class or fundamental right is involved. Congressional flexibility is so great that it was noted in the 1930s that "No tax has been held invalid under the Fifth Amendment because based on an improper classification . . ."[116] Tax invalidations have remained rare in the intervening years. Absent unusual circumstances, the broad discretion given Congress in formulating tax classifications renders the equal protection requirement insignificant as a limitation on the taxing power.

---

[112] *Taxation with Representation v. Regan*, 676 F.2d 715, 724 (D.C. Cir. 1982) (en banc).

[113] 461 U.S. at 547-48.

[114] *Ibid.* (quoting *Madden v. Kentucky*, 309 U.S. 83, 88 (1940) (footnotes omitted)).

[115] *Bell's Gap R.R. Co. v. Pennsylvania*, 134 U.S. at 237; see also *Allied Stores v. Bowers*, 358 U.S. at 528.

[116] *Heiner v. Donnan*, 285 U.S. 312, 338 (1932) (Stone, J., dissenting) (majority struck as violating due process a federal tax provision creating an irrebuttable presumption that gifts made within two years prior to death were made in contemplation of death).

Often overlapping with equal protection, a second type of due process analysis examines whether a tax is rationally related to legitimate purposes, and whether it reasonably may be expected to accomplish those purposes. Like equal protection, due process leaves Congress a wide scope of discretion in determining the purposes to be served by taxation.[117] The due process standard utilized in evaluating tax laws is whether the law comports with some notion of minimum rationality in the structure of taxation, whether the tax scheme is arbitrary and capricious.[118] Tax measures ordinarily have little difficulty satisfying the minimum rationality requirement. Courts have found that a tax measure has a rational justification if one of its main purposes is to raise revenue.[119]

A due process/rationality argument appears strongest when raising revenue directly conflicts with other clearly specified goals of a statute. It requires little knowledge of economics to realize that penalizing an activity will cause it to occur less often. When Congress states its intention to encourage an activity and then proceeds to tax that activity,[120] it has, in terms of economic policy, acted irrationally. However, this argument has been rejected.[121]

Even where congressional action is allegedly based on improper motives, if any rational purpose can be identified, the tax will be upheld.[122] The due process requirement may be used to strike a tax "only if the act be so arbitrary as to compel the conclusion that it does not involve an exertion of the taxing power, but constitutes, in substance and effect, the direct exertion of a different and forbidden power, as for example, the confiscation of property."[123] Virtually the only situation in which a due process/

---

[117] *Carmichael v. Southern Coal Co.*, 301 U.S. at 514.

[118] "This court has recognized that a statute purporting to tax may be so arbitrary and capricious as to amount to confiscation and offend the Fifth Amendment. And we must conclude that . . . the statute here under consideration . . . is arbitrary, capricious, and amounts to confiscation." *Nichols v. Coolidge*, 274 U.S. 531, 542-43 (1927) (citations omitted); see also *Brushaber v. Union Pacific R.R. Co.*, 240 U.S. 1 (1916).

[119] *Fox v. Standard Oil Co.*, 294 U.S. 87, 101 (1935); *A Magnano Co. v. Hamilton*, 292 U.S. 40, 44 (1934); *McCray v. United States*, 195 U.S. 27 (1904). "Because every economic regulation serves some purpose, the rational relation standard essentially presupposes judicial withdrawal" (B. Siegan 1980' p. 265). But see *Metropolitan Life Ins. Co. v. Ward*, 470 U.S. 869 (1985) (favoritism toward in-state business was not justified by a legitimate state purpose).

[120] Assuming that the tax is levied for general revenue purposes, not to finance programs that might arguably benefit the taxed industry.

[121] See, for example, *Ptasynski v. United States*, 550 F. Supp. 549, 555 (D. Wyo. 1982) (taxes may not be struck down because they are "unwise").

[122] *McCray v. United States*, 195 U.S. 27 (1904).

[123] *A. Magnano Co. v. Hamilton*, 292 U.S. 40, 44 (1934), (cited with approval in *Pittsburg v. Alco Parking Corp.*, 417 U.S. 369, 375 (1974).

rationality approach has successfully invalidated a tax is where a tax is placed on imputed income. Because of the "fundamental conceptions which underlie our system," attempts to measure the tax on one person's income by reference to the income of another is contrary to due process.[124]

Standing alone, the fact that a tax is extremely high and unduly burdensome does not provide grounds for Fifth Amendment challenge.[125] It is not the province of the judiciary to inquire whether a tax is reasonable in amount.[126] "A tax does not cease to be valid merely because it regulates, discourages, or even definitely deters the activities taxed."[127] This general proposition remains true even if a tax is so heavy that it halts legitimate commercial activities. "Even if the tax should destroy a business, it would not be made invalid or require compensation upon that ground alone. Those who enter upon a business take that risk."[128] A burdensome and destructive tax may be stricken only if "the form of taxation was adopted as a mere disguise."[129]

The range of possible challenges to taxation that fall under the rubric of due process is broad. Due process also includes assertions that taxing statutes should be invalidated because they are unduly vague,[130] retroactive,[131] or contain irrebuttable presumptions.[132] None of these claims, however, has played a significant role in limiting congressional tax actions. The Due Process Clause acts as a limit on taxation only when a tax

---

[124] *Hoeper v. Tax Commission*, 284 U.S. 206, 215 (1931); see also *Burnet v. Wells*, 289 U.S. 670, 683 (1933) (Sutherland, J., dissenting) ("The powers of taxation are broad, but the distinction between taxation and confiscation must still be observed. So long as the Fifth Amendment remains unrepealed and is permitted to control, Congress may not tax the property of A as the property of B, or the income of A as the income of B.").

[125] "The proposition that where a tax is imposed which is within the grant of powers, and which does not conflict with any express constitutional limitation, the courts may hold the tax to be void because it is deemed that the tax is too high, is absolutely disposed of by the opinions in the cases hitherto cited . . ." *McCray v. United States*, 195 U.S. 27, 60 (1904).

[126] See *Pittsburg v. Alco Parking Corp.*, 417 U.S. 369, 373 (1974) (Court refused to pass on "reasonableness" of a tax); see also *Patton v. Brady*, 184 U.S. 608, 623 (1902).

[127] *United States v. Sanchez*, 340 U.S. 42, 44 (1950).

[128] *Alaska Fish Salting & By-Products Co. v. Smith*, 255 U.S. 44, 48 (1921) (citations omitted); accord *Pittsburgh v. Alco Parking Corp.*, 417 U.S. 369 (1974); *Fox v. Standard Oil Co.*, 294 U.S. 87 (1935).

[129] *A. Magnano Co. v. Hamilton*, 292 U.S. 40, 44 (1934); see also *Pittsburgh v. Alco Parking Corp.*, 417 U.S. 369 (1974).

[130] See David Crump (1983), (citing *Weissinger v. Boswell*, 330 F. Supp. 615, 624 (M.D. Ala. 1971) (three judge court)); *Taxation with Representation v. Regan*, 676 F.2d. 715, 726 n. 22 (D.C. Cir.1982) (en banc).

[131] See *Nichols v. Coolidge*, 274 U.S. 531 (1927); *Milliken v. United States*, 283 U.S. 15, 21 (1931); *Welch v. Henry*, 305 U.S. 134, 144-45 (1938).

[132] *Heiner v. Donnan*, 285 U.S. 312 (1932).

interferes with some individual right beyond the right to own property[133] or to engage in legitimate business activities.

B. Taking

A taxing power limitation based on taking, or the requirement for just compensation, has considerable appeal from a political science standpoint.[134] It is rooted in the Founding Fathers' understanding of the weakness of a democratic system. A democracy always presents the danger that fifty-one percent of the people will use the force of law to seize the possessions of the other forty-nine percent. To prevent this, the Constitution requires just compensation whenever private property is taken for a public purpose.[135] The Taking Clause was "always understood to have been adopted for protection and security to the rights of the individual as against the government . . ."[136] It "stands as a shield against the arbitrary use of governmental power."[137]

The conceptual similarity of taxes, on the one hand, and takings of private property through the eminent domain power on the other hand, has been recognized in the scholarly literature. "Taxation and eminent domain indeed rest substantially on the same foundation, as each implies the taking of private property for the public use on compensation made . . . ," (Thomas Cooley 1927).

However, despite the similarity between taxation and eminent domain, courts have generally held that no compensation is required when private property is taken through taxation. This interpretation leads to the anomalous result that a person must be compensated if his home is condemned through the eminent domain power, but no compensation is necessary if, when an individual sells his home to another private individual, the entire proceeds of that sale are confiscated through taxation.[138] Although the practical result of a taking through eminent domain may be identical to that of taxation, the legal rules are quite different.

---

[133] *Lynch v. Household Finance Corp.*, 405 U.S. 538, 552 (1972) (reaffirmed ownership of property as a basic civil right).

[134] The author's application of eminent domain theories to taxation was inspired by Professor Richard Epstein. See Epstein, (1982).

[135] The Fifth Amendment Takings Clause (also termed the Just Compensation Clause or the Eminent Domain Clause) provides: "[N]or shall private property be taken for public use, without just compensation."

[136] *Pumpelly v. Green Bay Co.*, 80 U.S. (13 Wall.) 166, 177 (1871).

[137] *Webb's Fabulous Pharmacies v. Beckwith*, 449 U.S. 155, 164 (1980).

[138] If applied literally, a "compensation" requirement for taxation would demand the ridiculous result that a part of tax funds collected be paid back as compensation. The appropriate remedy in a tax situation would be the invalidation of taxes that did not adequately provide in-kind compensation to taxpayers, as described below.

The important issues in eminent domain analysis are (1) distribution of benefits and burdens, and (2) existence of a public purpose of a taking. Each of these points is also frequently addressed in tax decisions, but in a different manner than in eminent domain cases. We shall examine these two points and then consider the implications of applying a taking analysis to taxation.

In the area of eminent domain, the Takings Clause is intended to prevent the government "from forcing some people alone to bear burdens which, in all fairness and justice, should be borne by the public as a whole."[139] In the area of taxation, taxes are considered "the means of distributing the burden of the cost of government,"[140] and no citizen enjoys immunity from that burden.[141] Taxpayers receive compensation for their contributions by sharing in the benefits of society, including social and family rights and privileges,[142] public services, and the government's protection of life, liberty, and property.[143] The assumption that compensation is provided by general societal benefits is always implicit when tax funds are used for the general benefit of society, and the tax burden is distributed with some degree of generality.

When the placement of benefits and burdens is not roughly equal, judicial analyses have not been consistent. Some cases have rejected entirely any assertion that maldistribution of benefits and burdens could invalidate a tax: "The cases, both state and Federal, are numerous in which it has been held that taxes, otherwise lawful, are not invalidated by the allegation, or even the fact, that the resulting benefits are unequally shared."[144]

On the other hand, courts have sometimes invalidated government actions that created disproportionate benefits or burdens. One nineteenth century case colorfully expressed the prohibition against an inequitable distribution of benefits. "To lay, with the one hand, the power of the government on the property of the citizen, and with the other to bestow it upon favored individuals to aid private enterprises and build up private fortunes, is none the less a robbery because it is done under the forms of law and is called taxation."[145] In a considerably more recent case, the Supreme Court struck down an improper placement of a burden. It found an "obviously un-

---

[139] *Armstrong v. United States*, 364 U.S. 40, 49 (1960); accord, *Webb's Fabulous Pharmacies v. Beckwith*, 449 U.S. 155 (1980).

[140] *Carmichael v. Southern Coal Co.*, 301 U.S. 495, 508 (1936).

[141] *Welch v. Henry*, 305 U.S. 134, 143 (1938).

[142] *Thomas v. Gay*, 169 U.S. 264, 280 (1898).

[143] See Cooley (1927).

[144] *Thomas v. Gay*, 169 U.S. 264, 280 (1898).

[145] *Citizens' Savings & Loan Ass'n v. Topeka*, 87 U.S. (20 Wall.) 655 (1875).

compensated" taking where a government entity had "not merely 'adjust[ed] the benefits. Rather, the exaction is a forced contribution to general governmental revenues, and it is not reasonably related to the costs . . . "[146]

The balancing of benefits and burdens is discussed most frequently in cases on taxes assessed for particular public works projects.[147] For example, in *Myles Salt Co. v. Board of Commissioners*,[148] land was included within a drainage district that, because of its topography, could not possibly benefit from that district's activities. The only reason for including the area was to derive revenue from it. The Court labelled this "an act of confiscation," because it imposed "a burden without a compensating advantage of any kind."[149]

In balancing the distribution of benefits and burdens, courts have always upheld taxes on particular classes of taxpayers to pay for special benefits received by that class, or to compensate society for a special burden created by that class. The guiding proposition is "when particular individuals are singled out to bear the cost of advancing the public convenience, that imposition must bear some reasonable relation to the evils to be eradicated or the advantages to be secured."[150] The category of special benefits includes many taxes that are essentially user fees. For example, highway user taxes fall upon those who utilize the highways, and the proceeds are used to maintain those highways. The tax is an attempt to focus expenditures and revenue-raising on the same group.[151]

The inverse situation is exemplified by taxes that are regulatory in character, such as the perennial taxes on liquor and tobacco. Theoretically, at least, these taxes compensate society for the "evils" created by the taxpayers. Similarly, taxes on railroads to pay for the construction of highway overpasses were generally upheld, not because the railroads benefitted from the automobile overpasses, but because the overpasses remedied the

---

[146] *Webb's Fabulous Pharmacies v. Beckwith*, 449 U.S. 155, 163 (1980).

[147] It should be noted that assessments have been treated differently than general taxation. "While moneys raised by general taxation may constitutionally be applied to purposes from which the individual taxed may receive no benefit, and indeed, suffer no detriment, so called assessments for public improvements laid upon particular property owners are ordinarily constitutional only if based on benefits received by them." *Nashville, Chattanooga, and St. Louis Ry. v. Walters*, 294 U.S. 405, 429-30 (1935) (citations omitted). Nevertheless the benefit/burden analysis utilized by these cases is illustrative.

[148] 239 U.S. 478 (1916).

[149] *Myles Salt*, 239 U.S. at 485.

[150] *Nashville, Chattanooga & St. Louis Ry. v. Walters*, 294 U.S. 405, 429-30 (1935) (citation omitted).

[151] See also *Fernandez v. Wiener*, 326 U.S. 340-358 (1943) ("The tax burden thus laid is not so unrelated to the privileges enjoyed by the taxpayers who are owners of the property affected that it can be said to be an arbitrary exercise of the taxing power.").

inconveniences caused by the railroads.[152]

The second factor to be examined in a taking-style analysis of taxation is the purpose for which a tax is assessed. The general rule is that taxes can be levied for any proper public purpose.[153] Identification of a public purpose is related to a balancing of benefits and burdens because a compensating benefit is presumed whenever tax funds are used for a public purpose.[154] If the tax is not for a public purpose, then the benefits are not distributed in accordance with the burdens, and the tax may be invalidated.

A taking problem may arise when an industry is taxed to support government programs that, though they may be perceived as benefitting society as a whole, directly benefit the competitors of the taxpaying class. In one case, the Supreme invalidated an assessment against a railroad to pay for construction of an interstate highway overpass. Although a railroad can be taxed to pay for crossings that allow local traffic to cross the tracks, it could not be forced to finance the construction of a major interstate highway, since "[p]ractically all vehicles moving upon it will directly or indirectly compete for traffic with the Railway."[155] A more modern example is the Windfall Profit Tax Act,[156] which designates a portion of the proceeds from the tax on oil producers to be used for development of alternate energy sources, thereby lessening the dependence on petroleum products.

The analysis found in most judicial decisions attempts to draw a firm line between takings and ordinary taxes. Yet even where courts have been reluctant to view the Fifth Amendment as a limitation on the taxing power, they have acknowledged that an extremely egregious situation may rise to the level of a taking. Pronouncing that a tax is a taking is treated as equivalent to pronouncing that it is confiscation, beyond the power granted

---

[152] See *Atchison, Topeka & Santa Fe Ry. Co. v. Public Utility Commission*, 346 U.S. 346, 353 (1953) ("Having brought about the problem, the railroads are in no position to complain because their share in the cost of alleviating it is not based solely on the special benefits accruing to them from the improvements."). But see *Nashville, Chattanooga, & St. Louis Ry. v. Walters*, 294 U.S. 405 (1935) (railroad does not have to bear cost of grade crossing that would benefit only interstate highway).

[153] *Carmichael v. Southern Coal & Coke Co.*, 301 U.S. 495, 514 (1937); *A Magnano Co. v. Hamilton*, 292 U.S. 40, 44 (1934).

[154] *A. Magnano Co.*, 292 U.S. at 43 ("a tax designed to be expended for a public purpose does not cease to be one levied for that purpose because it has the effect of imposing a burden upon one class of business enterprises in such a way as to benefit another class....")

[155] *Nashville, Chattanooga & St. Louis Ry. v. Walters*, 294 U.S. 405, 426 (1935).

[156] 26 U.S.C. Sections 4986-98 (1982). The practice of "earmarking" proceeds of a tax allows Congress to justify the new level of taxation and to gain the support of those who benefit from the revenue allocation. See James Wetzler (1980). Earmarking is generally a strictly advisory activity, because Congress seldom binds itself to distribute actual revenues according to the earmarking. Unless Congress does commit itself to an allocation, earmarking probably would not influence the taking analysis.

hy the Constitution. According to this approach, benefits and burdens are examined only to see if there is an outrageous disproportionality.

An alternative analysis available to the court is to consider all taxes to be takings and thereby routinely subject them to limitation and justification. In other words, rather than distinguishing between taxes that are takings and taxes that are not takings, one would subject all taxes to the same scrutiny as takings. The implications of this approach are best described by Professor Epstein:

> The proposition [that all taxes are takings under the Eminent Domain Clause] does not command the absurdity that all taxes are refunded or that no future taxes be collected at all. It does not command that all, let alone even most, taxes be regarded as unconstitutional. It does not demand government grind to a halt. What it does do is lay the foundation for an examination of the tax to see whether it can pass muster upon the same constitutional principles applicable to other takings, an inquiry that could not commence if taxes were regarded as falling within one logical domain and takings were regarded as falling in quite another.[157]

An eminent domain analysis of taxation is consistent with the principle that the Fifth Amendment protects against abuses of governmental authority. It would prevent the burdens of expensive government programs from being borne by small groups that did not share in the benefits. However, employing this analysis to weigh the validity of tax measures requires a delicate balancing, without firm standards to guide judicial decision-making. Unless more definite standards can be enunciated, the courts will probably remain unwilling to systematically balance the benefits and burdens of taxation.

V. Procedural Obstacles Restricting Constitutional Challenges to Taxation

In addition to the unique constitutional standards applicable to federal tax cases, several unique procedural requirements also limit judicial review of tax matters. There is a particularly strong presumption in favor of the constitutionality of any tax statue.[158] Only "when the question is free from any reasonable doubt" does a court find a revenue act unconstitutional.[159] Furthermore, the burden on those challenging tax statutes is almost impossibly heavy: "The burden is on the one attacking the legislative

---

[157] Richard Epstein, untitled memorandum (Aug. 8, 1980) (unpublished memorandum, on file at the *Harvard Journal of Law & Public Policy*).

[158] *Madden v. Kentucky*, 309 U.S. 83, 87-88 (1940); *Regan v. Taxation with Representation*, 461 U.S. 540, 547-48 (1983).

[159] *Nicol v. Ames*, 173 U.S. 509, 515 (1899).

arrangement to negative *every conceivable basis* which might support it."[160]

Precise structures and procedural rules have been established for adjudicating tax questions. It is only through following these procedures that a taxpayer may overcome the bar of sovereign immunity.[161] A taxpayer may have his tax liability litigated in federal district court only if he waits until the end of the first taxable period, pays the disputed tax in full,[162] then files an administrative claim for refund with the Internal Revenue Service.[163] After this claim is denied or after the taxpayer has waited at least six months to give the IRS an opportunity to respond,[164] the taxpayer may file a suit for refund in federal district court or the Court of Claims.[165] Alternatively, if the taxpayer wishes to avoid paying the tax, he can wait for the IRS to issue a deficiency notice[166] and then proceed with an action in the United States tax court.[167]

Dating back to 1867, the Anti-Injunction Act is one of the most effective means for discouraging suits challenging the constitutionality of tax measures. It prohibits courts from granting injunctions in federal tax cases.[168] A second, parallel provision is of more recent origin. The Declaratory Judgments Act contains an exception preventing declaratory judgments on federal tax issues.[169] The scope of the Anti-Injunction Act

---

[160] *Madden v. Kentucky*, 309 U.S. 83, 88 (1940) (emphasis added); *Regan v. Taxation with Representation*, 461 U.S. 540, 547-48 (1983); see also *San Antonio Indep. School Dist. v. Rodriquez*, 411 U.S. 1, 40-41 (1973); *Lehnhausen v. Lake Shore Auto Parts Co.*, 410 U.S. 356, 359-60 (1973); *United States v. Maryland Savings-Share Ins. Corp.*, 400 U.S. 4, 6 (1970). The burden of invalidating a tax scheme runs counter to, and must be distinguished from, the presumption in interpreting taxes. "[W]hen the question has been one of construction and nothing more, a question as to the meaning of a taxing act [is] to be read in favor of the taxpayer." *Burnet v. Wells*, 289 U.S. 670, 678 (1933).

[161] See *Bailey v. George*, 259 U.S. 16, 20 (1922); *Flora v. United States*, 362 U.S. 145 (1960).

[162] See *Flora v. United States*, 362 U.S. 145 (1960).

[163] 26 U.S.C. Section 7422(a) (1982).

[164] 26 U.S.C. Section 6532(a)(1) (1982). This requirement is designed to allow the IRS an opportunity to audit the taxpayer's return and determine whether the claim is allowable and whether other taxes may be owed. See *Cherry Cotton Mills v. United States*, 327 U.S. 536, 539 (1946); *United States v. Memphis Cotton Oil Co.*, 288 U.S. 62, 70-71 (1933).

[165] 28 U.S.C. Section 1346(a)(1) (1982).

[166] Pursuant to 26 U.S.C. Section 6212 (1982).

[167] 26 U.S.C. Section 7442 (1982).

[168] 26 U.S.C. Section 7421(a) (1982) provides that, with some specific statutory exceptions, "no suit for the purpose of restraining the assessment or collection of any tax shall be maintained in any court by any person . . ."

[169] 28 U.S.C. Section 2201 (1982) (declaratory relief is not available "with respect to Federal taxes").

and the Declaratory Judgments Act exception is coterminous.[170] Both are intended to prevent taxpayers from circumventing the rigorous statutory scheme for adjudicating tax liability, and thereby "protect the government's ability to assess and collect taxes free from pre-enforcement judicial interference . . ."[171]

Courts have not always interpreted the Anti-Injunction Act quite as strictly as its language would indicate.[172] At one time, the Court found an exception to the Act when the legal remedy was inadequate, such as where collection of the tax "would destroy [the taxpayer's] business, ruin it financially, and inflict loss for which it would have no remedy at all."[173] Experience proved that this interpretation virtually negated the Anti-Injunction Act, as taxpayers could often prove that payment of taxes would inflict irreparable financial loss. Consequently, the Court adopted a stricter interpretation. Injunctive relief is permissible only in narrow circumstances: (1) where under the most liberal view of the law and facts the government could not ultimately prevail,[174] and (2) plaintiff would sustain irreparable injury for which there is no adequate remedy at law.[175]

An exception may also exist where "an aggrieved party has no access at all to judicial review."[176] When a denial of judicial review rises to the level of constitutional infirmity, due process requires that some judicial relief be provided.[177] If judicial review is merely delayed, or if no property rights cognizable under the Due Process Clause are affected, then injunctive relief remains barred.[178]

Despite these exceptions, in most situations a suit seeking to enjoin

---

[170] *Investment Annuity v. Blumenthal*, 609 F.2d 1, 4 (D.C. Cir. 1979), cert. denied sub nom.*First Investment Annuity Co. v. Miller*, 446 U.S. 981 (1980); *Eastern Kentucky Welfare Rights Org. v. Simon*, 506 F.2d 1278, 1285 (D.C. Cir. 1974), rev'd on other grounds, 426 U.S. 26 (1976).

[171] *Investment Annuity v. Blumenthal*, 609 F.2d at 5.

[172] The Court followed a "cyclical pattern of allegiance to the plain meaning of the Act . . ." *Bob Jones University v. Simon* 416 U.S. 725, 742 (1974).

[173] *Miller v. Standard Nut Margarine Co.*, 284 U.S. 498, 510-11 (1932).

[174] If the government clearly cannot prevail in its position, the "exaction is merely in 'the guise of a tax'," *Enochs v. Williams Packing & Navigation Co.*, 370 U.S. 1, 7 (1962) (quoting *Miller v. Standard Nut Margarine Co.*, 284 U.S. 498, 510-11 (1932)), so the Anti-Injunction Act would not apply.

[175] *Alexander v. "Americans United" Inc.*, 416 U.S. 752, 758 (1974); *Enochs v. Williams Packing & Navigation Co.*, 370 U.S. 1 (1962).

[176] *Bob Jones University v. Simon*, 416 U.S. at 746.

[177] *Investment Annuity v. Blumenthal*, 609 F.2d at 5; *California v. Regan*, 641 F.2d 721, 723 (9th Cir. 1981).

[178] *Investment Annuity v. Blumenthal*, 609 F.2d at 7.

collection of a tax must be dismissed.[179] The existence of the Anti-Injunction Act and Declatory Judgment exception have some practical effects beyond ensuring that the flow of vital funds to the federal treasury will not be interrupted pending a final determination of liability. Forcing litigants to follow standard procedures also provides a small measure of strategic assistance to the IRS. The most important strategic consideration is timing. A new tax statute is most vulnerable immediately after enactment, before the bureaucracy for collecting the tax has been established, before any public outcry about the tax has died down, and before the treasury has become dependent on the revenues it generates. Because of the time-consuming statutory procedures described above, a judicial proceeding usually cannot commence for at least a year after passage of a tax statute.

A second consideration is that these statutory procedures preclude the use of class actions in federal tax cases. Thus a tax issue especially suited to class litigation, i.e., an issue having a small impact on a large number of individuals, may not be litigated. These issues may be litigated through representative suits, financed by unions, trade associations, or other organizations of affected taxpayers. However, a victory in a representative suit may not have the desired effect because of the IRS's "non-acquiescence" procedure. The IRS has a formal procedure for determining whether it will "acquiesce" in lower court decisions. If the IRS acquiesces, the decision will be followed in tax collections throughout the nation. If not, the IRS will continue to follow its own interpretation of the tax statute. This procedure has practical benefits for an agency that may be faced with conflicting judicial decisions in various jurisdictions, but it can frustrate taxpayer litigants.[180] Lower courts are not empowered to enjoin IRS actions that conflict with their rulings, so an adverse decision may have very little impact on tax collections. Unless the IRS acquiesces in a lower court ruling, the only way to conclusively resolve a tax issue is for the matter to be decided by the Supreme Court.

VI. Conclusion

At some point, tax burdens become so heavy that they begin to undermine the free society they were intended to support. When that occurs, the nation

---

[179] See *Alexander v. "American United" Inc.*, 416 U.S. 752 (1974); *Bob Jones University v. Simon*, 416 U.S. 725 (1974); *Enochs v. Williams Packing & Navigation Co.*, 370 U.S. 1 (1962).

[180] For example, a few years ago, several hotels backed a suit by one hotel to obtain an interpretation of a particular tax provision. Although the hotel won its suit, *Hotel Conquistador v. United States*, 597 F.2d 1348 (Ct. Cl. 1979), cert. denied, 444 U.S. 1032 (1980), the IRS issued a notice of non-acquiescence. Rev. Rul. 80-41, 1980-1 C.B. 211. Thereafter, the IRS continued to assess and collect the tax against other hotels until the disputed statute was interpreted adversely to the IRS in *Rowan Companies v. United States*, 452 U.S. 247 (1981).

must determine whether the balance between protecting individual rights and ensuring necessary government revenues has been disrupted.

It is virtually beyond dispute that the Courts have not provided significant limits on the taxing power of Congress. Furthermore, they are not prepared to limit abuses that may arise as budgetary pressures become more acute. The preceding analysis reveals that the judiciary will uphold almost any tax classification or unequal placement of tax burdens. The constitutional requirements of uniform and apportioned taxation have been narrowed until they have only minimal impact. Furthermore, the fact that a tax is unwisely or destructively high is not grounds for invalidation under current constitutional standards.

However, the policy implications are not clear-cut. A shift by the judiciary to an aggressive enforcement of constitutional limitations upon the taxing power could limit the ability of special interest groups to obtain selective tax treatment. A requirement that the burden of taxation be shared in somewhat equal proportion by all taxpayers would do much to revitalize the safeguards necessary for a democratic system of government. Democratic institutions may provide a real limitation on excessive taxation, so long as the tax burden is equally distributed. It is perhaps particularly prudent for the courts to reexamine the explicit constitutional tax limitations, the Uniformity Clause and the Apportionment Clause, to determine whether their operation has been unnecessarily circumscribed.

On the other hand, existing constitutional doctrine presents no easy avenues for the courts to follow in evaluating the constitutionality of taxes. None of the theories discussed above may provide sufficient guidance for judicial enforcement. Amending the Constitution to provide more clearly drawn safeguards may ultimately be the only way to guard against abuses of the taxing power.

References

Anderson, Martin. "An Economic Bill of Rights." In *To Promote Prosperity*, edited by John H. Moore. Stanford: Hoover Institution Press, 1984.

Cooley, Thomas. *Constitutional Limitations.* 8th ed. Boston: Little, Brown and Co., 1927.

Crumbley, D. Larry, and Reese, Craig E. *Readings in the Crude Oil Windfall Profit Tax*, Tulsa, OK: Pennwell Books Division, 1982.

Crump, David. "The Crude Oil Windfall Profit Tax: Is It Unconstitutional?" *Texas Bar Journal* 46 (May 1983): 555-65.

Dow, J. Matthew. "The Windfall Profit Tax Exposed." *St. Mary's Law Journal* 14 (1983): 739-56.

Drapkin, Dennis B. and Verleger, Phillip K., Jr. "The Windfall Profit Tax: Origins, Development, Implications." *Boston College Law Review* 22 (May 1981): 631-704.

Epstein, Richard A. "Taxation, Regulation, and Confiscation." *Osgoode Hall Law Journal* 20 (1982): 433-53.

Hutchinson, David. *The Foundations of the Constitution*. Secaucus, NJ: University Books, 1975.

Interstate Oil Compact Commission. *Effects of Crude Oil Windfall Profit Tax* Oklahoma City, OK: Interstate Oil Compact Commission, 1980.

Johnson, Gregg D. "The Unconstitutional Exemption of North Slope Crude Under the Windfall Profit Tax Act: Exhuming the Direct Tax and Uniformity Provisions." *Tax Lawyer* 35 (Summer 1982): 717-45.

Miller, Barry R. and Easley, Dan G. "The Windfall Profit Tax—An Overview." *St. Mary's Law Journal* 12 (1980): 414-35.

Morrow, Dwight W. "The Income Tax Amendment." *Columbia Law Review* 10 (May 1910): 379-415.

National Petroleum Council. *U. S. Artic Oil and Gas*. Washington: National Petroleum Council, 1981.

Paul, Randolph E. *Taxation in the United States*. Boston: Boston, Little, Brown, 1954.

Reese, Craig E. "The Royalty Owner's Exemption from WindfallProfit Taxation." *Taxes* 60 (1982): 725-42.

Riddle, J. H. "The Supreme Court's Theory of a Direct Tax." *Michigan Law Review* 15 (May 1917): 566-78.

Robison, Douglas M. "The Misnamed Tax: The Crude Oil Windfall Profits Tax of 1980." *Dickinson Law Review* 84 (Summer 1980): 589-603.

Saterdal, A. and Marks, Jay Glenn. "Oil Industry Profits: Perception vs. Reality." *Mines Magazine* 70 (March 1980): 5-10.

Siegan, Bernard. *Economic Liberties and the Constitution*. Chicago: University of Chicago Press, 1980.

Story, Joseph. *Commentaries on the Constitution of the United States*, reprint of 1873 Ed. New York: De Capo Press, 1970.

Wetzler, James. "Energy Excise Taxes as Substitutes for Income Taxes." *National Tax Journal* 33 (1980): 321-29.

13

PROCEDURAL AND SUBSTANTIVE CONSTITUTIONAL PROTECTION OF ECONOMIC LIBERTIES

Peter H. Aranson

Introduction

Recent history and the Bicentennial of the U.S. Constitution have revived interest in long-standing questions about the Republic's constitutionally constructed political and judicial institutions. This paper focuses on the role of one institution—the federal judiciary, and especially the Supreme Court—to discern the nature of its place in setting the metes and bounds of the relationships between federal and state political branches on one side and citizens' economic rights on the other.

The first section describes and criticizes three currently prominent theories of constitutional interpretation: the interpretivist position, espoused most recently by Attorney General Edwin Meese III and Chief Justice William H. Rehnquist; the noninterpretivist position, often embodied in the opinions and other writings of Associate Justice William J. Brennan; and the procedural protections position, as developed in the work of Professor John Hart Ely. The essay then reviews the place of procedural and substantive protections in constitutional argument and discerns the fundamental weaknesses in the interpretivist, noninterpretivist, and Ely positions: None of the positions addresses the problem of rent-seeking, by which minority interests and their coalitions engage the political process to reduce the welfare of members of the majority. The analysis is then applied to two recent Supreme Court cases, *Supreme Court of New Hampshire v. Piper* (470 U.S. 274 [1985]) and *Metropolitan Life Insurance Co. v. Ward* (470 U.S. 869 [1985]). The essay concludes by examining some recently proposed constitutional correctives to the problem of rent-seeking.

Cato Journal, Vol. 7, No. 2 (Fall 1987). Copyright Cato Institute. All rights reserved.

The author is Professor of Economics at Emory University. He thanks Thomas Arthur, William Mayton, Fred McChesney, and Thomas Morgan of the Emory Law School for their helpful comments on an earlier draft of the paper.

The Search for Principles: Interpretivists, Noninterpretivists, and Proceduralists.

The central questions about the constitutionally derived relation between the government and the governed in the American Republic, which have for so long dominated constitutional argument, form a hierarchy of principal and subsidiary questions with respect to the federal judiciary. First, should federal courts apply the Constitution to such relationships in conformance with that document's words—the interpretivist position—or should they seek applications that rest on a discovery of other values, which arguably inhere in the document itself or that go beyond such values—the noninterpretivist position? Second, does the Constitution, so read, oblige or empower the federal judiciary to place procedural or substantive constraints on the actions of either the federal or the state political branches? Third, if the Constitution so obliges or empowers the federal judiciary to constrain any of the political branches with respect to citizens' rights, then what constraints are appropriate?[1]

The principal antagonists in today's debate concentrate on the first question and then perhaps too easily reach answers to the second and third questions. Interpretivists, for example, claim that judges in constitutional argument must interpret the Constitution as it is written and apply the resulting imperatives to the cases before them (*Marbury v. Madison*, 1 Cranch. 137, 2 L.Ed. 60 [1803]). Finding no plain meaning in the text, judges must then try to discern what the words of the original document meant to the Framers. Should that exercise fail, judges must come as close as they can to discovering the requirements that the text imposes, according to the Framers' original intentions about such matters as federal structure (*Gibbons v. Ogden*, 9 Wheat. 1, 6 L.Ed. 23 [1824]). At some point, however, judges must be willing to break off from this exercise, declare the rights pleaded for as not within the compass of the Constitution, and send the parties to a different forum (or none at all) for the resolution of their conflict.[2]

---

[1] My concern throughout this essay is with constraints limiting the ability of the political branches to erode citizens' economic liberties, but I suspect that much of the analysis applies as well to matters of civil rights and civil liberties. See infra, note 18.

[2] See, for example, *Jackson v. City of Joliet*, 715 F.2d 1200 (7th Cir.), *cert. denied*, 465 U.S. 1049 (1983), as discussed in Currie (1986). At issue was a suit brought against the City of Joliet, whose police officers chose to direct traffic instead of inquiring about the presence of and rescuing occupants of a burning car. The occupants died, and their heirs sued under the Fourteenth Amendment's due process clause, arguing that the city had deprived the victims of life without due process of law. In *Jackson*, Judge Posner wrote that the Constitution:

is a charter of negative rather than positive liberties . . . . The men who wrote the Bill of Rights were not concerned that Government might do too little for the people

To answer the second question, most interpretivists believe that the Constitution obliges or empowers federal judges and Supreme Court justices to interfere with the political branches only in extreme cases. In these bodies, interpretivists opine, resides the power to make laws, as Article I delegates it to the Congress and the Tenth Amendment "to the States respectively, or to the people." Said with firmer particularity, and to answer the third question, federal judges and Supreme Court justices must not substitute their own public policy preferences (or self-discovered "fundamental values") for those revealed by federal, state, or local political branches. Accordingly, many substantive economic policy problems seldom can elicit principled constitutional constraints from the federal judiciary.

Noninterpretivists, by contrast, regard the Constitution's "open texture" as an invitation to discover "fundamental values" emanating from the document. They take this perspective not merely to fill in the interstices that its passages leave empty, but to go beyond the text's plain meaning, sometimes extending to "penumbras formed by emanations from" the "specific guarantees in the Bill of Rights," which "help give them life and substance."[3] Hence, noninterpretivists answer the first question by asserting that plain meanings elude us, because the Framers' intentions are neither obvious nor unanimous; that plain meanings often are absent, because the Constitution does not speak specifically to a variety of issues; and that from time to time the document contradicts itself, even under the most narrow or alternatively expansive readings that are tailored to make interpretation coherent. Noninterpretivists then answer the second question affirmatively

---

but that it might do too much to them. The Fourteenth Amendment, adopted in 1868 at the height of laissez-faire thinking, sought to protect Americans from oppression by state government, not to secure them basic governmental services. (715 F.2d at 1203).

For an insightful discussion of related issues, see Williams (1983).

[3] In *Griswold v. Connecticut*, 381 U.S. 479 (1965), the Court reviewed the conviction under a Connecticut statute of the executive officers and medical directors of the Planned Parenthood League of Connecticut. The statute made the use of contraceptive devices a criminal offense, and the defendants had been convicted as accessories in giving out information and recommendations concerning contraceptive use. Justice Douglas struck down the Connecticut statute thus: "The foregoing cases suggest that specific guarantees in the Bill of Rights have penumbras, formed by emanations from those guarantees that help give them life or substance" (*id.* at 484). Douglas then invoked most of the Bill of Rights in describing various "penumbras" and "emanations," though the Framers plainly did not have birth control in mind when they wrote the Constitution, nor did the writers of the Bill of Rights or of the Fourteenth Amendment concern themselves with this issue.

In my view, Justice Douglas reached the correct result in *Griswold*, but he might have grounded the decision in a reinvigorated contracts clause instead of bending the Bill of Rights beyond recognition. On the potential importance and reach of the contracts clause, see Epstein (1984). Alternatively, Justice Douglas might have based his decision in *Griswold* on a reading of the First Amendment favorable to defendants.

and the third question most generously by discerning values that they find below, or even beyond, the text's written words.

The terms "interpretivist" and "noninterpretivist," of course, describe neither exhaustive nor exclusive categories. In the absence of textual clarity, the interpretivist sometimes must rely on finding values or structural implications in the body of the Constitution, and the noninterpretivist's task *perforce* must begin with interpreting the Constitution's words and the Framers' intent. More importantly, those speaking for either side of this debate easily can undermine the certainty of the law. An interpretivist position remains capable of finding in the document both majoritarian and antimajoritarian implications, while a noninterpretivist position can enshrine values distinctly at odds with those that many noninterpretivists now embrace.

Nor is that all. The hierarchical structure of our three questions leads us through paths whose end points are not independent of the questions' ordering. For example, if we place the third question first (how should courts constrain the political branches?), then a negative answer to the second question (can they do so?) would make the entire Constitution irrelevant to the subject of our inquiry. A positive answer would leave it to those who answer the first question to define the manner of discovering constraints on the political branches. If we begin with the second question, then we are led into the landscape in which the Court-versus-legislature debate ordinarily is waged, namely, the problem of judicial review in a democracy. Embedded in this second question are the other two: What, if any, legislative acts should the judiciary review (question three), and what does the language of the Constitution imply about judicial limitations on the political branches (question one)?

Interpretivists appear to distrust judicial review, because of the way in which they answer the first two questions. But in an earlier time, their conservative judicial forebears were eager to have the Supreme Court declare the New Deal unconstitutional on what now appear to be noninterpretivist (substantive due process) grounds.[4] Likewise, noninterpretivists now acquiesce in judicial review, although their liberal judicial ancestors earlier regarded it with as much distrust as interpretivists do today. The members of both camps appear to have consulted their policy preferences and fashioned their constitutional jurisprudence accordingly. At least the statistical correlation seems nigh on perfect.

John Hart Ely (1980), who has established the terms of much of this

---

[4] Concerning state ecnomic regulation, the key case if *Lochner v. New York*, 198 U.S. 45 (1905). This passage should not be read, however, to imply that one could not justifiably invalidate the New Deal on what turned out to be interpretivist grounds. See Epstein (1985).

debate, tries to find a dimension of judicial review orthogonal to those fought over by interpretivists and noninterpretivists. He begins his analysis by showing the inherent difficulties of interpretivism. He then rejects the search for fundamental values, whether they are derived from natural law, tradition, consensus, reason, neutral principles, or whatever other animating spirit the justices or commentators might seek to discover. Finally, he tries to reconcile the operation of judicial review with that of democratic governance by finding in the Constitution the judicial obligation to perfect democratic governance itself.

In searching for judicial amelioration, Ely would not have courts second guess legislative public policy decisions per se. Instead, he would have them ask: Has the majority not merely placed a minority at a relative disadvantage in terms of legislatively derived benefits conferred or costs imposed, but it has also done so because of imperfections in the system of representation, perhaps created by the majority itself? If so, the courts might try to fashion a remedy by relying on a theory of virtual representation, where representation is formally impossible. For instance, in cases involving state taxation or regulation of foreign (out-of-state) corporations or persons, courts might impose on state legislation the even-handedness required by the commerce, privileges and immunities, or equal protection clauses. A court might insist that a state legislature could not tax foreign liquor producers at a higher rate than it taxes domestic producers (*Bacchus Imports Ltd. v. Dias*, 468 U.S. 263 [1984]). When taxed at equal rates, the theory suggests, domestic producers will "virtually represent" foreign producers in the state's political process.

Where direct representation remains possible, courts might perfect it by requiring equal apportionment, eliminating discriminatory gerrymandering, and removing more explicit racial or property qualifications for the franchise. If representation, so perfected, fails to produce a parity of legislatively created benefits and costs, then the courts must examine the causes of the inequality, perhaps by discerning whether or not the disadvantaged group is a "discrete and insular" minority, that is, one whose representatives in the legislature enjoy no parity in the policymaking process because of preexisting prejudices (*United States v. Carolene Products Co.*, 304 U.S. 144, 153 n. 4 [1938]).

Two problems seriously afflict Ely's approach to resolving the dilemma of judicial review. First, if a court discovers that a disadvantaged group remains a "discrete and insular minority," even though it might share full participatory and representational rights, then the court may fashion a remedy in terms of public policy. That is, the court must go through the mental experiment of deciding what benefits or costs the group would have enjoyed or borne from the legislative process had it not been a discrete and insular minority; then the court must supply them. Such an experiment begs for unprincipled judicial construction. More importantly, as recent advances in public choice theory demonstrate, the task is daunting and ordinarily impossible.[5] Again, such a rule of judicial decisionmaking invites judges to substitute their own preferences for those that the legislature might have revealed, had it operated without prejudicial characteristics.

Second, Ely seriously misapprehends the problem of democratic governance (as do both interpretivists and noninterpretivists). Nearly all of Ely's analysis explains what courts should do to protect minorities, at least in their participational and representational rights, against an aggrandizing majority. He surely reads the *Federalist Papers* in this light, and all of his subsequent prescriptions address this problem. But that is not the only or even the most important problem of democratic governance, nor was it the problem that wholly concerned the Framers. The problem is that of minorities—cohesive interest groups—exacting benefits from the public sector at collective cost. But the reinforcement of this problem's institutional groundings is one of the principal solutions to impermissible majoritarian dominance over minorities that Ely would have the courts impose on the political branches.

In terms of actual values and preferences, Ely recognizes that majorities seldom arise in the legislative process. Instead, legislation reflects the act of coalition-building, in which a variety of groups, probably in disequilibrium, form and reform around certain issues. Pork-barrel politics provide a good example. Citizens of Boston have no particular wish to confer a new port facility on citizens of New York City, Baltimore, Savannah, or New Orleans. But the member from Boston votes for these other projects in an omnibus rivers-and-harbors bill, because it is the only way that he can get the other minorities to agree to have the public treasury underwrite his own city's harbor improvements. Legislative minorities coalesce in this process, providing benefits to each. Ely would have the courts "unblock" minority access to the legislature; if that strategy should fail to produce the benefits of representation for discrete and insular minorities, then courts must rectify public policy itself. Ely believes that the forming of temporary majorities on votes, but not on preferences, ordinarily will ensure that majorities do not exclude minorities from benefits nor impose undue concentrated costs.

In recognizing the interest-group nexus of the legislative process, Ely is uncommonly modern. He makes a partly convincing case that the courts, merely by unblocking access through perfecting process, will help to ensure

---

[5] If there is no equilibrium motion in the legislature (one that defeats or ties all other motions), then we cannot predict what the legislature would have done had the minority in question not been walled off from the give-and-take of legislative coalition-building politics. See, for example, Riker (1982a).

that all values emanating from the people will be heard, leaving the political branches to make sounder judgments with better information than otherwise might seem possible.[6] That is, the judiciary leaves value judgments to the legislature, but it seeks to ensure through procedural guarantees that all values (minority interests) find voice in the legislature.

Where Ely goes wrong is in believing that majority governance based on legislative votes bears a clear relationship to majority governance based on citizens' values. Reflecting the Framers' explicit concerns, public choice theory has (re)discovered a serious failure in the operation of the political branches. This failure—variously called hyper-pluralism, rent-seeking, and the collective provision of private benefits—focuses precisely on the nature of majority *voting* coalitions to show that they are not identical to majority *preference* or *value* coalitions.[7] Small, cohesive groups use the political process to accomplish the distributional goals of providing themselves with benefits (or lowered costs) that they cannot or would not purchase in the private sector. Cost-spreading through the "fisc" induces a rational ignorance of this process on the part of the disadvantaged *majority*. Legislators then face incentives to make decisions on distributional margins and not on allocative ones (Mayhew 1974; Fiorina 1977).

Ely persuades us that the Supreme Court's constitutional jurisprudence, perhaps at least partly through perfecting process, *inter alia* seeks to protect minorities from majorities.[8] But his judicially crafted solutions to the problems of disadvantaged minorities arguably are worse than the disease they seek to cure; they leave the majority even more unprotected against ever-shifting, predatory coalitions of minorities. Today's interpretivists also appear to form their constitutional preferences around distributional margins, as their variegated theories of interpretation tend to sanction redistribution of resources at the state level from uninformed majorities to cohesive minorities, usually to serve some imagined public purpose. Noninterpretivists, of course, look for standing in trees and every other interest group with a claim of positive rights against the majority's traditional claim to negative liberty.

The inescapable conclusion seems to be that neither the interpretivist nor the noninterpretivist nor Ely's position will do. The Constitution places both procedural and substantive limits on the political branches, derived from the Framers' explicit words and understanding that both kinds of limits

---

[6] On the incorporation of minorities into legislative majority coalitions, see Miller (1983) and Riker (1982b).

[7] See, for example, Aranson and Ordeshook (1985); Buchanan, Tollison, and Tullock (1980); and Weingast, Shepsle, and Johnsen (1981). The models reported in these essays differ materially from one another, but their conclusions remain surprisingly alike.

[8] See, for example, *Baker v. Carr*, 369 U.S. 186 (1962), and *Reynolds v. Sims*, 377 U.S. 533 (1964).

protect minorities *and* majorities. Today's interpretivists would ignore these limits in asserting a nearly unalloyed form of legislative power, which they mistakenly regard as embodying majority will. Noninterpretivists show less concern for majorities and more for particular kinds of minorities; but they consult their own preferences, not the Constitution, in deciding to further the interests of some minorities but to denigrate the interests of others. Ely's position, of course, largely ignores the Constitution's substantive limits, relying instead on the very imperfect instrument of naked procedural constraints, but only to protect minorities.

Nor do the interpretivist and noninterpretivist positions appear to be historically valid or principled. For example, with respect to some interpretivists' denial of Fourteenth Amendment incorporation of the Bill of Rights as limitations on the power of state governments, Senator Howard, chairman of the joint committee that drafted the amendment, stated:

> Such is the character of the privileges and immunities spoken of in the second section of the fourth article of the Constitution. To these privileges and immunities, whatever they may be—for they are not and cannot be fully defined in their entire extent and precise nature—to these should be added the personal rights guaranteed and secured by the first eight amendments of the Constitution. . . . [A]ll these immunities, privileges, rights, thus guaranteed by the Constitution or recognized by it, are secured to the citizen solely as a citizen of the United States and as a party in their courts. They do not operate in the slightest degree as a restraint or prohibition upon State legislation. . . . The great object of the first section of this amendment is, therefore, to restrain the power of the States and compel them at all times to respect these great fundamental guarantees.[9]

So much, then, for Attorney General Meese's (1986, p. 8) misplaced interpretivist claim that "since 1925 a good portion of constitutional adjudication has been aimed at extending the scope of the doctrine of incorporation. But the most that can be done is to expand the scope; nothing can be done to shore up the intellectually shaky foundation upon which the doctrine rests."

Justice Brennan, a noninterpretivist, does not fare much better against the historical record. His remark (1986, p. 23) that "as I interpret the Constitution, capital punishment is under all circumstances cruel and unusual punishment prohibited by the Eighth and Fourteenth Amendments," fails by any reasonable standard of constitutional interpretation. While we could imagine *some* circumstances in which capital punishment

---

[9] *Congressional Globe*, 39th Cong., 1st Sess. 1765-66 (1866). As quoted in Ely (1980, p. 26). It is only fair to point out, as Ely does in his discussion, that this speech appears to be the only mention of incorporation in congressional debates over adoption of the Fourteenth Amendment. But the quotation at least clearly puts to rest the notion that incorporation was on no one's mind.

is cruel and unusual punishment, it is surely is not so in *all* circumstances. The Constitution's text also makes plain the possibility of imposing such a penalty. Thus, Brennan seems no more persuasive than does Meese. Each reads the text and historical record in a most peculiar way to bring about the public policy results of which he approves. Neither Meese nor Brennan seems capable of laying a claim to principled or historically valid argument or judgment.

Should we try to award a victory in this debate between two positions that seem incorrigibly wrong? Some may find virtue in a debate that is not capable of resolution on its present terms. Perhaps political and economic stability, not to mention the preservation of rights, relies upon a degree of uncertainty in the persuasiveness of any argument at the constitutional level. If so, then that uncertainty, as well as the stability that relies on its existence, is always at risk from a different argument, one that completely refashions the fundamental dimensions on which the debate has proceeded. I do not suggest such a complete refashioning here, but I do suggest that we change the dimensions of the debate to consider what Brennan and Buchanan (1985, ch. 1) have called "constitutionalism" and that we thereby remove the debate to a different level of discourse.

The Constitution, Uncertainty, and Procedural Management

We begin by asking a question that remains surprisingly absent in constitutional dialogue: What is the function of a constitution? Lawyers, law professors, and judges are more interested in asking: What does *this* Constitution require? They answer that it requires that judges read it strictly, discerning original intent as closely as possible according to what is contained in the "four corners" of the document (Meese); that judges read it liberally and explore its fundamental values or other values and what those values imply under modern conditions (Brennan); or that judges not worry too much about values but instead reflect on process, making the institutions that the Constitution describes mirror more perfectly the preference of all citizens (Ely). These answers seem premature, because they preempt the answers to other questions—answers that might affect the derivative consequences for the nature of both interpretation and public policy judgments within constitutional argument. But a constitution serves, *inter alia*, both a managerial and a value function. It does so in a particular sort of way, involving uncertainty about the time-bound goals of the process to be managed and about what values are permissible outcomes from the process so managed.

It is difficult to overstate the central place of uncertainty in constitutional construction. Consider the managerial function. Our Constitution, as any constitution, sets up allocations of responsibilities and empowerments between and among the federal government, the state governments, and individual citizens. Our Constitution also develops very clear procedures for the federal political branches (Article I), although it speaks far less clearly with respect to the states, with the exception of its impact on election law and representation. These provisions plainly reflect some value judgments concerning appropriate limits placed on both value inputs (citizens' and legislators' preferences) and outcomes of the political branches (public policy).

But it is not those limits and values that we wish to consider just yet. Instead, we concentrate here on the document's managerial functions. The Constitution, for example, specifies with great precision the path that a bill must take to become a law. This path seems not to vary, as the Court most recently has pointed out in striking down the legislative veto (*I.N.S. v. Chadha*, 462 U.S. 919 [1983]) and parts of the Gramm-Rudman-Hollings Act (*Bowsher v. Synar*, 106 S. Ct. 3181 [1986]). Now, by exploring two separate informational conditions, we may describe the purposes that this constitutional procedural particularity serves in defining the manner in which the federal legislature and executive must enact legislation.

Suppose that the Framers enjoyed perfect foresight concerning all of the issues that would come before the President and Congress for the next century. Under these conditions, which correspond roughly to the perfect information condition in first semester price theory, the Framers at least would have varied the nature of the decision rules and legislative paths that each bill must take to reflect either their own preferences and known relative prices or the (perfectly known) preferences and relative prices that their progeny would face. This much we learn from public choice theory: given preferences, the rules of procedure determine the outcomes.[10] Failing that, and given perfect information but no transactions costs, the Framers even might have set out to settle all future political conflicts themselves, passing laws in 1787 to go into effect at appropriate times in the future. The century-long horizon may seem too great, but certainly a quarter-century or even a decade is not unimaginable. Yet, the Framers did not try to settle all future policy decisions through constitutional provisions. Instead, they imposed a difficult legislative decision process, one even more difficult to change, for *all* legislation.[11]

---

[10] For accessible discussions of this proposition, see Riker (1980); McKelvey and Ordeshook (1984); and Shepsle and Weingast (1984).

[11] The Farmers did set different procedural rules for the disposition of different kinds of legislative actions. The House issues an impeachment (Article I, section 2), but conviction requires a two-thirds vote of the senators present (Article I, section 3). The ratification of treaties similarly requires a two-third vote of senators present (Article I, section 2), and senatorial advice and consent is required for the confirmation of ambassadors, cabinet secretaries, and federal judges

This hypothetical situation may seem to be nonsensical, but it serves to indicate exactly why the Framers constructed the elaborate legislative process that they did.

1.They could not anticipate what issues would arise, so they saved future generations the substantial decision costs of creating decision procedures anew with each subsequent proposal. Because rules, given preferences, do determine outcomes, the Framers prevented what was likely to occur (and to some extent still does occur in arguments over procedure in each congressional chamber): a redundant dispute over rules that is really a dispute over outcomes.

2.The Framers could not anticipate the conditions (relative prices and production possibilities), and to some extent preferences, that the members of future generations might confront, but they reduced the possibility of legislative "experts" exploiting those less well informed by making the lawmaking process constant and explicit. That is, they increased the likelihood that more rather than fewer citizens could understand the lawmaking process, rely on its relative immutability, and thus have their preferences registered in the political process.[12]

The Framers did anticipate particular issues, and these anticipations stand behind certain procedural constitutional provisions in, for example, the population-based representation in the House but state-based representation in the Senate. The Framers might have resolved the expected policy

---

(Article I, section 2). "All bills for raising Revenue," furthermore, "shall originate in the house of Representatives . . ." (Article I, section 7).

We may explain these variations in decision rules by referring to the theory that Buchanan and Tullock develop in *The Calculus of Consent* (1962). What is important here is not that the Framers decided to impose different decision rules for different *kinds* of actions (e.g., ordinary legislation *versus* treaties). The hypothetical case of perfect information implies instead that the Framers should have imposed different decision rules, say, for different *kinds* of treaties or even for different treaties themselves. That they did not do so supports the claim that they could not know what kinds of treaties the Senate would consider, or that they did not trust the Senate not to classify a "significant" treaty (requiring a two-thirds vote, for example) as a "technical" one (perhaps requiring only a majority vote of those present).

[12] In an important series of papers, Ronald Heiner (1983, 1986, 1987, 1988) discerns a connection between the presence of uncertainty and the use of rules, as distinct from calculation, to guide choice. Heiner observes that as the decisional environment grows more complex or as the decision maker enjoys less competence with respect to the environment's complexity, there will be a substitution away from specific calculation attending each decision and toward the use of rules, sometimes heuristics, to make decisions. For example, lower animals that confront the largest gap between calculating ability and environmental complexity, rely far more heavily on the "rules of instinct" than do human beings. Heiner's insight has influenced much of my thinking about the function of a constitution and the importance of not departing from its prescribed rules. The lawmaking environment has grown increasingly complex in recent years, but human ability to calculate has improved much less. Hence, even with benevolent legislators, we should require a closer conformance with constitutional requirements. This appears to contradict arguments that the increasing complexity of modern government requires a "bending" constitution.

problems in a "nonconstitutional" way by tacking specific provisions onto the Constitution. They did so, to some extent in terms of substantive limits, by including Article I, Section 9, which prohibited congressional action against the importation of slaves before 1808.

If the managerial function of a constitution flows from uncertainty about the nature of future issues, relative prices, preferences, and other conditions, then we must understand (with Hayek 1981, vol. 3, ch. 17) that the *organization* of a government through constitutional design is preeminently a planning process that purposefully may suppress procedural spontaneity. That is, for some of the specific decisions that the political branches make, there may be better (less costly) ways to make them than the way the Constitution specifies. But adherence to constitutional processes, like adoption of strict liability in tort as compared with a rule of negligence that requires constant calculation, seems institutionally efficient (cf. Rizzo 1980) for governing decisions about future enactments whose subjects we cannot anticipate.

The Constitution, Uncertainty, and Values

Ely correctly discerns that the managerial regularization of procedure provides an important though imperfect check on the majority exploitation of minorities, but procedural safeguards do not work as well to check minority exploitation of majorities. This important asymmetry stands at the heart of most theories of rent-seeking through legislative processes, and it requires explanation. It also begins our explanation of the evident values, in terms of substantive limitations on the political branches, which we find throughout the Constitution.

Managerial regularization of procedures aids minorities in limiting their exploitation by majorities through the process of rational ignorance. Downs (1957, pp. 207-67) first explained this phenomenon with respect to the incentives that different kinds of persons and groups would have to gain information about the political process and about the positions on public policy issues held by various politicians. In Downs's view, the value of investing in additional political information is in distinguishing correct from incorrect decisions. For example, without better information a citizen might cast a vote for a candidate whose election would have worse consequences for him than would the election of the candidate's opponent. But because the probability that the citizen's vote might affect the election outcome is so small in large electorates, most of the time most citizens will remain "rationally ignorant": they will choose not to invest in acquiring additional political information.

Exceptions may occur if the citizen has paid a sunk cost of acquiring information with political content or if he belongs to an organization that will do so for him—one that enjoys substantial economies of scale in performing these tasks. Either possibility seems most likely if the citizen is a member of a specialized group, such as a producer group, but not if he is a member of the group of all consumers or taxpayers. Specialized consumer groups or groups of ethnic, racial, or religious minorities also might be in positions analogous to those of producer groups with respect to this mechanism.

It follows that the members of small, cohesive groups might enjoy relatively superior information about candidates' and officeholders' positions on issues that affect them differentially, about the stages in the legislative process wherein legislation that affects them now resides, and about the appropriate legislative body on which to exert influence. The regularization of procedure through constitutional design might make if less costly for minorities to protect themselves against aggrandizing majorities than for rationally ignorant and unorganized majorities to pass aggrandizing legislation against minority interests.

While this interpretation of procedural protection differs from Ely's by filling in the details in terms of an actual political explanation and mechanism, it also denotes the limits of such protection. First, a minority nested within a larger minority or a minority nested within a majority ordinarily may act alone to initiate lawmaking procedures. The configurations of political conflict commonly place these two kinds of minorities at odds over the passage of legislation. For example, specific occupational groups may represent minorities nested within the majority of white or native-born workers or of workers residing within a particular state. Minorities nested within the majority sometimes find themselves competing with price-cutting nonwhite or alien workers or with workers or firms residing elsewhere. Given the presence of rational ignorance, constitutionally prescribed federal legislative procedures and parallel procedures at the state level are likely to favor the minority nested within the majority over its new competition. Much federal immigration, state licensing, and regulatory legislation reflects the minority-within-majority's predicted political advantage. Hence, the procedural check remains most imperfect, because the outside minority will be disadvantaged in the legislative battle.

A procedural check also does not operate in the implicit contest of cohesive minorities against rationally ignorant and unorganized majorities. The occupational group that achieves legislative protection against the new, lower-cost producers has used the political process to restrict supply and, thus, to redistribute income (at some cost of efficiency in terms of deadweight loss) from the larger majority (as well as from the new entrants) to itself. More importantly, where the configuration of interests places a minority nested within the majority against the majority, the minority usually wins, as the example of pork-barrel rivers-and-harbors legislation indicates.

Concerning judicial control of the states' political branches, for example, the Supreme Court's recent decisions have substantially diminished the temporizing effects of virtual representation through the operation of the dormant commerce clause, the privileges and immunities clause, and the equal protection clause. The Court ordinarily will strike down state legislation that facially discriminates against foreign corporations;[13] and sometimes against residents of other states (see, e.g., *Supreme Court of New Hampshire v. Piper*, 470 U.S. 274 [1985]). But where the discrimination takes the form of incidence only—where it is not wholly facial—the Court tends to let the state legislation stand. Sometimes the discriminatory legislation reflects the political influence of a minority within the state (see, e.g., *Moorman Mfg. Co. v. Bair*, 437 U.S. 267 [1978]) and sometimes the operation of the majority of the legislature against all those beyond its borders (states may be small enough, in terms of resolving a majority's free-rider problem of political organization, to bring forth such out-of-state, minority-disadvantaging legislation, even when not called for by a minority within the state nested within the majority.)[14]

The Framers fully understood these possibilities. In *Federalist* No. 10, Madison plainly grasped the political possibilities:

> The most common and durable source of factions has been the various and unequal distribution of property. Those who hold, and those who are without property, have ever formed distinct interests in society. Those who are creditors, and those who are debtors, fall under a like discrimination. A landed interest, a manufacturing interest, a mercantile interest, with many lesser interests, grow up of necessity in civilized nations, and divide them into different classes, actuated by different sentiments and views.

But just as the Framers faced uncertainty about future preferences and relative prices concerning the structuring of legislative procedures for managerial purposes (but with some policy consequences in mind), they also faced uncertainty about the structure of preferences between majorities and minorities ("factions" in Madison's "extended republic"). This uncertainty seems especially pronounced in the case of state governments, about whose legislative and electoral procedures the original Constitution remained largely silent. Concerning both federal and state political branches, however, no one could predict how future interests might align themselves or what those interests might entail. All that remained certain was that these factions would emerge and that their political actions might place both

---

[13] See, for example, *Maryland v. Louisiana*, 451 U.S. 725 (1981), and *Metropolitan Life Insurance Co. v. Ward*, 470 U.S. 869 (1985); but cf. *Western and Southwestern Life Ins. Co. v. State Board of Equalization*, 451 U.S. 648 (1981).

[14] See, for example, *Commonwealth Edison Co. v. Montana*, 453 U.S. 609 (1981); but cf. *Kassel v. Consolidated Freightways Corp.*, 450 U.S. 662 (1981).

the majority and unknown minorities at a disadvantage. As Madison notes in *Federalist* No. 62.

> Every new regulation concerning commerce or revenue, or in any manner affecting the value of the different species of property, presents a new harvest to those who watch the change, and can trace its consequences; a harvest, reared not by themselves, but by the toils and cares of the great body of their fellow citizens. This is a state of things in which it may be said with some truth that the laws are made for the *few*, not for the many.

In sum, procedural guarantees cannot alone prevent a majority legislative coalition from placing a minority at a disadvantage or prevent a minority from placing either another minority or the majority at a disadvantage. As Ely correctly observes, the Framers of the Constitution, the Bill of Rights, and the Civil War Amendments anticipated that both majorities and minorities within majorities would try to sequester some minorities away from the political process. But they also anticipated that majorities, minorities within majorities, and sometimes minorities alone would try to use the political process to gain benefits for themselves and impose costs on both majorities and other minorities.

Again, we might argue as some interpretivists seem to imply that the Framers could anticipate the exact form of such private interest legislation and prevent it through procedural (managerial) aspects of the Constitution. But uncertainty characterizes this problem in constitution-writing as much as it does the problem of creating legislative managerial processes. The uncertainty of substance, however, grows out of two sources. First, the political process is highly entrepreneurial. One cannot predict the substantive course of legislation, because the interest groups that may arise in different circumstances remain unpredictable.[15] One even discovers in modern democracies that legislators pass laws that enable certain interest groups to arise against both majority and minority interests, in the face of an otherwise disabling free-rider problem (Berry 1977).

Second, even if one could predict the formation of particular interest groups, it is doubtful that one could predict the legislation-passing coalitions representing such groups that might form in the political branches. This problem grows out of the inherent instability of public policy decisions in majority-rule institutions. Legislators face games with no apparent equilibria; therefore, there is little theory with the power to predict the outcomes of these games and less confidence that constitution writers, even very wise ones, could foresee the nature of the coalitions or public policies that might emerge from these institutions (Riker and Weingast 1986). But

---

[15] See Hayek (1944) and Leoni (1971). I have expanded on this theme in Aranson (1987).

our very wise constitution writers could foresee the essentially redistributive nature of much legislation.

In the face of uncertainty about future legislative substance, the Framers attacked the substantive, or value, problem in two ways. First, in Article I, section 8, they delimited the scope of congressional enactments to set tasks, thus creating a national government of "enumerated powers," which look surprisingly like the desirable subjects for public policy listed in a modern public finance text. Second, they limited the powers of both federal and state governments by restricting national coalitions of some states against others. For example, Article I, section 9 requires uniformity among states in matters of taxation (but cf. *United States v. Ptasynski*, 462 U.S. 74 [1983]), prohibits the taxation of exports from any state, and provides for neutrality among states in the "regulation of commerce." Third, the Framers' immediate successors tried to prevent federal deprivations of citizens' economic, civil, and religious rights by ratifying the Bill of Rights, as the Framers had done at the state level through the contracts and interstate commerce clauses. Finally, the drafters of the Fourteenth Amendment tried to apply those same substantive limitations of the Bill of Rights to state legislation.

If Ely is correct that the Constitution calls on the courts to "clear the channels" of the democratic process so that the preferences of all groups may register therein, and if what he calls "procedural" values are part of the judiciary's list of protected values, then what about property? Notice that the Constitution protects property against governmental incursions in the most general sense. The Fifth Amendment announces that no person may ,"be deprived of life, liberty, or property, without due process of law; nor shall private property be taken for public use, without just compensation." Article I, section 9 reads: "No state shall . . . pass any law impairing the obligation of contracts." And the Ninth Amendment demands that "the enumeration in the Constitution of certain rights, shall not be construed to deny or disparage others retained by the people."

These provisions construct the broadest imaginable protections of private property. Placed in the context of a national government of enumerated powers along with the enshrinement of the common law in the Seventh Amendment, they protect the three necessary characteristics of a system of private property: universality, excludability, and transferability. Considering the very broad tendencies of federal and state political branches to erode the rights on which these characteristics rely, it seems beyond *peradventure* that the Framers intended the Constitution to be read narrowly with respect to the privileges of the political branches and broadly with respect to individual economic rights.

Some Cases

Most constitutional protections of property rights have not survived the Constitution's two centuries. For example, the Court's refusal to interpret exactly what a "taking" might be has narrowed the Fifth Amendment's protection of property beyond all recognition.[16] Its "public use" provision has been emptied of all meaning by a series of decisions culminating in *Hawaii Housing Authority v. Midkiff* (467 U.S. 229 [1983]). The contracts clause has gone to the same trash bin with decisions such as *Home Building and Loan Association v. Blaisdell.*[17] And the commerce clause has been gutted, as we mentioned earlier.

What about more recent cases? Economic regulation cases involving citizens' suits against a state government and its agents provide the best frame of reference for comparing Attorney General Meese's view of interpretivism with my own. This comparison seems especially noteworthy in cases involving interstate commerce, where a firm or citizen of one state finds his rights (under the commerce clause, the privileges and immunities clause, or the equal protection clause) denied by the political branches or courts of another state. Here we come up against Meese's recent list of approved and scorned decisions, of which we shall review two, beginning with *Supreme Court of New Hampshire v. Piper* (470 U.S. 274 [1985]), overturning the exclusion of nonresidents from membership in the New Hampshire Bar.[18]

---

[16] See, for example, Epstein (1982, 1985). One need not take Epstein's extreme view of the imperatives of the takings clause (though I am inclined to do so) to understand that the Supreme Court has bent over backwards to avoid making definitive judgments that seriously limit the states' power of eminent domain. See *Penn Central Transportation Co. v. New York City*, 438 U.S. 104 (1978), *Agins v. City of Tiburon*, 447 U.S. 255 (1980), and *Keystone Bituminous Coal Ass'n v. DeBenedictis*, 55 L.W. 4326 (1987).

The Court's two most recent takings decisions, *First Evangelical Lutheran Church of Glendale v. County of Las Angeles*, 55 L.W. 4781 (1987) and *Nollan v. California Coastal Comm'n,*55 L.W. 5145 (1987), were decided in the right direction, but they were not as potent against takings as some believe. *First Evangelical* only decided the question of remedy favorably for owners in "temporary" takings. But the Court remanded the case to the trial court, to decide if a taking actually had occurred. *Nollan* held that a building permit pursuant to a land use regulation could not be used to effect an actual taking unrelated to the purpose of the permit. But *Nollan* then left in place, and indeed may have strengthened, the ability of state and local governments to accomplish regulatory takings, as in *Penn Central, Agins,* and *Keystone Bituminous*. For a discussion of the Court's many problems with takings jurisprudence, see Krier (1982).

[17] 290 U.S. 398 (1934). See Epstein (1984).

[18] Attorney General Meese (1986, pp. 4-5) disapproved of this decision, noting:

The Constitutional status of the States further suffered as the Court [in its 1984 term] curbed state power to regulate the economy, notably the professions.... In *Supreme Court of New Hampshire v. Piper...* the Court held that the Privileges and Immunities Clause of Article IV barred New Hampshire from completely excluding a nonresident from admission to its bar. With the apparant policy objective of creating

Kathryn Piper submitted a statement of intent to become a New Hampshire resident at the time that she applied to take the New Hampshire Bar examination. She passed the examination and was found to be of good moral character. All was in order except for her resident status. Piper, who lived "about 400 yards from the New Hampshire border (470 U.S. at 275)," sought an exemption to Rule 42 of the New Hampshire Supreme Court requiring that a person be "a bona fide resident of the State... at the time that the oath of office... is administered."[19] Piper stated that "her house in Vermont was secured by a mortgage with a favorable interest rate, and [that] she and her husband recently had become parents" (*id.* at 276). On denial of her request by the clerk of the court, Piper formally petitioned the New Hampshire Supreme Court for an exception to Rule 42. That court denied her petition, and she filed an action in the United States District Court for the District of New Hampshire, asserting, *inter alia*, that Rule 42 violated her rights under the privileges and immunities clause of the United States Constitution, Article IV, section 2. The District Court granted Piper summary judgment (539 F.Supp. 1064 [1982]), and the Court of Appeals for the First Circuit split evenly, thus affirming the judgment below (723 F.2d 110 [1983]). The Supreme Court then sustained the courts below, with six justices joining Justice Powell's opinion, Justice White concurring, and Justice Rehnquist dissenting.

Public choice scholars will recognize that Rule 42 attempts to limit entry into the legal marketplace. In terms of our earlier analysis, the New Hampshire Bar is a minority nested in the majority of New Hampshire citizens. Kathryn Piper represents a minority beyond the state's representational, political institutions in this instance, the New Hampshire Supreme Court. By restricting entry, Rule 42 harmed Piper and her class and redistributed wealth from the majority of New Hampshire's citizens to the pockets of that state's attorneys. The essential public policy argument

unfettered national markets for occupations before its eyes, the Court unleashed Article IV against any State preferences for residents involving the professions or service industries.... Our view is that federalism is one of the most basic principles of our Constitution. By allowing the States sovereignty sufficient to govern, we better secure our ultimate goal of political liberty through decentralized governments.

In my discussion of these two cases, I focused on questions of economic rights because they help to illuminate many of the issues discussed in this paper. But I also wish to record my profound disagreement with the attorney general's characterizations and interpretations of cases involving civil rights and civil liberties, including the search and seizure cases and the establishment clause religion cases. Most of the argument advanced here goes forward to these other areas of constitutional law with few modifications.

[19] 470 U.S. at 277 n. 1 (affidavit of John W. King, App. 32). Surprisingly, a resident member of the New Hampshire Bar may move out of New Hampshire but still retain his membership in the Bar.*Id.* at 285 n. 19.

concerned whether there were external benefits from requiring New Hampshire lawyers to be residents or alternatively whether there would be external costs from allowing lawyers practicing in New Hampshire to live elsewhere. But it is not these matters that directly concern us here; it is the Court's disposition, and the reasons for that disposition, of the constitutional rights that Piper asserted.

Justice Powell's decision found, first, that the "right to practice law is protected by the *Privileges and Immunities Clause*" (470 U.S. at 283). Second, he went on to explore if the state had "a substantial reason for the difference in treatment" between residents and nonresidents and if "the discrimination practiced against nonresidents bears a substantial relationship to the State's objectives" (*id.* at 284). Powell found that New Hampshire had no justifiable reasons for discriminatory treatment. Moreover, the majority opinion held, the state could have fashioned "less restrictive means" to accomplish its goals (*id.* at 284-87). Concurring in the result (*id.* at 288-89), Justice White held that the application of Rule 42 to Piper was invalid but that the Court need not overturn the rule itself.

Justice Rehnquist, in his dissenting opinion (*id.* at 289-97), argued that there are essential differences between the practice of law and the plying of other trades, which give New Hampshire a legitimate state interest in providing an adequate supply of resident lawyers. He placed much greater weight on New Hampshire's substantive claims than did the majority and said of the majority's speculations:

> It is no answer to these arguments that many lawyers simply will not perform these functions [for example, pro bono work], or that out-of-state lawyers can perform them equally well, or that the State can devise less restrictive alternatives for accomplishing these goals. Conclusory second-guessing of difficult legislative decisions, such as the Court resorts to today, is not an attractive way for federal courts to engage in judicial review. . . . I find the Court's "less restrictive means" analysis both ill-advised and potentially unmanageable. . . . [T]he challenge of a "less restrictive means" should be overcome if merely a legitimate reason exists for not pursuing that path. And in any event courts should not play the game that the Court has played here—independently scrutinizing each asserted state interest to see if it could devise a better way than the State to accomplish that goal.[20]

---

[20] *Id.* at 294-95. In attacking the decision in Piper, Justice Rehnquist engaged in just the sort of social or economic calculation that he believes belongs in the hands of the state legislatures and that the Court should not second-guess. But in doing so, he employed arguments that are at once incorrect and fully destructive of his more basic claims. At one point, for example, he asserts, (*id.* at 292):

> Since at any time within a State there is only enough legal work to support a certain number of lawyers, each out-of-state lawyer who is allowed to practice necessarily takes legal work that could support an in-state lawyer, who would otherwise be

Justice Rehnquist's dissent is fully consistent with Attorney General Meese's preference for state sovereignty over *federal* judicial intervention. And despite the backdrop of privileges-and-immunities case law, it seems difficult to fault Rehnquist for chiding the Court on its willingness to act as a super-legislature. Thus, *Piper* appears to be yet another case where the federal government has subverted the plain meaning of the Tenth Amendment.

But Rehnquist's is a crabbed view of *Piper* and related cases. What is at issue is a claim by a citizen of one state that the government of another state has denied her rights under the privileges and immunities clause. On this reading, it is not the *result* in *Piper* that is at fault. As Justice Rehnquist points out, it is the Court's *reasoning* that seems faulty. Quoting from *Baldwin v. Montana Fish and Game Comm'n* (436 U.S. at 383 [1978]), Justice Powell wrote "that it is '[o]nly with respect to those "privileges and immunities" bearing on the vitality of the nation as a single entity' that a State must accord residents and nonresidents equal treatment" (470 U.S. at 279).

But one searches the privileges and immunities clause in vain to find such a gloss. Here is a constitutional right that is evident on its face: "No State shall make or enforce any law which shall abridge the privileges or immunities of citizens of the United States. . . ." Justice Rehnquist, then, roasted Justice Powell and the Court on an extra-constitutional spit of their own making. Yet, Justice Rehnquist's substantive reasoning in *Piper* seems as inapposite as does the majority's less-restrictive-means analysis.[21] As an

---

available to perform various functions that a State has an interest in promoting. In a footnote in this passage, he goes on to explain (*id.* at 293 n. 3):

> In New Hampshire's case, lawyers living 40 miles from the state border in Boston could easily devote part of their practice to New Hampshire clients. If this occurred a significant amount of New Hampshire legal work might end up in Boston, along with lawyers who might otherwise reside in New Hampshire.

This set of claims seems astonishing on its face. Justice Rehnquist essentially is arguing that the entry of more (out-of-state) attorneys into New Hampshire practice would have no effect on price and, therefore, on quantity of legal service demanded. More important for our purposes, he has set the groundwork for the counter-argument: that the people of New Hampshire should be free to choose higher quality or lower cost substitutes domiciled elsewhere. If they willingly would not so choose, then Rule 42 is unnecessary; if they would so choose, then Rule 42 is adverse to the interests of the majority, not to mention those of Kathryn Piper.

[21] Justice Rehnquist's dissent in *Piper* invokes the same kinds of substantive tests for state interest that the majority relies on. Neither his nor the majority's use of such speculations makes all that much sense, provided that one regards economic rights as being fundamental and as deserving of protection as are any other rights guaranteed under the Constitution. Were his position to prevail, the Court would have engaged in "conclusory second guessing" of the Fourteenth Amendment's express language. The problem, of course, is that through the years the Court has read into the Constitution a diminished concern for economic rights. See, for example, *New Orleans v. Dukes*, 427 U.S. 303-4 (1976).

interpretivist (but one whose interpretations differ fundamentally from those of the present attorney general and chief justice), I read the result in *Piper* to accord with the privileges and immunities clause's iron-clad constitutional guarantee, one that seems far more evident in its application here than does the Tenth Amendment's division of powers between the state and federal governments. The action in *Piper* was brought by a citizen against a state, not by the federal government. Hence, the privileges and immunities clause should control, and it should do so absolutely.

Next in Attorney General Meese's list of disfavored decisions is *Metropolitan Life Insurance Co. v. Ward* (470 U.S. 869 [1985]). Finding a violation of the equal protection clause of the Fourteenth Amendment, the Court overturned an Alabama statute that facially imposed a higher tax on premiums received by foreign (out-of-state) insurance companies than by domestic companies. The statute also forgave some of the difference in tax rates if a foreign corporation invested up to 10 percent of its total assets in Alabama.

Public choice scholars again will recognize in Metropolitan Life the same pattern of rent-seeking found in *Piper*. And again, the case presents the problem of a minority nested within a majority (Alabama's domestic insurance industry) benefiting from state legislation that distributes income from all other citizens of Alabama (the majority) and from foreign corporations (the minority without representation) to itself. Of course, the foreign firms' reduction in taxes pursuant to investments made in Alabama arguably also benefits the majority of Alabama's citizens, but it does so to the detriment of the foreign minority, which has had its investment decisions altered and distorted by the law.

Metropolitan Life contains two interesting peculiarities. First, appellants sued under the equal protection clause, because the McCarran-Ferguson Act exempts state regulation and taxation of insurance companies from commerce-clause (and anti-trust) attack and because the Court earlier had removed privileges-and-immunities clause protection from corporations, holding that they are not "citizens" within the language of that clause.[22] Second, during the appeals process in the Alabama courts, to expedite disposition of their suit the appellants had waived a hearing on the issue of whether or not the statutory classification "bore a rational relationship to the purpose found by the Circuit Court to be legitimate" (*id.* at 874). Hence, they asked the Supreme Court to decide only if these purposes alone were legitimate or constitutionally infirm. The case thus came on appeal shorn of the opportunity for the Court to exercise its proclivities

[22] *Metropolitan Life Insurance Co. v. Ward*, 470 U.S. 869 at 884 (1985) (O'Conner, J., dissenting) (citing *Hemphill v. Orloff*, 277 U.S. 537 [1928]).

for various balancing tests: plaintiffs merely asked the Court to decide whether or not the state's purposes were legitimate against an equal-protection clause challenge.

The Court, per Justice Powell, held that this form of discriminatory taxation to advance either of the state's purposes—encouraging the development of the domestic insurance industry and encouraging investment of capital in Alabama—impermissibly denied appellants their equal protection of the law, as guaranteed by the Fourteenth Amendment. The Court's decision is the soul of brevity, compared to those in earlier cases involving taxation of foreign corporations. The Court merely distinguished some earlier cases and acknowledged the rent-seeking aspects of the "parochial" interests involved. It also appeared to eschew tiresome comparisons of the equities as well as the derogations of rights that such comparisons often invite by observing (*id.* at 882, footnote omitted):

> Acceptance of its contention that promotion of domestic industry is always a legitimate state purpose under equal protection analysis would eviscerate the Equal Protection Clause in this context. A State's natural inclination frequently would be to prefer domestic business over foreign. If we accept the State's view here, then any discriminatory tax would be valid if the State could show it reasonably was intended to benefit domestic business. A discriminatory tax would stand or fall depending primarily on how a State framed its purpose—as benefiting one group or as harming another. This is a distinction without a difference.

The dissenting opinion (*id.* at 883-902), written by Justice O'Connor and joined by Justices Brennan, Marshall, and Rehnquist, produced the usual brief of those who would support state domination of economic regulation to the exclusion of citizens' constitutional guarantees. Justice O'Connor (*id.* at 844) wrote, "Our precedents impose a heavy burden on those who challenge local economic regulation solely on Equal Protection Clause grounds. In this context, our long-established jurisprudence requires us to defer to a legislature's judgment if the classification is rationally related to a legitimate state purpose."

In Justice O'Connor's view, the state's purposes were legitimate by default, because such a statutory classification "trammels" not on "fundamental personal rights" nor is it "drawn upon inherently suspect distinctions such as race, religion, or alienage. . . ." Therefore, the Court's decisions in such lesser economic matters "presume the constitutionality of the statutory discrimination."[23] The classification is also rationally related to this "legitimate' state interest. For example:

---

[23] *Id.* at 885 (quoting *New Orleans v. Dukes*, 427 U.S. 297, 303 [1976], and citing *Lehnhausen v. Lake Shore Auto Parts Co.*, 410 U.S. 356 [1973]).

Alabama claims that its insurance tax, in addition to raising revenue and promoting investment, promotes the formation of new domestic insurance companies and enables them to compete with the many large multistate insurers that currently occupy 75% to 85% of the Alabama insurance market. Economic studies submitted by the State document differences between the two classes of insurers that are directly relevant to the well-being of Alabama's citizens. Foreign insurers typically concentrate on affluent, high volume urban markets and offer standardized national policies. In contrast, domestic insurers...are more likely to serve Alabama's rural areas, and to write low-cost industrial and burial policies not offered by the larger national companies. Alabama argues persuasively that it can more readily regulate domestic insurers and more effectively safeguard their solvency than that of insurers domiciled...in other states.[24]

And then comes the now-expected passage from *New Orleans v. Dukes*:

the judiciary may not sit as a super-legislature to judge the wisdom or desirability of legislative policy determinations made in areas that neither affect fundamental rights nor proceed along suspect lines; in the local economic sphere, it is only the invidious discrimination, the wholly arbitrary act, which cannot stand consistently with the Fourteenth Amendment.[25]

But sitting "as a super-legislature" is exactly what the dissenting opinion in *Metropolitan Life* would have the Court do. Notice that the pertinent section of the Fourteenth Amendment simply reads: "No State...shall deny to any person within its jurisdiction the equal protection of the laws." There is no language about "invidious discrimination" or "fundamental rights" as distinct from rights that are in some sense "less fundamental" and therefore may be read out of the Constitution when they collide with "legitimate" state interests served through "rationally related" means. Again, as in Justice Rehnquist's dissent in *Piper*, the dissenters in *Metropolitan Life* ask the Court to sit as a super-legislature, a new constitutional convention, departing from the Constitution's express language

---

[24] *Id.* at 887-88 (citations and footnote omitted). Justice O'Connor's economics in *Metropolitan Life* are as problematic as Justice Rehnquist's reasoning in *Piper*. First, the differential tax may not increase the number of domestic firms writing the kinds of insurance that she enumerates. Foreign firms reportedly already had abandoned this market to locals (*id.* at 887, n.1), and local firms probably are at a competitive supply equilibrium. Second, the out-of-state firms might write lower-value insurance if their costs, including the tax, were smaller. Third, because foreign insurance companies write 75 percent to 85 percent of the policies in Alabama, the differential tax also redistributes income and wealth within the state from urban to rural areas, under the facts as given.

Discerning tax incidence is always a difficult problem (see, for example, McLure 1982), but the majority in *Metropolitan Life* has been properly attentive to doctrinal imperatives.

[25] 470 U.S. at 901-2 (O'Connor, J., dissenting) (quoting *New Orleans v. Dukes*, 427 U.S. 303-4; [1976]).

and reverting to faulty economic reasoning. Stated differently, Justice O'Connor departs from the interpretivist fold, and by implication, so does Attorney General Meese.

Meese reasons in these cases that the Constitution limits the federal government *and its judiciary* in economic jurisprudence to do only what Article I, section 8 requires. All other powers remain with the states. Hence, in his view the decisions in *Piper* and *Metropolitan Life* remain unprincipled. Of course, we search with little success to find the specific, interpretivist application of this principle to the federal judiciary. The line of reasoning pressed in these pages concerning constitutional imperatives regarding rent-seeking and uncertainty, not to mention that concerning a purified inter-pretivist jurisprudence based on doctrine, urges another interpretation.

One might agree with the attorney general that when the contest is just between the federal judiciary (upholding the Congress) and a state government *and its citizens*, then we would prefer state supremacy.[26] But cases such as *Piper* and *Metropolitan Life* involve much more: They find the states' political branches in constitutionally impermissible rent-seeking moves that disadvantage out-of-state minorities and their own citizens as well. In most of these cases, there is also a demonstrable absence of a relationship between the legislation's stated purposes and the statutory means employed to achieve them. More importantly, there is only one clear motive for such moves: to deprive the unrepresented of the opportunity to enter commerce in the protectionist, mercantile state.

Constitutional Correctives

A growing number of legal commentators, economists, and political scientists have become increasingly dissatisfied with the (in)ability of contemporary constitutional argument to suppress the rent-seeking, rights-degrading activities of the political branches (Aranson 1985). I have sought to outline the reasons for believing that doctrinal constitutional argument—a reliance on the Constitution's evident value-based constraints on the political branches—exercised by a reinvigorated judiciary should provide a welcome source of suppression. But a widely accepted judicial method for providing that source is not close at hand.

We enjoy only one positive economic theory of judicial review of legislative enactments: that developed by Landes and Posner (1975). Their

---

[26] One such instance arises in *Garcia v. San Antonio Metro.*, 469 U.S. 528 (1985), which over-turned the Court's exemption of municipalities from the Fair Labor Standards Act, as granted on Tenth Amendment grounds in *National League of Cities v. Usery*, 426 U.S. 833 (1976). While both *Garcia* and *National League of Cities* are difficult cases, I concur with Attorney General Meese's opinion that in *Garcia* the Court ignored the constitutional requirements of state sovereignty.

theory explains that the legislature gives independence to the judiciary in exchange for which the judiciary refrains from judicial review of legislation on *legislative* (value) grounds. The purpose of this bargain, at least in the minds of legislators, is to enhance the durability of special interest legislation. The judiciary (I would claim, though Landes and Posner do not) may review legislation on grounds orthogonal to legislative concerns (for example, on procedural grounds such as the requirements of separation of powers), but it agrees not to replace legislative policy values with its own. In all other instances the judiciary must defend bargains struck in the legislature (to avoid an end-run around the lawmaking process by dissatisfied lawmakers or interest groups) and avoid declaring an act of Congress unconstitutional.

As a *positive* theory, the Landes and Posner theory has several problems. First, it fails to acknowledge that the judiciary remains sufficiently decentralized so that individual federal judges may "chisel" on the implicit bargain. Second, the theory does not explain why or ask whether the federal judiciary would stay its hand from invalidating state legislation on constitutional grounds. Indeed, the federal judiciary sometimes does overturn state legislation on precisely such grounds. Third, most acts of Congress filter through a bureau or agency in the implementation process, and review of administrative actions thus remains an indirect but potent source for judicial control of the political branches. Fourth, Landes and Posner support their theory with the common observation that the Supreme Court seldom has invalidated congressional enactments on constitutional grounds. But that evidence (gathered before *I.N.S. v. Chadha*, 462 U.S. 919 [1983]) may indicate simply that the members of Congress anticipate invalidation and structure their enactments to avoid it.

Beyond this single positive theory, the legal literature contains several normative theories of how to engage the judiciary as a counterforce to rent-seeking and sometimes to the derogation of constitutional rights. Judge Easterbrook (1984), for example, would have the Court be a faithful agent of the legislature in enforcing any interest-group bargains that it reviews; but he would have the Court enforce such bargains narrowly, using the old doctrine that statutes in derogation of the common law should be strictly construed. The parties to the bargain should get what was enacted, no more and no less. Over time the existence of legislatively created rents will attract legally differentiated competitors and others beyond the statute's narrowed domain, who will help to dissipate any rents created.

For the most part, Professor Ely would use the judiciary to open up the political process, allowing the courts to make value judgments only when the legislature, to the detriment of a minority, is structurally and preferentially incapable of doing so. But Ely's gloss turns out to be a valiant yet ultimately unsuccessful attempt to read substantive values as procedural rights, and one that does nothing to protect unorganized majorities.

Unlike Judge Easterbrook, Jonathan Macey (1986) argues that the Court, in following its traditional approach to statutory interpretation, should not look for interest-group bargains, but instead should assume that each enactment has a benevolent public purpose, as stated in its preamble or as assumed to be the product of "reasonable men." The Court should then interpret the statute accordingly. In Macey's view, "where [there is] a sharp divergence between the stated public-regarding purpose of the legislature and the true special interest motivation behind a particular statute, courts will, under the traditional approach, resolve any ambiguities in the statute consistently with the stated public-regarding purpose" (p. 251). But this approach borders on substantive review.

Gellhorn, Robinson, and I (1982) have argued (as do Ely 1980 and Sunstein 1985) that the Court should pay attention to procedure and reinvigorate the delegation doctrine, to reduce the use of regulation for redistributive purposes. Our theory urges the courts to require legislative specificity, *inter alia*, to place the full political costs of its actions on the legislature, which it now escapes through delegating legislative tasks to bureaus and agencies.

Each of these proposals has some merit, though at least two of them (Easterbrook's and Macey's) contradict each other. The essential problem that all share, however, is a full reliance on process, a venerable legal fallback. Each, of course, is but an unsatisfactory substitute for substantive due process, a doctrine long held in disrepute. But though process standards may seem value-neutral—and, therefore, constitutionally principled answers to the dilemma of judicial review in a democracy—social choice theory demonstrates that they never can be so. Moreover, clever people can invent a hundred different ways to circumvent procedural guarantees, so that over time such guarantees will grow increasingly obsolete and only their managerial functions will remain.

Since the end of the *Lochner* era, the closest one comes to finding a frontal attack on rent-seeking is in the writings of Mashaw (1980) and Sunstein (1984, 1985). But even these scholars take an oblique approach to the problem, arguing for methods of review that ultimately turn aside from a direct constitutional attack on rent-seeking.

The burden of the argument in these pages, then, is that the Framers endowed the Constitution and its amendments with both process and value limitations on the political branches. The Court has upheld both kinds of limitations, but it has withdrawn from imposing most value limitations in economic litigation (though not yet fully in the area of civil rights and liberties). The time has come for the Court to recognize the Constitution's full protection of economic liberties (Epstein 1982, 1984, 1985; Siegan 1980). And as we grow increasingly dissatisfied with the limited protections that procedure alone can afford—special interests, which have solved the rational ignorance problem, will dominate *any* process that courts might impose except a random and constantly changing one—we might rediscover the full meaning and intent of the great clauses of the Constitution that the Framers designed explicitly to protect economic liberties against federal and state intervention.

References

Aranson, Peter H. "Judicial Control of the Political Branches: Public Purpose and Public Law." *Cato Journal* 4 (Winter 1985): 719-82.

Aranson, Peter H. "Calculus and Consent." In *Democracy and Public Choice*, pp. 60-65. Edited by Charles K. Rowley. New York: Basil Blackwell, 1987.

Aranson, Peter H.; Gellhorn, Ernest; and Robinson, Glen O. "A Theory of Legislative Delegation." *Cornell Law Review* 68 (November 1982):1-67.

Aranson, Peter H. and Ordeshook, Peter C. "Public Interest, Private Interest, and the Democratic Polity." In *The Democratic State*, pp. 87-177. Edited by Roger Benjamin and Stephen L. Elkin. Lawrence: University Press of Kansas, 1985.

Berry, Jeffrey M. *Lobbying for the People: The Political Behavior of Public Interest Groups.* Princeton: Princeton University Press, 1977.

Brennan, Geoffrey, and Buchanan, James. M. *The Reason of Rules: Constitutional Political Economy.* New York: Cambridge University Press, 1985.

Brennan, William J. Speech to the Text and Teaching Symposium, Georgetown *University, 12 October 1985.* In *The Great Debate: Interpreting Our Written Constitution*, pp. 11-25. Washington, D.C.: The Federalist Society, 1986.

Buchanan, James M., and Tullock, Gordon. *The Calculus of Consent: Logical Foundations of Constitutional Democracy.* Ann Arbor: University of Michigan Press, 1962.

Buchanan, James M.; Tollison, Robert D.; and Tullock, Gordon, eds. *The Theory of the Rent-Seeking Society.* College Station: Texas A & M University Press, 1980.

Currie, David P. "Positive and Negative Constitutional Rights." *University of Chicago Law Review* 53 (Summer 1986): 964-80.

Downs, Anthony. *An Economic Theory of Democracy.* New York: Harper and Row, 1957.

Easterbrook, Frank H. "Foreword: The Court and the Economic System." *Harvard Law Review* 98 (November 1984):4-60.

Ely, John Hart. *Democracy and Distrust: A Theory of Judicial Review.* Cambridge: Harvard University Press, 1980.

Epstein, Richard A. "Taxation, Regulation, and Confiscation." *Osgoode Hall Law Journal* 20 (September 1982):433-53.

Epstein, Richard A. "Toward a Revitalization of the Contract Clause." *University of Chicago Law Review* 51 (Summer 1984):703-51.

Epstein, Richard A. *Takings: Private Property and the Power of Eminent Domain*. Cambridge: Harvard University Press, 1985.

Hayek, Freidrich A. *The Raod to Serfdom*. Chicago: University of Chicago Press, 1944.

Hayek, Friedrich A. *Law, Legislation, and Liberty: The Political Order of a Free People*. Vol. 3. Chicago: University of Chicago Press, 1981.

Heiner, Ronald A. "The Origins of Predictable Behavior." *American Economic Review* 73 (September 1983):560-95.

Heiner, Ronald A. "Imperfect Decisions and the Law: On the Evolution of Legal Precedent and Rules." *Journal of Legal Studies* 15 (June 1986):227-61.

Heiner, Ronald A. "Imperfect Decisions in Organizations: Toward a Theory of Internal Structure." *Journal of Economic Behavior and Organization* (Spring 1987).

Heiner, Ronald A. "The Necessity of Imperfect Decisions." *Journal of Economic Behavior and Organization* (forthcoming, Spring 1988).

Krier, James E. "The Regulation Machine." *Supreme Court Economic Review* 1 (1982):1-37.

Landes, William M., and Posner, Richard A. "The Independent Judiciary in an Interest-group Perspective." *Journal of Law and Economics* 18 (December 1975):875-901.

Leoni, Bruno. *Freedom and the Law*. Los Angeles: Nash, 1971.

Macey, Jonathan R. "Promoting Public-Regarding Legislation through Statutory Interpretation: An Interest Group Model." *Columbia Law Review* 86 (March 1986): 223-68.

Mashaw, Jerry L. "Constitutional Deregulation: Notes Toward a Public-Public Law." *Tulane Law Review* 54 (June 1980): 849-976.

Mayhew, David R. *Congress: The Electoral Connection*. New Haven: Yale University Press, 1974.

McKelvey, Richard D., and Ordeshook, Peter C. "An Experimental Study of the Effects of Procedural Rules on Committee Behavior." *Journal of Politics* 46 (February 1984): 182-205.

McLure, Charles E., Jr. "Incidence Analysis and the Supreme Court: An Examination of Four Cases from the 1980 Term." *Supreme Court Economic Review* 1 (1982):69-112.

Meese, Edwin, III. Speech Before the American Bar Association, 9 July, 1985, Washington, D.C. In *The Great Debate: Interpreting Our Written Constitution*, pp. 1-10. Washington, D.C.: The Federalist Society, 1986.

Miller, Nicholas. "Pluralism and Social Choice." *American Political Science Review* 77 (September 1983): 734-47.

Riker, William H. "Implications from the Disequilibrium of Majority Rule for the Study of Institutions." *American Political Science Review* 74 (June 1980):432-47.

Riker, William H. *Liberalism Against Populism: A Confrontation Between the Theory of Democracy and the Theory of Social Choice*. San Francisco: W. H. Freeman, 1982a.

Riker, William H. "Democracy and Representation: A Reconciliation of Ball v. James and Reynolds v. Sims." *Supreme Court Economic Review* 1 (1982b):39-68.

Riker, William H., and Weingast, Barry R. "Constitutional Regulation of Legislative Choice: The Political Consequences of Judicial Deference to Legislatures." Working Paper P-86-11. Stanford University, Hoover Institution, Domestic Studies Program, 1986.

Rizzo, Mario J. "Law Amid Flux: The Economics of Negligence and Strict Liability in Tort." *Journal of Legal Studies* 9 (March 1980):291-318.

Shepsle, Kenneth A., and Weingast, Barry R. "When Do Rules of Procedure Matter?" *Journal of Politics* 46 (February 1984):206-21.

Siegan, Bernard H. *Economic Liberties and the Constitution.* Chicago: University of Chicago Press, 1980.

Sunstein, Cass R. "Naked Preferences and the Constitution." *Columbia Law Review* 84 (November 1984):1689-1732.

Sunstein, Cass R. "Interest Groups in American Public Law." *Stanford Law Review* 38 (November 1985):29-87.

Weingast, Barry R.; Shepsle, Kenneth A.; and Johnsen, Christopher. "The Political Economy of Costs and Benefits: A Neoclassical Approach to Distributive Politics." *Journal of Political Economy* 89 (August 1981):642-64.

Williams, Stephen F. "Liberty and Property: The Problem of Government Benefits." *Journal of Legal Studies* 12 (January 1983):3-40.

14

THE PUBLIC TRUST DOCTRINE
Richard A. Epstein

Private and Public Property

From the outset political and legal theory have long been divided on the question of whether various forms of natural resources are in the original position held in common ownership or, alternatively, are subject to private ownership by individual acts of appropriation. Locke, for example, tries to work both sides of the street. He first appeals to Biblical authority to demonstrate that God gave mankind the earth to be held in common: "God, as King David says, Psalm cxv.16, 'has given the earth to the children of men,' given it to mankind in common." (Locke 1690, ch. 5; para. 25). Thereafter he argues that individuals "fix" their property in that portion of the common good with which they mix their labor, even when they act without the consent of others.

Locke's argument rested in part on a theistic foundation. Once that is removed, however, accounting for property rights is far more difficult, for there is no obvious starting point for the analysis, as mankind in general cannot be regarded as joint donees who take by transfer, rather than by acquisition. Locke's argument does not tell us how to think about property when there are no rights, and no grantor, in the state of nature. No longer is the inquiry, how does one get private rights out of public ones, or indeed how to get public rights out of private ones. No longer is there any necessary presumption that all property rights should be either private or public. A mix of rights, some public and some private, is surely conceivable, even if their relative proportions are unclear. Historically, both the common law and Roman traditions were able to accommodate both forms of property, with the navigable waters being perhaps the most notable forms of public

---

Cato Journal, Vol. 7, No. 2 (Fall 1987). Copyright Cato Institute. All rights reserved.

The author is James Parker Hall Professor of Law at the University of Chicago. He wishes to thank Carol Rose for her extremely valuable comments on an earlier draft of the paper.

property — often "inherently" so (see Rose 1986; Sax 1970). The task for a unified theory of property is to develop an account of the original position which accomplishes two things. First, it allows for some property rights to be private and others to be public. Second, it permits correction of any initial allocative mistakes by providing a way for assets to move from one regime of property rights to another. In dealing with these two themes, my emphasis is on property that is owned by the public at large. The "public trust" title given to the paper refers to the legal rules that limit the power of the people, or (in time) the legislature, to dispose of public property.[1]

In addressing the original position, no government is already in place with the power to assign rights in property to single individuals or the public at large. Locke may not have established that mankind in common is the donee of all property, but surely he demolished the divine rights of kings. The inability to locate the original grantor of property in God or in the state has had profound consequences on the shape of political theory, for it has forced both legal and political thinkers to take a more explicit consequentialist view of legal rules and social arrangements. The task of justification has been to show what general set of legal institutions will advance the welfare of the public at large, when measured against its next best alternative. The task is surely daunting, as there is no obvious means to take information about individual utilities and combine them into any unique social welfare function. But by the same token that task is in some sense quite unavoidable: for if one does not look to *any* of the consequences of legal rules, however nebulous and uncertain, then what could furnish a justification for any practice?

In addressing the original position, I believe that the most fruitful line of inquiry stresses the relationship between the rules of transfer and the rules of original ownership (see Holderness 1985). In some logical sense rules of initial acquisition are necessarily prior to the rules of transfer. After all, how can anyone transfer property that he does not own? Yet in another sense one can determine the rules of original acquisition only with an appreciation of the importance of the rules of transfer. The needed explanation

---

[1] In more recent times efforts have been made to expand the scope of the public trust doctrine so that a public trust is impressed upon ordinary private property simply because individuals have notice of the types of regulations that might be imposed. "Expectations must be deemed to change as time, circumstances and public attitudes change, and expectations which might have been reasonable at one time can cease to be reasonable." See Sax (1981, p. 10). Stated in this form, the public trust doctrine strays from its original function, that of limiting government power over public assets, and addresses a new function, that of expanding government power over private property. The newer approach to the public trust doctrine is simply another unfortunate effort to create instability in private rights, in harmony with the modern efforts to eviscerate the eminent domain clause. I have said enough about eminent domain already (see Epstein 1985a) and do not address this constellation of issues further here.

rests in a single phrase: "mutual benefit." There are all sorts of reasons why someone who now owns one thing no longer wishes to keep it: I want to sell my house in Chicago because I have a new job out of town. A rule of voluntary exchange allows the owner to get rid of something he has in order to acquire something to which he has greater value. In the ordinary case, these rules of exchange leave both parties to the transaction better off than they were before; otherwise they would not enter into them. The mutual benefit between the parties creates a presumption that the transfer in question is a social good, for someone is better off and thus far no one is worse off. But this presumption is not absolute. In turn it could be rebutted by a showing that the transfer has created negative effects on some third parties.

Here there is need to be careful, for every transfer has *some* negative external effects on the welfare of at least one third person. Nonetheless the overall effect of voluntary exchange will usually be positive. The increase in wealth of the immediate parties will generally increase the opportunities for exchange left open to all third parties. The disappointed competitor in the one case may well turn out to be the successful bidder in the next, so a system of property rights which facilitates free exchange is one that will in the long run work to the advantage of all its participants by increasing the amounts of available goods and services. In marriage markets, for example, no one would (I hope) think that A's decision to marry B and not C, could justify a system of regulation that would oust the principle of joint consent. The usual libertarian line has been that between competition and violence, and it is a very accurate proxy for which rules have, in the aggregate, third party effects that are overall negative or positive. In the absence of force, or the threat of force against third parties (Epstein 1985b), it is very difficult to rebut the original presumption that ordinary voluntary exchanges (unlike contracts to kill or steal) should go forward.

Voluntary exchanges are then a critical part of any sensible legal system. The question of whether these exchanges in fact can take place is, however, critically a function of the original design of a system of property rights. Here of course it is quite impossible for any human being or human institutions to engage in self-conscious acts of deliberation that will yield some perfect set of original rights or for that matter a perfect set of legal institutions. The line between violence and competition is, for example, a first approximation, one which leaves open the limited possibility that further corrections can be made in the original allocation of rights should the circumstances require it: for example, some laws restricting the enforceability of cartel arrangements. The questions to be asked, therefore, are two: What rules will in general promote voluntary transactions? And what methods does the legal system have to "correct" those original allocations that turn out to be arguably wrong? The first of these questions addresses the mix of public and private property. The second addresses the role of the eminent domain principle and its analogue for public property, the public trust doctrine. The eminent domain rules govern the forced conversion of private to public property. Rightly understood, the public trust rules do the reverse, and govern the forced conversion of public to private property.

The Original Position

The first question is, why should some things be regarded as unowned in the original position and others subject to a common indivisible ownership? I believe that a *single* theory accounts for both types of ownership. In the original position property should be subject to that form of ownership that minimizes the bargaining problems associated with moving the asset to its highest-valued use. In most cases that proposition points to a system of private property, where a single person enjoys the right to the possession, use, and disposition of a given thing. The existence of a single owner means that normally one person is needed to sell, and only one to buy. Stated otherwise, two distinct people are the logically necessary minimum for any exchange to take place. The system of private ownership tends to ensure that any two people who choose to pair up are able to so act, without the consent of others.

This concern with voluntary exchanges helps explain the original distribution of rights to the person and many forms of real and personal property. With the person, that result is achieved under the traditional protection of individual autonomy, long associated with natural rights theory. Each person is the sole owner of himself, and hence can sell his labor without the consent of other individuals. Autonomy quite literally means capable of movement by the self — alone. There is no need in this view to have any rule which specifies how any person acquires ownership of himself; he has it by being in necessary possession of his own body: "every man has a property in his own person; this nobody has any right to but himself. The labor of his body and the work of his hands we may say are properly his." (Locke, ch. 5; para. 27).

No rule of original ownership for human talents could possibly operate at lower cost. Yet here too there are qualifications, for it is necessary to specify a guardian for individuals during infancy. Parents assume that role in part because they are in possession of the child at birth, and in addition have strong biological motives to protect the child until its maturity. The automatic selection of a very small number of guardians again facilitates the voluntary transactions entered into for the care and raising of the child.

With respect to land and chattels, there is no obvious assignment of any external things to any particular individual. In this context the first possession rule at common law allows persons to come forward and become single owners of external things (Epstein 1979). Once those things are reduced to single owners, they can then be disposed of in voluntary transactions that in the typical case involve two (or very few) persons. In both cases the distributional consequences of the first possession rule are distinctly secondary in importance. What matters is that resources with positive value not be left without any owners to fend for them, or with too many owners to squabble over them. In principle the entire process of assigning things to private ownership can take place, moreover, without the intervention of the extensive administrative state and its powers of centralized control. Initiation lies in the hands of private persons. The role of government is only to police the rules whereby ownership is acquired and transferred.

The desirability of this system of first possession changes radically when we consider, for example, the use of navigable rivers and lakes for transportation. Now any system of divided private ownership, based on first possession, tends to create the very bargaining and holdout problems that the institution of private property is designed to overcome. Each segment of the river is worth very little for transportation unless all segments could be subjected to uniform ownership. The risk is that the owner of one segment will hold out against all the others, so that bargaining breakdown will prevent any use of the river at all for navigation. It is precisely to overcome such difficulties that one of the most unproblematic uses of the eminent domain power has always been the condemnation of private lands for public highways, open to all. The formation of the highway removes, or at least controls, the risk of holdout which might otherwise dominate voluntary negotiations to lay out and construct roads.

If we need highways, then why is the land for public highways not owned by the public at large in the original position? The answer is quite simply this: while in the original position we know that there is some need for public highways, we do not know *where* they are best located. That decision turns on subsequent events, including the pattern of land use development and the emerging routes for internal and external trade. The location of the highway involves some degree of discretion and must necessarily await future events. In the interim, private ownership of the underlying land facilitates its beneficial use. At some later time when the land is needed for the road, it can be condemned, where the requirement of compensation offers an effective way to constrain the state into making wise decisions about what lands should be taken (see Epstein 1985a, pp. 12-17).[2]

---

[2] Note in some cases cash compensation will not be needed, because the very presence of the highway will increase the value of the retained lands, so that each landowner's reduced holdings are worth more with the road in place than his larger holdings are worth without the road. Note too that the allocation of this surplus is nonetheless important. If there is no system of transfer payments after the highway is put in place, each owner will have an incentive to try to get the road located on the land of a neighbor, but adjacent to his own land.

There is, however, no reason to wait for government action to dedicate navigable rivers to commerce. The location of the common highway is dictated by nature. There is no need to begin with private ownership, and then to allow the property to be taken for public use upon payment of just compensation to private owners. So long as there is good reason to think that navigation along the river will be socially beneficial — an easy call — then the original recognition of navigation servitude prevents the blockade of the river by any single riparian or interloper. No system of eminent domain is costless to administer. Sometimes it is difficult to identify the owner of a particular asset; it is always tricky business to value their interests; and someone must levy and collect the taxes necessary to pay the needed compensation. The transactions costs are quite considerable. In contrast, the questions of which rivers are navigable, and what conduct counts as their obstruction can be answered by ordinary common law litigation. It is therefore possible to have a system of public ownership without an extensive government to administer it. The recognition of the public's navigation servitude in the original position ironically serves to *reduce* the size of government while recognizing the customary public ownership of public goods, which was firmly established if imperfectly justified.

There will of course be some difficult questions of how to define the limit of the scope of public ownership over navigable waters. The bilateral monopoly problem does not extend to all use of the waterways (see Rose 1986, p. 749). There is no reason to adopt a system that speaks of some inherent right of public access to navigable waters over private riparian lands. While there may be only a single navigable river, there can be many places where access to that river can be gained. Competition between landowners will keep the price of entry down, and if public access points are desired, then individual landowners can be compensated for the loss of their exclusive possession. Unless that is done, each riparian will be prepared to undertake steps to influence government powers to place public access ways over the lands of others. Requiring compensation reduces the costs of these wasteful games, while at the same time public officials face a budget and a taxing constraint whenever they wish to expand the scope of access.

Issues like fishing and bathing in navigable rivers are closer calls (Rose 1986, pp. 754ff.), but in the end these, unlike access rights, should probably be regarded as public. Once there is a guaranteed access to the river in question, it is hardly conceivable to think of effective ways to prevent persons on the river from using it for these purposes, and very difficult

---

Requiring some fair division of the surplus created by the introduction of the road reduces this particular form of rent dissipation. In this context too there is a powerful correspondence between intuitive notions of fairness (that each person be treated equally) and the economic fear of rent dissipation.

to imagine how a principle of first possession could reduce fishing and bathing rights across the board to private ownership.[3] It is very difficult to exclude persons from using navigable waters when they cannot be excluded from gaining access to it. Navigable rivers are therefore a mixed asset, some of whose attributes should remain private and others should be public. In sorting out the various cases, the guiding principle throughout should remain constant: choose that form of ownership that minimizes the expected number of bargaining breakdowns. The historical divisions between public and private rights often followed that general rule.

Nor Shall Public Property Be Transferred To Private Use, Without Just Compensation

The parallels between public and private property can be extended to the second of our inquiries, the correction of individual allocative mistakes. In dealing with private property, the system of ownership created under the rule of first possession will not always prove optimal. To be sure, private bargains can often work the needed reassignment of property rights. Yet in other cases, when the bargains must touch the rights of multiple owners, the parties face the very set of bargaining barriers that private ownership was designed to avoid. The problems of the common fishery, of oil and gas, and even of bankruptcy are often taken as illustrations of cases where voluntary bargains are unable to correct allocative imbalances brought about in a system of private property based upon the principle of first possession.

In this world the use of government takings is thought to play an important role. The government takes property from private parties and pays them compensation, in cash or in kind, for what they have lost (Epstein 1985a, chaps. 14-15). The point of the system is that if the state can afford to pay the compensation for the losses that it imposes upon private owners, then there is good reason to believe that the entire set of coerced takings will benefit all (or virtually all) members of society simultaneously. The reason why compensation is strictly required is both prudential and universal. If takings could be made by state fiat alone, then, to avoid abuse, there would necessarily have to be elaborate administrative reviews to estimate, first, the value to the state of the property taken, and second, the losses the taking imposes upon the private owner. The taking should only go forward where the gains to the state (or the people it represents) exceed the losses that the taking imposes. But no administrative process is equal to that task. These investigations would be expensive to supervise, and in the end there would be little reason to have any confidence that only the "right"

---

[3] This is not to say that some form of regulation by the state will not in the end be necessary. Common fisheries present the obvious and classical common pool problem (see Hardin 1968).

takings were undertaken by the state. The requirement of just compensation thus serves as an effective bulwark against government abuse by making public officials back up speech with dollars. Questions of the size of public gain are largely removed by judicial review, leaving the price feature as a powerful deterrent to unwise state action. If the court sets the price of the taking correctly, then there is some insistent legal pressure for public officials to estimate accurately the benefits from their own takings. Where the prices are set incorrectly (as when losses to good will are improperly ignored in the calculations), then there will be too many takings brought about by the state.

The analogous problem of correcting imbalances could also arise with property that is originally held by the public in common. Suppose some property which is given to the state is more valuable in private hands. The question is how does one determine what property that is, and transfer control over it to some private person. Initially the problem is complicated because property that has been customarily held in common cannot be disposed of by the (disorganized) public at large. Some group of persons must have the power to dispose of it, and to control the use of the proceeds that has been so obtained. The need to transfer resouces from state control is just one reason why some organized system of collective ownership has been imposed upon public property. But whenever power is created, abuse may follow in its wake. The question is what rules, if any, should regulate those transactions that seek to move public property into private hands.

Two questions have to be addressed. The first is whether the transfer should be made, and the second is, when made, what level of compensation should be provided. The problem of disposing of public property thus raises the mirror image of public use and just compensation questions under the takings clause of the Fifth Amendment: "Nor shall private property be taken for public use, without just compensation." The underlying problems are not any simpler when dealing with property which was originally held by the public in common, for now the guiding principle is in a sense the converse of the original eminent domain clause, to wit: "No *public* property may be transferred to *private use*, without just compensation," payable to the public at large. This reverse eminent domain clause in turn reduces itself into the same two questions raised in the ordinary takings context, first, whether the state transfer should be made, and second, what compensation, if any, should be provided.

In dealing with the first of these issues, it is clear that the transfer is desirable only if it can improve the lot of everyone in society, that is, by the creation of general social improvement. In order for that conclusion to hold, there must be some reason to believe that the private owner of the asset can make better use of it than the public owner. In dealing with the navigation servitude over the river that conclusion does not seem very promising. Initially, any transfer of the navigable servitude to two or more persons, each entitled to do with his interest as he pleases, cannot have the desired effect, because it necessarily reintroduces the bilateral monopoly problems that the system of public ownership was designed to overcome.

In principle it might be possible to escape this problem by selling the navigation servitude to a single firm. But other problems remain. Surely the sale of the navigation rights limits the otherwise unlimited access to the public waters. In order to recoup the initial cost, the owner of the navigation servitude must charge a positive price to all users of the system — a price which will usually be in excess of the very low marginal cost that each additional user brings upon the system. And there would be a real skewing of benefits from privatization unless the new owner were required to accept *all* users at some nondiscriminatory price. The moment this condition of universal access is added, however, it becomes a doubtful question whether the navigation servitude has been really made private. The insistence upon universal access impresses the public trust upon the navigation servitude even after legal ownership is vested in private hands. The absolute right to exclude, long thought the essence of private property, is denied the purchaser who takes, as it were, subject to the original public trust.

The theoretical gains from this type sale are, then, very hard to see. Yet its practical difficulties are very great. First, there are considerable costs associated with trying to organize a sale of so complex an asset as a navigable river. Who does the packaging of the rights and measures their value? Is it possible to really sell off the entire Mississippi river system from Minnesota to New Orleans? Unlike the case of highways, there is no obvious way to allow the new monopolist to limit the use of the river by riparian owners, who have previously had unlimited access to it. It is for good reason, then, that privatization has not come to the navigation servitude. The social gains just do not seem to be there.

At this point the parallels to the ordinary principles of eminent domain become explicit. When it is said that public rights over navigable waters are "inalienable," then the law in effect has applied by analogy the "public use" limitation of the ordinary eminent domain clause to property held by the public. If the transfer of the navigation servitude into private owner-system of side payments, no system of just compensation, can make all individuals better off than before when all gains and losses are taken into account. Someone has to bear the bottom line losses of the contemplated change in ownership rights. Under these circumstances, it is better therefore simply to prevent the transfer from taking place. Exactly that result is obtained by saying that public waterways are inalienable, and must remain, "inherently" public.

Yet in some situations, it seems clear that public ownership of resources is not necessarily a good thing. Consider the important case of minerals located in the riverbeds of navigable rivers. In the original position, it is arguably a close question of whether these should be treated as property held in common by the public at large, or as unowned resources subject to acquisition under the principle of first possession. On the one hand, private ownership of minerals does not create the same type of blockade situation that would arise with private ownership of a river or a lake. Yet by the same token, the removal of minerals from a riverbed may well require an extensive dislocation of transportation along the river, for surface easements are needed to mine. The dangers posed to navigation by unlimited private access to mineral rights over public waters are not a trivial concern. Public ownership of the bed of the river and the mineral rights it contains avoids just that difficulty, and the general rule so provides (*Barney v. Keokuk*, 94 U.S. 324 [1876]).

Nonetheless it is doubtful that the public or the government has any natural advantage in the way in which it mines minerals. A system of ownership that treats the unorganized public as the owner of the minerals effectively withdraws them from gainful exploitation. The recognition that the state is the owner of these resources, in trust for the public at large, now endows a single group of individuals with the power to dispose of the minerals to private parties. The language of the public trust is far more than an idle metaphor because it is quite clear that the public officials in question cannot treat the proceeds of sale as their private property. Instead they are required to hold the moneys received as part of the public treasury, that is, for the benefit of all the individuals who had in the original position some undivided interests in the underlying mineral rights.

Some sales of public assets are for public benefit, but some are not. But which are which? Now attention has to be given to the question of what legal institutions will secure for members of the public at large the right price and the right terms for its asset. The first question raises the precise parallel to the "just compensation" requirement found in the eminent domain clause. If the transfer is simply made to private individuals without any restraint, there is the enormous temptation to use political influence and intrigue to divert public property to private hands. Requiring just compensation from the private acquirers of the mineral interests limits the possibility that the rights will be given away for a song, and strongly suggests that a competitive auction to maximize public revenues may be required as a constitutional matter.

This stringent compensation requirement, however, does not of itself answer the second question: What is the bundle of rights that the state itself should put up for auction? The problem is of great importance with minerals, where the structure of the access rights may alter the value of the navigation servitude that is retained. The pricing system is not able to handle this question because bids for the assets sold will not reflect the diminution in the value of the property rights retained by the public. Some form of administrative action is necessarily required. A division of power among various public officials is, accordingly, a necessary part of the program of any sale of public assets. That these additional steps are required should not be surprising. Private corporations often must confront the perils of self-dealing, and they take similar procedural precautions. If anything, the conflict of interest problem is far more acute with the disposition of publicly held assets. Unlike the corporation situation, there is no systematic selection of individuals into the public venture based upon their common attitude toward risk, or their attitudes on consumption. Still every member of the public is a beneficiary of the public trust. Their fundamental divergence of opinions and attitudes only makes it more difficult to decide whether, and if so how, these public assets should be disposed of. The procedural safeguards are as much a part of the program for the disposition of public assets as the just compensation requirement.

Illinois Central Railroad v. Illinois

The above framework should make it possible to explain the enormous intellectual difficulties in that most important of the public trust cases, *Illinois Central Railroad v. Illinois* (146 U.S. 387 [1892]). The history of the case should be recounted in some detail. An Illinois statute of 1852 had given the Illinois Central Railroad permission to construct a line along the shore of Lake Michigan. That original grant was then confirmed in a statute of 1869. More controversially, the 1869 statute also granted to the Illinois Central Railroad title to extensive submerged lands in Lake Michigan, about 1,000 acres in all, including all of the outer harbor along Lake Michigan, and some additional submerged lands as well (146 U.S at 454). The new grant provided that the railroad should hold title to the land in perpetuity, but should not have the power to grant, sell, or convey the fee, that is, outright ownership, therein to any other person. The state retained no express power to revoke the grant. Illinois Central was given the same freedom of control over the lands as if they were uplands, that is, lands not subject to the original navigation servitude. The grant also provided that Illinois Central could not "authorize obstructions to the harbor or impair the public right of navigation, or exclude the legislature from regulating the rates of wharfage or dockage to be charged" (*id*. at 451). In exchange for the conveyance of the land, Illinois Central agreed to carry over the compensation formula that the 1852 act used to set the moneys payable by the railroad to the state, and to pay some fraction of its gross earnings from its use, occupation, and control of the submerged lands in question. The 1869 grant, however, did not oblige the railroad to enter into any immediate efforts to make improvements on the lands so conveyed.

The entire arrangement under the 1869 statute was short-lived, for the original grant was revoked by new legislation, without compensation, four years later. In the interim period the Illinois Central had used some but not all of the waters conveyed to it for its railroad business, but did not appear to pay any revenues to the state. The challenge made to the 1873 act was, when all was said and done, that the revocation of the 1869 act was an illegal taking. The railroad's case was that the grant of the submerged lands had conveyed an indefeasible title in the railroad in accordance with the terms of the grant. At that point the state could still revoke, but only if it paid compensation for the property so taken. Once the state conveyance is made the private title is as good as that which is acquired from any other source.

The argument for the state was that its original conveyance was in violation of the public trust under which those submerged lands had been held. As such at most a mere license was created by the 1869 act, so that an asserted legal title in the railroad was void (or at least voidable) at the option of the state. The upshot was that no compensation was required when the new legislature reversed the field of the old one.

The decision in the case was close, but the state prevailed by a four to three vote.[4] The opinion for the Court was written by Justice Stephen J. Field, normally a staunch defender of individual liberty and private property. (See, e.g., his powerful dissent in *Munn v. Illinois* 94 U.S. 113 [1877]). His refusal to uphold the original legislative grant has been taken to be inconsistent with his general philosophical position. On reflection I believe this is a mistake. In order to understand the case, it is necessary to apply the two step analysis of public trust cases developed above.

The first question is whether the conveyance to Illinois Central is per se out of bounds because it necessarily is a losing proposition. However, it is hardly clear that the case falls into this category. The 1869 statute did not convey the entire lake itself to a private party. The use of Lake Michigan for navigation remains unimpaired, and the development of the harbor is consistent with the original use of the lake itself, for the grant itself prevented the railroad from obstructing navigation. In addition, there may be some efficiency gains in integrating the operations of the shipping and rail traffic. Finally, the risks that the railroad will abuse its position are reduced given that the state reserved powers to regulate its activities on the submerged lands. A categorical denunciation of the grant is hard to establish.

The question therefore turns on the second of the two issues identified

---

[4] Two justices were disqualified: Chief Justice Melville Fuller because he had represented the City of Chicago, and Justice Blatchford who was a shareholder in Illinois Central Railroad.

above: Did the state receive just compensation from the private party for
the lands which it had conveyed out? In order to answer this question it
is necessary to value the consideration received by the state for the submerged lands conveyed away.[5] By treating the question strictly as one of
the capacity of the city to convey its submerged properties, Justice Field
(and the dissent of Justice Shiras) did not explicitly address the compensation issue. But it is clear that this issue lies at the root of the case. Note,
initially, there was no competitive bidding situation for the rights to the
submerged land, and the price paid over was shrouded in mystery. Thus
the 1869 statute called for the payment of $800,000 in installments to the
city for the submerged lands, but the city comptroller refused to accept
the first payment from the railroad if acceptance meant a waiver of the
city's rights to challenge the grant. The remaining payments from the
railroad were only conditional upon its receiving revenue from its development of the project in question. None (it appears) had been paid over in
the interim four year period that the statute had been in effect, and the
railroad had complete control over the timing of any improvements that
it chose to make. Clearly there are always conflicts of interest between
the city and the railroad with the timing of improvements, and the 1869
act reduced the cost of delay to the railroad. Finally, the amount of land
conveyed in the 1869 grant had been quite considerable in extent and value.
It was as large as the docks along the Thames, much larger than those of
Liverpool, and nearly as large as those of New York (*id.* at 454). The consideration for so substantial a grant should be quite considerable indeed.

In spite of its critical importance the just compensation issue was never
addressed, except obliquely. Justice Field insisted that small grants of particular bits of waterfront for the development of piers and wharfs were well
within the power of the state to grant. For this he was chided forcefully
by the dissent of Justice Shiras, which said that if the state has the capacity
to convey out bits and pieces of the waterfront, it could convey out the
entire area at once. If the only issue had been the capacity to convey, then
Shiras's objection would have seemed well grounded, but once the focus
turns to the just compensation requirement, then the reverse is true. It
is easier to monitor whether the state is getting fair value if its sells off

---

[5] There is also a second takings issue hidden in the case. If the moneys received by the "state"
are paid into the state treasury, then there may well be an implicit transfer among citizens
of the state. The citizens of Chicago are the obvious beneficiaries of the use of the submerged
lands in Lake Michigan but the proceeds of sale inure only in part to their benefit, with the
remainder going to citizens downstate. The implicit wealth transfer between different segments
of the public creates rent seeking opportunities. The public trust doctrine does not only address
the opposition between the individual recipients of the trust property and the public at large,
but also the parallel tensions between different members of the public. I shall, however, not
pursue, these issues further here.

small parcels for immediate use by competitive bid. It is far harder to measure compensation with the giant deal that was organized here. The clear sense of the Court's majority was that the city had been "ripped off" by the railroad which had gotten the advantage of a bargain purchase under the 1869 statute. Once that is done, then only complete nullification of the original grant will set the situation aright. Condemning the lands back again only allows the railroad to cash out a gain to which it was not entitled in the first instance.

It might of course have been possible for the railroad to place a different gloss on these facts. The railroad, for example, could have tried to show that the city's retained power of regulation over its wharves and piers eliminates the dangers of monopoly profits, and that the percentage of future revenues reserved under the grant are substantial in character. And even if the railroad does not have perfect incentives to develop the property, it surely has some, for the longer it keeps the waterfront in its undeveloped state, the longer it has to wait to realize a return from its asset. In his argument, the railroad's lawyer made explicit reference to the fact that the common council of Chicago gave its consent "on conditions that were extremely burdensome, but they have been fully complied with" (*id.* at 416).

At this distance it is extremely difficult therefore to make a judgment about how the adequacy of consideration issue should be ultimately resolved. Yet when all is said and done there is no denying its relevance. Suppose a private corporation sold all its assets to one of its shareholders. The risk of self-dealing is so great that the transaction could always be challenged by the remaining shareholders on the ground that the corporation had not received adequate compensation for the property it had distributed. *Illinois Central Railroad* raises that same issue of self-dealing in the public sphere. When Justice Field struck down the grant to the railroad, he acted not to restrict the power of ordinary conveyances, but to prevent the abuse of legislative power that might well have transpired. His position is thus consistent with his own theory of limited government, which everywhere places limitations on public officials that are not imposed upon private individuals.

Notwithstanding the internal logic of Field's opinion, there are many disquieting elements about *Illinois Central*, both at an institutional and a constitutional level. As an institutional matter, it is surely a source of some disquiet that the case was finally resolved only 19 years after the 1873 statute. That delay works in no one's interest, for in the interim neither the city nor the railroad knows whether it is in a position to develop the land. The time to resolve doubts about public grants is before, or shortly after, they are made. In part this can be done by procedural protections. Public hearings about the terms and conditions of the grant, its costs and its benefits, seem clearly appropriate before the grant is made. Such deliberations are held before corporations sell substantial assets to shareholders.

There is, however, no certainty that these will be sufficient. The question therefore is what types of judicial challenges can be made to set aside the grant. *Illinois Central* reached the courts only because the subsequent legislature revoked the earlier grant, without paying compensation. But why should the grant remain beyond challenge if it is not revoked? The underlying fear is both familiar and recurrent: the first legislature has been bought off. If so, then the next legislature could be bought off as well. To condition challenge to the grant on its repeal means that in some cases needed challenges will never take place. *Any* citizen should have standing to challenge a major transfer of public assets. What seems to be called for is a system which allows a prompt (if that word can ever be used about the judicial system) challenge to the original grant on grounds of inadequacy, as by declaratory judgment. But the fuse should be short, and once the period has passed, the grant should be regarded as fully valid, and not subject to subsequent attack in any forum. Its future revocation would then require compensation.

Constitutional Issues

The constitutional issues raised by *Illinois Central* are, if anything, more puzzling. The public trust doctrine is the mirror image of the eminent domain clause. Both are designed to place limitations upon the power of legislature to divert property, whether held privately or in common, from A to B, or more generally from a group of As to a group of Bs. Both doctrines derive from a strong sense of equity that condemns these uncompensated transfers as a genteel form of theft, regardless of whether the original holdings are public or private. In each case the prohibition upon legislative behavior has beneficial allocative consequences as well, because it prevents the dissipation of valuable resources that are used to obtain or resist uncompensated transfers. In principle the public trust doctrine should operate at the constitutional level, as a parallel to the eminent domain clause. Nonetheless the basis for the public trust doctrine in the United States Constitution is difficult to identify.[6]

Consider the way the public trust question arose in *Illinois Central*. That action was brought by the railroad to challenge the revocation of the original grant under the 1873 statute. The railroad claimed that the earlier con-

---

[6] Many state constitutions have specific public trust provisions in them. See, e.g., Montana Constitution, Art. 9, sect. 3(3), which provides:

> All surface, underground, flood and atmospheric waters within the boundaries of the state are the property of the state for the use of its people and subject to appropriation for beneficial uses as provided by law.

veyance had made the submerged lands its private property, protected against the confiscation by any government action. If the railroad did indeed owns the lands, then its case was airtight. Accordingly, the state's defense rested on the proposition that the original grant was invalid under the public trust doctrine. The public trust question was thus raised by indirection only. At this point, the juridical status of the public trust doctrine in the legal hierarchy becomes critical to the analysis. If the doctrine applied only at common law, then the state legislature could trump it. If the principle were embodied only in the Illinois constitution, then the case should not be heard in the U.S. Supreme Court. If the public trust principle found its application in the U.S. Constitution, then Justice Field should have said where. But the opinion is not ,"clause-bound" (see Ely 1980) in any sense at all. Instead Field works very much in the "natural" or "higher" law tradition (see Grant 1931). *Illinois Central* contains no citations to particular constitutional provision, and the opinion reads like an essay that runs for 20 pages without case citation (146 U.S., at 436 to 456).

It is therefore an open question whether the public trust doctrine has a constitutional home. Here two alternatives present themselves, each with its own interpretative difficulties. The first is the standard due process clause of the Fourteenth Amendment: "Nor shall any State deprive any person of life, liberty, or property, without due process of law." There is a long but an uneasy tradition that reads the last phrase, "without due process of law" to be the equivalent of "without just compensation" (*Chicago, Burlington & Quincy Railroad Co. v. Chicago*, 166 U.S. 226, 236 [1986]). On that substantive reading, the due process clause seems to apply because the "property" to which it refers includes not only private property, but also the fractional share that each person holds in the trust property. At this point the outcome in *Illinois Central* depends upon the adequacy of consideration received by the state, just as this due process analysis appears to provide. to provide.

The second possible source of constitutional rights is the equal protection clause, which provides that no state shall "deny any person within its jurisdiction the equal protection of the laws." Unlike the due process clause this clause is not tied to the protection of any particular interest in property, public or private. The modern law of equal protection confers upon the states a massive degree of discretion for dealing with property and other economic issues (*Minnesota v. Clover Leaf Creamery Co.*, 449 U.S. 456 [1981]) because such is not regarded as either a "fundamental right" like voting (*Harper v. Virginia State Board of Elections*, 383 U.S. 663 [1966]); or a "suspect classification" like race (see *Brown v. Board of Education*, 347 U.S. 483 [1954]). Neither gloss on the clause, however, appears to be compelled by the text, or even consistent with its general language. The principle of equal protection is stated in universal terms:

no state shall deny *any person* equal protection of the laws. Accordingly the clause seems to prohibit any invidious classification that the state makes among its citizens, wholly without regard to fundamental right or suspect classification.

Viewed in this expanded light, the public trust cases appear to fall under the clause. When property is conveyed out of public trust for inadequate consideration, some citizens receive disproportionate benefits, while others receive disproportionate losses. The uncompensated transfer of public property to private use thus disadvantages some at the expense of others. Those who have come up short under the transfer have been denied the equal protection of the law. Success or failure under the equal protection clause thus turns on the presence or absence of compensation when property rights are taken. This close connection between disproportionate impact and just compensation is not simply invented for the occasion. It is quite explicit in the ordinary eminent domain cases. "The Fifth Amendment's guarantee that private property shall not be taken for a public use without just compensation was designed to bar Government from forcing some people alone to bear public burdens which, in all fairness and justice, should be borne by the public as a whole" (*Armstrong v. United States*, 364 U.S. 40, 49; [1960]; Epstein 1985a, p. 204). This "equal protection" dimension of the eminent domain problem arises with equal force in the public trust cases as well. The net losers under the transfer have not received equal protection of the law.

Conclusion

The preceding discussion has examined the public trust doctrine in the area of its birth. In closing it is worth asking how far the doctrine can be extended. From the above arguments the scope should be broad indeed. So long as one deals with property which is held by the people in common in the original position, then its disposition is governed by the public trust doctrine as formulated in *Illinois Central*. Some sense of the sweep of the doctrine is captured by Professor Sax (1970, p. 566) in his early and influential treatment of the subject:

> It is clear that the judicial techniques developed in public trust cases need not be limited either to these few conventional interests [e.g. rivers, streams or parklands] or to questions of disposition of public properties. Public trust problems are found whenever governmental regulation comes into question, and they occur in a wide range of situations in which diffuse public interests need protection against tightly organized groups with clear and immediate goals.[7]

The source of the danger is evident. Well organized political groups may

---

[7] Sax then adds rights of way for utilities, wetland regulation, and air pollution to the list of questions. But the comprehensive scope of the theory goes further.

well be able to obtain net transfers from legislation. As such, the connection between the defects of the political process and the public trust doctrine is as explicit as the connection between the defects of the political
process and the eminent domain clause (Epstein 1985a). As the takings
clause, in my view, reaches all forms of taxation and regulation, it should
not be surprising that the public trust doctrine has a similar scope.

The closeness of the public trust doctrine and the eminent domain power
can be shown in yet another way. Thus far the inquiry has taken place on
the assumption that all property held by the public was acquired by it in
the original position. That assumption is clearly false in the modern setting,
where enormous amounts of property held on the public account have been
acquired by either purchase (with tax dollars) or condemnation. With
respect to property so acquired the eminent domain principle and the public
trust principle now converge. The two principles impose identical limitations on the disposition that public officials can make of public property.
The nature of the limitations could be quite substantial, and it might be
appropriate in closing to mention a few illustrations of their reach. Assume
that land has been condemned for use as a public highway. If it is thereafter
held in public trust, then it is highly questionable whether the state may
allow some individuals free access to the highways which it denies to others.
There is thus serious doubt as to whether the state can issue licenses for
commercial transportation to some firms, while denying those licenses to
others. At the very least it should be required to sell those licenses in a
competitive market, so that the gain from the license remains with the
public at large. The elaborate prerogatives of licensing bus and taxi services on a favored basis is more than nettlesome. It is an impermissible
diversion of public assets to some persons to the exclusion of others.

The same point of course applies with respect to exclusive franchises
over public waters. The great case of *Gibbons v. Ogden* (22 U.S. [9 Wheat]
1 [1824]), for example, involved a grant by the state of New York to
Livingston and Fulton of the exclusive right to run steamships in New York
Harbor. The grant was held to be invalid because it was preempted by
federal statutes enacted pursuant to the power of Congress to regulate
commerce among the several states. If the analysis above is correct, exclusive grants of that sort are improper diversions of public resources under
the public trust, even if authorized by Congress. There is little reason to
believe that a system of monopoly control promises superior social results
to one of free entry, and in any event, there was no evidence that Livingston
and Fulton paid full value for the franchise that they so acquired.

Over a broad range of cases, then, the public trust and the eminent
domain theory impose in principle parallel restrictions upon the application
of government power, no matter what the original distribution of rights.
This is as it should be, for a comprehensive theory of governance should be

able to account for all forms of government control of property, regardless of whether that property is public or private in the original position.

References

Ely, John Hart. *Democracy and Distrust: A Theory of Judicial Review.* Cambridge: Harvard University Press, 1980.

Epstein, Richard A. "Possession as the Root of Title." *Georgia Law Review* 13 (1979): 1221-43.

Epstein, Richard A. *Takings: Private Property and the Power of Eminent Domain.* Cambridge: Harvard University Press, 1985a.

Epstein, Richard. "Why Restrain Alienation?" *Columbia Law Review* 85 (1985b): 970-90.

Epstein, Richard A. "An Outline of Takings." *Miami Law Review* 41 (1986): 3-19.

Grant, J.A.C. "The 'Higher Law' Background of the Law of Eminent Domain." *Wisconsin Law Review* 6 (1931): 67-85.

Hardin, Garett. "The Tragedy of the Commons." *Science* 162 (1968): 1243-48.

Holderness, Clifford. "A Legal Foundation for Exchange." *Journal of Legal Studies* 14 (1985): 321-44.

Locke, John. *Of Civil Government, Second Treatise* (1690).

Rose, Carol. "The Comedy of the Commons: Custom, Commerce, and Inherently Public Property." *University of Chicago Law Review* 53 (1986): 711-81.

Sax, Joseph. "The Public Trust Doctrine in Natural Resource Law: Effective Judicial Intervention." *Michigan Law Review* 68 (1970): 471-566.

Sax, Joseph. "Liberating the Public Trust Doctrine from its Historical Shackles." in *The Public Trust Doctrine in Natural Resources Law and Management.* Edited by Harrison C. Dunning. 1981.

15

ECONOMIC FREEDOM AND THE CONSTITUTION: THE DESIGN OF THE FRAMERS
Forrest McDonald

Among the mistakes historians tend to make when seeking to understand the past, one of the most common is that of judging intentions from results. Thus when we observe that a liberal economic order rapidly began to emerge after the adoption of the Constitution, it is easy to conclude that the authors of the Constitution had such an order in mind. This inference is lent credence by the fact that the Framers, almost to a man, agreed that the purpose of government is to secure men in their Lockean trilogy of rights to life, liberty, and property. John Adams, like most of the Founding generation, could wax eloquent on the subject:

> "The moment the idea is admitted into society, that property is not as sacred as the laws of god, and that there is not a force of law and public justice to protect it, anarchy and tyranny commence. If 'THOU SHALT NOT COVET,' and 'THOU SHALT NOT STEAL,' were not commandments of Heaven, they must be made inviolable precepts in every society, before it can be civilized or made free." [1850-56, Vol. 6, p.9)

As is usual with pivotal historical moments, however, the emergence of a free politico-economic system in America was considerably more complex than might appear in retrospect. It is true that broad and general forces had been moving America in that direction for a long time before 1787. Between 1697 and 1774 the volume of trade between Britain and its mainland colonies had increased almost tenfold, and despite Parliamentary enactments that trade had been carried on with but minimal restraint by government. Yet if we look more closely we see that economic activity in America was far more fettered than would at first appear and, indeed, that the weight of law, tradition, philosophical values, and—especially after 1776—ideology was such as to make the emergence of a liberal regime seem almost impossible.

Forest McDonald is a Professor of History at the University of Alabama.

I shall attempt to demonstrate, in the pages that follow, that the Framers were divided in their views as to the kind of economic order the United States should have; that, as a result, the Constitution leaves the question open; that it was only when the new government was put in place that the nation became committed to a developmental, entrepreneurial, capitalistic economy; and that resistance to that commitment persisted for many decades afterwards, providing a foundation for a return to statism in the twentieth century.

Obstacles to the Development of a Liberal Economy

Let us begin with the obstacles, of which the legal may be considered first. Property law in America was based upon English common law, which meant that it was based ultimately upon the medieval concepts of fair value and just price. Every state had adopted the English prohibitions of "offenses against public trade," which banned usury, regulated the price of bread, and forbade such practices as "forestalling" (buying or contracting commodities on their way to market), "regrating" (buying and reselling products in the same market), and "engrossing" (buying large quantities of commodities with intent to sell them again). The common law of contract was particularly incongruent with the free interchange of goods, for it made *choses in action*—evidences of money, goods, or services due but not in hand—unassignable. If, for example, Smith borrowed money from Jones and gave as security a note promising to repay the sum and lawful interest in one year, Jones could not sell the note to a third party. Such restrictions greatly impeded the development of paper credit, the life's blood of free commerce. Moreover, freedom of contract was further impaired by the jury system: under American law until after the War of 1812 (and much longer in some jurisdictions), juries retained the power to rule on matters of law as well as matters of fact, and interventions into contractual commercial relations, particularly efforts of creditors to collect from debtors, were extremely common. And on top of all the multitudes of legal restraints, there was mercantilism: vehemently as colonial Americans had protested the British mercantilist system, every American state enacted a mercantilist system of its own as soon as independence was won.

It has been argued, especially by the Canadian C.B. Macpherson (1962) and his disciples, that American's embracing of the philosophy of John Locke (which underlay the Declaration of Independence) amounted to acceptance of the theory of possessive individualism—the proposition that individuals have an absolute right to pursue private gain and that if they are allowed to do so the public interest will be served. But as a close reading of his work will reveal, Locke's theories of property rights were in spirit much more consonant with medieval communitarian economic ideas than with those of nineteenth century liberalism. Locke did maintain that natural law "gives every Man a Title to the product of his honest Industry, and the fair Acquisitions of his Ancestors descended to him"; but he also held that there were divinely imposed limits upon the amount that a man could accumulate. No man could amass such a "Portion of the things of this World" as to deprive "his needy Brother a Right to the Surplusage of his Goods." In other words, a man could only acquire and keep as much as he could consume, and natural law "gives every Man a Title to so much out of another's Plenty, as will keep him from extream want" (Locke, p. 188). That idea—that the poor have a natural right to the surpluses of the rich—was perpetuated in the late eighteenth century and the first few decades of the nineteenth through William Paley's *Principles of Moral and Political Philosophy* (1775), which was the textbook for the mandatory course in moral philosophy in every American college. This is hardly the stuff of which laissez-faire economic systems are made.

Another set of obstacles arose from the agrarian tradition and the mystique of the land. Jefferson's oft-quoted opinion—" . . . those who labor in the earth are the chosen people of God if ever He had a chosen people, in whose breasts He has made His peculiar deposit for substantial and genuine virtue"—was widely shared in America, as was its counterpart horror of the urbanization that attends economic growth: "the mobs of great cities add just so much to the support of pure government, as sores do to the strength of the human body." These prejudices found expression in a variety of ways. One was the ubiquitous landed property qualification for the suffrage and the larger such requirement for officeholders, which insured that government would be dominated by the landed interest, not the commercial, manufacturing, or financial. Another was that the only route to wealth that was universally acceptable, socially, was land speculation: the acquisition of large tracts of vacant land from government and the subsequent resale of farm-sized units to the hordes of immigrants who arrived throughout the century. Chronically, land speculation diverted capital, in a capital-starved country, from productive investment.

But the agrarian tradition stood in the way of economic development in more specific, explicitly anti-capitalistic ways as well. Though the tradition had its roots in a pastoral ideal that extended all the way back to Virgil if not beyond, the version of it most immediately absorbed by Americans was that formulated by Henry St. John, First Viscount Bolingbroke, and his circle of English Tory friends. Bolingbroke had led the opposition to the ministry of Sir Robert Walpole, which guided the Financial Revolution that transformed England into the first modern capitalistic state by monetizing its public debt during the 1720s and 1730s. Bolingbroke and His Circle glorified landholders and excoriated "money men," coining a veritable litany of opposition to finance capitalism that warped the perspective of Americans as they imbibed it and established among them what has aptly been described as a paranoid political style. Both style and language were evident when the Jeffersonians "discovered" that the Hamiltonian fiscal system was a "monocrotic plot," and the same would be true when the Jacksonians, the Populists, and the New Dealers discovered their particular plutocratic conspiracies. (One indication of the perdurance of the anticapitalistic vocabulary of Bolingbrokean agrarianism is that in 1727 John Gay, a member of the circle, penned a satirical "Beggar's Opera" attacking Walpole which, two centuries later, the German Marxists Kurt Weil and Bertolt Brecht could modify only slightly and stage as that most bitter of attacks on capitalism, the "Threepenny Opera.")

Powerfully reinforcing agrarianism was the American commitment to republicanism, which was made partly as a by-product of the classical revival and partly as a consequence of rejecting monarchy. Only recently have historians re-learned that classical republicanism and the commercial spirit were absolutely antithetical. Plato had recommended that no republic should be established either on the sea or on a large river, for that "would expose it to the dangers of commerce." Lycurgus, in establishing the much-admired republic of Sparta, had forbidden all trade. Montesquieu, the latest word on the subject, averred that if people were "allowed to dispose of [their] property to whom and how [they] pleased," then "the republic will be utterly undone" (Montesquieu 1949; Pocock 1975).

The reason for republicanism's incompatibility with free commercial activity lay in the concept that the life-giving principle of republics was virtue—not in a moral or ethical sense, but in the sense of manliness and unremitting devotion to the welfare of the republic. The opposite of manly virtue was effeminacy, a taste for luxury and refinements and voluptuous pleasures that commercial intercourse invariably induced. It was assumed without question that, once such a taste was acquired, a republic was doomed to corruption, decay, and death.

The hostility of republican ideologues toward commerce and credit was almost hysterical. John Adam's rantings on the subject were typical. "Credit has been the Inlet to most of the Luxury & Folly which has yet infected our People," he wrote. "He who could devise a method to abolish it forever, would deserve a Statue to his Memory" (King, p. 182). Benjamin Franklin, who did not agree with Adams on many things, nonetheless shared that attitude. He characterized all commerce as "generally cheating," and wrote bitterly of its corrupting and debilitating effects. Of Americans who wanted to forsake the simple life for the riches of manufacturing and trade, Franklin said "I can put them in a way to obtain a Share of it. Let them with three fourths of the People of Ireland, live the Year round on Potatoes and Buttermilk, without Shirts, then may their Merchants export Beef, Butter, and Linen. Let them, with the Generality of the Common People of Scotland go Barefoot, then may they make large Exports in Shoes and Stockings: And if they will be content to wear Rags like the Spinners and Weavers of England, they may make Cloths and Stuffs for all Parts of the World" (McCoy, p. 605-28). In that spirit, the legislatures of every state enacted sumptuary legislation, prohibiting the importation and consumption of luxuries; and the newspapers teemed with articles insisting that they should do more.

It is true that there was one model of a successful commercial republic available to Americans, that of Venice. But the image of the Venetian republic had become thoroughly tarnished by the time of the American Revolution (the Essex Result in 1778 points accusingly at the republics of Venice and Holland which "have degenerated into insupportable tyrannies"), partly because of the city's decline and partly because Thomas Otway's popular play *Venice Preserved* depicted it as a corrupt oligarchy, "where all agree to spoil the public good, And villains fatten with the brave man's labours."[1]

Ideas Influencing the Framers of the Constitution

The Framers of the Constitution were familiar with, though by no means uniformly sympathetic to, three bodies of thought which offered paths around these obstacles and toward a liberal regime. All, interestingly, were the work of Scotsmen: William Murray (Lord Mansfield), Sir James Steuart, and Adam Smith and David Hume.

Mansfield, in his capacity as chief justice of the Court of the King's Bench from 1756 to 1788, had wrought a revolution in English law. In a series of decisions he had wrenched the law from its medieval, land-centered roots and transformed it into a code well-calculated to facilitate free commercial intercourse. He reshaped the law of promissory notes, bills of exchange, bank drafts, and contracts to make them flexible and responsive to the market, and he established the new field of marine insurance. By the time he was done, the *lex mercatoria* (the informal body of practices which had long governed transactions among international merchants) had been systematized and made into a pervasive part of the domestic law of Great Britain.

Though none of Mansfield's innovations had been incorporated into American law, most American lawyers and many laymen were thoroughly aware of what he had done and how he had done it. South of the Potomac and in much of New England disapproval was widespread, not least because Mansfield had, as a necessary means to his end, contrived a number of devices for circumventing juries in civil cases—a practice which, as a

[1] For greater detail, see Horwitz (1977), Kramnick (1968), and Parker (1975).

Virginian put it, did not "accord with the free institutions of this country." It is important to understand that, as long as juries could decide the law the legal changes necessary for the triumph of capitalism could not take place; and Americans guarded the prerogatives of their juries jealously. As a Bostonian said, "to render the jury incompetent to law, is to depreciate the character of every other man in society but practitioners of it." But there were a number of lawyers and merchants, especially concentrated in New York and Philadelphia, who were eager to effect a Mansfield-style revolution in America. Possibly as many as a dozen men who were so inclined served as delegates in the Constitutional Convention, (Horowitz, p.142).

Steuart's oeuvre was a powerful treatise entitled *An Inquiry into the Principles of Political Oeconomy* (1767). In essence, the *Inquiry* is an extensive analysis of the means by which Britain had developed what Steuart called an "exchange economy," and a companion analysis of the reasons for the failure of John Law's efforts to accomplish the same thing in France. Four premises underlie Steuart's thinking. The first is that though there are "natural" economic "laws," disasters can result if economic activity is not carefully supervised. Therefore Steuart emphasizes that "I constantly suppose a statesman at the head of government, systematically conducting every part of it, so as to prevent the vicissitudes of manners, and innovations . . . from hurting any interest within the community," (p. 122). If that statement is taken literally, as contemporaries tended to take it, Steuart's meaning is lost. Steuart's "statesman" is not one who attempts to direct the economy in its day to day operations, which are best left to individual bargainers in the marketplace. Rather, his "statesman" is a minister who attends to general trends and takes measures to prevent violent disruptions in the course of trade. Moreover, Steuart rejects a regime of absolute power; he insists that any exchange economy is incompatible with arbitrary government and is most compatible with liberty, law, and free government.

Steuart's second premise is that different policies are appropriate at different phases in the growth of an exchange economy. In what he calls the "infant" phase, industries are to be encouraged through protective tariffs, bounties, and the whole range of mercantilist devices. Once industries are well established, however, all such encouragements are to be withdrawn, because they impede growth in the next phase—the "foreign" phase, or the period of international trade, when the interest of the nation requires freedom of trade. During this phase, rulers are to "banish luxury," which was encouraged during the infant phase, and to "fix the lowest standard of prices possible." Luxury continues to advance industry by stimulating workers to produce it, but the statesman's role is now "to remove the seat of it from his own country." Finally, when the country reaches the mature phase, that of "inland" trade, it can once again encourage domestic luxury and consumption, (Steuart, pp. 260-65).

Steuart's third underlying principle is that bullion is an inadequate money supply and that provision must be made for the paper monetization of all alienable things, goods, and services. This is done by developing institutionalized forms of credit, whereby "solid property" is made liquid. "Symbolic money"—bonds, notes, mortgages, accounts, and other instruments—enables those who own the land and other properties "which by their nature cannot circulate (and which, by-the-bye, are the principle cause of inequality), to give, to the full extent of all their worth, an adequate circulating equivalent for the services they demand. In other words, it is a method of melting down, as it were, the very causes of inequality, and of rendering fortunes equal," (Steuart, pp. 316-17).

The fourth premise is that the most efficacious way of monetizing the whole economy is by establishing a monetized public debt, which will create a huge fund of "symbolic money" that can supply the means with which banks and other institutions can "melt down" all the rest. Steuart insists that no new property is created by doing this. If a nation collects 5 million pounds a year in revenues and spends it, or if it borrows 100 million pounds at five percent to pay perpetual interest, it has not created any new wealth, but has only allocated the same resources differently. Yet is has increased the circulating medium greatly by "melting down" the taxing power, (Steuart, pp. 532-63, and pp. 599-609).

Steuart's ideas were obviously incompatible with both the agrarian ideal and republican ideology; but even so they gained a number of American adherents, most importantly Alexander Hamilton. Moreover, during the 1780s the main ingredient necessary for fashioning an economy of the kind Steuart described—a large public debt—was present in America for the first time. During the colonial era, American governments had expended minimal sums except in times of war, and they had financed their wars by issuing fiat money that depreciated rapidly and could be painlessly taxed out of existence. Huge amounts of fiat money were also issued during the Revolutionary War, but in addition the Continental Congress and the states took on public debts which, in 1787, amounted to nearly $80 million and had proved to be a crushing burden upon normal economic activity, (U.S. Department of Commerce, 1975). Hamilton and everyone else who had read Steuart knew how to use the debts in a liberating way—provided that government were given the necessary powers.

The third route toward a liberal regime, that charted by Hume and Smith, was quite an opposite one: whereas Steuart proposed that the power of government be used to cause such a regime to come into being, Hume and Smith insisted that if government left things alone a free and expanding economy would emerge spontaneously because every individual "necessarily endeavors" to direct his industry so "that its produce may be of the greatest possible value" (Smith, p. 455). Thus human industry, "if left to itself, will naturally find its way to the most useful and profitable employment." Indeed, it was at least in part a desire to stem the influence of Steuart's *Inquiry* that led Smith to publish *The Wealth of Nations,* as is attested by one of Smith's best-known lines: "The statesman, who should attempt to direct people in what manner they ought to employ their capitals, would not only load himself with a most unnecessary attention, but assume an authority which could safely be trusted, not only to no single person, but to no council or senate whatever, and which would nowhere be so dangerous as in the hands of a man who had folly and presumption enough to fancy himself fit to exercise it" (p. 456). Smith and Hume also lambasted Steuart for his endorsement of a monetized public debt, both being convinced that the ever-growing British national debt would lead to bankruptcy.

Smith and Hume met with a favorable reception in the United States, the warmth of the response generally increasing as one moved from North to South. Their writings, however, contained a disturbing feature. Both believed in the natural progress of society from primitive hunting and gathering economies up through a succession of stages to herding, to tillage agriculture, to commerce, and so on. Each stage is accompanied by improvements and refinements, but beyond a certain point the bad begins to outweighs the good; for ultimately all the land is taken up, the dispossessed drift into cities, and the drudgery of factory life begins for the masses. Smith's well-known example of the increased productivity resulting from the division of labor in a pin factory is counter-balanced by the appalling picture he draws of the consequences for factory workers. Every worker "becomes as stupid and ignorant as it is possible for a human creature to become." They are the worst of citizens, and yet "in every improved and civilized society this is the state into which . . . the great body of the people, must necessarily fall, unless government takes some pains to prevent it" (Smith, p. 782).

The Political Economy of the Constitution

Let us now bring all this to bear on the question, what kind of system of political economy did the Framers of the Constitution have in contemplation? A casual reading of the document is sufficient to indicate that its adoption did not terminate the old order in a single stroke. Somewhat closer attention will reveal that it did make a transformation to a liberal regime possible. Still more careful scrutiny, including some consideration of the debates in the Constitutional Convention, is necessary if we are to ascertain which if any of the Founding Fathers intended that such a transformation should take place.

Broadly speaking, those features of the Constitution which bear upon the question are of two general descriptions. One group of provisions is specific, being built directly into the instrument itself; the others, establishing the rules for the levying of taxes and making provision for the public debts, are more open-ended, leaving a large measure of discretion to Congress.

Several of the specific features of the Constitution were tilted strongly in favor of a free market system. One consisted of the provisions which made the United States the largest area of free trade, meaning trade unimpeded by tariff barriers or other restrictions, in the world. Others include the prohibition of the taxing of exports and those provisions that empower Congress to establish uniform weights and measures. (Equally important was the rejection by the convention, over the protests of the Old Republican from Virginia, George Mason, of a proposal to give Congress power to enact sumptuary legislation.) Perhaps the most important specific provisions are those in Article I, Section 10, which restrict the powers of the states. Some of the prohibitions on the states are political rather than economic, but the crucial clause in the section, and the one which pointed the United States most directly toward a capitalistic future, is the contract clause: "No state shall pass any Law impairing the Obligation of Contracts." If it be read broadly, literally, unequivocally, and without regard to the context of the times, the contract clause alone would seem to indicate that the Founding Fathers rejected the existing economic order and endorsed the order that was to come. How they meant it to be read, however, was far from self-evident; two full generations of adjudication would be required to establish a free-market-oriented interpretation of it.

As for provisions concerning the taxing power, these evolved in the convention with surprisingly little friction. With a minimum of discord, the delegates agreed to vest Congress with a full range of taxing powers, limited only by the requirements that taxes be levied solely for national purposes, that they be uniform throughout the United States, and that direct taxes be proportionate to population. The prohibition of state taxes on imports and exports also met with little resistance.

Agreement on provision for the public debts was far less readily attained. When the matter was first broached on July 18, 1787, general dissatisfaction was expressed with the phraseology and the subject was dropped. It came up again several times in August, amidst Bolingbrokean charges that public securities had been bought at greatly depreciated prices by "Blood-suckers who had speculated on the distresses of others," and amidst demands that provision be made for discrimination between original creditors and speculators. Finally, to cool the tempers that the issue raised, Edmund Randolph of Virginia proposed the neutral wording which, with minor modifications, was approved in the finished Constitution: "All Debts contracted and Engagements entered into, before the Adoption of this

Constitution, shall be as valid against the United States under this Constitution, as under the Confederation."

That method of dealing with the emotionally laden issue of the public debts—in essence, by passing the buck to the First Congress—accomplished its purpose, for the question was not frequently agitated during the contests over ratification. Unfortunately, it also obscured the intentions of the Framers in regard to how the public debt should figure in the future course of American economic development. Even so, it is possible to reconstruct the attitudes of most of the delegates. By my reckoning, Alexander Hamilton and sixteen more of the fifty-five members of the convention—slightly fewer than a third—viewed, or were persuaded to view, the constitutional provisions regarding public debts as the instrument for the creation of a modern capitalistic order. On the other hand, thirteen delegates indicated during the convention, in the course of their opposition to ratification, or by their opposition in the First Congress, that they were hostile to that view. The views of the remaining twenty-five delegates cannot be definitely ascertained, but from what is known of them it seems probable that all but six or eight would have been in the opposition.

Hamilton's Fiscal Program[2]

The public debt was not the only potentially divisive issue that the convention avoided by passing the buck to the First Congress. The Constitution was left uncompleted in several other important particulars: the bill of rights, the appointment and removal powers of the president, the structure of the judiciary, the makeup and responsibilities of the executive departments. In each of these areas the work of the First Congress amounted to a continuation of the labors of the Constitutional Convention; and so it was, too, with the enactment of the fiscal program devised by Alexander Hamilton. Indeed, Hamilton's program may justly be regarded both as the completion of the Constitution and as the means by which life was breathed into the document. For that reason, and because it is central to the question at hand, a brief review of Hamilton's system is necessary, together with an analysis of what he intended it to accomplish and of what it did accomplish.[3]

Hamilton regarded the public debt as a means of effecting a social revolution. He proposed to use it to erect a system in which the value of all things would be measured in the marketplace, with money as the criterion—and thus to create a social order in which success, status, and power would derive from merit and industry rather than, as in the existing

[2] The section borrows freely from McDonald (1982).
[3] This section is developed in McDonald (1979).

scheme of things, from inherited property or social position. In so doing he would be rewarding effort and punishing idleness, and thereby rousing his countrymen from what he saw as "voluptuous indolence" and stimulating them to do the work that would make themselves rich and their nation great.

The first step in Hamilton's grand undertaking was to transform the public debt into the basis of a stable but elastic currency system. Though a number of congressmen had, by the end of 1789, come to think along those lines, a considerable majority had something quite different in view: they wanted to extinguish the debt in the simplest and most expeditious way possible, provided that the means were consistent with national honor and justice to the creditors. Several, in fact, wanted to extinguish it by means that were not consistent with honor and justice: repudiating all or part of the debt, devaluing it, buying it on the open market at deflated prices, and/or discriminating against present holders of the securities if they were not the original creditors. A goodly number of congressmen were therefore surprised when Hamilton, in his "First Report on the Public Credit," did not suggest ways of paying the debt, at par or otherwise, but instead proposed that it be "funded"—that is, that Congress should provide for regular interest payments by a permanent appropriation of essentially mortgaged revenues, rather than by making annual appropriations, and that the question of retiring the principal of the debt be left to the discretion of government. Hamilton made his aim specific—to transform the public debt into a *substitute for money.*

His proposal was as follows. The foreign debt would be placed on a regular interest-paying basis and, as principal payments came due, be refinanced in the Netherlands. The domestic debt would be refinanced on a different basis. Holders of the outstanding public securities of various kinds, including creditors of the states as well as the nation, would be invited to subscribe to a new loan by exchanging their old paper for new government securities. The pledging of permanent revenues for interest payments on the new securities would help raise their market value. To augment that rise, Hamilton provided in his plan for the establishment of a "sinking fund," whose purpose was not to retire the debt but to buy and sell public securities on the open market with the intention of stabilizing their market prices at par. To prevent the debt from increasing in future beyond the capacity of the government to service it, Hamilton insisted that adequate new revenues be pledged specifically to cover any new debts that might be taken on.

The genius of the system lay in Hamilton's understanding of the nature of money. Money is whatever people believe is money and use as money; as Hamilton put it, "opinion" is the soul of it. If it became a fixed opinion in the public mind that government securities were equal in value to and readily interchangeable with gold and silver, people would accept the securities in most transactions as the equivalent of money, and they would therefore be money.

After a long and acrimonious debate Hamilton's proposals were enacted into law on August 4, 1790. The result was the almost instantaneous transformation of the public debt from a paralyzing economic liability into highly liquid capital. Moreover, an enormous store of new capital was created in the bargain: the market value of the entire domestic public debt a few months before Hamilton took office had been around $15 million, and by the end of 1790 it was around $45 million. And then, during the next two years, a second transformation took place. Forty new corporations—as many as had been chartered in the entire period before the Constitution—were created, nine for banks which further multiplied the supply of capital, the remainder for manufacturing and canal companies; and public securities furnished almost all the capital.

Meanwhile, Hamilton had proposed and Congress had enacted the next phase of his plan, the establishment of the Bank of the United States (Syrett, Vol. 7, pp. 236-342). The key feature of the banking system lay in the using of the public debt as the basis for the nation's currency. Investors could pay four-fifths of their subscriptions to the bank's stock in government securities at par, which incidentally increased the market value of the securities still further. Against its total capital of $8 million in government securities and $2 million in specie, the bank could circulate $10 million in notes which, together with the notes of the state-chartered banks, would serve as the country's principal medium of exchange. Basing the currency upon bank notes instead of gold and silver had profound consequences. The crucial characteristic of banking currency is that it is money created in the present, not out of past savings but out of the expectation of future income. Furthermore, since it was inherent in Hamilton's system that money and capital were interchangeable, capital as well as money could be created through the institutionalization of future expectations. This meant that the nation's economic development could be financed on credit without the need for collateral: the collateral was the future.

It is to be observed that Hamilton had followed Sir James Steuart's guidelines in every respect but one. Hamilton did not propose to establish a system that a "statesman" would need to guide at every turn. Rather, he was (in the jargon of economists) structuring market alternatives, rechanneling the flow of commercial activity in the directions that Smith and Hume thought "natural" but which experience had shown to require human artifice to bring about. Once that great engineering feat was accomplished, the statesman's job was done. As someone mistakenly said of the Constitution, Hamilton had created "a machine that would go of itself."

The bill to establish the Bank of the United States met with a celebrated constitutional debate. James Madison and Thomas Jefferson both contended that Congress, in the absence of specific constitutional authorization, had no power to create a bank Hamilton's rebuttal, which persuaded President Washington to sign the bill into law, was devastating, profound, and conclusive: to those who would understand what the Constitutional Convention had wrought—whatever its members had intended to do or thought they were doing—his opinion on the constitutionality of the bank is indispensable reading. The convention's crucial action was the very establishment of a government, for from that action a great deal else necessarily flowed. "Every power vested in a Government," Hamilton pointed out, "is in its nature sovereign, and includes by force of the term, a right to employ all the means requisite, and fairly applicable to the attainment of the ends of such power" unless such means are expressly forbidden by the Constitution, (Syrett, Vol. 8, p. 98). As Chief Justice John Marshall was to rule in *McCulloch v. Maryland* (1819): "The powers of government are limited, and its limits are not to be transcended. But let the end be legitimate, let it be within the scope of the constitution, and all means which are appropriate, which are plainly adapted to that end, which are not prohibited, but consist with the letter and spirit of the constitution, are constitutional."

Given such extensive powers, and given the convention's open-ended language regarding matters of public finance, the First Congress had been vested with the awesome choice of determining what kind of political economy the nation should have. Most Americans, in all likelihood, would have chosen otherwise, but Congress opted for the Hamiltonian way. The United States would be built under a government-channeled, government-encouraged, and sometimes government-subsidized system of private enterprise for personal profit, in which the market would be the ultimate arbiter.

From the Founding to the Present

The choices made between 1787 and 1791 guided the course of American development for more than a century and a half, and during that time the American nation marched to greatness—as the richest, freest, and most powerful political society in the history of the world, and as a beacon light unto mankind. After that began another and sadder story. Both stories are beyond the scope of this essay, but there is space to suggest their general outlines.

To do so one must start, as people were fond of saying in the eighteenth century, with a consideration of first principles, with the Founding Fathers' basic assumptions about the nature of man and society. In regard to both political and economic life, their first premise was that man is governed not by virtue or reason but by his passions, meaning desires for self-gratification, and is happiest when left alone to pursue those desires. The secondary premise of the syllogism, however, was different in politics from what it was in economics. In politics the secondary premise was that none are safe in pursuing their desires for self-gratification unless all are restrained by a government of laws. The conclusion was that government is therefore necessary to provide a maximum of liberty consistent with the safety and well-being of both individuals and society. In economics the secondary premise was that men are interdependent and, in pursuit of self-gratification, find it necessary to gratify others. As Adam Smith (p. 27) put it, "It is not from the benevolence of the butcher, the brewer or the baker that we expect our dinner, but from their regard of their own interest." The conclusion was that the material prosperity of a society will therefore be best served if all its members are at liberty, under law, to pursue their personal gain.

The Constitution and the Hamiltonian system of political economy embodied these principles into fundamental law. Now, the idea of fundamental law can most readily be understood if one conceives of political and economic activity as games played in accordance with rules: fundamental law is the rule book, defining the objects of the game and specifying how it is to be played. The constitution was the rule book for government, the Hamiltonian system for the economy. But the political and economic games, as played in America, differ from ordinary games in two key respects. One is that they are open-ended rather than zero-sum: there can be many winners and there need not be any losers. The other is that the games are interrelated: winners in the money game can influence the course of the political game, and winners in the political game can change the rules of the money game.

These arrangements proved to be remarkably stable. They remained essentially intact despite wars, territorial expansion, population growth, and a technological revolution that transformed the world into something the Founding Fathers would not have recognized. There were changes in the system, to be sure. The Supreme Court under Roger Brooke Taney interpreted the Constitution differently from the way it had been under John Marshall, and Taney's successors interpreted it differently still. The Jeffersonians and Jacksonians attacked and temporarily destroyed the Hamiltonian fiscal apparatus, and the Hamilton-Jefferson feud was, in different forms, repeatedly refought in the twentieth century. But what was happening, as long as the American story was a success story, was that the rules of the game were being changed to expand the base of players who could compete successfully; the object of the game remained the same. This continued to be true even through Franklin Roosevelt's New Deal and Harry Truman's Fair Deal. Despite the stretching of the Constitution during those administrations, the federal government over which Dwight Eisenhower presided in the 1950s was still recognizably the one over which George Washington had presided in the 1790s; and despite Roosevelt's and

Truman's rhetorical attacks on big business, both were seeking to make capitalism work more effectively and equitably, not to destroy it.

Then came the sadder story. In the 1960s the federal government, under the presidency of Lyndon Johnson and the chief justiceship of Earl Warren, launched a massive, all-out effort to extend the system far beyond the limits of what was possible. The fruits of the effort, besides a general loss of faith in the system when the effort failed, were a Court that legislates rather than adjudicates and a metastasized federal bureaucracy. The Court, driven by a mindless compulsion to legislate equality, has all but abolished the idea of a written constitution which means what it says. The bureaucracy, driven by a mindless compulsion to run everything, has all but abolished the idea that rewards are to be commensurate with effort as measured in the marketplace.

Between them, the Court and the bureaucracy have made government as oppressive and arbitrary as under a feudal baron, and the resemblance to feudalism does not end there. Despite some deregulation during the presidency of Ronald Reagan, government edicts continue to drive us toward zero economic growth (a goal that no small number of bureaucratic agencies actively espouse). Zero economic growth necessarily makes economic activity a zero-sum game; and that, in turn, locks people into the relative socio-economic positions into which they were born. Along the way, the "exploitation rate," meaning the percentage of a producer's output that is taken away from him, reaches in the form of taxes alone more than 40 percent—as much as the exploitation rate under serfdom, and twice the rate under antebellum Southern slavery.

To conclude: The Constitution was not originally designed to establish capitalism in America, but constitutional government and capitalism became inextricably intertwined at the outset. They were born together, they lived together, they prospered together, and—unless we return to first principles, and soon—they will die together.

References

Adams, John. *The Works of John Adams*. Vol. 6 , edited by C. F. Adams. Boston: Little, Brown, & Co., 1850-56.

Farrand, Max, Ed. *The Records of the Federal Convention of 1787*, 4 Vols. New Haven: Yale University Press, 1937.

Horwitz, Morton J. *The Transformation of American Law*, 1780-1860. Cambridge: Harvard University Press, 1977.

Jefferson, Thomas. *Basic Writings of Thomas Jefferson*. Vol 1., edited by P. S. Foner. New York: Wiley Book Co., 1944.

Jefferson, Thomas. *The Papers of Thomas Jefferson*. 21 Vols., edited by Julian P. Boyd, et. al. Princeton, N. J.: Princeton University Press, 1950-1982.

King, Rufus. *The Life and Correspondence of Rufus King.* 6 Vols., edited by Charles R. King. New York: 1894-1900.

Kramnick, Issac. *Bolingbroke and His Circle.* Cambridge: Harvard University Press, 1968.

Locke, John. *Two Treatises of Government.* Edited by Peter Laslett. Cambridge: Cambridge University Press, 1960.

Macpherson, C. B. *The Political Theory of Possessive Individualism: Hobbes to Locke.* Oxford: Clarendon Press, 1962.

McCoy, Drew R. "Benjamin Franklin's Vision of a Republican Political Economy for America." *William and Mary Quarterly* 35 (1978): 605-28.

McDonald, Forrest. *The Phaeton Ride: The Crisis of American Success.* New York: W. W. Norton and Co., 1974.

McDonald, Forrest. *Alexander Hamilton: A Biography.* New York: W. W. Norton and Co., 1979.

McDonald, Forrest. "The Constitution and Hamiltonian Capitalism." In *How Capitalistic is the Constitution?* Edit by Robert A. Goldwin and William A. Schambra. Washington: American Enterprise Institute, 1982.

McDonald, Forrest. *Novus Ordo Seclorum: The Intellectual Origins of the Constitution.* Lawrence: University Press of Kansas, 1985.

Montesquieu, Charles Louis de Secondat, Baron de. *The Spirit of the Laws.* Translated by Thomas Nugent. New York: Hafner Publishing Co., 1949.

Paley, William. *The Principles of Moral and Political Philosophy.* Reprint. Boston: St. Thomas, 1977.

Parker, Roger D. "The Gospel of Opposition: A Study in Eighteenth-Century Anglo-American Ideology." Ph.D. dissertation, Wayne State University, 1975.

Pocock, J. G. A. *The Machiavellian Moment: Florentine Political Thought and the Atlantic Republican Tradition.* Princeton: Princeton University Press, 1975.

Smith, Adam. *An Inquiry Into the Nature and Causes of the Wealth of Nations,* Liberty Classics Edition. Indianapolis: Liberty Press, 1981.

Steuart, James. *An Inquiry Into the Principles of Political Oeconomy,* reprint. Edited by Andrew S. Skinner. Chicago: University of Chicago Press, 1966.

Syrett, Harold C., et. al. ed. *The Papers of Alexander Hamilton,* 26 Vols. New York: Columbia University Press, 1961-1979.

U. S. Department of Commerce. *Historical Statistics of the United States: Colonial Times to 1970.* Washington, D. C.: Government Printing Office, 1975.

16

FEDERALISM: A MARKET ECONOMICS PERSPECTIVE
Robert L. Bish

Introduction

Two very good years were 1776 and 1787. The first of these years saw the publication of Adam Smith's *Wealth of Nations* and the Declaration of Independence, two of the most influential documents in Western thought. The second of these years saw not just the drafting of the U.S. Constitution but, even more important, the initiation of a series of essays by Alexander Hamilton, John Jay, and James Madison, which came to be known, as the *Federalist Papers*. The sense in which these essays may be considered of greater importance than the Constitution rests on the notion that how we think about complex phenomena is usually more important than some objective "truth" about that phenomena; and while any constitution will have problems over time, a way of thinking about it, which is what the *Federalist* presents, may help us find solutions.

During the past dozen years, bicentennial celebrations of Smith's *Wealth of Nations*, the Declaration of Independence, and the Constitution have been publicized extensively, but there has been very little recognition of how close intellectually the ideas in these works are. Indeed, a good case can be made that they are so complementary that an understanding of their implications can be reached only if they are examined together rather than separately. This is especially the case for understanding the *Federalist Papers*; without some understanding of complex systems, such as markets or multi-organizational structures, these essays do not appear to have a con-

Cato Journal, Vol. 7, No. 2 (Fall 1987). Copyright Cato Institute. All rights reserved.

The author is Professor of Public Administration and Economics at the University of Victoria. This paper has benefited from discussions with and comments by Buzz Boschken, Laura Langbein, Vincent Ostrom, Mark Sproule-Jones, and Jeffrey Wallin.

consistent theoretical framework.[1]

In the analyses that follow, the similarities and differences between Smith's approach to markets and social coordination will be compared with the *Federalist's* approach to government. While this method results in some obvious conclusions, they might not be so obvious without the benefit of the last 30 years of intellectual revival, which was based on self-consciously using the logic of economics for institutional analyses. Many of the conclusions of these analyses could be derived as well from the work of James Buchanan, Gordon Tullock, Mancur Olson, Vincent Ostrom, and others associated with public choice theory.

Basic Theory

All theories are abstractions, and any summary of a theory or body of related theories must be selective in features chosen for comparison. For purposes here, I will summarize a few elements of market and federalist theory, including both assumptions and generally recognized conclusions.[2]

Market Economics

Many important elements of market economics have remained unchanged since economics began to emerge as a discipline during the 18th century, including assumptions of scarcity and rational, self-interested behavior.[3] For example, in his *Wealth of Nations*, Smith demonstrated how self-interested behavior could result in a more efficient use of scarce resources and, hence, a higher standard of living for citizens than was likely to be achieved in a society where the sovereign directed the allocation of resources.

---

[1] An analysis of the difficulty political scientists have had in dealing with the theoretical structure of the *Federalist* is presented in Ostrom (1971). There are also political scientists who consider the *Federalist* to possess a well-integrated theoretical structure. See, for example, Ostrom's (1971) discussion and Martin Diamond's writings. For an integrated interpretation by an organization theorist, see Boschken (1982).

[2] For a more detailed analysis, see Bish (1977).

[3] Justification of the assumption of rational behavior — that is, reasoned behavior to relate means to ends—includes its predictability and the fact that only *some* people need be rational for models to yield good predictions, in addition to the notion that survivors in a competitive system must have acted as if they were rational. Rational choice does not require assumptions of perfect information and equilibrium, and the rationality postulate can be applied to any situation of scarcity and choice.

The assumption of self-interested, rational behavior in a world of imperfect knowledge appears to be identical to the way Hamilton, Madison, and Jay viewed individuals and their environment. The authors of the *Federalist* also emphasized (pp. 226-30) that humans are fallible and can learn. Their conception of rational behavior does not imply a mechanistic "irrational" passion for rational calculation in a world of perfect information, nor does it imply social aggregates, such as governments. Thus, the Smithian and the *Federalist* view of man is significantly different from the view held by many contemporary economists.

There are both positive and normative components to Smith's argument. Normatively, the economic system was to be judged by the degree to which it resulted in citizen/consumer satisfaction, not by how well it satisfied the preferences of producers or the sovereign. In the positive or predictive argument, the division of labor was important for achieving a higher standard of living; the complexity of a system of specialized individuals and businesses was too great for the sovereign to obtain information about consumers' preferences and how to organize production. Smith anticipated that a market economy would include a great number of cooperating and competing individuals and organizations. He also was among the first to discuss a key theme in the theory of markets, namely, how social coordination can occur without central direction. Subsequently, Hayek (1945) and other economists continued to emphasize "information" as one of the most important outputs from market exchange. Furthermore, only by seeing preferences "revealed" through voluntary choices could an outside observer infer what people really want (Buchanan 1959).

Smith was also concerned with the problem of monopoly. He specifically warned that a popular use of government was merchants advocating laws that create monopolies, which in turn reduce benefits to consumers. According to Smith, all suggestions for government involvement in business should be viewed with skepticism. Smith did recognize and advocate using government to maintain the legal system and to provide military security and public works. His major concern, however, was with explaining the operation of markets, and his analysis of government consists primarily of identifying the consequences of governmental policies or recommending that the government should or should not do certain things. Smith provided no real analysis of how government could be organized so that it would be more likely to do the things he recommended rather than those he recommended against.[4]

Since Smith's *Wealth of Nations*, the dominant developments in economics, especially in the United States, have been less concerned with information, monopoly, and social coordination. The focus has shifted to the logical development of implications of different conditions within a known environment where government was abstracted from, or treated as if it were run by a benevolent despot who would accept and implement an economist's advice. Only recently have economists extended their postulate of rational self-interest to the public sector and begun to examine the problems of information, monopoly, and social coordination in govern-

---

[4] Smith's arguments are virtually identical to those of Mancur Olson in his *Rise and Decline of Nations* (1982), which applies the logic of collective action and public goods to interest group formation and activity. Olson also lacks an answer to the dilemmas he poses.

ment. It is within this framework that modern economists can learn from the authors of the *Federalist*.

Federalist Theory

Scholars of federalism seem to agree less on a common paradigm than do scholars of market economics.[5] It does seem clear, however, that federalism as a system of government is viewed as a potential solution to Hobbes's problem of constraining the Leviathan, that is, of maintaining a constitutional government where government officials operate within the law and have no power to change the law to suit their own self-interest (Hobbes [1651] 1962). This normative objective is clearly set out in the Declaration of Independence and repeated throughout the *Federalist*. Contained within this analysis is the explicit assumption that people, including government officials, act in their own self-interest. Furthermore, they will use government to advance their own interests unless they are constrained by persons who have recourse to other government officials to protect them from those officials who would abuse their authority (*Federalist* No. 5). In economic terms, monopolies in government are to be avoided just as are monopolies in the market. Hobbes's problem of the Leviathan could also be labeled "a monopoly problem."

The authors of the *Federalist* also address market economics in their analysis of information problems, especially knowledge of the preferences of individuals that the government is to serve. They argue that the economy and policy are so complex that issues should be debated and scrutinized in several forums to be certain that the viewpoints from people with different information are considered before adoption (*Federalist* No. 69). They also emphasize how difficult it is for an external observer to know or understand an individual's preferences, stressing that each person is the best judge of his own self-interest but not possessing the capacity to judge his own interests in relation to the interests of others (*Federalist* No. 10). It also seems clear that the authors of the *Federalist* anticipated both cooperation and rivalry among governments (for example, rivalry with concurrent taxation and cooperation in tax administration (*Federalist* No. 35), just as Smith recognized cooperation and competition among individuals and organizations in the market. Competition among and within governments is critical to prevent monopolization and to preserve a governmental system with an enforceable constitution. At the same time, cooperation emerges because related activities are often performed more effectively by organizations of

---

[5] My own theory of federalism and interpretation of the *Federalist* have been heavily influenced by the work of and association with Vincent Ostrom, especially *The Political Theory of a Compound Republic* (1987).

different sizes; hence, citizens could be made better off by the same kind of specialization and trade that occurs among manufacturers, wholesalers, and retailers in the market. It is also important to recognize that in the *Federalist* (No. 36) local governments—called "the system of each state within that state"—are included as part of federalism. This inclusion is a natural additional division of labor that recognizes thousands of governments instead of just those at state and national levels. It is this vast system of governments that is viewed in the same manner that Smith viewed markets, and it is this extension of Smith's logic to the analysis of constitutions and institutions that is the critical contribution of the *Federalist* to an understanding of the problem of social coordination among governments when no single government or group is "in charge."

There is one area, however, where the authors of the *Federalist* specifically differ from at least the "laissez-faire" economists. There is nothing "automatic" about the creation of a governmental system where governments serve citizens and not themselves. In fact, even the authors of the *Federalist* viewed the creation of such a government as a rare experiment in a world populated primarily by governments whose structure was dependent on accident and force (*Federalist* No. 1).

Smith's market economics and the constitutional analysis of the *Federalist* reflect a similar way of thinking. Both view individuals in the same way, both have a similar normative perspective, and in both the issues of competition, monopoly, information, and coordination among many independent individuals and organizations are central to the analysis. These similarities indicate that further application of market economics concepts may enhance our understanding of federal systems.

Voluntary Agreements and Exchange

The market economy runs on voluntary agreements, most of which are of an exchange nature. In its simplest sense, individuals choose to enter into agreements with other individuals where they perceive that they will obtain the greatest net gain. Societal coordination occurs when each person selects among substitutes, and competition stimulates individuals to be efficient and to try to offer more than their competitors. This process works best when there are many buyers and sellers, freedom of entry and exit, well-specified and enforceable property rights, and relatively high levels of information. It is important to consider whether we can transfer applications of the concept and conditions of exchange that lead to mutually beneficial social coordination in the use of scarce resources to a federal system.

By definition, in a federal system there are multiple individuals and organizations that need to interact with one another without central direction. In addition, this interaction occurs within a set of rules (a constitution) analogous to the rules of property that operate in markets.

So far so good. But is there anything automatic about voluntary exchanges among different components of a federal system or between citizens and different components of a federal system leading to the kind of social coordination and efficient resource usage that Smith envisaged for private markets? Is it possible that a constitution could create a federal system that resolved the Hobbesian problem, that is, could it prevent any monopoly organization from taking over the system, while failing to create a system where an individual's responses to incentives lead to lower rather than higher levels of citizen consumer satisfaction? The answer to both these questions is yes.[6] The more important question is how an understanding of exchange helps us recognize how we can achieve either beneficial or perverse outcomes from the operation of a federal system.

One need look no further than Smith for an answer to how voluntary agreements can lead to poor outcomes for consumers. Smith explicitly recognizes that although competition is good for consumers, it is anathema to businessmen and that whenever possible they will collude to legally rig the market or seek monopoly status. In short, individuals and organizations are just as likely to enter into agreements with each other that disadvantage third parties as they are to enter agreements that create social well-being unless consumers always have substitute suppliers available to them.

[6] Two important questions need to be asked to demonstrate this. First, can citizens effectively articulate their demands and be responded to; second, can citizens avoid costs imposed on themselves when benefits accrue to others? Both questions are equally important for evaluating the performance of a political system. Yes or no answers to these questions provide for four potentially different situations:

		Responsive to Citizens	
		No	Yes
Citizens Can Avoid Polical Externality Costs	No	Tyranny	Gargantua
	Yes	No Government	Contractarian Ideal

If a governmental system does not respond to citizens and yet citizens must pay for it, it can only be described as a tyranny. This is the kind of system the Framers wanted to avoid, and for the most part they were successful. If a government were not responsive and citizens could avoid paying for anything that did not benefit them, the result would be no government.

There are also two possibilities for responsive governments. If a government were responsive to the requests of all groups and yet citizens could avoid political externality costs, those individuals and groups that benefited from governmental policies would have to pay for them. Individuals and groups would only demand programs where there were net benefits because they bear the costs. This is the system that would be expected to generate the greatest mutual benefits and could be called the contractarian ideal.

The final possibility is that government is responsive to citizens and organized groups but that other citizens cannot avoid paying the costs of the responsiveness; thus, very high political externality costs are generated. This "gargantua" outcome is most likely when political decision-making is primarily through bargaining among organized interests to obtain special benefits, yet costs are spread out over all citizens.

Although federalism is designed to provide "substitute" governments so that the officials of different governments or branches of a government watch each other, there is nothing intrinsic in federalism that would prevent collusion among government officials or between government officials and some citizens. In fact, because governments wield coercive power, the incentives to engage in such collusion may be even stronger than may occur among Smith's businessmen. But given the normative content of the *Federalist*, with its focus on protecting citizens against the state, is there any reason to be concerned about such collusion in the American federal system? The work of Anthony Downs, James Buchanan, Gordon Tullock, Mancur Olson, and other public choice theorists provides considerable insight into this question.

Downs, Buchanan and Tullock, and Olson all analyze situations where large numbers of people have difficulty striking mutually beneficial agreements because of high decisionmaking costs. Downs (1957) describes how politicians seeking office would seek a "median voter" position in small political units; but as the size of government increases, parties will be formed, specific information will be less visible, and ideologies and appeals to special interests will emerge. Buchanan and Tullock (1962) explain how lowering decisionmaking costs with less than the unanimous support required for political decisions may result in costs being imposed on those whose consent is not needed in the decisionmaking process. Mancur Olson (1965, 1982) analyzes how special interests can come to dominate political decisionmaking.

The conclusion emerging from these analyses is that a federal system can be one where narrow interests and governments act like Smith's cartels and monopolists, except that the situation may be worse because governments have the power to regulate and to tax — powers that Smith's monopolists lacked. In addition, because of the nature of political competition in large governments, there is no reason to predict that elected officials will make mutually beneficial decisions instead of catering to special interests at some cost to citizens. This does not mean that such costs can be infinite, because citizens can "vote with their feet" (Tiebout 1956) to escape tyranny; but, as with any "monopolist," if substitutes are more costly than they would be under competitive conditions, there is some transfer of wealth from consumers and excluded suppliers to the monopolist with a net loss in the process. Voluntary agreements within and among governments can lead to both positive and negative consequences.

Bureaucratic Production and Contracting-Out

Public choice theory implies that local governments, which are relatively small, homogeneous, and have a limited range of functions, should have the fewest problems in electing politicians who represent and have incen-

358 THE ECONOMY AND THE CONSTITUTION

tives to respond to citizens' preferences (Bish 1971). Local governments, however, face some unique production problems, because they are either too large or too small to produce all of their activities at the lowest average cost. There is also the problem that all producing organizations face in ensuring that their managers are efficient. Local governments usually respond to scale problems by recommending that the governments be made larger to capture economies of scale and that they decentralize internally for those activities lacking economies of scale. While appearing to be based on "economic analysis," these recommendations pay no attention to whether or not the managers of the organizations (who are like Smith's businessmen) have any incentive to produce efficiently. The best empirical evidence is that they apparently do not.[7] Many studies of the production of local government services indicate that after a local government makes a policy decision on what to provide to its citizens it can obtain much less costly production of the goods by contracting-out in a competitive bidding process.[8] For example, a recent study of garbage collection in all Canadian municipalities with over 10,000 in population indicates that municipally managed collection averages $42.29 per household and contracted-out collection averages $28.02 (McDavid 1985). The cost difference is a result of private contractors using large trucks with two-man crews who collect twice as many tons per man per day as do municipal crews using small trucks and three-man crews (who also spend a large proportion of the day riding back and forth to the dump). This is not unusual, as a recent survey of contracting-out in the United States and Canada indicates (Bish 1986).

Contracting-out occurs not just between local governments and the private sector but among governments as well. Robert Warren's (1964, 1966) studies of Lakewood Plan cities in California indicate that governments can compete with private sellers when they have the incentives to do so and that governments of different levels can resolve both incentive and scale problems by contracting with one another and with private firms. Contracting-out with competitive bids eliminates the monopoly position of the government bureaucracy and introduces more information and competition into the system. These changes contribute to better results for citizens, as both Smith and the *Federalist* would predict.

Government Collusion

Smith emphasizes that businessmen will form cartels that disadvantage

---

[7] For an analysis of the Reform Tradition in local government, a tradition that recommended one local government for each metropolitan area on the assumption that it would produce local services at lower cost, see Bish and Ostrom (1973).

[8] For a recent analysis of evidence on contracting-out, see Bish (1986).

consumers. So will government officials. One striking example of empirical research on a "cooperative agreement" among government officials is Dolores Martin's (1976) analysis of Local Agency Formation Commissions (LAFCOs) in California and similar arrangements restricting the creation of local governments in other states. LAFCOs are comprised of the representatives of existing government units that must approve new governments and government boundary changes. Many economists would argue that LAFCOs would reduce public service costs by simplifying and rationalizing the local government structure. Others would hypothesize that because they are comprised of officials of existing local governments, LAFCOs would act as a cartel and simply exclude competition from the market, resulting in higher local government costs over time. Martin found significantly higher annual cost increases for local government after LAF-COs were created in California relative to the cost before their creation. Her nationwide, cross-sectional study also indicates that states with this kind of arrangement face significantly higher local government costs than found in non-LAFCO or "free-entry" states.

It is precisely this kind of hypothesis building and empirical testing that is critical to understanding the relationship between intergovernmental relations and outcomes in federal systems. It is also direct evidence that Smith's logic is as applicable to the public sector as it is to the private sector. There are many more examples of market-like behavior, including exchanges for mutual benefit, such as contracting-out production and collusive behavior, which impose net costs on citizens.[9] The important point here is that thinking with a market economics model helps us understand how federal systems operate.

Fiscal Federalism

Neither studies of contracting-out nor collusion among government officials would generally be considered to be studies of federal systems in the context of a body of literature generally referred to as "fiscal federalism."[10] Historically, fiscal federalism has considered tax coordination and competition; more recently, it has included grant programs and functional responsibilities for different levels of government. These later analyses have been facilitated by the theory of public goods and externalities and the recognition that most public goods and externalities affect areas

---

[9] For example, revenue-sharing has been viewed as a collusive agreement to raise all local government revenues while avoiding the competition that would come from "voting with one's feet" (Bish and Ostrom 1973, p. 64; McKenzie and Staaf 1978). For further analysis of governmental cooperation that benefits citizens and cooperation (collusion) that disadvantages citizens, see Bish (1978).

[10] Some of the points made in this section are treated in Bish (1977).

smaller than the entire country. This work, however, poses interesting problems for conclusions based on market economics and federalist models, because fiscal federalism studies arrive at conclusions that are directly contrary to conclusions based on market economics and the political theory of federalism.[11] Not only are the conclusions different, but their normative recommendations would also eliminate the most distinguishing feature of a federal system, competition among governments.

In *Fiscal Federalism*, Wallace E. Oates (1972) reaches the same conclusions as have other major economists, including Musgrave (1969), Tiebout (1961), and Head (1974). Oates presents a highly simplified and essentially normative model of the public sector: "In this pure model there is a *clear division of functions among levels of government*, one that leads to the attainment of a welfare optimum" (p. vii, emphasis added). Oates's conclusion does not follow from basic economic theory unless we are willing to assume that a monopoly behaves in the same way as does an organization where citizens have alternatives. Oates has focused only on scale problems; that is, different government activities may most efficiently be provided for different sized geographic areas or produced by different sized organizations. Oates simply ignores the monopoly problem, which is so important (and which provides the very rationale for a federal system) as presented in the *Federalist*.

Analyses of federalism that ignore the monopoly problem and focus only on scale problems are indistinguishable from analyses of decentralized unitary government systems—a point Oates (pp. 16-17) recognizes explicitly, without concern. There are, however, reasons for neglecting the monopoly problem. One could assume that public officials would not act in their self-interest and instead be benevolent monopolists, like Plato's philosopher king. I do not think Oates intends to make that assumption, because his analysis of intergovernmental grants and taxation requires self-interested officials to respond to particular incentive systems, and they cannot all be schizophrenic. A second reason could be that electoral competition alone will keep public officials responsive, but this argument is not stated and could easily be refuted by drawing on economic analyses of the problems of managing government bureaucracies (Tullock 1965; Niskanen 1971; Ahlbrandt 1973). Thus, a critical question remains: Are Oates and other economists who study fiscal federalism logically inconsistent in their behavioral assumptions and neglectful of empirical evidence on political competition, or does the introduction of the concept of a public

---

[11] Three significant exceptions are the work of Nathan (1975), Scott (1973), and Wagner (1971). None of them, however, directly confronts the dilemma posed by the application of public goods theory to federal systems.

good really force the conclusion that a system of monopolies producing public goods on an appropriate scale is superior to a federal system characterized by competition among governments that provide substitutes for one another? Were Smith, the Framers of the Constitution, and the authors of the *Federalist* that wrong? Or do serious problems exist in "fiscal federalism"?

Public Goods Theory and Federalism

Public goods are defined as goods, services, or valued states of affairs that when once provided no one can be excluded from benefiting (nonexclusion) and no one's consumption reduces another person's consumption (nonsubtractability). The nonexclusion characteristic generates a free-rider problem; that is, voluntary contributions will not support provision because noncontributors cannot be excluded from benefits. Public goods are predicted to remain unprovided (or underprovided) in a purely market economy. The solution to the free-rider problem is through coercive taxation, where all beneficiaries are forced to pay, with the power to tax being a general characteristic of government. If a public good is pure — that is, if the characteristics of nonexclusion and nonsubtractability are extended nationwide—then the potential low-cost provision system, *ceteris paribus*, would be a single governmental unit. By adding different kinds of "impurities," such as geographically confined benefits or geographic differences in people's preferences, one can develop arguments for provision by smaller governmental units.

What is being discussed here is provision, that is, demand articulation and collection of taxes, not actual production. Production may be undertaken by an organization either larger or smaller than the government that provides the service through intergovernmental agreements and contracting. Some economists have assumed that provision and production are undertaken only by the same organization; thus, they have combined the economies-of-scale criterion with the provision criteria to determine the variety of optional-sized governments in a system (Rothenberg 1970). This reasoning process is equally appropriate for either decentralized unitary or federal governments.

But does this logic lead to the conclusion that different public functions should be provided exclusively by different levels of government? What constitutes the "public good" here is critical. For example, if public safety means providing a night watchman, a small government may be efficient. If public safety means capturing bank robbers, then a large organization — or at least one covering a larger geographic area — may be more efficient. If public safety means bringing criminals to trial, a prosecutor and a court system may be appropriate. If public safety consists of all these elements, then the function may be best provided by multiple governments at the same time. Just what is the public good? If we apply our definition of public good only to single activities — for example, the patrol by the night watchman — and not to groups of activities constituting functions, we can conclude that a single organization should provide a single activity within its area of benefits. This approach is consistent with a logic of different activities for different levels of government and is implicit in the work of Head (1974), Tiebout (1961), and Musgrave (1969). It is also consistent with Oates if we assume that his terms, services, activities, functions, and programs describe only single activities. From this, Oates concludes that an economist's theoretical model should indicate a clear division of functions but that the "real world" appears to be one of increasing participation of different levels of government providing the same functions. If Oates had applied his public goods theory to only specific activities and recognized that different activities comprising the same function could be undertaken by different levels of government, his ideal model would be consistent with observed trends in multilevel fiscal activity and permit him to go much further in analyzing federal systems than he has been able to do. He could also avoid trying to justify an ideal type that obviously does not fit. In addition, it is precisely the observation that different activities of functions may be provided by different levels of government that makes a solution to the monopoly problem — which Oates totally neglects — possible in federal systems.

Public Goods and Monopoly

The logic of a public good is such that provision by a single organization in an area is most efficient. If there are multiple organizations, then it is rational for each to let others provide the good; members of the non-providing organization may then consume the good without having contributed to its cost. When there are multiple organizations, some organizations will be free-riders.

The logic that a single organization is needed for a public good poses a monopoly problem: If the officers of the organization do not efficiently provide the public good to meet citizens' preferences, the citizens have no substitutes to turn to. For example, if one organization provides all public safety activities and its officers harass citizens when they call for help, there is no other source of assistance, including protection from harassment by the officials themselves. In contrast, even if patrolling activities are provided by a single law enforcement agency, if other public safety activities are provided by employees of other organizations (such as sheriffs, federal marshals, state patrols, prosecutors, and the FBI), then there are substitutes; if local police do not perform well, citizens will have recourse to an alternative organization. Thus, it is precisely because no single organization provides all public safety activities or can prevent others from performing similar activities that a monopoly over public safety activities is avoided. Each activity can be adjusted to an appropriate scale and the resulting overlapping of organizations can resolve the monopoly problem. Public goods theory, then, when applied to activities rather than entire functions, aids our understanding of federal systems in a way that is consistent with federalist theory and market economics.

The substitutes that preclude monopolization in the public sector are not the same as "perfect substitutes" or identical products so popularized in developing welfare conclusions from models of "perfect competition." Substitutes need not be perfect (e.g., a fence and guard dogs may substitute for a police patrol) to stimulate competitive behavior among producers. This concept of competition is associated with Smith and is well express-ed in Hayek's "The Meaning of Competition" (1948); it is not the much narrower view of a perfectly competitive market.

Competition

Competition is a key theme in Smith and in the *Federalist*, and a closer look at how the concept of public goods is used in the fiscal federalism literature shows that competition can be included in that analysis as well. Given the importance of competition, it is important to ask if there are situations where competition goes wrong. Two such situations are directly relevant: problems of common property and imperfect information.

The Problem of the Commons

In economic theory, competition "goes wrong" when users compete to use a commons, which is a resource for which property rights are only par-tially defined (a right to use but no right to exclude others from use). The "tragedy of the commons" occurs when the value to users is sufficiently great that users overuse and destroy the commons, leaving everyone worse off than they would be had they been able to agree on a more complete assignment of property rights for rationing purposes. The problem of the commons, which arises because of an inadequate specification of basic pro-perty rights, clearly creates a situation where competition leads to undesirable results.

Studies of the commons began with an examination of "unowned" natural resources, such as fisheries and groundwater (Gordon 1954), but the analyses have been expanded to include the destruction of public goods after congestion sets in, as occurs in public parks. The general principle is simple: Whenever the benefits of something exceed its realized costs, people will choose to have it, even if the sum of their costs plus the costs imposed on others exceed their total benefits. In government, the most striking example of this problem is that many politicians, bureaucrats, and citizens appear to view the public treasury as a commons that each wants to use for his or her own benefit. Special interest groups find that their special benefits exceed their tax increase (which is spread over all taxpayers) for their special project, even though all citizens may end up paying to finance all special interests that exceed their own benefits. This problem is likely to be even more severe if expenditures are financed with deficits.

The usual suggestions for resolving the "commons problem" are either assigning complete property rights or introducing a monopoly regulatory agency with the coercive power to limit access. Both suggestions constitute fundamental changes in the legal structure and are analogous to effective changes in the Constitution. This problem is clearly one that can emerge from competition among politicians and bureaucrats to satisfy citizen preferences in a federal system.[12]

The Problem of Imperfect Information

A second area where competition may appear to go wrong is where consumers or producers possess only biased or imperfect information. In order to make good decisions on the use of scarce resources it is necessary to have a system that produces and makes available information on demands, opportunity costs, and production alternatives. A major argument in Smith and refined in Hayek (1945) is that markets produce and transmit this information in the form of prices more effectively than could a mercantilistic state or a central planning agency. In fact, it is because markets operate on the basis of decisions made in response to prices that many economists call market systems "price systems," and most economists would be at a loss to explain how a market system could work without prices. Applying the logic of markets to federalism then leads to very important questions: Are prices really necessary for the operation of complex systems? And what are the prices in a federal system?

The first question can be answered in the negative. An example would be the ecological survival of the fittest model where organisms or species are adapted to fit the environment and may not engage in any purposeful behavior. If there were tighter control between citizens and preferred policies so that governments that did not meet expectations were eliminated, the system would adapt to citizen preferences even without prices or conscious attempts by management to meet citizen preferences. Both Alchian (1950) and Tiebout (1957) have explained such a model in economics, but most of us would expect purposeful human behavior with the right incentives to result in an improvement over a pure no-information random adaptive system. We should be aware, however, that a large federal system can

---

[12] The literature often refers to the negative consequences of competition within government as resulting from "rent seeking" (Buchanan *et. al.* 1980).

operate—and may be operating—without the kind of prices that economists consider necessary to get efficient resouce allocation.

The problems of introducing prices that reflect values and opportunity costs into the public sector are serious ones. In order to intentionally undertake production to satisfy customers, managers have to know demand prices, resource prices, and the production function (the relationship between resources and the value they add to the output). Given the nature of many governmental activities, the prices necessary to make these decisions are largely unknown. For example, there is no quantitative measure for "public safety," let alone a demand price; nor is there precise information on the contribution of different resources — such as police cars, policemen, computers, and crime laboratories — toward the objective. In short, managers do not know either the demand price or the production function for many government activities. Of course, there are other activities, such as water supply or garbage collection, where prices can be identified and the production function specified without difficulty, although the way in which the public sector is organized makes it possible that such information will not be as readily available to managers or elected officials as it would be for comparable activity in the private market. Given the range of activities in which governments are engaged, such diversity in government activities should be anticipated.

Federal systems do not produce the same price information as do "ideal" market systems, nor are they likely to produce as much price information as do real market systems. The information problems, however, may be more a matter of degree than of fundamental difference. For example, large corporations undertake many activities internally and must make management decisions without knowing the precise contribution to output of some activities. It is also difficult to measure the outputs of many private firms, such as a law firm. In these cases, the conditions of "perfect competition" are not met; but as long as markets are competitive, those businesses that do relatively better are most likely to survive and provide net benefits to consumers. Thus, while one must recognize the difficulty of developing ideal prices in federal systems (and try to improve difficulty where possible, such as with contracting-out), the lack of ideal prices is not a barrier to using market models to understand federalism. Explicit recognition of the lack of ideal prices, however, reemphasizes the potential lack of relevance of economic models that include as a basic assumption the availability of perfect information.

Implications of a Market Perspective

The major arguments of the paper can be summarized as follows:

> 1. The basic way of thinking in market economics, such as is presented in Adam Smith's *Wealth of Nations*, is highly congruent with the way of

thinking about government presented in the *Federalist*. Both view people as acting in their own self-interest; both are aware of the difficulty of producing and transmitting information; both place considerable importance on competition to get good results for consumer/citizens; and both oppose the creation of monopolies.

2. Empirical evidence supports the position that greater competition can improve production efficiency (contracting-out) and that governments will engage in collusive behavior to the disadvantage of citizens (LAFCOs).

3. Recognition of the difference between functions and activities when applying the concept of public good can reconcile federalist and market approaches with the fiscal federalism literature. This approach also indicates the importance of a broad definition of substitutes, not just the identical substitutes of perfectly competitive models.

4. Competition may lead to undesirable results when it is for a commons, and the public treasury may be analogous to a commons when viewed by special interests.

5. Federal systems do not generally produce as much price information as do private markets, but they still function more like markets than like single firms or hierarchical bureaucracies.

The Constitutional Convention of 1787 created a framework that has facilitated economic development and has left the United States one of the best governed nations in the world. While that was no small achievement and should not be underrated, social scientists who study the public and private sectors should be proposing ideas that will improve things. If they are right, there may even be some changes.

Before one can make recommendations, however, it is necessary to understand how something works. In order to understand the U.S. constitutional system, it is necessary to understand federalism. The *Federalist* provides an excellent basis for understanding how federalism works, but the logic of economics also makes a major contribution because of the congruence between the theoretical framework presented in the *Federalist* and the theory of markets. This does not mean that we can simply adopt Smith's conclusions, even if supplemented by the analyses of public choice theorists, and apply them to the public sector; but it does mean that we can use the logic of market economics to understand federalism more fruitfully than has been done in the past.

References

Ahlbrandt, Roger S. Jr. *Municipal Fire Protection Services: Comparison of Alternative Organizational Forms.* Beverly Hills: Sage, 1973.

Alchian, Armen. "Uncertainty, Evolution and Economic Theory." *Journal of Political Economy* 58 (June 1950):211-21.

Bish, Robert L. "The Assumption of Knowledge in Policy Analysis." *Policy Studies Journal* 3 (Spring 1975):256-62.

Bish, Robert L. *The Public Economy of Metropolitan Areas.* Chicago: Markham Rand McNally, 1971.

Bish, Robert L. "Economic Theory, Fiscal Federalism, and Political Federalism." Paper presented at the Annual Meeting of the American Political Science Association, Washington, D.C., 1-4 September 1977.

Bish, Robert L. "Competition and Collusion: Some Implications From a Public Choice Perspective." In *Intergovernmental Policymaking.* Edited by K. Hans and F. W. Sharps. Beverly Hills: Sage, 1978.

Bish, Robert L. "Competition and Collusion: Some Implications from a Public Contracting Out." In *Responses to Economic Change*, pp. 203-37. Edited by David Laidler. Toronto: University of Toronto Press, 1986.

Bish, Robert L., and Ostrom, Vincent. *Understanding Urban Government: Metropolitan Reform Reconsidered.* Washington, D.C.: American Enterprise Institute, 1973.

Boschken, Herman L. "Organization Theory and Federalism: Interorganizational Networks and the Political Economy of 'The Federalist'." *Organization Studies* 3, no. 4 (1982): 355-73.

Buchanan, James M. "Positive Economics, Welfare Economics, and Political Economy." *Journal of Law and Economics* 2 (1959):124-38.

Buchanan, James M., and Tullock, Gordon. *The Calculus of Consent.* Ann Arbor: University of Michigan Press, 1962.

Buchanan, James M.; Tollison, Robert D.; and Tullock, Gordon, eds. *Toward a Theory of the Rent-Seeking Society.* College Station: Texas A & M University Press, 1980.

Downs, Anthony. *An Economic Theory of Democracy.* New York: Harper and Row, 1957.

Gordon, H. Scott. "The Economic Theory of a Common-Property Resource: The Fishery." *Journal of Political Economy* 62 (April 1954):124-42.

Hamilton, Alexander; Jay, John; and Madison, James. *The Federalist Papers.* New York: Modern Library Edition, n.d.

Hayek, Friedrich A. "The Use of Knowledge in Society." *American Economic Review* 35 (September 1945):519-30.

Hayek, Friedrich A. "The Meaning of Competition." In *Individualism and Economic Order*, pp. 92-106. Chicago: University of Chicago Press, 1948.

Head, John G. "Public Goods and Multilevel Government." In *Public Goods and Public Welfare*, pp. 263-84. Durham: Duke University Press, 1974.

Hobbes, Thomas. *Leviathan.* 1651. London: Collier-Macmillan, 1962.

Martin, Dolores Tremewan. "The Institutional Framework of Community Formation: The Law and Economics of Municipal Incorporation in California." Ph.D. diss., Virginia Polytechnic Institute and State University, Blacksburg, 1976.

McDavid, James C. "The Canadian Experience with Privatizing Solid Waste Collection Services." *Public Administration Review* 45 (September/October 1985):602-8.

McKenzie, Richard B., and Staaf, Robert J. "Revenue Sharing and Monopoly Government." *Public Choice* 33, no. 3 (1978):93-97.

Musgrave, Richard A. "Theories of Fiscal Federalism." *Public Finance* 24, no. 2 (1969):521-32.

Nathan, Richard P. "Federalism and the Shifting Nature of Fiscal Relations." *Annals* 419 (May 1975):120-29.

Niskanen, William A. *Bureaucracy and Representative Government.* Chicago: Aldine-Atherton, 1971.

Oates, Wallace E. *Fiscal Federalism.* New York: Harcourt Brace Jovanovich, 1972.

Olson, Mancur. *The Logic of Collective Action.* Cambridge, Mass.: Harvard University Press, 1965.

Olson, Mancur. *The Rise and Decline of Nations.* New Haven: Yale University Press, 1982.

Ostrom, Vincent. *The Political Theory of a Compound Republic: Designing the American Experiment.* Lincoln: University of Nebraska Press, 1987.

Rothenberg, Jerome. "Local Decentralization and the Theory of Optimal Government." In *The Analysis of Public Output*, pp. 31-64. Edited by Julius Margolis. New York: Bureau of Economic Research, 1970.

Scott, Anthony. "The Defense of Federalism, or, The Attack on Unitary Government." *American Economist* 17 (Fall 1973):162-69.

Smith, Adam. *The Wealth of Nations.* 1776. New York: Modern Library, 1937.

Tiebout, Charles M. "A Pure Theory of Local Expenditures." *Journal of Political Economy* 64 (October 1956): 416-24.

Tiebout, Charles M. "An Economic Theory of Fiscal Decentralization." In *Public Finances: Needs, Sources, and Utilization*, pp. 79-96. National Bureau of Economic Research. Princeton: Princeton University Press, 1961.

Tiebout, Charles M. "Location Theory, Empirical Evidence and Economic Evolution." *Papers and Proceedings of the Regional Science Association* 3 (1957): 75-82.

Tullock, Gordon. *The Politics of Bureaucracy.* Washington, D.C.: Public Affairs Press, 1965.

Wagner, Richard E. *The Fiscal Organization of American Federalism.* Chicago: Markham Rand McNally, 1971.

Warren, Robert. "A Municipal Services Market Model of Metropolitan Organization." *Journal of the American Institution of Planners* 30 (August 1964):193-214.

Warren, Robert. *Government in Metropolitan Regions: A Reappraisal of Fractionated Political Organization.* Davis: Institute of Governmental Affairs, University of California, 1966.

17

CAN THE CONSTITUTION PROTECT PRIVATE RIGHTS DURING NATIONAL EMERGENCIES?
Robert Higgs

[F]ew indeed have been the invasions upon essential liberties which have not been accompanied by pleas of urgent necessity advanced in good faith by responsible men . . . .

—Justice Frank Murphy

The answer is no. The historical record is quite clear; and in regard to this question there is no reason to suppose that the future will differ from the past. The outlook, therefore, can only dishearten those who believe that the fundamental purpose of the Constitution is to protect private rights to life, liberty, and property. The founders of the United States established the Constitution to "secure the Blessings of Liberty" to themselves and their posterity. But time and chance have been unkind to their hopes. They intended their framework of freedom and government to endure through the ages, through storm as well as sunshine.[1] But the dead could not forever bind the living, and the unfolding of our history during the twentieth century has brought into being a second Constitution. Besides the Normal Constitution, protective of private rights, we now have a Crisis Constitution, hostile to private rights and friendly to the unchecked power of governmental officials. In national emergencies the Crisis Constitution overrides the Normal Constitution. The great danger is that in an age of permanent emergency—the age we live in, the age we are likely to go on living in—the Crisis Constitution will simply swallow up the Normal Constitution, depriving us *at all times* of the very rights the original Constitution was created to protect *at all times*.

The Historical Record

The development of the Crisis Constitution has been described in

---

[1]Robert Higgs is the William E. Simon Professor of Political Economy at Lafayette College.

[2] See *The Federalist Papers* (1787-1788), Ex parte Milligan, 4 Wallace 2 (1866), *Home Building and Loan v. Blaisdell*, 290 U.S. 398 (1934) at 448-83 (Sutherland dissenting).

detail elsewhere. [2] Here I shall review only a few of the outstanding events and leading Supreme Court decisions.

Though earlier events, especially during the Civil War, foreshadowed the Crisis Constitution (Rossiter 1948, pp. 223-239, 241-242; Kelly, Harbison, and Belz 1983, pp. 229-327), World War I witnessed its unmistakable emergence. Even before the United States formally entered the war, the railroad labor troubles of 1916-1917 provoked unprecedented governmental actions. Facing the prospect of a nationwide railroad strike when the operating brotherhoods and the railroad managers could not agree on wages and hours, President Woodrow Wilson turned to Congress, gaining passage of the Adamson Act in September 1916. In effect the act simply imposed on the interstate railroad industry a 25 percent increase in the wage rates of operating employees. The employers challenged the law, but the Supreme Court upheld its constitutionality in *Wilson v. New* (243 U.S. 332 [1917]). The court's decision emphasized the gravity of the situation—"the impediment and destruction of interstate commerce which was threatened" (p. 352) and "the infinite injury to the public interest which was imminent" (p. 348)—but justified the government's actions by arguing that, while the government has no emergency power as such, it has a reservoir of reserved power upon which it may legitimately draw during emergencies. The outcome: railroad owners were deprived of a great deal of property, without compensation, for a use not public, namely, the enrichment of unionized railroad workers holding hostage the American economy.

After the United States formally entered the war, the government enacted legislation providing for conscription of soldiers. Though men had been drafted during the Civil War, the Supreme Court had never ruled on the constitutionality of the draft. Besides, the issues now differed: men were being drafted not to defend the government against violent domestic rebellion or invasion but to do battle in the trenches of faraway France, ostensibly to foster such abstract ideological aims as "making the world safe for democracy" and securing the "autonomous development" of various European ethnic groups (Corwin 1947, pp. 87-88; Murphy 1972, p. 13, n. 34). The Supreme Court readily affirmed, however, the constitutionality of sending men against their will to fight and die in a remote power struggle. Said Chief Justice Edward White: "It may not be doubted that the very conception of a just government and its duty to the citizen includes the reciprocal obligation of the citizen to render military service in case of need and the right to compel it" (*Arver v. United States*, 245 U.S. 366 [1918] at 378). The court refused to consider seriously the claim that conscription

---

[2] See Corwin (1947), Rossiter (1948), Murphy (1972), Belknap (1983), Bigel (1986), Higgs (1987), and Higgs and Twight (1987).

constitutes a form of involuntary servitude forbidden by the Thirteenth Amendment. The outcome: draftees were deprived of liberty and—tens of thousands of them—consequently deprived of life itself by the actions of political authorities intent on the prosecution of war but unwilling to impose enough explicit taxes to hire the desired military personnel.

The Great Depression, which Justice Louis Brandeis called "an emergency more serious than war," prompted a welter of emergency actions by governments at all levels. In 1932-1934 twenty-five states enacted legislation providing for moratoria on mortgage foreclosures (Alston 1984, p. 446). Such laws appeared to be unambiguous impairments of the obligation of contract and therefore in clear violation of the U.S. Constitution. But when Minnesota's mortgage moratorium law came before the Supreme Court for review (*Home Building and Loan Association v. Blaisdell*, 290 U.S. 398 [1934]), the majority pronounced this self-declared emergency legislation a valid exercise of the state's police powers. Harkening back to the precedent of *Wilson v. New*, Chief Justice Charles Evans Hughes reasoned that "[w]hile emergency does not create power, emergency may furnish the occasion for the exercise of power" (p. 426). The Contract Clause's protection of private rights, said Hughes, "is not to be read with literal exactness" (p. 428). Those mysterious "reserved powers" of the government are "read into contracts" (p. 435). In sum, "[a]n emergency existed in Minnesota which furnished a proper occasion for the exercise of the reserved power of the State . . . " (p. 444). The outcome: many thousands of mortgagees were deprived of the rights of foreclosure stipulated in their contracts and compelled to make do with the alternatives provided by emergency statutes.

Also in the depths of the Great Depression the federal government abandoned the gold standard, nationalized the monetary gold stock, and abrogated the gold clauses of all contracts, public and private, past and future. This "act of absolute bad faith" astonished even some members of Congress. Senator Thomas P. Gore told President Franklin D. Roosevelt: "Why, that's just plain stealing, isn't it, Mr. President?" (quotations from Anderson 1979, pp. 316-17). Stealing or not, it certainly smacked of what Justice James McReynolds called "arbitrary action, whose immediate purpose and necessary effect is destruction of individual rights" (294 U.S. at 372). But McReynolds was speaking in dissent. The majority, for whom Chief Justice Hughes spoke, held that "[i]f the gold clauses . . . interfere with the policy of the Congress in the exercise of that [monetary] authority they cannot stand." The court recognized that "express stipulations for gold payments constitute property," but "[c]ontracts, however express, cannot fetter the constitutional authority of the Congress" (*Norman v. Baltimore and Ohio Railroad Co.*, 294 U.S. 240 [1935] at 307, 311). The outcome: certainly thousands, perhaps millions, of parties to contracts containing gold clauses, including the many holders of U.S. government bonds, stipulating payment in gold, were deprived of property rights, victimized by their own government's unprincipled rapaciousness.

In the war emergency that followed the Japanese attack on Pearl Harbor the government built an awesome command economy, suspending many private property rights. As Clinton L. Rossiter (1948, p. 279) noted, "Of all the time-honored Anglo-Saxon liberties, the freedom of contract took the worst beating in the war." Ten million men were conscripted. The Supreme Court refused even to review challenges to the constitutionality of the draft. Some 110,000 Japanese-Americans, two-thirds of them U.S. citizens and not one of them proven guilty of a crime, were herded into concentration camps, sustaining property losses estimated at some $400 million (Howard 1968, p. 301). All quite constitutional, said the justices (*Hirabayashi v. United States*, 320 U.S. 81 [1943]; *Korematsu v. United States*, 323 U.S. 214 [1944]). Raw materials and plants were allocated by governmental order; production facilities, sometimes entire industries, were seized and operated by the government; many consumer goods were officially rationed. None of these actions elicited so much as a ruling from the Supreme Court (Mason 1956, pp. 696-97). The sweeping price and rent controls exercised by the Office of Price Administration did come before the court, but the cases focused on procedural not substantive questions, and even then the court found no reason to deny the government any of the many powers it was exercising at the expense of private rights (Rossiter 1976, pp. 97-100). Said Justice Wiley Rutledge, one of the *least* single-mindedly bellicose justices, "Citizens must surrender or forego [sic] exercising rights which in other times could not be impaired" (321 U.S. at 461).[3] Justice Owen J. Roberts, in notable dissents, pronounced the court's review of the government's price and rent controls a sham, "a solemn farce."

During the Korean War emergency the government reinstituted controls over raw materials, production, shipping, credit, wages, and prices. When the wage-price controls created a collective-bargaining impasse in the steel industry, threatening a nationwide strike, President Harry Truman ordered the Secretary of Commerce to seize the industry. In *Youngstown Sheet & Tube Co. v. Sawyer* (343 U.S. 579 [1952]) the Supreme Court, unconvinced that a genuine national emergency existed, ruled that the President had no constitutional authority for the seizure (Marcus 1977, pp. 225-27). The *Youngstown* ruling, however, in no way signified a triumph of private rights or a significant check on the exercise of the government's emergency powers

[3] Leading cases were *Yakus v. United States*, 321 U.S. 414 (1944), *Bowles v. Willingham*, 321 U.S. 503 (1944), and *Steuart v. Bowles*, 322 U.S. 398 (1944).

(Corwin 1974, pp. 112, 157). The case actually arose from a power struggle between Truman, by then a very unpopular President, and the Congress (Marcus 1977, pp. 17-37, 83-101, 258-59). Finding the available legislative bases for a seizure either inconvenient or impolitic, Truman had chosen to base the seizure on a vague claim of inherent presidential power under the Constitution. The court's decision, really a ruling on separation of powers rather than emergency power as such, found intolerable the President's failure to cite specific legislative authority for his action. On emergency powers, however, the justices' multiple opinions—seven in all—spoke more in favor than in opposition. The three dissenters argued that "a [presidential] power of seizure has been accepted throughout our history" (343 U.S. at 700). Justice Tom Clark, who supported the result but not the reasoning of the majority's ruling, agreed (p. 662). Justice Robert Jackson, in a concurring opinion, emphasized "the ease, expedition and safety with which Congress can grant and has granted large emergency powers" (p. 653). Only two justices (Black and Douglas) explicitly rejected the claim of inherent presidential power to seize the industry in the absence of congressional authorization (Marcus 1977, p. 216; Bigel 1986, pp. 135-150). The outcome: the steel seizure itself was forbidden; but, given the reasoning of the justices and the fragmentation of their opinions, the vulnerability of private property rights to emergency suspension remained virtually as great as before.

In the 1970's, passage of the National Emergencies Act (1976) and the International Emergency Economic Powers Act (1977) placed new procedural requirements on the exercise of emergency powers by the President but did little to detract from the substance of such powers, which continue to be employed routinely (Higgs and Twight 1987; Belknap 1983, pp. 100-101). Under emergency decrees American citizens recently have been forbidden to engage in a variety of travel, commercial, and financial transactions with the citizens or governments of designated countries, including Cuba, Iran, Libya, Syria, South Africa, and Nicaragua.

Recent Supreme Court rulings have sustained a wide scope for the exercise of presidential emergency powers. The congressional veto case (*Immigration and Naturalization Service v. Chadha*, 103 S.Ct. 2764 [1983]) effectively demolished the check of a concurrent resolution as provided in the National Emergencies Act. In *Dames & Moore v. Regan* (101 S. Ct. 2972 [1981]) the court gave broad construction to the President's power to act under the International Emergency Economic Powers Act, endorsing President Jimmy Carter's use of that act first to block Iranian funds and later to compel their return to Iran (thereby nullifying certain attachments issued by U.S. courts) as part of his effort to secure release of American hostages. Equally significant was the court's ruling on the scope of executive power to deal with such foreign policy disputes in the absence of statutory authority. While holding that President Ronald Reagan lacked statutory authority under the International Emergency Economic Powers Act to "suspend" U.S. citizens' claims against Iran pursuant to President Carter's agreement with the Iranian government, the court nevertheless ruled that the President did not lack *constitutional* power to terminate the claims. Further erosion of the restraints on the President stipulated in the National Emergencies Act and the International Emergency Economic Powers Act came in *Regan v. Wald* (104 S.Ct. 3026 [1984]), where the court allowed the executive branch to impose a major new curtailment of private travel to Cuba without a declaration of national emergency or compliance with the procedural requirements of the National Emergencies Act (Higgs and Twight 1987).

The outcome: during the past decade, American citizens have been forbidden to travel to various countries, to borrow or buy from, lend or sell to the citizens or governments of various countries, to fulfill the terms of valid contracts, to pursue in U.S. courts legal remedies for injuries and takings. Far from having their rights to life, liberty, and property upheld by the federal government, Americans have been routinely deprived of such rights under declarations of emergency.

Three Loci of the Constitution

Instructed to find the Constitution, most people probably would go to the bookshelf and take down a copy of the Constitutional Document. "This," they would devoutly declare, "is it. And it says right here that . . . ." For some purposes the Constitutional Document is all we need to consult. It says that every state shall have two senators, that the Vice President shall be President of the Senate, that only natural-born citizens may become President, and so forth. And sure enough, one may confidently expect that all these unambiguous prescriptions will be observed in practice—at all events they have been for two hundred years.

One will search the Constitutional Document in vain, however, for provisions relating to emergency powers. Such powers are not mentioned. If the Framers intended the powers of governmental officials or the rights of private citizens to be any different in national emergencies, it is curious that they neglected to express that intention in the Sacred Text.

A more sophisticated searcher, however, would look for the Constitution not just in the Document itself but in the several hundred volumes of U.S. Supreme Court reports. The Constitution, as Charles Evans Hughes once bluntly said, "is what the judges say it is" (quoted in Corwin 1974, p. xv). And so it necessarily must be. After all, the meanings to be given to such expressions as "commerce among the several states," "due process of law," "necessary and proper," or "cruel and unusual punishments" are far from transparent. Charles A. Beard (1936, p. 30) observed that "dispute has raged among men of strong minds and pure hearts over the meanings of these cloud-covered words and phrases." The verbal ambiguities must be clarified if the terms of the Constitutional Document are to have practical application. The Supreme Court makes the final determination of contested meanings. All but the naive and the disingenuous recognize, however, that the justices do not—indeed cannot—merely "interpret" the Constitution, doing no more than "finding" the law it contains. As Lawrence M. Friedman (1984, p. 181) has written, "The Court goes far beyond interpretation. The Court invents and expands constitutional doctrine; some of this doctrine is connected to the text by gossamer threads, if at all." There is nothing especially modern about such judicial practice; the Supreme Court has been making law throughout its history.

The court has been reluctant to pronounce a clear national-emergency doctrine. To do so would reveal too starkly that the court effectively disappears from the governmental scene from time to time, an embarrassing admission that would detract from judicial majesty. Even when validating extraordinary governmental powers—and therefore the suppression of personal rights ostensibly protected by the Normal Constitution—as in *Wilson v. New* and *Blaisdell*, the court has taken pains to deny that emergency as such alters the Constitution. But in constitutional matters, too, actions speak louder than words.

Which brings us to the third locus of the Constitution. Unlike the Document or the Supreme Court's pronouncements, this Constitution is diffuse; it is all around us; it is the Constitutional System. Recognition of a constitution in this sense goes back at least as far as Aristotle, who remarks in his *Politics* that "[t]he words constitution and government have the same meaning." In this most fundamental sense the Constitution is, as Beard (1936, p. 34) said, "what living men and women think it is, recognize as such, carry into action, and obey." The Constitutional System comprises "the entire network of attitudes, norms, behaviors, and expectations among elites and publics that surround and support the written instrument" (Burnham 1982, p. 78)—and, one might add, the court's pronouncements, too. Herman Pritchett (1968, p. 298) has observed that "[t]he constitutional system is not separate from the political system, but a necessary part of it, performing the vital function of giving order and structure to the processes of policy formation." The Constitutional System, then, is nothing less than the conglomerate of beliefs, behaviors, and institutions that actually determine the structure of governmental powers and private rights and the processes whereby these powers and rights are altered (Belz 1972, p. 664; Davidson 1984).

Clearly the Crisis Constitution is, and long has been, an integral part of the American Constitutional System. Were you making bets, you could be confident in placing your money on the prospect that, in the next national emergency—real or contrived—the federal government will extend its powers at the expense of private rights to life, liberty, and property.

Why The Crisis Constitution?

Perhaps the best way to understand how the Crisis Constitution has become embedded in the Constitutional System is to examine the major episodes of its development, asking of each: Might it have been different? For each episode one can scarcely imagine that, given the political realities and the prevailing crisis conditions, the actual outcome could have been avoided. By considering why these events were so likely to happen as they did, one may gain a deeper appreciation of the American Constitutional System and the role of the Supreme Court in it.

Consider first whether the court might have found the Adamson Act unconstitutional in 1917. What would have been the consequence of such a ruling? Presumably a national railroad strike would have occurred, causing the "destruction of interstate commerce" and the "infinite injury to the public interest" that the court considered imminent. Bad enough, but even greater disaster loomed. The United States stood on the brink of war. (The court announced its decision on March 20; the United States declared war on April 6.) Thomas Gregory, the Attorney General at the time, later recalled: Chief Justice White "knew, as we all knew, that we were on the very verge of War; for the moment he forgot the facts of the case that was before him and his prophetic eye was resting on the immediate future when every proper energy of our country would be called upon to sustain it in its hour of greatest need" (quoted by Belknap 1983, p. 80, n. 93). The majority simply was not willing to issue a ruling fraught with danger to the military strength of the nation, no matter what the Normal Constitution might require. In retrospect the most remarkable aspect of *Wilson v. New* is that four justices dissented, William R. Day and Mahlon Pitney recording vigorous opposition to the majority's derogation from private property rights in the crisis.

The division within the court disappeared completely when the justices ruled on the constitutionality of the military draft in 1918: the decision was unanimous. Under the prevailing political and social conditions, permeated by war hysteria, superheated patriotism, and vigilante attacks on "slackers," the ruling was well-nigh inevitable.[4] Men were, after all, being thrown into jail merely for questioning the constitutionality of the draft. (The Attorney General went so far as to request the aid of the American Protective League, a private organization of superpatriots, to locate draft

---

[4] See Rossiter (1976, p. 95), Murphy (1972, pp. 12-13), Kelly, Harbison and Belz (1983, pp. 447, 526-30), and Higgs (1987, pp. 123-58).

resisters. Members of the league conducted numerous "slacker raids," made some forty thousand citizens' arrests, and investigated about three million suspected subversives [McCloskey and Zaller 1984, p. 40].) Leon Friedman (1969 as reprinted in Anderson 1982, p. 233) has argued that the draft-law cases "were based upon superficial arguments, disregard of substantial historical evidence, and undue deference to the exigencies of the First World War—in short, that they were incorrectly decided." Nonetheless, one can easily understand why the justices chose to transcend the Normal Constitution and uphold the draft: without it the government's war effort would have collapsed. The 2,820,000 draftees made up about 70 percent of the Army (U.S. Bureau of the Census 1975, p. 1140); and no doubt many of the volunteers came forward only because of the draft. Patriots themselves, the justices simply were not willing to pay such a high price to sustain the Normal Constitution, especially when political elites throughout the land were howling for conscription. Besides, had the court declared the draft unconstitutional, the executive branch would probably have ignored the ruling, leaving the court defeated, embarrassed, and diminished in constitutional status. "[I]t is an axiom of constitutional justice that any decision which the Court thinks will not be enforced will probably not be made" (Strum 1974, p. 4); "judges who find themselves 'powerless in fact' are apt to declare themselves 'powerless in law'" (Howard 1968, p. 337).

Might the Supreme Court have upheld private property rights in the Minnesota mortgage moratorium case? Of course, it might have—where human judgment is determinative anything is possible, and the actual decision rested on only a 5-to-4 margin. Again, however, the court's ruling accords well with a view of the court as belonging to, rather than hovering above, the Constitutional System. Farmers had suffered disproportionately in the Great Contraction. Caught between drastically reduced farm prices and less deflated nonfarm prices, and faced with fixed dollar obligations for taxes and for interest and principal on mortgage loans, hundreds of thousands had lost their homes and sources of livelihood at a time when the number of alternative opportunities was diminishing daily. Angry and frustrated, some had resorted to violence. Many others brought ominous political pressures to bear on state legislatures.[5] To strike down, in January 1934, the mortgage moratorium laws already enacted by twenty-two states would have risked setting off an explosion of farm protest and perhaps widespread violence. The court's ruling, in Chief Justice Hughes' words (290 U.S. at 440, would allow Minnesota—and by implication all other states—to

---

[5] See Paschal (1951, p. 167), Leonard (1971, p.82), Murphy (1972, p. 110, n. 28), Alston (1983, p. 886), and Alston (1984, p.447).

prevent "the immediate and literal enforcement of contractual obligations by temporary and conditional restraints where vital public interests would otherwise suffer." Forced to choose between upholding the Normal Constitution and averting a potential social and political calamity, the five-man majority decided to avert the calamity (Hendel 1951, pp. 180-81).

When the court ruled on the gold-clause cases, early in 1935, it faced—as it often does in cases involving public policies with pervasive impacts—an executive fait accompli. The government had taken possession of the nation's monetary gold stock; it had voided all contractual gold clauses and thereby prompted a multitude of changes in specific contractual performance. Was the court now to say that the government must return the gold coins and certificates to the millions of citizens who had surrendered them, and that all those who had paid legal tender instead of gold must turn around and pay the gold as initially stipulated in their contracts? The far-reaching economic consequences of such a ruling—the business chaos of which Attorney General Homer Cummings had warned the court—must have given the justices pause.[6] Contracts valued at some $100 billion were at stake. (So disastrous did the President consider an adverse court ruling on the gold clause of government bonds that, in anticipation, he prepared a radio address announcing that he would not enforce such a ruling [Pusey 1963, pp. 735-36].) Beyond the utter confusion of the marketplace lay the disruption of the administration's monetary policy, now almost two years old. The Attorney General's argument before the court emphasized the doctrine of emergency powers and the gravity of the prevailing depression crisis; the "power of self-preservation," he declared, required transcending the "supposed sanctity and inviolability of contractual obligations." Again, given the prevailing economic and political conditions, the remarkable aspect of the decision is that four justices dissented—Justice McReynolds read their objections with muttered asides that "the Constitution is gone" and "this is Nero at his worst" (all quotations from Murphy 1972, pp. 137-38).

The Supreme Court's virtual abdication during World War II reflected, even more clearly than the gold-clause cases, a fait accompli by the legislative and executive branches of government. The political branches had created a full-blown command economy, complete with conscription of soldiers, physical allocations of raw materials, confiscation of private facilities, controls of wages, prices, and rents, rationing of consumer goods, and a great deal more (Higgs 1987, pp. 196-236). Was the court, deciding cases in 1944 after such policies had been in force for years, to say that

---

[6] See Paschal (1951, p.181), Leonard (1971, p. 57), and Kelly, Harbison, and Belz (1983, p. 489).

they were unconstitutional? It is inconceivable. It would, in any event have been futile; and the court appreciated that fact quite well. "[M]ost judicial leaders hoped at all cost to avoid finding themselves in situations of judicial defiance of measures and actions clearly geared to the war effort and national security" (Murphy 1972, p. 224). The court occupied "the position of a private on sentry duty accosting a commanding general without his pass" (Mason 1956, p. 665). The best that it could do was to continue to go through the motions of judicial review, biding its time in anticipation of the return of normal conditions, when the Normal Constitution would reassert itself over the Crisis Constitution and genuine judicial review would again become feasible (Corwin 1947, p. 177).

Besides, as Rossiter (1976, p. 91) noted, "the Court, too, likes to win wars." Edwin Corwin (1947, pp. 177, 131), expressing himself somewhat more circumspectly, observed that "in total war, the Court necessarily loses some part of its normal freedom of decision and becomes assimilated, like the rest of society, to the mechanism of the national defense." Thus, "the restrictive clauses of the Constitution are not . . . .automatically suspended, but the scope of the rights to which they extend is capable of being reduced in the face of the urgencies of war, sometimes even to the vanishing point. . . . [T]he Court will not intrude its veto while war is flagrant." For the most part the suppression of private rights during the war was not even challenged in the courts—or, if challenges arose, the Supreme Court, dominated by the so-called War Hawks (Frankfurther, Stone, Black, and Douglas), chose not to review them (Mason 1956, pp. 675, 679-81).

Events during World War II demonstrate in its clearest form the logic of the Crisis Constitution (Higgs 1987, pp. 62-67). When elites and masses alike believe that national emergency is upon them, they call on the government to "do something." The political branches, acting more or less autonomously, adopt policies. By their very nature such policies entail costs, virtually all of which fall on nongovernmental people. The greater the costs, the more likely is public resistance. In the extreme, public resistance jeopardizes the government implementing the policy. Anticipating resistance, governments take steps to conceal or obscure the costs of their policies. One device invariably adopted is the substitution of (cost-hiding) command-and-control measures for (cost-revealing) fiscal-and-market means of resource allocation. The necessary implication of this substitution is the attenuation or destruction of private rights—rights previously protected by the Normal Constitution.

After the fall of France and even more so after the Japanese attack on Pearl Harbor and the ensuing declarations of war, Americans demanded effective military action to defend the nation and subdue its powerful enemies. The political branches responded by imposing a sweeping command-and-control system. The Supreme Court simply could not have prevented this development even had it wanted to do so. "The country at large was prepared to accede to the law of [perceived] necessity rather than to cogent constitutional analysis" (Kelly, Harbison, and Belz 1983, p. 553). The court must rely on the executive branch for enforcement of its rulings.[7] As Aristotle said, "[T]hose who carry arms can always determine the fate of the constitution." But even more fundamental than arms themselves—because arms must be wielded by people conscious of what they are doing—is the dominant ideology. As James Davidson (1984, p. 68) has said, "[m]etaconstitutional limits determine what constitutional provisions could be tolerated if enacted." These limits change during national emergencies. People anxiously seeking security against imminent threats to the economic viability, independence, or survival of the nation submit far more readily to a deprivation of normal private rights. Many people who ordinarily would have refused to comply with intrusive governmental directives accepted them during World War II as appropriate to the prevailing national condition (Rossiter 1948, pp. 4, 11, 276, 305; Schwartz 1957, p. 293). Only because of such public support did the government's emergency measures prove reasonably effective.

In sum, the Crisis Constitution, like the Normal Constitution, rests on a broad ideological base. Public attitudes, values, norms, and expectations condition the structure and processes of governmental powers and private rights in both cases (Olson 1984, pp. 93-94). In the twentieth century the American people have come to expect, tolerate, and in many instances demand that the Normal Constitution be displaced during national emergencies (Kelly, Harbison, and Belz 1983, pp. 554, 556). Governmental officials understand this public disposition and act accordingly, seeking their own objectives within the altered constraints. Conceivably the dualism of our fundamental institutions could be unproblematical: we would act according to the Crisis Constitution during national emergencies and according to the Normal Constitution at all other times.[8] But history has not conformed to such a simple pattern.

A Merger of the Two Constitutions?

In fact the Normal Constitution to which we revert after a national emergency has ended is never the same as it was before the crisis. To some degree, aspects of the Crisis Constitution, as expressed in judicial inter-

---

[7] See Strum (1974, p. 3), Friedman (1984, p. 196), and Bigel (1986, pp. 190-93).

[8] Strangely, in view of the voluminous evidence to the contrary in their own book, Kelly, Harbison, and Belz (1983, p. 571) assert that the American Constitutional System has in fact demonstrated such "remarkable flexibility." They claim that "it could adjust rapidly to the requirement of war and then return as rapidly to the institutions of peace."

pretation and even more so in the Constitutional System, are incorporated into the Normal Constitution.[9]

Such legacies marked the aftermaths of both world wars and the Great Depression. After World War I the Normal Constitution included massive governmental participation in credit markets, communications, and transportation industries as well as enduring precedents for rent controls, military conscription, and the suppression of free speech (Higgs 1987, pp. 148-56). The Great Depression, of course, brought a profusion of governmental restraints and regulatory agencies and a corresponding constriction of private property rights. Rossiter (1948, p. 264) noted also that "the emergency practices of the Year of Crisis [1933] wrought several lasting alterations in the Constitutional structure," including "important permanent delegations of crisis power . . .; a greatly expanded administration; a marked breakdown of the federal principle; and a general increase of presidential power based on executive leadership in the lawmaking process and the delegation of power." During 1937-1942, as all constitutional scholars acknowledge, a veritable Constitutional Revolution took place—"the product of emergency conditions, the threat to the Court and the reconstruction of its personnel by President Franklin D. Roosevelt" (Hendel 1951, p. 275)—submerging the doctrine of economic substantive due process and giving unrestricted scope to the federal regulatory power. Then the events of World War II carried the Crisis Constitution to new heights, and the legacies were legion. Even after enactment of a joint resolution repealing many of the wartime statutes in July 1947, more than a hundred wartime statutory provisions remained active; official states of emergency continued in force; and various new emergency measures, including a rent-control act and a peacetime military-conscription law, were enacted (Kelly, Harbison, and Belz 1983, pp. 574-75). Corwin (1947, pp. 172, 179) observed that after the war, for the first time in American history, the country did not return to a "peacetime Constitution." Now the Normal Constitution included:

(1) the attribution to Congress of a legislative power of indefinite scope;
(2) the attribution to the President of the power and duty to stimulate constantly the positive exercise of this indefinite power for enlarged social objectives;
(3) the right of Congress to delegate its powers ad libitum to the President for the achievement of such enlarged social objectives. . . .;
(4) the attribution to the President of a broad prerogative in the meeting of "emergencies" defined by himself and in the creation of executive agencies to assist him;

[9] See Corwin (1947, p. 172), Rossiter (1948, pp. 13, 295, 313), Kelly, Harbison, and Belz (1983, pp. 517, 519, 565, 574-75), and Higgs (1987).

(5) a progressively expanding replacement of the judicial process by the administrative process in the enforcement of the law—sometimes even of constitutional law.

In the four decades that have passed since Corwin made this summary, nothing he mentioned has changed (Higgs 1987, pp. 237-57). Thus the Normal Constitution of the post-World War II era has fully validated Big Government in the sense of an active, powerful, highly arbitrary government far less restrained by the constitutional checks and balances of the old Normal Constitution, a system that once restrained the interventions if not the ambitions of governmental officials.

Emergency powers as such continue to undergird the government's denial of numerous private rights, especially in relation to international travel, commercial, and financial transactions. Senators Frank Church and Charles Mathias noted in 1974 that "[e]mergency government has become the norm." Their committee report identified "at least 470 significant emergency powers statutes without time limitations delegating to the Executive extensive discretionary powers, ordinarily exercised by the Legislature, which affect the lives of American citizens in a host of all-encompassing ways" (quoted in Belknap 1983, pp. 68-69, n. 17). Recent presidents, Republican and Democratic alike, have dipped repeatedly into this vast reservoir of emergency powers, most recently to constrain or deny the rights of Americans to travel or do business with, *inter alia*, the citizens or governments of Cuba, Libya, Iran, Nicaragua, South Africa, and Syria (Higgs and Twight 1987).

The Supreme Court in the 1980's, as before, has made no attempt to constrain the emergency suppression of private rights. In *Dames & Moore v. Regan* (101 S. Ct. 2972 [1981] at 2982) the court quoted with approval a lower-court decision as follows: "The language of IEEPA [the International Emergency Economic Powers Act] is sweeping and unqualified. It provides broadly that the President may void or nullify the 'exercising [by any person of] any right, power or privilege with respect to. . . . any property in which any foreign country has any interest. . . .'" Further, "both the legislative history and cases interpreting the TWEA [Trading with the Enemy Act, first enacted in 1917] fully sustain the broad authority of the Executive when acting under this congressional grant of power" (p. 2983). Thus, even in the early 1980's, as normal a time as one can expect in our era, the Crisis Constitution overrides and displaces the Normal Constitution.

Should a genuine national emergency arise, there can be no doubt about how the government would react. (Recall its actions in dealing with the partly spurious, partly self-inflicted "energy crisis" in the 1970's).The private rights of Americans—such as remain—are balanced on a very thin constitutional edge. A wide variety of crises, real or contrived, could easily knock them into oblivion.

Can Anything Be Done?

Effective protection of private rights against future governmental invasion under color of emergency is unlikely. The experience of the past decade has shown that the procedural safeguards stipulated in the National Emergencies Act have no real effect. Procedural requirements are easy enough to comply with—White House flunkies can handle such book-keeping chores. When the President does not bother to comply, however, nothing happens. As *Regan v. Wald* (104 S. Ct. 3026 [1984]) has recently shown, the Supreme Court will not hold the Executive responsible even for going through the formal motions of compliance with the procedural requirements enacted by Congress. In any event the problem is not procedure; it is substance—and the abuse of substantive powers.

Not much more hope can be placed in a reconstituted Supreme Court, one more devoted to private rights and to the restoration of the old Normal Constitution. Even if such judges could be found and appointed—an unlikely prospect—their resistance to the Crisis Constitution could not have more than temporary effect in a national emergency. This lesson we have learned from the constitutional crisis of the mid-1930's.[10] Even a court containing the Four Horsemen, a court willing to plunge a constitutional dagger into the collectivist heart of the New Deal, could not hold out indefinitely in the face of preponderant public support for the government's policies. Even if stubborn justices do not buckle under to public opinion in an emergency, they must eventually retire or die—to be replaced by more "cooperative" judges (e.g., Black, Reed, Frankfurther, Douglas). Although the court does not simply follow the election returns, neither does it completely ignore them. It certainly does not ignore social, political, and economic events or public opinion. Even George Sutherland, as staunch a friend as the Normal Constitution ever had, expressed doubt that judges "are indifferent to what others think about their decisions" and avowed that he himself was not indifferent (Paschal 1951, p. 200). Justice Roberts, the "swing man" who more than anyone else bore responsibility for the court's turnaround in 1937, later observed: "Looking back, it is difficult to see how the Court could have resisted the popular urge. . . ." He referred obliquely to "the tremendous strain and the threat to the existing Court, of which I was fully conscious. . ." (quotations from Leonard 1971, pp. 144, 155). On the court, as in other branches of government, good men are not enough. Before the fierce winds of adverse political actions and

[10] For the pressures that promoted the Constitutional Revolution, see Hendel (1951, pp.250-53), Paschal (1951, p.206), Mason (1956, pp. 437-39, 456, 463), Pusey (1963, p. 747), Leonard (1971. pp. 2, 56, 92-3, 124-25, 136-57), Murphy (1972, pp. 154-69), and Frankfurter as quoted in Marcus (1977, p. 334, n. 25).

Ultimately the preservation of the Normal Constitution against the inroads of the Crisis Constitution can be accomplished only if the politically influential elites who make policies and mold the opinions of the masses are willing to resist the passions of national emergency. (Such resistance is, or at least once was, possible. Recall how Grover Cleveland's administration and the Supreme Court dealt with the crisis of the 1890's [Higgs 1987, pp. 77-105].) People must understand that reversion to the *status quo ante* will not occur, that private rights once surrendered are unlikely ever to be recovered fully. If such understanding, and a concomitant commitment to private rights, were widespread, we would have little to fear. As Abraham Lincoln said, "With public sentiment nothing can fail; without it, nothing can succeed. Consequently, he who molds public sentiment goes deeper than he who enacts statutes or pronounces decisions. He makes statutes and decisions possible or impossible to be executed" (quoted in Rhoades 1985, p. 204). If the dominant ideology gives strong support to the Normal Constitution, it will survive, no matter what else happens.

But if the dominant ideology does not give strong support to the Normal Constitution, it will eventually be overwhelmed by the Crisis Constitution. Step by step, a ratcheting loss of private rights will attend each episode of national emergency—and we may as well admit that such emergencies are inevitable. Unfortunately, elites and masses in the United States today, with only a few notable exceptions, have neither an appreciation of the ratchet process nor a strong commitment to private rights to life, liberty, and property.[11] Therefore, the most likely prospect is for further expansion of the Crisis Constitution and a corresponding loss of private rights.

References

Alston, Lee J. "Farm Foreclosures in the United States During the Interwar Period." *Journal of Economic History* 43 (December 1983): 885-903.

Alston, Lee J. "Farm Foreclosure Moratorium Legislation: A Lesson from the Past." *American Economic Review* 74 (June 1984): 445-57.

Anderson, Benjamin M. *Economics and the Public Welfare: A Financial and Economic History of the United States, 1914-46.* Indianapolis: Liberty Press, 1979.

Beard, Charles A. "The Living Constitution." *Annals of the American Academy of Political and Social Sciences* 185 (1936): 29-34.

Belknap, Michal R. "The New Deal and the Emergency Powers Doctrine." *Texas Law Review* 62 (1983): 67-109.

Belz, Herman. "Changing Conceptions of Constitutionalism in the Era of World War II and the Cold War." *Journal of American History* 59 (December 1972): 640-69.

---

[11] See McClosky and Zaller (1984), Scalia (1985, pp. 708-09), Higgs (1987, pp. 192-5, 233-4, 256-7).

Bigel, Alan I. *The Supreme Court on Emergency Powers, Foreign Affairs, and Protection of Civil Liberties, 1935-1975.* Lanham, Md.: University Press of America, 1986.

Bork, Robert H. "A Lawyer's View of Constitutional Economics." In *Constitutional Economics: Containing the Economic Powers of Government,* pp. 227-34. Edited by Richard B. McKenzie. Lexington, Mass.: Lexington Books, 1984.

Burnham, Walter Dean. "The Constitution, Capitalism, and the Need for Rationalized Regulation." In *How Capitalistic Is the Constitution?,* pp. 75-105. Edited by Robert A. Goldwin and William A. Schambra. Washington, D.C: American Enterprise Institute, 1982.

Corwin, Edward S. *Total War and the Constitution.* New York: Knopf, 1947.

Corwin, Edward S. *The Constitution and What It Means Today.* Revised by Harold W. Chase and Craig R. Ducat. Princeton, N.J.: Princeton University Press, 1974.

Davidson, James Dale. "The Limits of Constitutional Determinism." In *Constitutional Economics: Containing the Economic Powers of Government,* pp. 61-87. Edited by Richard B. McKenzie. Lexington, MA: Lexington Books, 1984.

Friedman, Lawrence M. *American Law.* New York: Norton, 1984.

Friedman, Leon. "Conscription and the Constitution: The Original Understanding." *Michigan Law Review* 67 (May 1969). Reprinted in *The Military Draft: Selected Readings on Conscription.* Edited by Martin Anderson. Stanford: Hoover Institution Press, 1982.

Hendel, Samuel. *Charles Evans Hughes and the Supreme Court.* New York: King's Crown Press, 1951.

Higgs, Robert. *Crisis and Leviathan: Critical Episodes in the Growth of American Government.* New York: Oxford University Press, 1987.

Higgs, Robert, and Twight, Charlotte. "National Emergency and the Erosion of Private Property Rights." *Cato Journal* 6 (Winter 1987).

Howard, J. Woodford, Jr. *Mr. Justice Murphy: A Political Biography.* Princeton, N.J.: Princeton University Press, 1968.

Kelly, Alfred H., Harbison, Winfred A., and Belz, Herman. *The American Constitution: Its Origins and Development.* New York: Norton, 1983.

Leonard, Charles A. *A Search for a Judicial Philosophy: Mr. Justice Roberts and the Constitutional Revolution of 1937.* Port Washington, N.Y.: Kennikat Press, 1971.

McClosky, Herbert, and Zaller, John. *The American Ethos: Public Attitudes toward Capitalism and Democracy.* Cambridge, Mass.: Harvard University Press, 1984.

Marcus, Maeva. *Truman and the Steel Seizure Case: The Limits of Presidential Power.* New York: Columbia University Press, 1977.

Mason, Alpheus Thomas. *Harlan Fiske Stone: Pillar of the Law.* New York: Viking Press, 1956.

Murphy, Paul L. *The Constitution in Crisis Times, 1918-1969.* New York: Harper Torchbooks, 1972.

Olson, Mancur. "Comment." In *Constitutional Economics: Containing the Economic Powers of Government,* pp. 89-94. Edited by Richard B. McKenzie. Lexington, Mass.: Lexington Books, 1984.

Paschal, Joel Francis. *Mr. Justice Sutherland: A Man Against the State.* Princeton, N.J.: Princeton University Press, 1951.

Pritchett, C. Herman. "Constitutional Law: I. Introduction." *International Encyclopedia of the Social Sciences* 3 (1968): 295-300.

Pusey, Merlo J. *Charles Evans Hughes.* New York: Columbia University Press, 1963.

Rhoads, Steven E. *The Economist's View of the World: Government, Markets, and Public Policy.* New York: Cambridge University Press, 1985.

Rossiter, Clinton L. *Constitutional Dictatorship: Crisis Government in the Modern Democracies.* Princeton, N.J.: Princeton, University Press, 1948.

Rossiter, Clinton. *The Supreme Court and the Commander in Chief.* Expanded edition with additions by Richard P. Longaker. Ithaca, N.Y.: Cornell University Press, 1976.

Scalia, Antonin. "Economic Affairs as Human Affairs." *Cato Journal* 4 (Winter 1985): 703-709.

Schwartz, Bernard. *The Supreme Court: Constitutional Revolution in Retrospect.* New York: Ronaid Press, 1957.

Strum, Philippa. *The Supreme Court and "Political Questions": A Study in Judicial Evasion.* University Ala.: University of Alabama Press, 1974.

United Bureau of the Census. *Historical Statistics of the United States, Colonial Times to 1970.* Washington, D.C.: U.S. Government Printing 1975.

18

HELPING THE POOR THROUGH GOVERNMENTAL POVERTY PROGRAMS: THE TRIUMPH OF RHETORIC OVER REALITY
Dwight R. Lee and Richard B. McKenzie

In the view of many social-policy analysts, the mere existence of poverty, per se, justifies an expanded role for government. While more government may not be a sufficient condition to reduce poverty, government-provided poverty relief in some form is seen as a necessary condition, if poverty is ever to become a less-pressing social issue.

Of course, among economists, governmental poverty programs have been conventionally justified as being efficent and equitable. Relief programs enhance the efficiency of the economy because they "internalize the externalities" of improving the welfare of the disadvantaged sectors of the citizenry. Through taxes, the citizenry pays for the benefits, for example, of reduced blight associated with low-income areas. Relief programs also improve equity in the income distribution by more accurately aligning income shares with assumed income entitlement. Supposedly, market-determined incomes do not capture the full economic value of the contributions to production of many workers.The central proposition of this paper is that the reality of the political process results in a direct relationship between the size of government (particularly the size of the transfer sector) and the incidence of poverty. Thus, in the long run, increasing the scope of government (without regard for external constraints on the political process) will do nothing to improve the relative well-being of the poor, but instead will almost surely reduce the absolute well-being of the needy.

Unfortunately, in our view, the very reasons why an expanding government typically undermines the progress of the poor also explain why politicians and bureacrats are so effective at selling government programs

---

Dwight Lee and Richard McKenzie are Professors of Economics at the University of Georgia and Clemson University, respectively. They are the authors of *Regulating Government: A Preface to Constitutional Economics* (Lexington Books, 1987).

as the best hope for the poor. And the very failure of government "solutions" to poverty also helps explain why these "solutions" are so pervasive and so politically persuasive. In today's political environment, any genuine attempt to help the poor will require reversing the growth of government. But success in this effort requires a methodological perspective that extends beyond that typically employed in examination of ordinary politics.

The perspective of "constitutional economics" must replace the more conventional one of "policy economics." From this methodological perspective, any real hope for government action that assists, rather than retards, the well-being of the poor critically depends on constitutional limits on the scope and discretion of political action.

Inequality and Political Impotence

The case for government programs designed specifically for the purpose of helping the poor depends on two separate claims. First, the private market fails to generate an acceptable distribution of income and leaves in its trail a residual of poor. Second, government has the motivation and ability to reduce income inequality by helping the poor. The first claim is difficult to refute. This so-called "market failure" stems, in part, from the fact that the "acceptable" distribution of income is seldom precisely specified. At the same time, no one can argue convincingly that the market will eliminate poverty, certainly not in a relative sense. For the very reasons that this charge against the market is actually a substantive one, the claim that government can, in fact, help the poor is questionable, if not downright wrong. In a relative sense, government should be no better able than the market to achieve an unspecified, "fair" income distribution or eliminate poverty.

Consider explanations given for why the market fails to generate a distribution of income that social critics feel is "fair" (or even one that eliminates egregious cases of poverty). The marketplace can reasonably be characterized as a setting in which people attempt to advance their individual objectives by competing against each other for limited resources. The general outcomes that result from this competitive process are not ordained by any individual or group of individuals who participate in the process. Instead, general market outcomes simply emerge as the unintended consequence of individual actions. The advantage of the market is that the unintended outcomes of market activity are typically beneficial to the community at large. However, the income distribution that emerges from the competitive interplay of market forces will not necessarily be one that is widely seen as desirable. Indeed, one of the features of the market that makes it so generally efficient is the constant threat of poverty it imposes on all. Unless an individual uses resources in ways that satisfy the demands of others, the individual will experience a reduction in resources (and therefore wealth) as resources are transferred to those who are better able to accommodate the demands of others. Those who, for whatever reason, lack the skills necessary to employ resources efficiently will be unable to compete effectively in the marketplace and will be left behind.[1]

The view of the market process as one which makes the potential for failure instructional lies behind the pervasive notion that government should alter the distribution of income in favor of the poor. There might be a justification for government poverty relief on such grounds if individuals experienced a moral metamorphosis when they move from market roles to government roles (or, as discussed later, if workable restrictions on government transfer powers were in place). But there is no reason to believe that this metamorphosis takes place. And in the absence of evidence to the contrary, there can be little reason for expecting that government can correct the distributional "failures" of the marketplace. Government will fail to reduce the income inequality generated by market competition for the very reason the market distribution is considered unfair: the inability of some to compete successfully for limited resources. As a social institution for accomplishing social and economic objectives, the "government" is neither less degenerate nor more degenerate than the "market." Outcomes emerge from both through the interaction of equally imperfect people.

A realistic view of government has to recognize that, just as in the marketplace, it is not overarching social objectives that dominate the motivations of individual decision-makers. The political process can best be understood as a competitive arena in which individuals vie for resources with far more concern over promoting narrow personal objectives than broad social objectives. General outcomes do emerge from individual actions, but as with market outcomes, they are best described as the unintended consequences of this action. Political outcomes will generally differ from market outcomes because the rules of the competitive inter-action are different, not because the underlying motives of the individual decision-makers are different.

There is no *a priori* reason, however, for believing the distributional outcome of political activity will differ much, if any, from that of market activity. The income distribution that results from any competitive process depends to an overwhelming degree on the distribution of relevant skills

---

[1] Being left behind by the private market does not mean being left behind by the private sector, broadly defined. Individuals generally do not alter their purchasing decision in order to assist inefficient producers and workers, but they commonly provide charitable assistance to those who are poor. While private charity may not be as generous as some would like, neither is it insignificant. For example, in 1982 private contributions of money and volunteer time to community service (much of which, though not all, assisted the poor) was valued at $100 billion. This figure is cited and referenced in Steinberg (1987).

and incentives within the population. Somewhat different skills may be required for success in political competition than for success in market competition. Therefore, political competition and market competition may rank individuals differently. Nevertheless, even if rankings differed under the two regimes, it is still likely that politically relevant skills would be no more or no less evenly distributed throughout the population than market relevant skills, and the distribution of income would be the same, more or less, whether determined through the political process or through the market process. Whether under market or political competition, the more aggressive, ambitious, articulate, hardworking and persistent individuals are, the more likely they are to be successful. Thus, people who are poor because they lack the skills to succeed in the marketplace are unlikely to be compete successfully for resources in the public sector.

Given our underlying premise that it is narrow private objectives instead of broad community concerns that motivate political action, it follows that expanding government for the stated purpose of improving the relative position of the poor will almost surely fail to do so. This is true, at least in the long run, after all people have adjusted the allocation of their efforts to the new institutional setting. Again, our premise is that the income distribution is not chosen by some monolithic entity known as "government," just as it is not chosen by the "market." The distribution of income emerges from the competitive interaction of interests within the political economy, and there is no reason for believing that expanding government will have an appreciable influence on this competitive interaction as it pertains to the income distribution.

Our underlying premise, may be difficult for many to accept, since the rhetoric of the political process is almost exclusively organized around the professed desire to achieve noble social objectives, such as reducing poverty. And people may be easily convinced that public-interest political rhetoric provides an accurate reflection of political reality.[2] This gullibility is explained by certain incentives built into the political process that, in turn, explain why public interest rhetoric is such an effective tool of politically organized special interests. However, in political attempts to reduce poverty—before considering the reasons for, and significance of, the triumph of rhetoric over reality—it is useful to consider further the impotence of poverty programs.

---

[2] Consider, for example Lawrence Tribe's [of Harvard Law School] criticism of safeguarding existing property rights with the comment, "immunizing from majoritarian arrangement extant distributions of wealth and economic power, almost as though such patterns and distributions of capital reflected something decreed and indeed sanctified by nature rather than something *chosen by the polity*" (emphasis added). Cited in Sowell (1987; p. 188).

The Eroding Effectiveness of Poverty Programs

The inference to be drawn from this discussion is not that a government transfer program, in and of itself, is incapable of helping the poor. Surely there are particular programs that have, at least temporarily, transferred wealth from the relatively wealthy to the relatively poor. But such transfers are completely consistent with our view that expanding government for the purpose of helping the poor will fail to do so in the long-run. The effectiveness of government attempts to transfer wealth to the poor tends to erode over time. The explanation for this erosion can be grouped under two headings; 1) the response of those who are not poor to poverty programs and 2) the response of the poor to poverty programs.

The Response of the Nonpoor

Poverty programs, even when they initially serve to transfer resources exclusively from the nonpoor to the poor, seldom continue to do so. Government programs that are effective at transferring wealth attract the attention of non-recipients who see themselves as potential recipients. Given time, these groups are able to mobilize sufficient political influence to begin capturing some of the wealth transfer for themselves.

In the case of government programs initially justified as a way of helping the poor, there are numerous examples of their effectiveness being diluted as they were expanded to include the nonpoor. Medicaid, which was established in the 1960s to finance the medical care of the poor, was immediately accompanied by Medicare that financed medical care for those over age 65, the vast majority of whom are nonpoor. Of the two programs, it is Medicare that has grown the more rapidly.[3] Subsidized student loans were initially justified as a means of helping deserving but poor students continue their education at the college and university level. Soon after the subsidized loan program went into effect, however, Congress responded to political pressure and effectively removed income as a consideration in granting the loans. Loan volume increased immediately by a factor of five with the nonpoor receiving the bulk of the funds (See Quinn, 1982). Likewise, the political justification for farm subsidies has always rested heavily on the notion that these subsidies provided assistance to poor farmers who would otherwise be driven off their land. The facts of the case are that government farm assistance goes overwhelmingly to nonpoor farmers and the primary effect of government farm policy is to increase the price of food, an item on which the poor spend a far higher percentage of their budget than do the nonpoor.

---

[3] In Canada government transfers aimed at the medical needs of the poor have been recently expanded to include the nonpoor. The empirical evidence suggests rather strongly that the effect of this expansion was to reduce the well-being of the poor. See Lindsay and Zycher (1984).

The political pressure to expand transfer programs to include the non-poor comes not only from nonpoor recipients, but also from the suppliers of the transfer programs, including bureaucrats and private suppliers of the services. For example, the farm lobby wants the food stamp program expanded and it has been both aggressive and effective in pushing for such expansion. The American Medical Association lobbies actively for expansion in Medicaid and Medicare. Similarly, construction industry associations exert political influence on behalf of federal spending on construction, some of which is directed toward the provision of low-income housing but most of which has nothing to do with helping the poor. The political effectiveness of supplier groups at structuring poverty programs in ways that serve the interest of the supplier is evidenced by the fact that, between 1965 and 1981, of those transfers that did go to the poor, in-kind transfers increased 13 times faster than did cash transfers.[4]

The political competition among different interest groups will, no doubt, result in some programs that help the poor, even in the long-run, and even though these programs lose some of their effectiveness over time. However, these beneficial programs are invariably coupled with other programs that, though justified with the rhetoric of helping the poor, on balance take from the poor.

Furthermore, even when government manages to transfer wealth to the poor, predictably this gain will be at least partially offset by a decline in the private charitable response of the nonpoor. Decisions on private contributions to the poor will be influenced by the perception of how much the poor are being assisted by public transfers. Therefore, public sector transfers will crowd out private transfers—at least to some degree. The evidence is supportive of this view. Based on data from 1948-72, Abrams and Schmitz (1978) conclude that for every dollar increase in public welfare expenditures, private charity is reduced by 28 cents.[5] This understates the "crowding-out" effects on the poor according to evidence uncovered by Roberts (1984). Roberts argues that as the federal government has taken on more responsibility for assisting the poor, the composition of private charity has shifted away from donations to the poor and toward donations to nonpoor recipients, such as religious, educational, and artistic organizations. It should also be emphasized here that it is the public perception

---

[4] See Table 7.2 of Goodman (1984), It should be pointed out here that in 1983 only 16 percent of direct government transfers (both money and in kind) were means tested—specifically aimed at the poor.

[5] In a more recent paper, Abrams and Schmitz (1984) reached a similar conclusion using 1979 cross sectional data. In this study they find from every dollar increase in public welfare expenditure, a 30 cent reduction in private charity.

of how much government transfers are helping the poor that determines the "crowding-out" effect, not how much government transfers are actually helping the poor. And for reasons that will be discussed later, politicians are motivated to overstate the benefits the poor receive from public transfers, and taxpayers quite rationally accept these overstatements at their approximate face value.

The Response of the Poor

In spite of points just discussed, some wealth from government transfers may still trickle down to the poor. Even if this implied "trickle-down theory of poverty relief" were the case, it does not follow that the poor are made relatively better off. Any program that transfers income to the poor will reduce, to some extent, the incentive the poor have to provide for themselves. Perverse incentive effects are expected even under transfer arrangements such as the negative income tax—a program designed by economists seeking to minimize the waste and inefficiencies emanating from tax-transfer programs. When we consider the type of transfer programs that emerge from the special-interest competition of the real world of politics rather than those coming from the drawing boards of economists, then we are considering transfer programs that are both extremely costly in terms of budgets and extremely inefficient in terms of the accompanying disincentives.

The most effective way for an individual to overcome poverty is through the acquisition of productive skills and attitudes, an acquisition that invariably requires work-related experiences. For the poor, any program that reduces an individual's incentive to seek such experience also reduces that individual's chance of escaping poverty. With this point in mind, consider the fact that recipients of Aid for Dependent Children (AFDC) lose 67 cents for every dollar they earn (and report). And this 67 percent tax on (reported) earned income, albeit implicit, actually understates the disincentive effects because it does not include the possible loss of in-kind benefits, such as food stamps and Medicaid that are phased out as earned income increases beyond certain thresholds. When the loss of the in-kind benefits is considered, AFDC recipients often confront implicit marginal tax rates on additional earnings that approach, or in some cases even exceed, 100 percent.

More generally, consider the likely effect of the proliferation of Great Society welfare programs on labor-force participation rates. According to figures compiled by Murray (1982 and 1984, chapter 5), the labor-force participation rate for low-income males began a sharp decline in 1966, a time of economic prosperity and generally low unemployment rates. Despite historical similarity in labor-force participation rates across income classes, the gap between the low-income labor force participation rate and middle to upper-income labor force participation rates has continued to widen since 1966. Murray concludes that, "Without doubt, *something* happened in the mid-1960s that changed the incentives for low-income workers to stay in the job market. The Great Society reform constitutes the biggest, most visible, most plausible candidate" (Murray 1982, p. 13; emphasis in the original).

There seems to be a strong tendency for welfare recipients to substitute publicly provided income for privately earned income. The money that does filter down to the poor through government-transfer programs (which will be only a fraction of the income extracted from other higher income tax-payers) will not necessarily constitute additional income for the poor. While the poor may not be any better off financially because of transfer programs, they will be worse off by virtue of becoming dependent on these programs. Additionally, there is an insidious tendency for the dependency to be passed on from one generation to the next.

Consider the fact that as AFDC and other transfer benefits have grown, so has the percentage of unwed mothers among the poor. This does not suggest that the availability of public transfers for unwed mothers is the only thing that influences the rate of illegitimate births. Nonetheless, one study of unwed pregnant teenagers concluded that after controlling for such demographic considerations as age, religion, school enrollment, and ethnic origin, those eligible for public assistance were significantly more likely to deliver their babies out of wedlock (Fuchs 1983, pp. 105-06). Couple this finding with the fact that children born out of wedlock are more likely to be neglected and abused, and it is easy to understand why the welfare dependency of one generation tends to generate welfare dependency in the next.

There exists even more direct evidence that welfare dependency is bequeathed from one generation to the next. The Department of Health, Education and Welfare concluded (from a 1967 study) that over 20 percent of the AFDC mothers whose welfare history was known were, as children, in homes receiving welfare (Glicken 1981). Subsequent studies of the Department have failed to follow up on what it surely considered the embarrassing growth in intergenerational welfare dependency. It has been conjectured, however, that "trans-generational recipients" made up approximately 40 percent of all AFDC mothers in 1980 (Glicken 1981, pp. 28-29).

Apparently, public transfers create perverse responses on the part of the recipient poor and reduce the poor's ability to climb out of poverty and become productive members of society. These perverse incentives erode the government's ability to improve the well-being of the poor over time, and the erosion that extends, and probably intensifies, over future generations.

The Poor of the Future

A common presumption of traditional poverty relief proposals is that if net transfers are actually made to the poor, the income or wealth subject to transfer comes directly or indirectly from the nonpoor. Without much question, the taxes to support transfers are levied primarily on the nonpoor. However, contemporary poverty relief programs can through their effects on incentives, cause a transfer of income from the poor of the future to the poor of today. This is true to the extent that the poor of today obtain relief at the cost of lower incomes for the future poor (and nonpoor).

What is especially interesting about a political process unconstrained in the types of policies that can be adopted is that the poor and the nonpoor of the future do not have a vote—because they do not yet exist. Unconstrained democracy is an uncontrolled form of special-interest politics, with only the existing citizenry empowered with the right to vote. Of course, we should expect the current generation of poor and nonpoor alike to exploit their favored political positions to the disadvantaged of future generations —including future poor generations. As a consequence, we should not be surprised to find that in an unconstrained democracy, any gains in poverty reduction within the current generation will tend to be offset (or more than offset) by poverty increases over the course of time.

Again, such a conclusion should not be unexpected. It flows inexorably from a generalized principle: All favored politically powerful interest groups should be expected to exploit the political power at hand within competitive politics. As economists have conventionally argued, truckers, farmers, and teachers should be expected to exploit the political power at their disposal to the disadvantage of others within the current generation of voters. Similarly, to the extent feasible, we should expect the current generation of voters to exploit their political power to the detriment of any group not given equal political power, namely, those who do not exist and do not now have a vote.

In other words, in an unconstrained political world, there can be "too much" poverty relief in the sense that adopted governmental programs cause a net increase in poverty over the course of several generations. At the very least, government powers to relieve poverty need to be restricted for much the same reason that its powers to grant monopoly privileges need to be strictly contained: to prevent the politically influential from obtaining benefits that are worth less than the costs they impose on others. More will be said below on the need for constitutional checks on government relief powers.

A Matter of Evidence

There are compelling reasons for accepting the proposition that the poor receive far less benefit from public transfer programs than is indicated by the rhetoric that provides political justification for these programs or by the large sums of money that flow through these programs. Still, nothing we have said so far rules out the possibility that, on balance, the poor are made better off because of public transfer programs. This is an empirical question, and it is one of crucial relevance to the central proposition of this paper; i.e., a necessary condition for improving the welfare of the poor is the reduction of government.

Before presenting evidence that strongly suggests that the poor have not, on balance, benefitted by transfer programs, it is important to emphasize that we are concerned with the long-run consequences of these programs. It is undeniably true that if all transfer programs were suddenly terminated, the many poor (and nonpoor) people who have made educational, employment, and general life-style decisions in response to these programs would be much "worse off"; in some cases, for an extended period of time. Welfare recipients, for example, cannot instantly develop the skills and earning potential needed to replace welfare income. If one measures the benefits provided by welfare programs by simply comparing the current net income of welfare recipients with what their current net income would be if their welfare income was eliminated, everything else remaining the same, then it would appear that welfare programs are providing enormous benefits. It is precisely these types of comparisons that are made by those who argue that government transfers have been successful at helping the poor. However, this is not a measure of success. Rather, it is a measure of the dependency created by government transfers and, therefore, a measure of their long-run failure.

In order to evaluate accurately the long-run effect of government transfers on income inequality, we would have to know what the distribution would have been in the counter-factual world of no government-transfer programs. In other words, how does the existing income distribution that includes current government-transfer programs compare with the income distribution that would exist if there had never been any government-transfer programs? Unfortunately, there is no way to know with complete confidence the answer to this question because there is no way to observe a world that does not now exist.

Given the difficulty of determining counter-factual states of the world, the best hope for assessing government's long-run influence on the distribution of income is to look at this distribution over an interval of time during which government welfare programs have expanded. The evidence obtained from such an approach indicates that goverment-transfer programs have done little, if anything, to reduce income inequality in the United States.

Since the 1950s there has been a significant increase in the amount of resources that have been channeled through the federal government for the stated purpose of helping the poor. If one is optimistic that government can help the poor, then one would expect to observe some reduction in U.S. income inequality since 1950. Yet the evidence provides reasons for doubting that this has been the case. The most widely reported figures on the U.S. distribution of income are found in the Current Population Survey (CPS) undertaken by the Census Bureau. The CPS income measure includes salaries and wages, net income from self-employment, Social Security incomes, interest and dividends, net rental income, government cash transfers, private pensions, alimony, and regular gifts. Based on the CPS income measure, the share of income going to those families in the lowest quintile of the surveyed families declined from 4.9 percent in 1952 to 4.7 percent in 1984. At the other end of the spectrum, the share of income going to those families in the top quintile increased from 42.0 percent in 1952 to 42.9 percent in 1984. While relative income shares fluctuated slightly from year to year during the 1952-1984 period, the long-run trend for all quintiles has shown almost no movement. Economists Morgan Reynolds and Eugene Smolensky made a number of adjustments to the CPS measure to account for the value of all government transfers, in kind as well as cash, and looked at the resulting distribution of net income from 1950 through 1970. They detected no trend in the degree of income inequality.[6]

Unless one is prepared to believe that, in the absence of government-transfer programs, the distribution of income would have become even more unequal since 1950 (and there is no compelling reason for this belief), then it appears that government has done little, if anything, to help the poor. Some programs have without doubt helped the poor but others have made the poor worse off. Still other programs have had the effect of depressing the incomes of all, rich and poor. Some programs have helped particular segments of the poor while, at the same time, they have harmed other segments of the poor. On balance, it would appear that the poor would be just as well off if government had stayed out of the business of transferring wealth to "deserving" groups (deserving as determined by the political process). This is not to say that poverty would not be a problem in a world without government transfers and poverty programs. In such a world, there would surely be desperate cases of poverty. However, poverty is also a problem in a world with substantial public sector transfers. The government at all levels currently devotes 15 (or more) percent of the gross national product to programs ostensibly designed to combat poverty, yet there is no shortage of desperate cases of poverty.

Given the tremendous increase in government transfers over the last

[6] See Reynolds and Smolensky (1977; especially Chapter 5).

few decades, the evidence on the stability of the distribution of income is rather startling. But this evidence is completely consistent with the view that government, just as the market, is a competitive arena in which the distribution of competitive skills determines income shares. The noble goals and lofty rhetoric of government poverty programs have done little to alter the distribution of political and market skills within society and, therefore, these programs have failed to alter appreciably the distribution of income.

Helping the Poor By Reducing Government

So far we have been discussing the effect government transfers have had on the relative wealth position of the poor. Certainly of equal, if not greater, importance is the effect government transfers have had on the absolute wealth position of the poor. The unfortunate conclusion is that if government transfers have failed to increase the relative wealth of the poor, they have also failed to increase the absolute wealth of the poor. In fact, the transfers would probably reduce the absolute well-being of the poor even if they altered the income distribution somewhat in favor of the poor.

Government transfer expenditures adversely effect economic efficiency and the growth of income. The taxes necessary to finance transfer expenditures reduce the return to labor, saving and investment, thereby reducing the incentive to engage in these productive activities. Similarly, the payment of welfare benefits reduces the incentive of recipients to engage in productive activities. Just how large these efficiency costs are cannot be known with great precision. A large number of empirical studies have attempted to measure the size of the negative productivity effects of taxes and transfers and, not surprisingly, the estimates vary.[7] No one, however, has found the effects to be either neutral or positive. So, with government-transfer programs reducing the overall size of the economic pie, they are reducing the *absolute* wealth of the poor if the proportion of the pie going to the poor remains the same. Even if, contrary to the evidence, government-transfer programs are altering the *distribution* of income in favor of the poor, it would still be likely that the poor are absolutely worse off.

Our analysis suggests that the only effective way of helping the poor in absolute terms over the long-run is to reduce the size and scope of government by phasing out government-transfer programs. Such a reduction would probably have no noticeable long-run effect on the percentage of national income going to the poor, but would surely result in a larger national income. This is the essential logic that lies behind our introductory statement that a reduction in government is necessary for improving the growth in the poor's absolute wealth.

---

[7] Many of these studies are surveyed in Danziger et al. (1981).

Welfare reformers imagine that the system can be improved to the benefit of the poor. How? By reducing only those programs that, on balance, hurt the poor, while maintaining those that, on balance, help the poor. However, a major objective of this paper is to point out that it is naive to expect the political powers to implement only those programs that promote broad social goals, such as helping the poor, while ignoring special interest programs that do not. Once political transfers are made available to one group, no matter how deserving that group may be, economic rents (or profits) are generated that will motivate competition among politically organized groups. The result of this competition is, invariably, a package of programs that serve a variety of narrow interests, but which reduce general economic efficiency without improving the relative position of the persons the transfers were *originally* intended to help.

As opposed to the prevailing view, we argue that it is only by reducing government that it is possible to provide genuine help to the poor. Restrictions on the transfer authority of government translate into restrictions on the politically powerful nonpoor who are relatively more efficient than the poor at exploiting the government's transfer powers.

The Politics of Poverty Programs

If it is true that government transfers are doing little or nothing to help the poor, and are indeed hurting the poor, why is it that the tax paying public tolerates the enormous expense these transfers impose? What is it about the political process that allows politicians and bureaucrats to extract tens of billions of dollars from the American public year after year for the stated purpose of helping the poor? In considering this question, it cannot be denied that the public does provide political support for government programs that claim to assist the poor. If citizens refused to vote for such programs, or for the politicians who support them in the legislature, the programs would soon cease to exist.

An important element in understanding public support for failed poverty programs can be found in the simple arithmetic of voting. Whether considering an election of a few thousand voters or millions of voters, the probability is effectively zero that any one citizen will cast a decisive vote: that the election would be a tie in the absence of the citizen's vote. This lack of decisiveness has been used to explain why voters tend to be "rationally ignorant" of political issues and why it is often only a small percentage of eligible voters who bother to go to the polls. One often noted problem with this explanation of voter behavior is that it is difficult to square it with the number of people who actually do vote. If the only reason people voted was to influence political outcomes, then it is hard to explain why voter turnout is not far smaller than it actually is.

Obviously, people vote for reasons other than the hope of controlling election outcomes. The expressive urge is a strong one—people vote for the satisfaction of making a statement in favor of things of which they approve and in opposition to things of which they disapprove. Voting for a favored candidate (or the position the candidate claims to support) has much in common with cheering for the home team or sending a get-well card to a sick friend. There is no expectation that the cheering will make the difference between victory and defeat or that a get-well card will determine whether or not the sick friend recovers. People simply receive satisfaction from the act of expression.

Most people have some concern for the plight of the poor and realize positive satisfaction from expressing that concern. This concern can be expressed in several ways, for example, casual conversation and private contributions to the poor. Yet another way of expressing concern for the poor is by voting in favor of programs which purport to help them. It happens that this is one of the cheapest ways for an individual to express concern for the poor. An individual incurs little or no cost but realizes a satisfying sense of moral virtue by voting for a poverty program, even an extremely costly poverty program. If the program passes, the individual's share of the cost may be significant. However, the amount an individual has to pay is completely independent of how he votes, unless, of course, his vote is the decisive one. Since the probability that any one vote will be decisive is effectively zero, each voter can vote in favor of poverty programs and completely ignore the cost.

Voting for public charity is, therefore, quite different from contributing to private charity. When making a private contribution one has to confront the full cost of the choice made. The private cost is sure to serve as a moderating influence on expressing concern for the poor through private gifts. This moderating influence is inoperative when expressing concern for the poor through voting. If one gets even the slightest satisfaction from voting for a poverty program, or suffers even the slightest pang of conscience from voting against it, then the rational thing to do is vote yes, no matter how expensive the program. Expressing concern for the poor at the polls is much like expressing concern for the poor in polite conversation; it feels good and it costs nothing.[8]

Political action magnifies the result of our charitable feelings. Considering each poverty program one at a time, majorities tend to obligate themselves, along with everyone else, to far greater expenditures in the name of helping the poor than the sum of what each would be willing to give privately. Furthermore, it is one thing to vote in favor of money for the alleviation of poverty and quite another to make sure that the money is effectively

---

[8] For an early discussion of this point, see Tullock (1971).

used to that end. As opposed to voting in support of poverty programs, it is extremely costly for an individual to acquire the information and perform the monitoring necessary to insure that the programs primarily serve the interests of the poor.[9] Therefore, having voted for poverty programs, the typical citizen will give the problem of poverty little thought other than to reflect occasionally with satisfaction on his or her "proven" commitment to and concern for the poor. Remaining ignorant and apathetic as to the actual functioning of poverty programs is completely rational for the average citizen.

Our point is not that no one will take an active interest in the technical details of the design and implementation of poverty programs. As discussed earlier, those groups that are politically organized around interests which can be promoted by poverty programs will be actively involved in attempts to structure these programs in ways that best serve those interests. Typically, these attempts, when successful, will reduce if not eliminate entirely the effectiveness of the programs as an anti-poverty weapon. Furthermore, the rational ignorance and apathy of the average citizen will provide wide latitude for the special interests to work their political will successfully.

The special interests cannot be successful at structuring poverty programs primarily for their narrow advantage by being blatant in this effort. As is always the case, political coalitions can successfully promote their special-interest programs only by presenting them as public-interest programs. If the public were to see through the public-interest rhetoric that glosses over most poverty programs to the private-interest reality that lies behind them, it is doubtful that these programs would command the broad electoral support upon which their survival depends.

Poverty programs, even when their net effect is to make the poor worse off, will still appear to be helping the poor. It will be easy for supporters of a program to point to identifiable individuals who receive benefits and who would, at least in the short-run, be thrown into poverty (or greater poverty) if the program were eliminated. Similarly, identifiable beneficiaries will emerge from an expansion in existing programs or adoption of new ones. The fact that poverty programs have the long-run effect of generating dependency, rather than providing income over and above what recipients would otherwise have earned, will not be readily apparent. The visible

---

[9] The individual who did take on this responsibility would be contributing to the public good, the reduction of poverty. There is no reason to believe that individuals will make such contributions to any significant degree, and indeed a major argument in favor of government programs to help the poor, that of Friedman (1962; p. 191), is that individuals will not contribute to the public good of poverty reduction. This suggests, rather paradoxically, that the standard case for government poverty programs is based on considerations that explain why these programs will tend to be ineffective.

benefits a poverty program provides to some poor will invariably come at the expense of others, including other poor, in the form of generalized reductions in economic productivity. However, since this cost is diffused, it will go largely unnoticed even when it is substantially larger than the visible benefits. Even if the cost is noticed, it will not necessarily be connected to the programs causing the damage. Successful politicians are successful in large measure because of their ability to call attention to the benefits derived from the programs they sponsor while obscuring, or shifting the blame for, the costs of these programs.

The most effective way of helping the poor would be to reduce the role of the political process in economic decisions, allowing for an expansion in the role of the market process. Yet poverty programs are politically successful because the general public holds exactly the opposite opinion. The perception widely held is that the market generates poverty and the government has the ability to help the poor.

The irony is that the market process is seen as the source of poverty for precisely the reason that it creates wealth and that the political process is seen as the cure for poverty for precisely the reason that it destroys wealth.

The market generates wealth and distributes it widely because it does not permit one to ignore failure. Markets hold people accountable for their use of resources—rewarding those who develop and use resources in ways that are highly valued by others, while penalizing those who fail to do so. The treatment of both success and failure is important. Understandably, to the casual observer, any system that highlights failure may be seen as unfair even if it achieves general prosperity. After all, failures stand out against the general prosperity which, precisely because it is so general, is frequently taken for granted. Furthermore, the prospects of failure would not be nearly so constructive if failure were not, from time to time, realized with considerable force—that is, at a considerable personal cost to real people.

In contrast, the political process retards wealth creation because it focuses attention on benefits while obscuring the resulting costs. By allowing well-organized groups to obtain visible benefits by imposing generalized costs on others, the political process suppresses information and incentives required for accountability in the use of resources. Because of visible benefits and obscured costs, political action appears to be the means to greater fairness. Because the benefits of government programs are concentrated, they are applauded and appreciated; because their costs are general, they go unnoticed.

Political Buyouts in the Name of the Poor

A common presumption of humanitarian backers of poverty-relief programs is that all citizens do share, or should share, their heart-felt concern for the poor. Hence, democracy *should* structure legislation to pursue poverty relief in the most cost-effective manner. The social policy analysts, however, must consider the political world as it is—not as some may think it should be. The real political world is one in which some people care about the poor, but it is also a world in which at least some citizens are not very interested in paying taxes to assist the poor. Still other voters may have feelings toward the poor that are largely neutral. That is to say, they have no strong feelings about whether or not the poor should be helped.

In order to become law, programs must be supported by majorities. While majorities at times emerge "naturally," forming around shared values and goals, they often must be concocted—organized through logrolling, a nice-sounding word for political buyouts. The supporters of poverty-relief programs must buyout the opponents with concessions to vote for programs that transfer income to the nonpoor, for example, the people who are hostile toward poverty relief programs. While we can be sure that the political operatives who negotiate the political trades will be better off because of their deals, we cannot be sure that the poor will necessarily be better off, unless, of course, we can assume that the poor (or their representatives) are superior political wheelers and dealers—at best, a dubious proposition.

Constitutional Restraints on Government

The explanation for why government-transfer programs continue to receive public support as a means of helping the poor—despite their failure to do so—also explains why it will be difficult to reduce the size of government and thereby genuinely assist the poor. We have argued that the poor are likely, on balance, to be harmed in the long run by a large government because of the dominance of special (nonpoor) interests over the general interest in political decisions—and that this is the precise reason why reducing the size of government is so difficult. In addition to special-interest influence, it has to be recognized that, for reasons previously discussed, real (short-run) harm would be imposed on large numbers of people, poor as well as nonpoor, if government transfers were scaled back or eliminated quickly. This harm increases the political difficulty that will be encountered by any serious effort to reduce the size of government. A successful reduction in government-transfer programs would surely require a "phasing out" rather than a "cold turkey" approach. And even a gradual reduction in transfers will cause disruptions that, in the short-run, may generate more costs than benefits.

Clearly, success at reducing government transfers requires a long-run perspective, a perspective that extends far beyond that normally associated with ordinary politics. Unfortunately, but just as clearly, those vying for special-interest transfers have no motivation to look beyond short-run considerations. The government's general fund, the primary source of transfers, is analogous to a common property resource (for example, the air people breathe) in which the only ownership rule is the rule of capture.[10] Just as with any common property resource, the individual who exercises restraint and patience in exploiting current government revenues will not be rewarded with an additional claim in future revenues. What one individual does not grab will simply be grabbed by someone else. The end result of this myopic process is a form of "social pollution," a pattern of government expenditures that fails to accomplish any worthy social goal, such as reducing poverty, and which no one would choose if it were judged as a complete package.

In such a situation, each special interest begins to perceive the advantage in moderating and deferring its political demands if, in return, similar moderation and patience would be exercised by all other interest groups. But how can one group be sure that its willingness to reduce demands on government will be matched by a corresponding willingness on the part of others? As opposed to the market process, it is difficult, regrettably, for individuals to communicate commitments to each other in such a way as to motivate honest and reciprocal responses.

The best and only hope for achieving political restraint and the resulting long-run benefits is by subjecting political activity to restrictive rules imposed at the constitutional level. Because constitutional rules are intended to extend far into the future and apply to a long series of particular political decisions, they encourage a far-sighted perspective. When long-run adverse consequences will be the result of decisions that are sure to be made if discretion is allowed in the face of short-run temptations, commitment to a constitution that restricts available options and cannot be easily abandoned is advantageous. Over the long-run, more will be realized from government, collectively, by imposing constitutional rules of political conduct that frustrate our attempts to acquire more from government, individually.

Effective constitutional restrictions on the political process do not simply materialize. They result from a conscious public deliberation that is informed by an understanding of their need. Even if constitutional restrictions did simply fall from the heavens, they would be ineffective in the absence of public understanding of their importance. In fact, we have in the United States a constitution that has been handed down to us over a

---

[10] For an interesting discussion of politically controlled resources as common property see Baden and Fort (1980).

two-hundred-year history, and which served to restrain government (and government transfers) effectively until well into this century. What we do not have currently is the wisdom of our Founding Fathers who understood that while government was necessary for a free and prosperous society, it would abuse our freedom and reduce our prosperity unless tightly constrained. The Founders recognized that the greatest good from government came when it confined itself to the establishment of a legal and economic framework within which people could pursue their individual purposes in productive cooperation with each other. Over the years this understanding has eroded until today the prevailing view is that government has the ability and the responsibility to solve particular problems for particular groups. The unfortunate consequence of this view is that people attempt increasingly to solve their problems (extract special privileges) at the expense of their fellow citizens rather than in cooperation with them.

We understand why the political process has yielded to the temptation to do "good" by trying to help the poor. Our repeated point is that in order for the poor ultimately to benefit from government powers, proponents of poverty relief through government must understand the necessity of checks on the transfer powers of government, just to insure that the poor are not made worse off by the very process created to help them. Unfortunately, proponents of poverty relief have paid scant attention to the problem of erecting workable political checks on governmental powers.

Constitutional Solutions

In order to re-establish effective constitutional restraints on government, we have to return to the cautious view of government that guided the Founders. Over recent decades the tremendous growth of costly government programs that have clearly failed to promote their stated objectives provides ample evidence that the Founder's fears of an overreaching government are as relevant today as they were two hundred years ago. That constitutional amendments designed to limit government (for example, the balanced budget amendment and tax limitation amendment) have been widely discussed, and seriously considered at the federal level (and already contained in many state constitutions) is an encouraging sign that public perceptions are changing. Our existing Constitution, even without the enactment of new constitutional limits on government, will become a more effective restraint as the public becomes more aware of the desirability of that restraint. But, given the erosion of constitutional barriers to government profligacy, it is useful to consider constitutional amendments that would reinforce these barriers.

The purpose of the constitutionally imposed checks and balances that characterize our system of political decision making is to make it difficult for special interests (particularly, nonpoor special interests) to get their proposals enacted into law. One proposal for increasing this difficulty would be to require that proposed legislation receive super majorities in both houses of the U. S. Congress before becoming eligible for the president's signature and the status of law. For example, a bill could require at least two-thirds approval in both the House and the Senate (instead of the current majority approval) before it cleared the congressional hurdle. Congressional super majorities would obviously frustrate many otherwise successful attempts by special interests to get legislation passed.

One method by which intensely interested minorities obtain legislative approval for their proposals is through logrolling. A group that fervently wants a proposal passed will obtain votes for the proposal from other groups of intensely interested minorities by agreeing to vote for their proposals. It is therefore possible to logroll a series of proposals into law even though, if considered individually, each would be voted down by overwhelming majorities. A common and effective way of engaging in logrolling is to put together one bill which contains a sufficient number of special interest proposals—a number sufficient for its receiving a majority vote in the legislative body. Such omnibus bills will typically contain at least one proposal that the President anxiously wants passed. This suggests that the requirement that any piece of legislation contain but one proposal would somewhat diminish the influence of special interests. This is already a requirement in many state constitutions.

Each of these changes in the rules of the political process would increase the cost of using the power of government to transfer wealth from one group to another. This would reduce the wealth transferred by government and increase the wealth of the overall economy. And by doing so, constitutional restrictions on government would improve the well being of the poorest among us.

Concluding Comments

Those who advocate expanding government-transfer programs invariably do so in the name of concern and compassion. The implication, often stated quite explicitly, is that those who oppose expanding government transfers and who want to limit government lack concern and compassion. They are depicted as calloused, self-seeking individuals who are interested only in promoting economic efficiency and who are willing to sacrifice the less-fortunate members of society in order to do so. Unfortunately, advocates of limited government often do little to counter the Scrooge-like caricature being painted of them by their adversaries. No doubt, some readers have concluded from the detached analysis provided in this essay that the authors of this essay lack compassion, which is a total misinterpretation of the line of argument developed.[11]

Classical liberals—those who understand that both freedom and prosperity are enhanced by constitutionally limited government—not only can, but should, take the high road of compassion when making their case. While there is no reason to believe that classical liberals are, as a group, more compassionate than are those who favor expanding government transfers, there is certainly no reason to believe that classical liberals are less compassionate. And classical liberals have more reason to express their concern for the poor because it is their proposals for constitutional limits on government, rather than the government-transfer proposals of their opponents, that will do the most to reduce the problem of poverty.

References

Abrams, Burton and Schmitz, Mark. "The 'Crowding-Out' Effect of Government Transfers on Private Charitable Contributions." *Public Choice* 33 (1978): 28-40.

Abrams, Burton and Schmitz, Mark. "The 'Crowding-Out' Effect of Government Transfers on Private Charitable Contributions: Cross-Section Evidence." *National Tax Journal* 38 (December 1984): 563-68.

Baden, John and Fort, Rodney D. "National Resources and Bureaucratic Predators." *Policy Review* (Winter 1980): 69-81.

Danziger, Sheldon, Havemen, Robert and Plotnick, Robert. "How Income Transfer Programs Affect Work, Saving and the Income Distribution: A Critical Survey." *Journal of Economic Literature* 19 (September 1981): 975-1028.

Friedman, Milton. *Capitalism and Freedom.* Chicago: The University of Chicago Press, 1962.

Fuchs, Victor R. *How We Live: An Economic Perspective on Americans from Birth to Death.* Cambridge: Harvard University Press, 1983.

Glicken, Morley D. "Transgenerational Welfare Dependency." *Journal of Contemporary Studies* 4 (Summer 1981): 31-41.

Goodman, John C. "Poverty and Welfare." In John H. Moore, *To Promote Prosperity: U. S. Domestic Policy in the Mid-1980s.* Stanford: Hoover Institution Press, 1984.

Lee, Dwight R., and McKenzie, Richard B. *Regulating Government: A Preface to Constitutional Economics.* Lexington: Lexington Books, 1987.

Lindsay, C. Matt, and Zycher, Benjamin. "Substitution in Public Spending: Who Pays for Canadian National Health Insurance?" *Economic Inquiry* (July 1984): 337-59.

McKenzie, Richard A. *The Fairness of Markets: A Search for Justice in a Free Society.* Lexington: Lexington Books, 1987.

---

[11] For an extended discussion of the connection between actual poverty relief and constraints on government's transfer authority, see McKenzie (1987).

Murray, Charles A. "The Two Wars Against Poverty: Economic Growth and the Great Society." *The Public Interest* (Fall 1982): 3-16.

Murray, Charles A. *Losing Ground: American Social Policy, 1950-80.* New York: Basic Books, 1984.

Quinn, Jane B. "The Student Loan Scare." *Newsweek.* (May 24, 1982): 68.

Reynolds, Morgan and Smolensky, Eugene, *Public Expenditures, Taxes, and the Distribution of Income: The United States, 1950, 1961, 1970.* New York: Academic Press, 1977.

Roberts, R. D. "A Positive Model of Private Charity and Public Transfers." *Journal of Political Economy* 92 (February 1984): 136-48.

Sowell, Thomas A. *Conflict of Visions: Ideological Origins of Political Struggles.* New York: William Morrow and Company, Inc., 1987.

Steinberg, Richard. "Voluntary Donations and Public Expenditures in a Federalist System." *The American Economic Review* 77 (March 1987): 24-36.

Tullock, Gordon. "The Charity of the Uncharitable." *Western Economic Journal* 9 (December 1971): 379-92.

INDEX OF CASES

INDEX OF NAMES

413

INDEX OF TOPICS